Samuel Johnson

Debates In Parliament

Samuel Johnson

Debates in Parliament

ISBN/EAN: 9783741133008

Manufactured in Europe, USA, Canada, Australia, Japa

Cover: Foto ©Thomas Meinert / pixelio.de

Manufactured and distributed by brebook publishing software
(www.brebook.com)

Samuel Johnson

Debates In Parliament

DEBATES

IN

PARLIAMENT.

By SAMUEL JOHNSON, LL.D.

IN TWO VOLUMES.

VOL. I.

LONDON:

PRINTED FOR JOHN STOCKDALE,

OPPOSITE BURLINGTON HOUSE, PICCADILLY.

M,DCC,LXXXVII.

PREFACE.

A Compleat collection of the writings of the late Dr. Samuel Johnson was desired by the Public with an ardour almost equal to the high opinion which was entertained of his talents and his morals. The London Bookfellers undertook, in conjunction with the deceafed's executors, to gratify this defire with an alacrity, which proceeded from a conviction how much their own interest would be promoted by punctual compliance.

But, from whatever caufe, the prefent edition of the works of that great writer and illuftrious moralift, does not compre-hend his Parliamentary Debates, which, every competent judge muft allow, exhibit a memorable fpecimen of the ex-tent and promptitude of his faculties. Thefe Debates, as the intelligent have for fome time known, and as the world is now authentically told by the prefent hiftorian of his life, were originally compiled for the Gentleman's Magazine. And thefe Orations, which have induced learned foreigners to compare Britifh with ancient eloquence, were haftily fketched by Johnson, while he was not yet thirty-two, while he was little acquainted with life, while he was ftruggling, not for diftinction, but exiftence.

The

The illuminations of JOHNSON's Oratory were however obscured by the jargon, which CAVE thought it prudent to adopt, in order to avoid Parliamentary indignation. It is at length safe to substitute the real for the fictitious speakers. The present Editor thought it a duty he owed to the Author and the Reader, to lay aside the barbarous terms, which had been contrived as much by the vanity as the caution of CAVE, that the finest sense might conspicuously appear in the most brilliant language. As these Debates appeared originally without any regard to chronological order, it was deemed respectful to the public to restore this order, according to the dates, when the real Debates actually happened; beginning with the first of Johnson's on the 19th of November 1740, and ending with his last, on the 23d of February 1742-3. That this beginning and this end to the Parliamentary effusions of this successful rival of ancient Orators have been properly adjusted, might be determined from the superiority of style to the speeches of Guthrie and Hawkesworth, the precursor and follower of Johnson in this department of compilation, if Sir John Hawkins had not fixed the dates from the diary of the friend, to whose memory he has paid a proper tribute, by doing justice to his virtues and his failings.

It is undoubtedly true, that the Parliamentary motions, which are contained in the following sheets, were made, and that they were supported and opposed by the assigned speakers: but, it must be acknowledged, that Johnson did not give so
much

much what they refpectively faid as what each ought to have faid. Thefe debates, then, may be confidered as fo many diftinct dramas, in which, on extraordinary occafions of public expectation, known characters of confiderable confequence were brought forward to act their particular parts. As dramas thefe Debates have received a juft eulogy by the remark of competent judges, *how eafy it was to affign to every fpeaker his proper fpeech without knowing the name.* As dramas they may be perufed by the old, who read for amufement rather than inftruction.

As Parliamentary Debates thefe volumes may be regarded as ftill more ufeful: for, like the Orations of Cicero and Demofthenes, they ought to be ftudied by the Britifh youth as fpecimens of fplendid eloquence, nervous argument, and Parliamentary decorum. Though few can hope to rival Johnfon's performances, every youth, who from his birth or fortune expects to fit in Parliament, ought to aim by ftudious perufal at Johnfon's perfections in oratory and reafoning. And thefe volumes may be ufefully infpected by every public man for felicities of expreffion, for the ftructure of fentences, happy at once for point, dignity, and elegance.

Few of the collections of *Parliamentary Debates* can be juftly regarded as much more authentic than Johnfon's Orations. The moft ancient are probably the moft authen-

A 4   tic.

tic. D'Ewes' Journals of Elizabeth's Parliaments, as they contain the oldest Parliamentary speeches, are assuredly the most curious. The first volume of the Commons Journals contains several important Debates during the interesting period from the accession of James I. till the cessation of Parliaments under his unhappy son. The authentic Debates of the Session 1621 were published in 1766, from a Member's manuscript. The collections of Rushworth contain many of the Parliamentary Debates during the civil wars. To these follow Gray's Debates, which are still more authentic. But, as to those various collections, which profess to give the Parliamentary Debates, during that disputatious period from the Restoration to late times, they can be deemed of little more authority than the subjoined speeches of Johnson.

It was the Revolution which finally unshackled the press. But it was still criminal, at least dangerous, to publish Parliamentary proceedings without Parliamentary permission. During King William's reign the newspapers sometimes gave a detached speech of a particular speaker, who wished, by contributing the outlines, to gratify his vanity or secure his seat.

It was in the factious times, which immediately succeeded, when Parliamentary Debates were first distributed through the land in monthly pamphlets. Then it was that Boyer's zeal

propagated

propagated the *Political State*. This was succeeded, on the
accession of George I. by the *Historical Registers*, which were
published by soberer men, and may be supposed therefore
to contain more satisfactory information.

The Gentleman's Magazine soon after furnished the
public with still more finished Debates, which were first
compiled by GUTHRIE, then by JOHNSON, and afterwards
by HAWKESWORTH. The success of this far-famed mis-
cellany prompted many competitors for public favour, who
all found an interest in propagating what the people read,
however contrary to Parliamentary resolves. And these resolves have at length silently given way to the spirit of the
people, who, as they enjoy the right of instructing their
representatives, seem to have established the privilege of
knowing what their representatives say.

That the public, then, might not be deprived of writings,
thus worthy of their author, or excluded from the easy perusal
of Parliamentary Orations, thus amusing and instructive, the
two following Volumes were published. And, they are given
to the world in a form so convenient, that they may either be
considered as a proper SUPPLEMENT to the Works of Dr.
SAMUEL JOHNSON, at the same time published by the London Bookfellers, or regarded merely as the PARLIAMENTARY
DEBATES of that celebrated Orator, at the most interesting
period in our history. Actuated by these fair motives, the
                                                        Editor

Editor humbly fubmits thefe volumes to the reader, trufting to his candour for that favourable reception, which well-meant endeavours to inftruct and pleafe may always expect from a public, at once intelligent, refined, and generous.

LONDON,
March 1ft, 1787.

** Some gentlemen, for whofe tafte and difcernment the Editor has a high refpect, having obferved, that the barbarous jargon, which had been employed by the vanity or caution of the Editor of the Gentleman's Magazine, was mentioned too generally in the foregoing Preface, and that the Lilliputian terms, which once obftructed the reader's progrefs, would now gratify his curiofity, the Editor has fubjoined the fictious names of perfons and places with the real ones, as they occur in the Debates of that mifcellany.

The

The List of fictitious *Terms used by* CAVE *to disguise the real* NAMES *that occur in his Debates.*

A.

Abingdon, Ld.-Adonbing or Plesdrahn
Ambrose, Captain - Ambrefo
Archer - Arech
Argyle, Duke of - Agryl
Arthur - Aruth
Anne - Nuna
Adon - Anots
Aylesford, Lord - Alysfrop

B.

Baltimore, Lord - Blatirome
Barnard, Sir John - Branard
Barrington - Birrongtan
Bath, Earl of - Baht
Bathurst, Lord - Bruftath
Bedford, Duke of - Beflort
Berkeley, Lord - Berelky
Bishop - Flamen
Bladen, Mr. - Bledna
Bootle, Mr. - Butul
Bowles, Mr. - Bewlos
Bristol, Lord - Brollit
Bromley, Mr. - Bormlye
Brown Mr. - Brewon or Buron
Burleigh - Bruleigh
Burrell, Mr - Berrull

C.

Campbell - Campobell
Carew, Mr. - Cawer
Carlisle, Earl of - Carfilel
Carteret, Lord Quadrert
Caftres, Monf. - Cahftrehs
Cavendish - Candevith
Charles - Chorlo
Chesterfield, Earl of - Caftroflet
Cholmondeley, Earl of - Sholmlüg
Churchill - Chillchurch
Clutterbuck, Mr. - Cluckerbutt
Cocks - Cofck
Coke, Mr. - Qroke
Cooke - Cocko

Cooper, Mr. - Quepur.
Corbet, Mr. - Croteb
Cornwall, Mr. - Carnwoll
Cromwell - Clewmro

D.

Danes - Danians.
Danvers - Dranevs
Delawarr, Lord - Devarlar
Devonshire, Duke of - Dovenfhire
Digby - Dibgy
Drake, Mr. - Dekra

E.

Earle, Mr - Erel
Edmund - Endend
Edward - Eddraw
Elizabeth - Ezila
Erskine, Mr. - Eferkin
Eugene, Prince - Eunege

F.

Falconberg, Lord - Flacnobrug
Falkland - Flakland
Fanthaw, Mr. - Fathnaw
Fazakerly - Fakazerly
Fenwick, Mr. - Finweck
Ferrol - Ferror
Fox, Mr. - Feoux
Francis - Faracis or Friftan

G.

Gage, Lord - Gega
George - Gorgenti
Gibbon, Mr. - Gibnob
Gloucester, Duke o. - Gluftre
Godolphin, Lord - Golphindo
Gore - Gero
Gower, Lord - Gewor
Grenville, Mr. Grevillen
Gybbon, Mr. - Gybnob

H

Halifax, Lord - Haxilaf
Haddock, Admiral - Hockadd
Handalyd, Mr. - Hafandyd
Harding, Mr. - Hadringe
Hardwick, Lord - Hickrad
Harrington - Hargrinton
Hay, Mr. - Heagh
Heathcote - Whethtoe
Henry - Hynree
Herbert - Hertreb
Hervey, Lord - Heryef
Heffian - Hycffian
Hind Cotton - Whind Cotnot
Hindford - Honfyd
Hinton - Hwenton
Hobart - Hobrat
Holderneffe, Lord - Hodrelaefs
Hooper - Horcop
Hoffer, Admiral - Hozeri
Howe - Hewo

I.

Illay, Lord - Yaii
Ilham - Ihma
Ilchefter - Itcileffer

J.

James - Jacomo
Jekyl - Jelyco
Jenkins - Jenkino
John - Juon
Joleph - Jofippo.

K.

Keene, Mr. - Knee.

L.

Ledbury, Mr. - Lebdury
Lindfey - Linfyd
Litchfield - Lichfidd
Lockwood - Lockwoock
Lombe - Lobon
Lonsdale, Lord - Ledntal
Lovel - Lvol
Lymericks, Lord - Lyromick's
Lyttleton - Lottyltns

M.

Marlborough, Duke of - Maursllurgh
Malton, Lord - Marlon
Mawley - Mawly
Mary - Marya

Montrofe, Duke of - Morontoffe
Mordaunt - Madrount
Morton - Motron

N.

Newcaftle, Duke of - Nardac fecretary
Noel - Neol
Norris, Admiral - Nifror
Nugent - Netgun

O.

Ogle, Admiral - Oleg
Onflow - Olfwon
Orange - Organe
Ord, Mr - Whord
Orford, Earl of - Orfrod
Orleans - Olreans
Ormond, Duke of - Omrond
Oxford, Earl of - Odfrox
Oxenden - Odnexen

P.

Paxton - Pantox
Pelham, Mr. Plemahm
Perry - Prerur
Peterborough - Petraborauch
Pitt, Mr. - Ptit
Plumer Mr. - Plurem
Polworth - Polgarth
Portland, Duke of - Poldrand
Powlett - Pewlet or Pletow
Prince - Rednetrcp
Puffendorf - Pudendforf
Pulteney - Palnub

Q.

Quarendon - Quenardon

R.

Rainsford - Rainsfrod
Ranelies - Ranies
Raymond - Ramonyd
Robert - Retrob
Rochefter - Roffca

S.

St. Aubyn - St. Aybun
Salisbury - Samra
Samuel - Salvem
Sandwich, Earl of - Swandick
Sandys, Mr. - Snadfy
Scarborough, Lord - Sarkbrugh
Scroop, Mr. - Screop
Sidney, Lord - Sedyin

Selwin,

Selwin, Mr. - Slenwy
Shaftſbury, Lord - Shyſtaſbrug
Shippen, Mr. - Skeiphen
Sloper - Slerop
Somers - Soſrem
Somerſet - Soſermet
Southwell - Suthewoll
Strafford - Stordraff
Stair - Stari
Staniſlaus - Staſinlaus
Sundon - Snodyn

T.

Talbot - Toblat
Thomas - Tſahom
Thomſon, Mr. - Thoſmon
Tracey - Tryace
Trenchard - Trachnerd
Trevor, Mr. - Tervor
Turner - Truron
Tweedale, Marquis of - Tewelade
Tyrconnel, Lord - Trinocleng

V.

Vernon, Admiral - Venron

Viner, Mr. - Vynre or Venry

W.

Wade - Weda
Wager, Admiral - Werga
Wakefield - Waſekeild
Waller Mr. - Welral
Walpole, Sir Robert - Walelop
Walpole, Mr. - Walelop
Walter, Mr. Guſbret
Watkins, Mr. - Waknits
Wendover - Wednevro
Weſtmoreland - Weſtromland
William - Wimgul
Willimot, Mr. Guillitom
Winchelfea, Lord - Wichenſale
Winnington, Mr. - Wintinnong
Wortley Mr. - Wolreſyt or Werotyl
Wyndham - Gumdahm
Wynn - Ooyn

Y.

Yonge - Yegon.

_____

The Liſt of fictitious *Characters uſed by* CAVE *to diſguiſe the* PLACES *that occur in his Debates.*

A.

Almanza - Almanaz
America - Columbia
Amſterdam - Amſtredam
Achaffenburg - Aſchaſneſburg
Auſtria - Auriſta

B.

Barbadoes - Bardoſba
Barcelona - Bracolena
Brittany - Bratoney
Bavaria - Baravia
Blenheim - Bichneim or Bienhem
Bourbon - Buorbon
Brandenburg - Brangburden
Briſtol - Broſlit
Britain - Lilliput

C.

Cadiz - Cazid
Cambridge - Guntar
Campechy - Capemchy
Carolina - Carolana
Carthagena - Carthanega
Cologne - Colgone
Commons - Clinabs
Connecticut - Coatedlicnu
Creſſy - Cerſſy
Cuba - Cabu

D.

Dancram - Denmark
Dettingen - Detteneg
Dunkirk - Denkirk
Dutch - Belgians

E. Edin-

E.

Edinburgh - Edina
Europe - Degulia

F.

Flanders - Flandria
France - Bleraica

G.

Georgia - Gorgentia
Germany - Athenrou
Gibraltar - Grabutra
Guadlalla - Gua. Stalla
Guernfey - Guenfrey

H.

Hanover - Hanevro
Haverfham - Havremarfh
Heffe Caffel - Hyeffe Cleffa
Hifpaniola - Iberionola
Holland - Belgia
Hungary - Hungruland

I.

India - Idnia
Ireland - Irne
Italy - Italia

J.

Jamaica - Zamengel
Jucatan - Jucacan

K.

Leghorn - Lehgron
Leiden - Mot Valo

M.

Madrid - Mardit
Malplaquet - Malpalquet
Mardyke - Moravike
Marocco - Maronico
Mediterranean - Middle Sea
Minorca - Minorca

Munfter - Munftru
Mufcovy - Maufqueeta

N.

New York - Noveborac

O.

Orkney - Orkyen
Orleans - Oreans
Oftend - Odften

P.

Parma - Par Ma
Pennfylvania - Peavanfia
Poland - Polrand
Portugal - Lufrania
Port Mahon - Port Mohan
Pruffia - Prefhy
Prague - Praga

S.

Sardinia - Sadri.la
Schellmbourg - Schemelbourg
Seville - S. Itule
Sicily - Ciliy
South Sea - Pacific Ocean
Spain - Iberia
Streights - Narrow Seas
Sweden - Suefe

T.

Turkey - Korantce

U.

Utrecht - Ukralt

V.

Vienna - Vinena
Virginia - Veginia

W.

Wedminder - Belliborac
Wolfenbuttle - Webcaruffle

The List of fictitious *Characters used by* CAVE *to disguise the Name of* THINGS *that occur in his Debates.*

A.

Admiral - Galbet

B.

Baronet - Hurgolen

C.

Commons - Clinabs

D.

Duke - Nardac

E.

Earl - Cofern
Esquire - Urg

G.

Gentleman - Urgolen

H.

High Heels or Tory - Tramecfan

K.

Knight - Hurgolet

L.

Legal - Snilpal
Lord - Hurgo

P.

Penny - a Grull
Popery - Miffalfm
Prophet - Luftrug

S.

Sprug - a Pound
Squire - Urg

V.

Viscount - Comvic

Y.

Years - Moons.

CON-

gle

CONTENTS.

R E-

D E

DEBATES

IN

PARLIAMENT.

HOUSE OF COMMONS.

November 19, 1740.

PROCEEDINGS AND DEBATE, WITH REGARD TO THE BILL FOR
PROHIBITING THE EXPORTATION OF CORN, &c.

*O*N *the firſt day of the Seſſion, his Majeſty, in his ſpeech from the throne, recommended to Parliament to conſider of ſome good law to prevent the growing miſchief of the exportation of corn to foreign countries.*

On the fourth day, a bill for preventing for a limited time the exportation, &c. was read a firſt time in the Houſe of Commons, and the queſtion put, whether it ſhould be printed, which paſſed in the negative.

This day the agent for the colonies of Penſylvania and New Jerſey, preſented a petition againſt the ſaid Corn Bill, which was referred to the Committee.

Another petition was alſo preſented by the agent for the colony of Connecticut, in New England, ſetting forth that the chief trade of that colony aroſe from ſupplying other Britiſh colonies with corn, ſo that unleſs that colony be excepted from the reſtraints intended by this bill, both that and thoſe which are ſupplied by it will be reduced to great diſtreſs, and praying therefore that ſuch exception may be allowed.

The allegations in this petition were confirmed by another, from one of the provinces ſupplied by the colony of Connecticut.

Another petition was preſented by the agent for South Carolina, ſetting forth, that unleſs the rice produced in that province were allowed to be

B   *exported,*

exported, the colony must be ruined by the irretrievable loss of their whole trade, as the countries now supplied from thence, might easily procure rice from the French settlements already too much their rivals in trade.

This petition was supported by another, offered at the same time by the merchants of Bristol.

A petition was likewise presented by the agent for the sugar islands, in which it was alleged, that if no provisions be imported thither from Britain, they must in one month suffer the extremities of famine.

All these petitions were referred to the Committee for the bill.

A printed paper was also delivered to the members, entitled, Considerations on the Embargo, which enumerated many dangerous consequences likely to be produced by an embargo on provisions, and suggested that it was no better than a wicked scheme for private profit, with other reflections, for which the paper was deemed a libel, and the author committed to prison.

The bill being read in the Committee, produced the following memorable debate.

M R. PULTNEY spoke to this effect :—Sir, after all the attention which has been bestowed upon the bill now before us, I cannot yet conceive it such as can benefit the nation, or such as will not produce far greater inconveniencies than those which it is intended to obviate, and therefore as those inconveniencies may be prevented by other means, I cannot but declare that I am far from approving it.

Our ancestors, Sir, have always thought it the great business of this house to watch against the encroachments of the prerogative, and to prevent an increase of the power of the minister, and the Commons have always been considered as more faithful to their trust, and more properly the representatives of the people, in proportion as they have considered this great end with more attention, and prosecuted it with more invariable resolution. If we enquire into the different degrees of reputation, which the several assemblies of Commons have obtained, and consider why some are remembered with reverence and gratitude, and others never mentioned but with detestation and contempt, we shall always find that their conduct, with regard to this single point, has produced their renown or their infamy. Those are always by the general suffrage of mankind applauded as the patterns

of

of their country, who have struggled with the influence of the crown, and those condemned as traytors, who have either promoted it by unreasonable grants, or seen it increase by slow degrees without resistance.

It has not indeed, Sir, been always the practice of ministers to make open demands of larger powers, and avow, without disguise, their designs of extending their authority; such proposals would in former times have produced no consequences but that of awakening the vigilance of the senate, of raising suspicions against all their proceedings, and of embarrassing the crown with petitions, addresses, and impeachments.

They were under a necessity in those times of promoting their schemes, those schemes which scarcely any ministry has forborn to adopt, by more secret and artful and silent methods, by methods of diverting the attention of the publick to other objects, and of making invisible approaches to the point in view, while they seemed to direct all their endeavours to different purposes.

But such, Sir, have been the proofs of implicit confidence, which the administration has received from this assembly, that it is now common to demand unlimited powers, and to expect confidence without restriction, to require an immediate possession of our estates by a vote of credit, or the sole direction of our trade by an act for prohibiting, during their pleasure, the exportation of the produce of our lands.

Upon what instances of uncommon merit, of regard to the publick prosperity, unknown in former times, or of discernment superior to that of their most celebrated predecessors, the present ministers found their new claims to submission and to trust, I am indeed at a loss to discover; for however mankind may have determined concerning the integrity of those by whom the late memorable convention was transacted, defended, and confirmed, I know not that their wisdom has yet appeared by any incontestable or manifest evidence, which may set their abilities above question, and fix their reputation for policy out of the reach of censure and enquiries.

The only act, Sir, by which it can be discovered that they have any degree of penetration proportionate to their employments, is the embargo lately laid upon provisions in Ireland, by which our enemies have been timely hindred from furnishing themselves from our dominions with necessaries for their armies and their navies, and our fel-

low

low fubjects have been reftrained from expofing themfelves to the
miferies of famine, by yielding to the temptation of prefent profit;
a temptation generally fo powerful as to prevail over any diftant intereft.

But as nothing is more contrary to my natural difpofition, or more
unworthy of a member of this houfe than flattery, I cannot affirm
that I afcribe this ufeful expedient wholly to the fagacity or the caution of the miniftry, nor can I attribute all the happy effects produced
by it to their benign folicitude for the publick welfare.

I am inclined to believe that this ftep was advifed by thofe who
were prompted to confider its importance by motives more prevalent than that of publick fpirit, and that the defire of profit which
has fo often dictated pernicious meafures, has for once produced,
in return, an expedient juft and beneficial; and it has for once
luckily fallen out, that fome of the friends of the adminiftration
have difcovered that the publick intereft was combined with their
own.

It is highly probable, Sir, that the contractors for fupplying the
navy with provifions, confidering with that acutenefs which a quick
fenfe of lofs and gain always produces, how much the price of victuals would be raifed by exportation, and by confequence how much
of the advantage of their contracts would be diminifhed, fuggefted
to the miniftry the neceffity of an embargo, and laid before them
thofe arguments which their own obfervation and wifdom would never have difcovered.

Thus, Sir, the minifters, in that inftance of their conduct, on
which their political reputation muft be founded, can claim perhaps
no higher merit, than that of attending to fuperiour knowledge, of
complying with good advice when it was offered, and of not refifting
demonftration when it was laid before them.

But as I would never afcribe to one man the merit of another, I
fhould be equally unwilling to detract from due commendations,
and fhall therefore freely admit, that not to reject good counfel is a
degree of wifdom, at which I could not expect that they by whom
the convention was concluded would ever have arrived.

But whatever proficiency they may have made in the art of government fince that celebrated period, however they may have encreafed
their maxims of domeftick policy, or improved their knowledge of
foreign affairs, I cannot but confefs myfelf ftill inclined to fome degree

gree of fufpicion, nor can prevail upon myfelf to fhut my eyes and deliver up the publick and myfelf implicitly to their direction.

Their fagacity, Sir, may perhaps of late have received fome improvements from longer experience, and with regard to their integrity, I believe at leaft that it is not much diminifhed; and yet I cannot forbear afferting the right of judging for myfelf, and of determining according to the evidence that fhall be brought before me.

I have hitherto entertained an opinion that for this purpofe only we are deputed by our conftituents, who, if they had repofed no confidence in our care or abilities, would have given up long fince the vexatious right of contefting for the choice of reprefentatives. They would have furnifhed the miniftry with general powers to act for them, and fat at eafe with no other regard to publick meafures, than might incite them to animate with their applaufes the laudable endeavours of their profound, their diligent, and their magnanimous governours.

As I do not therefore check any fufpicions in my own mind, I fhall not eafily be reftrained from uttering them, becaufe I know not how I fhall benefit my country, or affift her counfels by filent meditations. I cannot, Sir, but obferve that the powers conferred by this bill upon the adminiftration are larger than the nation can fafely repofe in any body of men, and with which no man who confiders to what purpofes they may be employed will think it convenient to inveft the negociators of the convention.

Nor do my objections to this act arife wholly from my apprehenfions of their conduct, who are intrufted with the execution of it, but from my reflections on the nature of trade, and the conduct of thofe nations who are moft celebrated for commercial wifdom.

It is well known, Sir, how difficult it is to turn trade back into its ancient channel, when it has by any means been diverted from it, and how often a profitable traffick has been loft for ever, by a fhort interruption, or temporary prohibition. The refentment of difappointed expectations, inclines the buyer to feek another market, and the civility to which his new correfpondents are incited by their own intereft, detains him, till thofe by whom he was formerly fupplied, having no longer any vent for their products or their wares, employ their labours on other manufactures, or cultivate their lands for other purpofes.

Thus, Sir, if those nations who have hitherto been supplied with corn from Britain, should find a method of purchasing it from Denmark or any other of the northern regions, we may hereafter see our grain rotting in our storehouses, and be burthened with provisions which we can neither consume ourselves, nor sell to our neighbours.

The Hollanders, whose knowledge of the importance or skill in the arts of commerce will not be questioned, are so careful to preserve the inlets of gain from obstruction, that they make no scruple of supplying their enemies with their commodities, and have been known to sell at night those bullets which were next day to be discharged against them.

Whether their example, Sir, deserves our imitation I am not able to determine, but it ought at least to be considered whether their conduct was rational or not, and whether they did not by a present evil, ensure an advantage which overbalanced it.

There are doubtless, Sir, sometimes such exigencies as require to be complied with at the hazard of future profit, but I am not certain that the scarcity which is feared or felt at present, is to be numbered amongst them ; but, however formidable it may be thought, there is surely no need of a new law to provide against it : for it is one of those extraordinary incidents, on which the king has the right of exciting extraordinary powers. On occasions like this the prerogative has heretofore operated very effectually, and I know not that the law has ever restrained it.

It is therefore, Sir, in my opinion, most prudent to determine nothing in so dubious a question, and rather to act as the immediate occasion shall require, than prosecute any certain method of proceeding, or establish any precedent by an act of the senate.

To restrain that commerce by which the necessaries of life are distributed is a very bold experiment, and such as once produced an insurrection in the empire of the Turks, that terminated in the deposition of one of their monarchs.

I therefore willingly confess, Sir, that I know not how to conclude : I am unwilling to deprive the nation of bread, or to supply our enemies with strength to be exerted against ourselves ; but I am on the other hand afraid to restrain commerce, and to trust the authors of the convention.

Mr. PELHAM spoke next, to the following purport :—Sir, I am always in expectation of improvement and instruction when that gentleman

gentleman engages in any discussion of national questions, on which he is equally qualified to judge by his great abilities and long experience, by that popularity which enables him to sound the sentiments of men of different interests, and that intelligence which extends his views to distant parts of the world; but on this occasion I have found my expectations frustrated, for he has enquired without making any discovery, and harangued without illustrating the question before us.

He has satisfied himself, Sir, with declaring his suspicions without condescending to tell us what designs or what dangers he apprehends. To fear without being able to shew the object of our terrors, is the last, the most despicable degree of cowardice; and to suspect without knowing the foundation of our own suspicions, is surely a proof of a state of mind, which would not be applauded on common occasions, and such as no man but a *patriot* would venture to confess.

He has indeed, Sir, uttered some very ingenious conceits upon the late convention, has alluded to it with great luxuriancy of fancy, and elegance of diction, and must at least confess that whatever may be its effects upon the interest of the nation, it has to him been very beneficial, as it has supplied him with a subject of raillery when other topics began to fail him, and given opportunity for the exercise of that wit which began to languish for want of employment.

What connection his wonderful sagacity has discovered between the convention and the corn-bill, I cannot yet fully comprehend, but have too high an opinion of his abilities to imagine that so many insinuations are wholly without any reason to support them. I doubt not therefore, Sir, but that when some fitter opportunity shall present itself he will clear their resemblance, and branch out the parallel between them into a thousand particulars.

In the mean time, Sir, it may be proper for the house to expedite the bill, against which no argument has yet been produced, and which is of too much importance to be delayed by raillery or invectives.

Mr. SANDYS spoke next, in substance as follows:—Sir, the Bill before us, as it is of too great importance to be negligently delayed, is likewise too dangerous to be precipitately hurried into a law.

It has been always the practice of this house to consider money-bills with particular attention, because money is power in almost the

the highest degree, and ought not therefore to be given but upon
strong assurances, that it will be employed for the purposes for
which it is demanded, and that those purposes are in themselves
just.

But if we consider, Sir, the bill now before us, it will appear
yet more than a money-bill, it will be found a bill for regulating
the disposal of that, which it is the great use of money to procure,
and is therefore not to be passed into a law without a close attention
to every circumstance that may be combined with it, and an accurate examination of all the consequences that may be produced
by it.

Some of these circumstances or consequences, it is the duty of
every member to lay before the house, and I shall therefore propose,
that the inducements to the discovery of any provisions illegally exported, and the manner of levying the forfeiture, may be particularly
discussed ; for by a defect in this part, the regulation lately established by the regency, however seasonable, produced tumults and
distractions which every good government ought studiously to obviate.

By their proclamation, Sir, half the corn that should be found designed for exportation was to be given to those who should discover and
seize it.   The populace, alarmed at once with the danger of a famine, and animated by a proclamation that put into their own hands
the means of preventing it, and the punishment of those from
whose avarice they apprehended it, rose in throngs to execute so
grateful a law.   Every man, Sir, whose distress had exasperated him,
was incited to gratify his resentment ; every man, whose idleness
prompted him to maintain his family by methods more easy than
that of daily labour, was delighted with the prospect of growing rich
on a sudden by a lucky seizure.   All the seditious and the profligate
combined together in the welcome employment of violence and
rapine, and when they had once raised their expectations there was
no small danger, lest their impatience of disappointment should determine them to conclude, that corn, wherever found, was designed
for exportation, and to seize it as a lawful prize.

Thus, Sir, by an imprudent regulation, was every man's property brought into hazard, and his person exposed to the insults of
a hungry, a rapacious, and ungovernable rabble, let loose by a
publick proclamation, and encouraged to search houses and carriages
by an imaginary law.

That we may not give occasion to violence and injustice of the same kind, let us carefully consider the measures which are proposed before we determine upon their propriety, and pass no bill on this important occasion without such deliberation as may leave us nothing to change or to repent.

Mr. EARLE spoke next to this effect:—Sir, notwithstanding the dangers which have been represented as likely to arise from any error in the prosecution of this great affair, I cannot but declare my opinion, that no delay ought to be admitted, and that not even the specious pretence of more exact enquiries, and minute considerations, ought to retard our proceedings for a day.

My imagination, Sir, is perhaps, not so fruitful as that of some other members of this House, and therefore they may discover many inconveniencies which I am not able to conceive. But as every man ought to act from his own conviction, it is my duty to urge the necessity of passing this bill till it can be proved to me, that it will produce calamities equally to be dreaded with the consequences of protracting our debates upon it, equal to the miseries of a famine, or the danger of enabling our enemies to store their magazines, to equip their fleets, and victual their garrisons.

If it could be imagined, that there was in this assembly a subject of France or Spain, zealous for the service of his prince, and the prosperity of his country, I should expect that he would summon all his faculties to retard the progress of this bill, that he would employ all his sophistry to shew its inconveniency and imperfections, and exhaust his invention to suggest the dangers of haste; and certainly he could do nothing that would more effectually promote the interest of his countrymen, or tend more to enfeeble and depress the power of the British nation.

If this would naturally be the conduct of an enemy, it is unnecessary to prove that we can only be safe by acting in opposition to it, and I think it superfluous to vindicate my ardour for promoting this bill, when it is evident that its delay would be pleasing to the Spaniards.

Mr. BURREL then spoke as follows:—Sir, if this law be necessary at any time, it cannot now be delayed, for a few days spent in deliberation, may make it ineffectual, and that evil may be past of which we sit here contriving the prevention.

That

That many contracts, Sir, for the exportation of provisions are
already made in all the maritime parts of the empire, is generally
known; and it requires no great sagacity to discover that those by
whom they are made, and made with a view of immense profit,
are defirous that they may be executed; and that they will foon
compleat the execution of them, when they are alarmed with the
apprehenfion of a bill which in a few days may take from them
the power of exporting what they have already collected, and fnatch
their gain from them when it is almoft in their hands.

A bill for thefe purpofes, Sir, ought to fall upon the contractors
like a fudden blow, of which they have no warning or dread;
againft which they therefore cannot provide any fecurity, and which
they can neither elude nor refift.

If we allow them a fhort time, our expedients will be of little
benefit to the nation, which is every day impoverifhed by the exportation of the neceffaries of life, in fuch quantities, that in a
few weeks the law, if it be paffed, may be without penalties,
for there will be no poffibility of difobeying it.

Sir JOHN BARNARD fpoke next to the following purpofe :—Sir, I
cannot difcover the neceffity of preffing the bill with fuch precipitation,
as muft neceffarily exclude many ufeful confiderations, and may produce errors extremely dangerous ; for I am not able to conceive what
inconveniencies can arife from a fhort delay.

The exportation of provifions from Ireland is at prefent ftopped
by the proclamation ; and the beef which was defigned for other nations, has been prudently bought up by the contractors, by which
thofe murmurs have been in a great meafure obviated which naturally arife from difappointments and lofies.

There is therefore, Sir, no danger of exportations from that part
of our dominions, which is the chief market for provifions, and from
whence our enemies have been generally fupplied : in Britain there
is lefs danger of any fuch pernicious traffick, both becaufe the
fcarcity here has raifed all provifions to a high price, and becaufe
merchants do not immediately come to a new market.

The bill, at leaft, ought not to be paffed without regard to the
general welfare of our fellow fubjects, nor without an attentive confideration of thofe petitions which have been prefented to us ; petitions
not produced by panic apprehenfions of imaginary dangers, or diftant
profpects of inconveniencies barely poffible, but by the certain fore-
sight

fight of immediate calamities, the total deftruction of trade, and the fudden defolation of flourifhing provinces.

By prohibiting the exportation of rice, we fhall, Sir, in one year, reduce the colony of South Carolina below the poffibility of fubfift-ing; the chief product of that country, the product which induced us originally to plant it, and with which all its trade is carried on, is rice. With rice the inhabitants of that province purchafe all the other neceffaries of life, and among them the manufactures of our own country. This rice is carried by our merchants to other parts of Europe, and fold again for large profit.

That this trade is very important appears from the number of fhips which it employs, and which, without lading, muft rot in the har-bours, if rice be not excepted from the general prohibition. With-out this exception, Sir, it is not eafy to fay what numbers, whofe ftations appear very different, and whofe employments have no vi-fible relation to each other, will be at once involved in calamity, re-duced to fudden diftrefs, and obliged to feek new methods of fup-porting their families. The failor, the merchant, the fhipwright, the manufacturer, with all the fubordinations of employment that depend upon them, all that fupply them with materials, or receive advantage from their labours, almoft all the fubjects of the Britifh crown, muft fuffer at leaft in fome degree, by the ruin of Carolina.

Nor ought the danger of the fugar iflands, and other provinces, lefs to alarm our apprehenfions, excite our compaffion, or employ our confideration, fince nothing is more evident than that by paffing this bill without the exceptions which their petitions propofe, we fhall reduce one part of our colonies to the want of bread, and con-fine the other to live on nothing elfe; for they fubfift by the ex-change of thofe products to which the foil of each country is pecu-liarly adapted: one province affords no corn, and the other fupplies its inhabitants with corn only.

The neceffity of expediting this bill, however it has been exag-gerated, is not fo urgent but that we may be allowed time fufficient to confider for what purpofe it is to be paffed, and to recollect that nothing is defigned by it, but to hinder our enemies from being fup-plied from the Britifh dominions with provifions, by which they might be enabled more powerfully to carry on the war againft us.

To this defign no objection has been made, but it is well known, that a good end may be defeated by an abfurd choice of means, and I

am

am not able to difcover how we fhall encreafe our own ftrength, or diminifh that of our enemies, by compelling one part of our fellow fubjects to ftarve the other.

It is neceffary, Sir, to prohibit the exportation of corn to the ports of our enemies, and of thofe nations by which our enemies will be fupplied, but furely it is of no ufe to exclude any part of our own dominions from the privilege of being fupplied from another. Nor can any argument be alleged in defence of fuch a law, that will not prove with equal force, that corn ought to remain in the fame granaries where it is now laid, that all the markets in this kingdom fhould be fufpended, and that no man fhould be allowed to fell bread to another.

There is, indeed, Sir, a poffibility that the liberty for which I contend may be ufed to wicked purpofes, and that fome men may be incited by poverty or avarice to carry the enemy thofe provifions, which they pretend to export to Britifh provinces. But if we are to refufe every power that may be employed to bad purpofes, we muft lay all mankind in dungeons, and diveft human nature of all its rights; for every man that has the power of action, may fometimes act ill.

It is, however, prudent to obftruct criminal attempts even when we cannot hope entirely to defeat them, and therefore I am of opinion, that no provifions ought to be exported without fome method of fecurity, by which the governors of every place may be affured that they will be conveyed to our own colonies. Such fecurities will eafily be contrived, and may be regulated in a manner that they fhall not be defeated without fuch hazard, as the profit that can be expected from illegal commerce, will not be able to compenfate.

It is therefore, Sir, proper to delay the bill fo long at leaft as that we may produce by it the ends intended, and diftrefs our enemies more than ourfelves; that we may fecure plenty at home, without the deftruction of our diftant colonies, and without obliging part of our fellow-fubjects to defert to the Spaniards for want of bread.

Mr. BOWLES fpoke in this manner :—Sir, the neceffity of excepting rice from the general prohibition is not only fufficiently evinced by the agent of South Carolina, but confirmed beyond controverfy or doubt, by the petition of the merchants of Briftol, of which the juftice and reafonablenefs appears at the firft view to every man acquainted with the nature of commerce.

How

How much the province of South-Carolina will be diftreffed by this prohibition, how fuddenly the whole trade of that country will be at a ftand, and how immediately the want of many of the neceffaries of life will be felt over a very confiderable part of the Britifh dominions, has already, Sir, been very pathetically reprefented, and very clearly explained; nor does there need any other argument to perfuade us to allow the exportation of rice.

But, from the petition of the merchants of Briftol, it appears that there are other reafons of equal force for this indulgence, and that our regard for the inhabitants of that particular province, however neceffary and juft, is not the only motive for complying with their requeft.

It is fhewn, Sir, in this petition, that the prohibition of rice will very little incommode our enemies, or retard their preparations; for they are not accuftomed to be fupplied with it from our plantations. We ought therefore not to load our fellow-fubjects with embarraffments and inconveniencies, which will not in any degree extend to our enemies.

It appears, Sir, not only that a very important part of our commerce will be obftructed, but that it will probably be loft beyond recovery; for, as only a fmall quantity of the rice of Carolina is confumed at home, and the reft is carried to other countries, it is eafy to conceive that thofe who fhall be difappointed by our merchants will procure fo neceffary a commodity from other places, as there are many from which it may be eafily purchafed; and it is well known that trade, if it be once diverted, is not to be recalled, and therefore, that trade which may be without difficulty transferred, ought never to be interrupted without the moft urgent neceffity.

To prove, Sir, that there is now no fuch neceffity, by a long train of arguments, would be fuperfluous, for it has been fhewn already, that our enemies will not fuffer by the prohibition, and the miferies that inevitably arife from a ftate of war, are too numerous and oppreffive, to admit of any encreafe or aggravation upon trivial motives.

The province of Carolina, Sir, has already fuffered the inconveniencies of this war beyond any other part of his Majefty's dominions, as it is fituate upon the borders of the Spanifh dominions, and as it is weak by the paucity of the inhabitants in proportion to its extent; let us therefore pay a particular regard to this petition, left
we

we aggravate the terror which the neighbourhood of a powerful enemy naturaly produces, by the feverer miferies of poverty and famine.

Sir ROBERT WALPOLE fpoke next in fubftance as follows :—Sir, nothing is more abfurd than for thofe who declare on all occafions, with great folemnity, their fincere zeal for the fervice of the publick, to protract the debates of this houfe by perfonal invectives, and delay the profecution of the bufinefs of the nation, by trivial objections, repeated after confutation, and perhaps after conviction of their invalidity.

I need not obferve how much time would be fpared, and how much the difpatch of affairs would be facilitated by the fuppreffion of this practice, a practice by which truth is levelled with falfhood, and knowledge with ignorance ; fince if fcurrility and merriment are to determine us, it is not neceffary either to be honeft or wife to obtain the fuperiority in any debate, it will only be neceffary to rail and to laugh, which one man may generally perform with as much fuccefs as another.

The embargo in Ireland was an expedient fo neceffary and timely, that the reputation of it is thought too great to be allowed to the adminiftration, of whom it has been for many years the hard fate, to hear their actions cenfured only becaufe they were not the actions of others, and to be reprefented as traytors to their country for doing always what they thought beft themfelves, and perhaps fometimes what was in reality approved by thofe who oppofed them.

This, Sir, they have born without much uneafinefs, and have contented themfelves with the confcioufnefs of doing right, in expectation that truth and integrity muft at laft prevail, and that the prudence of their conduct and fuccefs of their meafures would at laft evince the juftice of their intentions.

They hoped, Sir, that there would be fome occafions on which their enemies would not deny the expedience of their counfels, and did not expect that after having been fo long accufed of engroffing exorbitant power, of rejecting advice, and purfuing their own fchemes with the moft invincible obftinacy, they fhould be fuppofed on a fudden to have laid afide their arrogance, to have defcended to adopt the opinions, and give themfelves up to the direction of others, only becaufe no objection could be made to this inftance of their conduct.

How unhappy, Sir, muft be the ftate of that man who is only allowed

lowed to be a free agent, when he acts wrong, and whose motions, whenever they tend to the proper point, are supposed to be regulated by another!

Whether such capricious censurers expect that any regard should be paid by the publick to their invectives, I am not able to determine; but I am inclined to think so well of their understandings, as to believe that they intend only to amuse themselves, and perplex those whom they profess to oppose. In one part of their scheme I know not but they may have succeeded, but in the other it is evident how generally they have failed. It must at least, Sir, be observed of these great patrons of the people, that if they expect to gain them by artifices like this, they have no high opinion of their discernment, however they may sometimes magnify it as the last appeal, and highest tribunal.

With regard, Sir, to the manner in which the embargo was laid, and the expedients made use of to enforce the observation of it, they were not the effects of a sudden resolution, but of long and deliberate reflection, assisted by the counsels of the most experienced and judicious persons of both nations; so that if any mistake was committed, it proceeded not from arrogance or carelessness, but a compliance with reasons, that if laid before the house, would, whether just or not, be allowed to be specious.

But, Sir, it has not appeared that any improper measures have been pursued, or that any inconveniences have arisen from them which it was possible to have avoided by a different conduct; for when any expedient fails of producing the end for which it was proposed, or gives occasion to inconveniences which were neither expected nor designed, it is not immediately to be condemned; for it might fail from such obstacles as nothing could surmount, and the inconveniencies which are complained of might be the consequences of other causes acting at the same time, or co-operating, not by the nature of things, but by the practices of those who prefer their own interest to that of their country.

But though it is, in my opinion, easy to defend the conduct of the ministry, I am far from thinking this a proper time to engage in their vindication. The important business before us, must now wholly engage us, nor ought we to employ our attention upon the past, but the future. Whatever has been the ignorance or knowledge, whatever the corruption or integrity of the ministry, this bill is equally useful,

uſeful, equally neceſſary. The queſtion is now concerning an act
of the ſenate, not of the miniſtry, and the bill may proceed without
obſtructing future examinations.

If the bill, Sir, now before us be ſo far approved as to be conceived of any real benefit to the nation, if it can at all contribute to the
diſtreſs or diſappointment of our enemies, or the prevention of thoſe
domeſtic diſturbances which are naturally produced by ſcarcity and
miſery, there is no need of arguments to evince the neceſſity of
diſpatch in paſſing it. For if theſe effects are to be produced by preventing the exportation of proviſions, and a law is neceſſary for that
purpoſe, it is certain that the law muſt be enacted, while our proviſions are yet in our own hands, and before time has been given for
the execution of thoſe contracts which are already made.

That contracts, Sir, are entered into for quantities that juſtly
claim the care of the legiſlative power, I have been informed by ſuch
intelligence as I cannot ſuſpect of deceiving me. In one ſmall town
in the weſtern part of this kingdom fifty thouſand barrels of corn are
ſold by contract, and will be exported, if time be allowed for collecting and for ſhipping them.

A few contracts like this will be ſufficient to ſtore an army with
bread, or to furniſh garriſons againſt the danger of a ſiege ; a few
contracts like this will produce a conſiderable change in the price of
proviſions, and plunge innumerable families into diſtreſs, who might
ſtruggle through the preſent difficulties, which unſucceſsful harveſts
have brought upon the nation, had we not ſold the gifts of Providence
for petty gain, and ſupported our enemies with thoſe proviſions which
were barely ſufficient for our own conſumption.

I have not heard many objections made againſt the intention of the
bill, and thoſe which were offered, were mentioned with ſuch diffidence and uncertainty, as plainly ſhewed, that even in the opinion of
him that propoſed them, they were of little weight ; and I believe
they had no greater effect upon thoſe that heard them. It may therefore be reaſonably ſuppoſed that the propriety of a law to prevent the
exportation of victuals is admitted, and ſurely it can be no queſtion,
whether it ought to be preſſed forward, or to be delayed till it will be
of no effect.

Mr. FAZAKERLY ſpoke next to this effect :—Sir, as the bill now
under our conſideration is entangled with a multitude of circumſtances
too important to be paſſed by without conſideration, and too nu-

merous to be fpeedily examined; as its effects, whether falutary or pernicious, muſt extend to many nations, and be felt in a few weeks to the remoteſt parts of the dominions of Britain, I cannot but think, that they who fo much prefs for expedition on this occaſion, conſult rather their paſſions than their reaſon, that they diſcover rather enthuſiaſm than zeal, and that by imagining that they have already traced the effects of a law like this to their utmoſt extent, they diſcover rather an immoderate confidence in their own capacity, than give any proofs of that anxious caution, and deliberate prudence, which true patriotiſm generally produces.

There is another method, Sir, of proceeding more proper on this occaſion, which has been already pointed out in this debate, a method of exerting the prerogative in a manner allowed by law, and eſtabliſhed by immemorial precedents, and which may therefore be revived without affording any room for jealouſy or complaints.

An embargo impoſed only by the prerogative may be relaxed or enforced as occaſion may require, or regulated according to the neceſſity ariſing from particular circumſtances; circumſtances in themſelves variable, and fubject to the influence of a thouſand accidents, and which therefore cannot be always foreſeen, or provided againſt by a law poſitive and fixed.

Let us not ſubject the commonwealth to a hazardous and uncertain ſecurity, while we have in our hands the means of producing the fame end, with lefs danger and inconveniency; and ſince we may obviate the exportation of our corn by methods more ſpeedily efficacious than the forms of making laws can allow, let us not oppreſs our fellow-ſubjects by haſty or imprudent meaſures, but make uſe of temporary expedients, while we deliberate upon the eſtabliſhment of a more laſting regulation.

Mr. CAMPBELL ſpoke to the following purpoſe:—Sir, That an embargo on merchandize or proviſions may, upon ſudden emergencies or important occaſions, be impoſed by the prerogative, cannot be doubted by any man whoſe ſtudies have made him acquainted with the extent of the regal power, and the manner in which it has been exerted in all ages. The chief uſe of the prerogative is to ſupply the defects of the laws, in cafes which do not admit of long conſultations, which do not allow time to convoke ſenates, or enquire into the ſentiments of the people.

For this reaſon, in times of war the imperial power is much enlarged,

larged, and has still a greater extent as exigencies are more pressing. If the nation is invaded by a foreign force, the authority of the crown is almost without limits, the whole nation is considered as an army of which the king is general, and which he then governs by martial laws, by occasional judicature, and extemporary decrees.

Such, Sir, is the power of the king on particular emergencies, and such power the nature of human affairs must sometimes require; for all forms of government are intended for common good, and calculated for the established condition of mankind, but must be suspended when they can only obstruct the purposes for which they were contrived, and must vary with the circumstances to which they were adapted. To expect that the people shall be consulted in questions on which their happiness depends, supposes there is an opportunity of consulting them without hazarding their lives, their freedom, or their possessions, by the forms of deliberation.

The necessity of extending the prerogative to the extremities of power, is, I hope, at a very great distance from us; but if the danger of the exportation of victuals be so urgent as some gentlemen have represented it, and so formidable as it appears to the whole nation, it is surely requisite that the latent powers of the crown should be called forth for our protection, that plenty be secured within the nation, by barring up our ports, and the people hindered from betraying themselves to their enemies, and squandering those blessings which the fertility of our soil has bestowed upon them.

Sir ROBERT WALPOLE replied in the following manner:—Sir, it is so unusual among the gentlemen who have opposed my opinion to recommend an exertion of the regal authority, or willingly to intrust any power to the administration, that, though they have on this occasion expressed their sentiments without any ambiguity of language, or perplexity of ideas, I am in doubt whether I do not mistake their meaning, and cannot, without hesitation and uncertainty, propose the motion to which all their arguments seem necessarily to conduct me, arguments of which I do not deny the force, and which I shall not attempt to invalidate by slight objections, when I am convinced in general of their reasonableness and truth.

The necessity of that dispatch which I have endeavoured to recommend, is not only universally admitted, but affirmed to be so pressing, that it cannot wait for the solemnity of debates, or the common forms of passing laws. The danger which is every
moment

moment encreafing, requires, in the opinion of thefe gentlemen, to be obviated by extraordinary meafures, and that pernicious commerce, which threatens the diftrefs of the community, is to be reftrained by an immediate act of the prerogative.

If this be the opinion of the houfe, it will be neceffary to lay it before his majefty by a regular addrefs, that the nation may be convinced of the neceffity of fuch extraordinary precautions, and that the embargo may be impofed, at once with the expedition peculiar to defpotick power, and the authority which can be conferred only by fenatorial fanctions.

Whether this is the intention of the members, from whofe declarations I have deduced it, can only be difcovered by themfelves, who, if they have any other fcheme in view, muft explain it in clearer terms, that the houfe may deliberate upon it, and reject or adopt it, according to its conformity to the laws of our country, and to the prefent ftate of our affairs.

Mr. PULTENEY fpoke thus :— Sir, whatever may be the meaning of other gentlemen, who muft undoubtedly be left at full liberty to explain their own expreffions, I will freely declare, that I am fufficiently underftood by the right hon. gentleman, and that, in my opinion, no remedy can be applied to the prefent diftemper of the nation, a diftemper by which it is hourly pining away, by which its vitals are impaired, and the neceffary nourifhment withdrawn from it, that will operate with fufficient efficacy and fpeed, except an embargo be impofed by the prerogative.

That this opinion, if received by the houfe, muft be the fubject of an addrefs, is in itfelf manifeft, and the reafon for which an embargo is required, proves that an addrefs ought not to be delayed.

I cannot omit this opportunity of remarking, how plainly it muft now appear that many of us have been unjuftly charged with obftructing the progrefs of the bill for pernicious purpofes, with views of raifing difcontents in the nation, of expofing the adminiftration to publick hatred, of obftructing the meafures of the government, or hindering the fuccefs of the war, when we have receded from our general principles, and fufpended the influence of our eftablifhed maxims, for the fake of facilitating an expedient which may promote the general advantage, by recommending his majefty to the affections of his people.

Mr. PELHAM here replied to this effect :—Sir, I am far from

blaming

blaming any gentleman for afferting, on all occasions, the integrity of his defigns, or difplaying the reafonablenefs of his conduct; and of what I do not difapprove I fhall not decline the imitation.

It is not uncommon, in the heat of oppofition, while each man is convinced of his own honefty, and ftrongly perfuaded of the truth of his own pofitions, to hear each party accufed by the other of defigns detrimental to the publick intereft, of protracting debates by artful delays, of ftruggling againft their own conviction, and of obfcuring known truth by objections which difcover themfelves to be without force.

Thefe accufations, which are on both fides frequent, are, I hope, on both fides generally falfe; at leaft it muft appear on this occafion, that thofe who prefs the bill had no views of ftrengthening their party by a victory, of wearying their opponents by obftinacy, or of promoting any private purpofes by a new law; fince an expedient, by which time may be gained, and the avowed end of haftening this neceffary bill fecured, is no fooner propofed on one part, than received on the other.

At the clofe of the debate, a form of an addrefs was propofed by Mr. Clutterbuck; which, being approved by the houfe, was prefented to his majefty: and an embargo was laid on all provifions accordingly.

On the 17th day of fitting the houfe proceeded on the bill for preventing exportation; and ordered an account of the corn which had been exported for fix years laft paft to be laid before the committee.

The houfe alfo addreffed his majefty to take off the embargo on fhips laden with fifh or rice, which his majefty had before ordered to be done.

On the 21ft the Corn Bill was again the fubject of deliberation, and fome amendments were offered by Mr. Sandys, containing not only exceptions of rice and fifh, which had been before admitted, but likewife of butter, as a perifhable commodity, which, if it were not allowed to be exported, would corrupt and become ufelefs in a fhort time.

He propofed likewife, that the two iflands of Jerfey and Guernfey might continue to be fupplied, with certain reftrictions, from the port of Southampton.

It was propofed likewife, in favour of fome other colonies, that they might receive provifions from Britain, left there fhould be a neceffity for the inhabitants of thofe provinces to abandon their fettlements.

The penalties of this law, and the manner in which they fhould be recovered and applied, were likewife fettled on this day.

November

November 25, 1740.

The confideration of the Corn Bill was refumed; and it was particularly
debated from what time it fhould commence, which fome of the members
were inclined to fix on the 9th day of the feffion, on which occafion
Mr. CAMPBELL *fpoke as follows:*

Sir, that the laws may be obferved by the nation without daily
violence and perpetual compulfion, that our determinations may be
received with reverence, and the regulations which we eftablifh confirmed by the concurrence of our conftituents, it is neceffary that we
endeavour to preferve their efteem, and convince them that the
publick profperity may be fafely trufted in our hands.

This confidence is to be gained as well in high ftations, as in lower
conditions, by large affemblies as by individuals, only by a conftant
practice of juftice, and frequent exertion of fuperior wifdom. When
any man finds his friend oppreffive and malicious, he naturally with-
draws his affections from him; when he obferves him advancing abfurd opinions, and adhering to them with obftinacy incapable of
conviction, he falls unavoidably into a diftruft of his underftanding,
and no longer pays any deference to his advice, or confiders his conduct as worthy of imitation.

In the fame manner, Sir, if the legiflative powers fhall, in making
laws, difcover that they regard any motives before the advantage of
their country, or that they purfue the publick good by meafures inadequate and ill-concerted, what can be expected from the people, but
that they fhould fet up their own judgment in oppofition to that of
their governors, make themfelves the arbiters in all doubtful queftions,
and obey or difregard the laws at difcretion?

If this danger may arife from laws injudicioufly drawn up, it may
furely be apprehended from a compliance with this propofal; a propofal that the operation of the law fhould commence eleven days before the law itfelf is in being.

I have hitherto, Sir, regarded it as a principle equally true in politics as in philofophy, that nothing *can act* when it does *not exift*;
and I did not fufpect that a pofition fo evident would ever ftand in
need of a proof or illuftration.

We live indeed in an age of paradoxes, and have heard feveral
notions ferioufly defended, cf which fome would, not many years
ago, have condemned their abettor to a prifon or a madhoufe, and
would have been heard by the wifeft of our anceftors with laughter or

detestation;

deteftation; but I did not expect that the moft hardy innovator would have fhocked my underftanding with a pofition like this, or have afferted that a law may operate before it is made, or before it is projected.

That where there is no law there is no tranfgreffion, is a maxim not only eftablifhed by univerfal confent, but in itfelf evident and undeniable; and it is, Sir, furely no lefs certain, that where there is no tranfgreffion there can be no punifhment.

If a man may be punifhed, Sir, by a law made after the fact, how can any man conclude himfelf fecure from the jail or the gibbet? A man may eafily find means of being certain that he has offended no law in being, but that will afford no great fatisfaction to a mind naturally timorous; fince a law hereafter to be made, may, if this motion be fuppofed reafonable, take cognizance of his actions, and how he can know whether he has been equally fcrupulous to obferve the future ftatutes of future fenates, he will find it very difficult to determine.

Mr. PELHAM rofe and fpoke thus:—Sir, notwithftanding the abfurdity which the honourable gentleman imagines himfelf to have difcovered in this propofal, and which he muft be confeffed to have placed in a very ftrong light, I am of opinion, that it may with very little confideration be reconciled to reafon and to juftice, and that the wit and fatire that have been fo liberally employed, will appear to have been loft in the air, without ufe and without injury.

The operation of the law may very properly commence from the day on which the embargo was laid by his majefty's proclamation, which furely was not iffued to no purpofe, and which ought not to be difobeyed without punifhment.

Sir JOHN BARNARD fpoke next to this effect:—Sir, I cannot but be fomewhat furprifed, that a gentleman fo long converfant in national affairs, fhould not yet have heard or known the difference between a proclamation and a penal law.

By a proclamation his majefty may prevent in fome cafes what he cannot punifh; he may hinder the exportation of our corn by ordering fhips to be ftationed at the entrance of our harbours; but if any fhould efcape with prohibited cargoes, he can inflict no penalties upon them at their return.

To enforce this prohibition by the fanction of punifhments is the intention of the prefent bill, but a proclamation can make nothing criminal,

criminal, and it is unjuft and abfurd to punifh an action which was
legal when it was done.

The law ought, Sir, in my opinion, not to commence till time
is allowed for difperfing it to the utmoft limits of this ifland ; for as
it is unreafonable to punifh without law, it is not more equitable to
punifh by a law, of which, they who have unhappily broken it,
could have no intelligence.

A future day was agreed to.

HOUSE OF COMMONS.

December 2, 1740.

DEBATE RELATING TO A SEDITIOUS PAPER OF THE SAME KIND WITH THE CONSIDERATIONS ON THE EMBARGO ON PROVISIONS.

Lord THOMSON *took notice of a paper which he had in his hand, and faid
he received it at the door, where it was given to the members as they came
in, and, complaining of it as an indignity offered to the houfe, defired
that it might be read. Which being done, he rofe up, and fpoke in fubftance as follows :*

SIR, the crime of exafperating the people againft their governors,
of raifing difcontent, and exciting murmurs in a time of general
danger, and of attempting to reprefent wife and falutary meafures,
which have received the approbation of the whole legiflature, as
mean artifices, contrived only to raife the fortunes of fome favou-
rites of the minifter, and aggrandize the officers of ftate by the miferies of the people, is a crime too enormous to require or admit any
aggravation from rhethoric, and too dangerous to hope from any excufe from candour and lenity.

To read or hear this paper is fufficient for a full conviction of its pernicious tendency, and of the malice of its author ; a charge not fixed
upon particular expreffions capable of a doubtful meaning, and which
heat or inadvertency might cafually have produced, but fupported by
the general defign of the whole paper, and the continued tenor of
the argument, which is evidently intended to fhew, that an act
of government, which cannot but appear neceffary and feafonable
in the prefent ftate of our affairs, an act ratified by the concurrence

C 4

of all the powers of the leg flature, is nothing but a fcheme of avarice to grow rich by oppreffion.

Nor is this fcandalous libel written with more confidence and infolence than it is difperfed. Not content, Sir, with vilifying the proceedings of the ftate, the author has induftrioufly publifhed his calumny at our door: the time has been when defamation fkulked in
fecret, and calumnies againft the government were difperfed by
whifpers or private communication; but this writer adds infults to
his injuries, and at once reproaches and defies us.

I beg leave to move, therefore, that the houfe do cenfure this paper
as " a malicious and fcandalous libel, highly and injurioufly reflect-
ing upon a juft and wife act of his majefty's government, and alfo
upon the proceedings of both houfes of fenate; and tending to
create jealoufies in the minds of the people." I alfo move, " that
the author may be ordered to attend, to be examined at our bar." .

[This was unanimoufly agreed to by the houfe. The door-keeper
was called in, and being fhewn the paper, was afked from whom he
received it? who anfwered, that he believed the perfon who delivered it to him, was then detained in one of the committee rooms,
upon which he was ordered to look for, and fetch him to the bar.

Mr Sandys, taking notice that the perfon was already in cuftody,
faid, that he fhould be glad to know by what authority. It was not
reafonable to punifh firft, and judge afterwards.

Upon which Sir W. Doge replied, that he had caufed him to be
detained, in order to know the pleafure of the houfe; and that he
thought it his duty to fecure fo enormous an offender from efcaping.

Soon after the door-keeper brought the man in, when he declared,
upon examination, his name, and his profeffion, which was that of
a fcrivener, and owned, with great opennefs, that he was the author of the paper. He was then afked, who was the printer, and
anfwered, that he printed it himfelf. Which he explained afterwards, by faying, that as he had carried it to the printer's, he might
be faid, in the general acceptation of the term, as applied to an
author, to be the printer. He then difcovered the printer, and was
afked, where was the original manufcript, which he faid he had
deftroyed, as he did any other ufelefs paper.

It having been obferved by fome of the members, that it was
printed in one of the daily papers, he was afked, who carried it
thither? and anfwered, that he carried it himfelf. It was then demanded,

manded, what he gave for having it inferted, and he anfwered
that he gave nothing.

After many queftions, Mr. *Henry Archer* defired that he might be
afked, Whether on the Friday before he was in the gallery? at
which fome of the members expreffed their difapprobation, and the
man being ordered to withdraw, the following debate enfued upon
the propriety of the queftion.]

Mr. SANDYS fpoke firft in fubftance as follows : —Sir, thofe who are
entrufted by their country with the authority of making laws, ought
undoubtedly to obferve them with the utmoft circumfpeftion, left
they fhould defeat their own endeavours, and invalidate by their
example their own decrees.

There is no part, Sir, of our civil conftitution more facred, none
that has been more revered by thofe that have trampled upon other
forms of juftice, and wantoned in oppreffion without reftraint, than
that privilege by which every Briton is exempted from the neceffity
of accufing himfelf, and by which he is intitled to refufe an anfwer
to any queftion which may be afked, with a view to draw from him a
confeffion of an offence which cannot be proved.

Whether this great privilege, Sir, is not violated; whether the
unalienable right of a free fubjeft is not infringed, by the queftion
put to the perfon at our bar, the houfe muft decide. The punifhment
to which intruders are fubjeft by the orders of this houfe, proves that
his prefence in the houfe is confidered as a crime, of which, as we
have no proof of it, a confeffion ought not to be extorted by an artful and infidious queftion, of which he may not difcover the intention or the confequence. Such treatment, Sir, is rather to be ex-
pefted by flaves in the inquifition of Spain, than a Briton at the bar
of this houfe ; a houfe inftituted to preferve liberty, and to reftrain
injuftice and oppreffion.

Mr. CAMPBELL fpoke next to this effeft :—Sir, I cannot but concur with the opinion of the Honourable Gentleman, that, in requiring an anfwer to this queftion, we fhall expofe a man to a punifhment againft whom we have no evidence but what is extorted from
himfelf; and confequently no knowledge of his crime upon which
we can proceed to inflift cenfures or penalties, without the manifeft
infraftion of our conftitution.

It cannot be imagined, Sir, that he intends to confefs himfelf
guilty of a crime of which no proof has been brought, or that he
will voluntarily fubjeft himfelf to punifhments. It muft, therefore,

follow that he is intrapped in his examination, by an artifice, which, I hope, will never find any countenance in this houfe.

Mr. WINNINGTON anfwered to the following purpofe :—Sir, it is not impoffible that the honourable gentlemen, having not lately looked into the orders of the houfe, may miftake the tendency of the queftion ; I therefore move, that the order may be read.

[*The order being read by the clerk, he proceeded.*]

It is evident, Sir, that, by the order now read, the ferjeant at arms attending on this houfe, may take into cuftody all ftrangers that fhall be found in the houfe or gallery while we are affembled ; and that this order is not always put in practice, muft be attributed to the lenity of the houfe. But that this order extends to paft offences, and fubjects any man to imprifonment for having been prefent in fome former day, cannot be conceived. For how far may fuch a retrofpect be extended ? or at what time after having intruded into the houfe, can any man prefume to confider himfelf as exempt from the danger of imprifonment ?

Our order, Sir, only decrees prefent punifhment for prefent offences, and therefore the queftion afked by the honourable gentleman, may be infifted on without fcruple, and anfwered without hazard. Let then the honourable gentlemen referve their laudable zeal for our conftitution till it fhall be invaded by more important occafions.

Mr. SANDYS replied :—Sir, what victory the honourable gentleman imagines himfelf to have gained, or whence proceeds all his wantonnefs of exultation, I am not able to difcover. The queftion only relates to the interpretation of one of our own orders, and is therefore not of the higheft importance ; nor can his fuccefs in fo trivial a debate entitle him to great applaufe from others, or produce, in a perfon of his abilities, any uncommon fatisfaction to himfelf.

But whatever may be the pleafure of the victory, it muft at leaft be gained before it can be celebrated ; and it is by no means evident that he has yet any reafon to affure himfelf of conqueft.

His interpretation, Sir, of the order, which he has fo confidently laid before the houfe, feems to me to have no foundation in reafon or juftice ; for if it be an offence againft the houfe to be prefent at our confultations, and that offence be juftly punifhable, why fhould any man be exempt from a juft cenfure by an accidental efcape ? or what makes the difference between this crime and any other, that this alone muft be immediately punifhed, or immediately obliterated, and that lucky flight is equivalent to innocence ?

..... It

It is furely, Sir, more rational to believe, that the houfe may punifh any breach of its orders at a diftant time, that if our cenfure is once eluded, it may be afterwards enforced ; and, therefore, that the queftion put to the perfon at the bar ought not to be afked, becaufe it cannot fafely be anfwered.

Mr. PULTENEY fpoke next in words to this effect :—Sir, I cannot but conceive that our order may extend its influence beyond the prefent moment, and that intrufions may be punifhed by the houfe on another day than that on which they were committed.

I am fo far, Sir, from being of opinion, that, to make the execution of this order valid, the houfe muft fit without interruption from the time of the offence to that of the punifhment, that if the gentlemen in the gallery were to be taken into cuftody, I fhould advife the ferjeant to wait till the houfe fhould break up, and feize them as they fhould come out.

Sir WILLIAM YONGE fpoke next in the manner following :—Sir, if any fuch punifhment were now intended, I fhould advife the gentlemen in the gallery to retire, indeed, but not to hide themfelves like felons, or men profcribed by proclamation ; for as the power of feizing any man in the houfe is fufficient to fecure us from intrufion, there is no reafon to extend it farther; and penalties are not without reafon to be inflicted, neither has the houfe ever coveted the power of oppreffing ; and what elfe is unneceffary punifhment ?

If, therefore, an intruder is not feized in the act of intrufion, he cannot legally be imprifoned for it. And any of the ftrangers who now hear this debate may retire to a very fmall diftance from the houfe, and fet the ferjeant at arms at defiance.

Sir ROBERT WALPOLE then fpoke to this effect :—Sir, whether the queftion be proper or not, it feems very unneceffary to debate ; becaufe, however it be anfwered, it cannot be of great importance : the man has already confeffed himfelf the author of the libel, and may, therefore, be punifhed without farther examination.

That he is the real author, Sir, I am not indeed convinced by his affertion, with whatever confidence it was made ; for fo far as his appearance enables me to judge of his education and fphere of life, it is not probable that he fhould be much verfed in political enquiries, or that he fhould engage in the difcuffion of queftions like this.

There appears, Sir, in the paper before us, a more extenfive knowledge of facts, a more accurate attention to commerce, more artful reafoning, and a more elevated ftile, than it is reafonable to expect from this man, whom, without pretending to determine the limits of his capacity, or the compass of his knowledge, I am, for my part, inclined to look upon as an agent to some other person of higher station, and greater accomplishments.

It is not uncommon, Sir, for gentlemen to exercise their abilities and employ their pens upon political questions, and when they have produced any thing, which their complaisance for themselves equally hinders them from owning and suppressing, they are known to procure some person of inferior rank to take upon him in publick the character of the author, and to stand the danger of the prosecution, contenting themselves with the applause and admiration of their chosen friends, whom they trust with the important secret, and with whom they sit and laugh at the conjectures of the publick, and the ignorance of the ministry.

This, Sir, is a frequent practice, not only with those who have no other employment, but, as I have sufficient reasons to believe, among some gentlemen who have seats in this house, gentlemen whose abilities and knowledge qualify them to serve the publick in characters much superior to that of lampooners of the government.

Mr. PULTENEY answered in terms to the following purpose :—Sir, whether the man who confessed himself the author of the paper has accused himself of what he did not commit, or has ingenuously and openly discovered the truth, it is beyond my penetration absolutely to decide; the frankness and unconcern with which he made the declaration, give it at least the appearance of truth, nor do I discover any reason for doubting his sincerity. Is there any improbability in the nature of the fact that should incline us to suspect his veracity? Is there any apparent advantage to be gained by assuming a false character? Neither of those circumstances can be produced against him, and an assertion is to be admitted for its own sake, when there is nothing to invalidate it.

But the honourable gentleman, Sir, appears to have a very particular reason for his doubts; a reason, which will, I hope, have no weight with any but himself. By denying the paper to this man, he gives room for conjecture and suspicion to range far and wide, and wanton with whatever characters he shall think proper subjects for his amusement. An author is now to be sought, and many diverting arguments may be brought by the dullest enquirer for fixing it upon one man, or denying it to another.

The

The honourable gentleman, Sir, has given us a bold specimen of this kind of wit, by infinuating that it is the production of some one of the members of this house ; a conjecture of which I am not able to find the foundation, and therefore imagine, that raillery rather than argument was intended. But let the honourable gentleman recollect, that the chief excellence of raillery is politeness, to which he has surely paid little regard, in suppofing that what has been unanimoufly condemned as a libel, has one of thofe who cenfured it for its author.

If I am particularly hinted at in this fagacious conjecture, I take this opportunity of declaring that I am equally ignorant of the whole affair with any other gentleman in this house ; that I never faw the paper, till it was delivered to me at the door, nor the author till he appeared at the bar. Having thus cleared myfelf, Sir, from this afperfion, I declare it as my opinion, that every gentleman in the houfe can fafely purge himfelf in the fame manner ; for I cannot conceive, that any of them can have written a libel like this. There are, indeed, fome paffages which would not difgrace the greateft abilities, and fome maxims true in themfelves, though perhaps fallacioufly applied, and at leaft fuch an appearance of reafoning and knowledge, as fets the writer far above the level of the contemptible fcriblers of the minifterial vindications : a herd of wretches whom neither information can enlighten, nor affluence elevate ; low drudges of fcurrility, whofe fcandal is harmlefs for want of wit, and whofe oppofition is only troublefome from the pertinacioufnefs of ftupidity.

Why fuch immenfe fums are diftributed amongft thefe reptiles, it is fcarce poffible not to enquire ; for it cannot be imagined that thofe who pay them expect any fupport from their abilities. If their patrons would read their writings, their falaries would quickly be withdrawn ; for a few pages would convince them, that they can neither attack nor defend, neither raife any man's reputation by their panegyric, nor deftroy it by their defamation.

Sir ROBERT WALPOLE then fpoke in the following manner:—I hope it is not expected, that the heat with which one clafs of our political writers have been attacked by the honourable gentleman, fhould engage me to undertake their defence with the fame earneftnefs. I have neither intereft enough in the queftion to awaken my paffions, nor curiofity or leifure fufficient for fuch an examination of the

writings

writings on each fide, as is neceffary, before the fuperiority of any
author above his brethren can be juftly afferted.

It is no part, Sir, of my employment or amufement to compare
their arguments, or to balance their abilities; nor do I often read
the papers of either party, except when I am informed by fome that
have more inclination to fuch ftudies than myfelf, that they have
rifen by fome accident above their common level.

Yet that I may not appear intirely to defert the queftion, I cannot forbear to fay, that I have never, from thefe accidental infpec-
tions of their performances, difcovered any reafon to exalt the authors who write againft the adminiftration, to a higher degree of reputation than their opponents. That any of them deferve loud applaufes, I cannot affert, and am afraid that all, which deferves to be
preferved of the writings on either fide, may be contracted to a very
few volumes.

The writers for the oppofition appear to me to be nothing more
than the echoes of their predeceffors, or, what is ftill more defpicable,
of themfelves, and to have produced nothing in the laft feven years,
which had not been faid feven years before.

I may, perhaps, be thought by fome gentlemen of each clafs to
fpeak contemptuoufly of their advocates, nor fhall I think my own
opinion lefs juft for fuch a cenfure; for the reputation of controverfial writers arifes, generally, from the prepoffeffion of their readers in
favour of the opinions which they endeavour to defend. Men eafily
admit the force of an argument which tends to fupport notions, that
it is their intereft to diffufe, and readily find wit and fpirit in a fatire
pointed at characters which they defire to deprefs: but to the oppofite party, and even to themfelves, when their paffions have fubfided,
and their intereft is difunited from the queftion, thofe arguments
appear only loud affertions, or empty fophiftry; and that wit which
was clamouroufly praifed, difcovers itfelf to be only impudence or
low conceits; the fpirit evaporates, and the malignity only remains.

If we confider, Sir, what oppofition of character is neceffary to
conftitute a political writer, it will not be wondered, that fo few
excel in that undertaking. He that will write well in politicks,
muft at the fame time have a complete knowledge of the queftion,
and time to digeft his thoughts into method, and polifh his ftile into
elegance; which is little lefs than to fay, he muft be at once a man
of bufinefs, and a man of leifure; for political tranfactions are not
easily

:afily underftood, but by thofe who are engaged in them, and the irt of writing is not attainable without long practice, and fedentary ipplication.

Thus it happens that political writings are generally defective : for they are drawn up by men unacquainted with publick bufinefs, and who can therefore only amufe their readers with fallacious re-:itals, fpecious fophiftries, or an agreeable ftile ; or they are the hafty productions of bufy negociators, who, though they cannot but excel the other clafs of writers in that which is of moft importance, the knowledge of their fubject, are yet rarely at leifure to difplay that knowledge to advantage, or add grace to folidity.

Writers of the latter fort appear but feldom, and moft of our po-litical papers, are the amufements of leifure, or the expedients of want.

Whether the paper now before us, is the produce of eafe, or of neceffity, I fhall not determine ; I have already offered my opinion, that the man who claims it, is not the author, nor do I difcover any reafon for changing my fentiment : the queftion is a queftion merely of conjecture, fince neither I nor the honourable gentleman attempt to offer any demonftrative proofs of our opinion. If he has any to produce in favour of his own notions, let him lay them before you, but let him always forbear to impute to me affertions which I never uttered, and beware of reprefenting me as declaring that I believe this paper the compofition of fome member of this houfe.

[*It was then debated, whether this offence fhould be punifhed by the au-thority of the houfe, or referred to the cognizance of fome of the courts of judicature in Weftminfter Hall, on which occafion Mr. Howe fpoke as follows :*]

Sir, it is the duty of every part of the legiflature, not only to pre-ferve the whole fyftem of our government unaltered and unimpaired, but to attend particularly to the fupport of their own privileges, privileges not conferred upon them by our anceftors but for wife pur-pofes.

It is the privilege of this houfe that we, and we only, are the judges of our own rights, and we only, therefore, can affign the proper punifhment when they fhall be prefumptuoufly invaded.

If we remit this offender, who has attempted to debafe the houfe in the opinion of the nation, to any inferior court, we allow that court to determine, by the punifhment that fhall be inflicted, the

importance

importance of this assembly, and the value of the collective character of this house.

It therefore concerns us, in regard to our own dignity, and to the privileges of our successors, that we retain the cognizance of this crime in our own hands, in which it is placed by perpetual prescription and the nature of our constitution.

[The house agreed to this, and the libeller was sent to the common gaol of Middlesex, by warrant from the Speaker.]

Sir WILLIAM YONGE then spoke to this effect:—Sir, I am pleased with finding that the malice and indecency of this libel, has raised in the house a just resentment, and that the wretch, who, with a confidence so steady, and such appearance of satisfaction in his countenance, confesses, or rather proclaims himself the author, is treated as he deserves. But let us not forget that the same degree of guilt always requires the same punishment, and that when the author of scandal is in prison, the printer and propagator of it ought not to be at liberty.

The printer of the daily news is surely the proper object of your indignation, who inserted this libel in his paper, without the fondness of an author, and without the temptation of a bribe; a bribe, by the help of which it is usual to circulate scurrility. To this man the expence or labour of aspersing the government was recompensed by the pleasure, and he could not prevail on himself to omit any opportunity of incensing the people, and exposing at once the whole legislature to censure and contempt.

Those, therefore, that have concurred in the imprisonment of the author, will doubtless join with me in requiring the attendance of his officious accomplice, and I cannot forbear expressing my hopes, that he will not meet with kinder treatment.

It is far from being the first offence of his licentious press; and the lenity of the government, by which he has been so long spared, has had no other effect upon him, than to add confidence to his malice, and incite him to advance from one degree of impudence to another.

He has for several weeks persisted in misrepresenting the intention of the embargo, by letters pretended to be written by friends of the government who are injured by it. He has vented his insinuations hitherto, as without impunity, so, as it appears, without fear. It

it

is time, therefore, to diſturb his ſecurity, and reſtrain him from adding one calumny to another.

Sir JOHN BARNARD roſe up hereupon, and oppoſed this motion in terms to the following effect :—Sir, the end of puniſhment is to prevent a repetition of the ſame crime, both in the offender, and in thoſe who may have the ſame inclinations, and when that end is accompliſhed, all farther ſeverities have an appearance rather of cruelty than juſtice.

By puniſhing the author of this libel, we have, in my opinion, ſufficiently ſecured our dignity from any future attacks, we have cruſhed the head of the confederacy, and prevented the ſubordinate agents from exerting their malice. Printers can do no injury without authors ; and if no man ſhall dare to write a libel, it is not worthy of our enquiry how many may be inclined to publiſh it.

But if the printer muſt neceſſarily be puniſhed before the reſentment of the houſe can be ſatisfied ; if it ſhall not be thought ſufficient to puniſh him without whoſe aſſiſtance the other could not have offended; let us at leaſt confine our animadverſion to the preſent fault, without tracing back his life for paſt miſdemeanors, and charging him with accumulated wickedneſs ; for if a man's whole life is to be the ſubject of judicial enquiries, when he ſhall appear at the bar of this houſe, the moſt innocent will have reaſon to tremble when they approach it.

Even with regard, Sir, to the offence of which he is now accuſed, ſomewhat may, perhaps, be ſaid in extenuation of his guilt, which I do not offer to gratify any perſonal affection or regard for him, to whom I am equally a ſtranger with any other gentleman in this houſe, but to prevent a puniſhment which may be hereafter thought diſproportioned to the crime.

It is, Sir, to be remembered, that he was not the original printer of the libel, which he only reprinted from a paper, of which he knew that it was to be diſperſed at our door, and in which he could not naturally ſuſpect any ſeditious or dangerous aſſertions to be contained. It is, therefore, probable that he fell into the offence by ignorance, or, at worſt, by inadvertency; and, as his intention was not criminal, he may properly be ſpared.

Mr. WINNINGTON ſpoke in anſwer to this effect :—Sir, I cannot but think the honourable gentleman betrayed by his zeal for the defence of this man, into ſome aſſertions not to be ſupported by law or reason. If it be innocent to print a paper once printed, will it not inevitably follow, that the most flagitious falshoods, and the moft enormous infults on the crown itself, the moft feditious invectives, and moft dangerous pofitions, may be difperfed through the whole empire, without any danger but to the original printer? And what reafon, Sir, can be affigned, why that which is criminal in one man, fhould be innocent in another?

Nor is this the only pofition which has been advanced contrary to the laws of our country; for it has been afferted, that the general character of an offender is a confideration foreign from that of his immediate crime; and that whatever any man's paft life has been, he is only to be judged according to the evidence for the offence which is then the fubject of examination.

How much this opinion is confiftent with the practice of our courts, a very flight knowledge of their methods of proceeding will readily difcover. Is any villain there convicted but by the influence of his character? And is not the chief queftion at a trial the paft conduct of the perfon at the bar?

Sir JOHN BARNARD rofe here and fpoke thus :—Sir, I rife up only to anfwer a queftion, which is, whether properly or not, put to me, and hope the irregularity will not be imputed to me by the houfe, but to the occafion which produces it.

I am afked, whether it is not the chief queftion at the bar of our courts of juftice, what is the character of the prifoner? and cannot but feel fome amazement that any man fhould be fo ignorant of common proceedings, and fo much unacquainted with the execution of our laws, as to have admitted a notion fo chimerical.

The character of the prifoner is never examined, except when it is pleaded by himfelf, and witneffes are produced to offer teftimony in his favour; that plea, like all others, is then to be examined, and is fometimes confuted by contrary evidence. But the character of a criminal, though it may be urged by himfelf as a proof of his innocence, is never to be mentioned by his profecutor as an aggravation or proof of his guilt. It is not required by the law, that the general character of a criminal, but that the particular evidence of the crime with which he ftands charged, fhould be examined; nor is his character ever mentioned but by his own choice.

Sir WILLIAM YONGE fpoke next to the effect following :—Sir, to prove the malignity of the intention with which this libel was inferted

ferted in the daily paper, it cannot be improper to obferve, that the embargo has been for many days paft the favourite topic of this printer, and that, therefore, it was not by accident that he admitted fo zealous an advocate for his opinions to be feafonably affifted by the circulation of his paper, but that he doubtlefs was delighted with an opportunity of difperfing fedition by means of greater abilities than his own.

Nor can it be juftly pleaded, Sir, in his favour, that he was encouraged to publifh it by the confidence with which he faw it difperfed; for it was printed by him in the morning, and not brought hither till the afternoon. I cannot, therefore, but conclude, that his intentions were agreeable to his practice, and that he deferves to acompany the author in his prefent confinement.

The Advocate CAMPBELL fpoke next to this purpofe:—Sir, I hope it will not be imputed to me as difregard of the government, or neglect of the honour of this houfe, that I declare myfelf, on all occafions like this, inclined to lenity, and think it neceffary always to proceed by regular methods, and known forms of juftice, not by capricious determinations, and orders variable at pleafure.

I oppofed the imprifonment of the man who juft now appeared at the bar of our houfe, and am ftill more unwilling to proceed to feverities againft another, who is criminal only in a fubordinate degree. The loudeft declaimers againft thefe men cannot have ftronger deteftation of falfhood and fedition than myfelf; but however flagrant may be the crimes, they may be punifhed with unjuftifiable rigour, and, in my opinion, we have already proceeded with feverity fufficient to difcourage any other attempts of the fame kind.

Whether it will promote the advantage of the publick, and the efficacy of our deliberations, to deter any man from the common practice of giving us information by delivering paper at our door, muft be confidered by the houfe.

Nor is it lefs worthy of our moft attentive enquiry, whether it is not more reafonable to profecute this offender in the common forms of juftice, than to punifh him by any act of uncontrollable, unaccountable authority? Whether it is not more reafonable to have him profecuted before a judge unprejudiced, and a difinterefted jury, than to act at once as party, evidence, and judge? I have no defire, Sir, of diminishing the privileges of this house; and yet, less would I contribute to establish any precedents of unlimited power or arbitrary punishments.

The ATTORNEY GENERAL then spoke to the following effect:— Sir, whence so much tenderness can arise for an offender of this kind I am at a loss to discover, nor am I able to conceive any argument that can be produced for exempting from punishment the printer of a paper, which has been already determined, by the vote of the house, to be a scandalous libel, tending to promote sedition.

It has been, indeed, agreed, that there are contained in the paper some true positions, and some passages innocent at least, and perhaps rational and seasonable. But this, Sir, is nothing more than to say, that the paper, flagitious as it is, might have been swelled to a greater degree of impudence and scurrility; that what is already too heinous to be born, might by greater virulence become more enormous.

If no wickedness, Sir, is to be checked till it has attained the greatest height at which it can possibly arrive, our courts of criminal judicature may be shut up as useless; and if a few innocent paragraphs will palliate a libel, treason may be written and dispersed without danger or restraint; for what libel was ever so crowded with sedition, that a few periods might not have been selected, which, upon this principle, might have secured it from censure.

The danger of discouraging intelligence from being offered at the door of our house, does not alarm me with any apprehensions of disadvantage to the nation; for I have not so mean an opinion of the wisdom of this assembly as to imagine that they can receive any assistance from the informations of their officious instructors, who ought, in my opinion, Sir, rather to be taught by some senatorial censure to know their own station, than to be encouraged to neglect their proper employments, for the sake of directing their governors.

When bills, Sir, are depending, by which either the interest of the nation, or of particular men, may be thought to be endangered, it is indeed the incontestable right of every Briton to offer his petition at the bar of the house, and to deliver the reasons upon which it is founded. This is a privilege of an unalienable kind, and which is never to be infringed or denied; and this may always be supported without countenancing anonymous intelligence, or receiving such

papers

papers as the authors of them are afraid or ashamed to own, and which they, therefore, employ meaner hands to distribute.

Of this kind, Sir, undoubtedly is the paper now under our consideration, of which I am far from imagining that it was drawn up by the man who declares himself the writer, and am therefore convinced of the necessity of calling the printer to the bar, that whatever the lenity or justice of this assembly may determine with regard to his punishment, he may be examined with respect to the real authors of the libel; and that our resentment may fall upon him, who has endeavoured to shelter himself by exposing another.

Counsellor ORD spoke to this effect:—Sir, I am inclined to believe, that the persons associated in writing and dispersing this paper, whosoever they may be, are of no high rank, or considerable influence; as it is not likely that any man who had much to hazard, would expose himself to the resentment of the whole legislature; but let us not for that reason exert our superiority in wanton punishments, or tyrannize merely because we cannot be resisted. Let us remember that the same justice and the same humanity is due to the meanest, as the highest of our fellow subjects; and that there is even less necessity of rigorous measures, as the attack is less formidable.

But, Sir, there is one motive to moderation that has seldom been found less efficacious than the consideration of the laws of justice or humanity. We ought to be withheld by regard to our posterity, and even to ourselves, from any exorbitant extension of our privileges. We know, that authority once exerted, is claimed afterwards by prescription. And who knows by what sudden rotation of power he may himself suffer by a precedent which he has concurred to establish, and feel the weight of that oppressive power which he first granted for the punishment of another?

Mr. HOWE spoke thus:—Sir, I am always unwilling to oppose any proposal of lenity and forbearance, nor have now any intention of heightening the guilt of this man by cruel exaggerations, or inciting the house to rigour and persecution.

But let us remember, Sir, that justice and mercy are equally to be regarded, and while we pity the folly of a misguided or perhaps a thoughtless offender, let us not suffer ourselves to be betrayed by our compassion, to injure ourselves and our posterity.

This house, Sir, has always claimed and exerted the privilege of judging of every offence against itself, a privilege so long established,

D 3 and

and so constantly exercised, that I doubt whether the inferiour courts of judicature will take cognizance of an attack upon us; for how can they venture to decide upon a question of such importance without any form or precedent for their proceedings.

There seems also to be at this time, Sir, an uncommon necessity for tenaciousness of our privileges, when, as some whispers, which have been wafted from the other house, inform us, a motion has been made in terms which might imply the subordination of this assembly, an assertion without foundation either in reason or justice, and which I shall always oppose as destructive to our rights, and dangerous to our constitution.

Let us, therefore, Sir, retain in our hands the cognizance of this affair, and let the criminal either suffer his punishment from *our* sentence, or owe his pardon to *our* mercy.

It was agreed that the printer of the daily paper should attend next day, when being called in, it was proposed that he should be asked, whether he printed the paper complained of. It was objected to, for the same reason as the question about the author's being in the gallery, because the answer might tend to accuse himself; and he being withdrawn, a debate of the same nature ensued, and the question being put whether he should be asked, if he be the person that printed the daily paper shewn to him, which paper the house the day before resolved to contain a malicious and scandalous libel, &c. it was on a division carried in the affirmative, by 222 against 163: accordingly he was called in again, and being asked the question, he owned that he printed the said paper from a printed copy which was left for him with one of his servants; and being asked what he had to allege in his justification or excuse for printing the said libel, he said that as he had before printed several other things which he had received from the said person, which had not given offence, he inserted part of the paper in his news, and which he should not have inserted, if he had thought it would have given offence to the house, and that he forbore to print the remainder, having heard that it had given offence. Upon which he withdrew, and the house, after some debate, on a division 188 to 145, not only ordered him into the custody of the serjeant, but resolved to present an address to his majesty, that he would be pleased to give directions to his attorney general to prosecute him at law.

The first printer of the libel was also ordered into custody. This was on the 3d December, but the next day presenting his petition, expressing his
sorrow

forrow for the offence, whereby he had juftly incurred the difpleafure of the
houfe, and praying to be difcharged, he was brought to the bar on the fol-
lowing day, received a reprimand on his knees, and was ordered to be dif-
charged, paying his fees.

On the 12th Lord Barrington *prefented a petition from the printer of the*
daily paper, expreffing his forrow, promifing all poffible care not to of-
fend for the future, and praying to be difcharged.

This petition being read, a motion was made, that the ferjeant at arms do
carry the petitioner to fome court of law, to give fecurity for his appear-
ance to the profecution to be carried on againft him by the attorney general,
which done, that he be difcharged, paying his fees,

Sir WILLIAM YONGE fpoke to this effect : —Sir, I know not for
what reafon this enormous offender is entitled to fo much regard, or
by what intereft he has engaged fo many, who, I doubt not, abhor
his crimes to pity his fufferings.

Had he been young and unexperienced, and feduced into the commiffion of this offence by artifice, or perfuafion, his act might have
been reafonably confidered rather as an error than a crime, and it
might have been proper to treat with lenity a delinquent neither obftinate nor malicious.

But how, Sir, can this plea be urged in favour of a man, whofe
daily employment it has been, for thefe two years paft, to mifrepre-
fent the public meafures, to difperfe fcandal, and excite rebellion,
who has induftrioufly propagated every murmur of difcontent, and
preferved every whifper of malevolence from perifhing in the birth.

The proper judge, Sir, of this affair, is his majefty's attorney general, who is not now in the houfe. I am, therefore, for detaining him
in cuftody, and for referring the confideration of farther proceedings
againft him to that gentleman whofe proper province it is to profecute
for the crown.

Mr. WALLER fpoke next to the following purpofe :—Sir, it is
undoubtedly the duty of every man to oppofe the introduction of new
laws, and methods of oppreffion and feverity, which our conftitution
does not admit; and what elfe is the mention of a prifoner's character
as an aggravation of his prefent offence ?

It is well known, and has been already afferted, upon this occafion, that in the lower courts of juftice, though the prifoner may
plead his character in his own defence, his profecutor is not at liberty

to produce it to his difadvantage. Even thofe who are cited to the bar for murder or for treafon, are tried only by the evidence of that crime for which they are indicted.

That this houfe is not bound to ftrict forms, and is not accountable for the exercife of its power, is eafily granted; but authority cannot change the nature of things, and what is unjuft in a lower court, would be in us not lefs unjuft, though it may not be punifhable.

It was replied that this queftion had been before fufficiently difcuffed.

The attorney general not being prefent, the debate was adjourned to the next fitting.

On the next day of the feffion, the lord Barrington *propofed, that the adjourned debate might be refumed, and feveral members interceded for the petitioner, that he might be releafed; to which it was objected, that it was not proper to releafe him, unlefs an information was lodged againft him, without which he could not be held to bail; and the queftion being put, whether he fhould be releafed, was determined in the negative.*

At the 6th fitting the author of the libel, who was committed to the common prifon of Middlefex, petitioned the houfe to permit him to implore pardon on his knees, and, promifing by the ftrongeft and moft folemn affurances not to offend again, was ordered to be difcharged the next day, paying his fees.

On the 47th fitting, the printer of the daily paper again petitioned the houfe, reprefenting, that he moft heartily bewailed his offence, that he was miferably reduced by his confinement, having borrowed money of all his friends to fupport himfelf, his wife and children, and praying the mercy of the houfe. He was then ordered to be difcharged, paying his fees, and giving fecurity for his appearance to anfwer the profecution.

On the 85th day Mr. George Heathcote *offered another petition for the faid printer, and reprefented, that the fees amounting to £.121 he was not able to pay them, that, therefore, he hoped the houfe would confider his cafe; but the petition was not allowed to be brought up. On which he remained in cuftody 14 days longer till the end of the feffion, and, the authority of the fenate ceafing, had his liberty without paying any fees.*

HOUSE

HOUSE OF COMMONS.

December 4—11, 1740.

ON INCORPORATING THE NEW-RAISED MEN INTO THE STANDING REGIMENTS.

On the 4th of December, Sir William Yonge, *secretary at war, having presented to the house of commons an estimate of the expence of raising ten thousand men, the same was taken into consideration in a committee on the supply, and after debate agreed to. At the report of this proceeding, on the* 11th, *another debate happened on a motion that the new raised men should be incorporated into the standing regiments, &c.*
As in these two debates the arguments were the same, they are thrown into one, to prevent unnecessary repetitions.

SIR WILLIAM YONGE opened the debate with respect to what he had delivered in the estimate after the manner following :—Sir, as this estimate has been drawn up after very accurate calculations and careful enquiries, I hope that no objections will be raised against it, and that the sum necessary for raising the new regiments will be very readily granted by that house, which voted the war necessary for which they are designed.

I hope, it will be admitted as some proof of frugality, that this estimate requires less money than one that was laid before the senate in the reign of king William; for if it be considered, that since that time the necessaries of life are become dearer, and that, therefore, all expences are encreased, it will appear to be the effect of the exactest oeconomy, that the sum required for the same service is less.

I have heard indeed, Sir, that in conversation, the method of raising troops on this occasion has been censured as improper, and that in the opinion of some, whose judgment cannot be entirely disregarded, it would be more reasonable to add more men to our regiments already established, than to raise new regiments with new officers.

The chief argument, Sir, produced in support of their method of augmentation, is drawn from the necessity of public frugality, a very popular topic, which never fails to produce favour and attention ; for every man is naturally inclined to hear his friend, and to consider

fider that man as performing the office of friendſhip, who propoſes methods of alleviating his taxes.

Frugality is undoubtedly a virtue very neceſſary to the happineſs of the nation, and ſuch as there occur frequent occaſions of inculcating to thoſe who are intruſted with the ſuperintendence of publick diſburſements, but I am far from thinking that this eſtimate affords any opportunity for declamations of this kind, and am of opinion that the addition of new ſoldiers to each regiment, would, in reality, be more expenſive.

It cannot be denied, Sir, that by augmenting the regiments, there would be immediately ſaved to the public the expence of the officers which are neceſſary in the method now propoſed ; but it is to be conſidered how much the number of officers contributes to the regularity and diſcipline of the troops, and how much diſcipline and order promote their ſucceſs. It is to be conſidered, Sir, that the moſt ſucceſsful method of making war is undoubtedly the cheapeſt, and that nothing is more expenſive than defeats.

If by raiſing the ſame number of men under fewer officers, we ſhould give our enemies any advantage, if a ſingle party ſhould be cut off, a garriſon forced, an expedition rendered fruitleſs, or the war protracted but a few months, where will be the advantage of this admired frugality ? What would be the conſequence, but the ſame or a greater expence, not to gain advantages, but to repair loſſes, and obviate the effects of our former parſimony ?

In private life, Sir, it is common for men to involve themſelves in expence only by avoiding it, to repair houſes at greater charges than new ones might be built, and to pay intereſt rather than the debt. Weak minds are frighted at the mention of extraordinary efforts, and decline large expences, though ſecurity and future affluence may be purchaſed by them; as tender bodies ſhrink from ſevere operations, though they are the certain methods of reſtoring health and vigour. The effects of this timidity are the ſame in both caſes, the eſtate is impaired inſenſibly, and the body languiſhes by degrees, till no remedy can be applied.

Such examples, Sir, are frequent, and the folly of imitating them is therefore greater, for who would purſue that track by which he has ſeen others led to deſtruction ? Nor need we ſearch for remote illuſtrations to diſcover the deſtructive tendency of unſeaſonable tenderneſs for the publick, for I believe the whole hiſtory of the wars of

king

ing William will prove, that too close an attention to parsimony is inconsistent with great atchievements.

It may be expected that I who cannot claim any regard in this disquisition from my own experience, should produce some decisive evidence in favour of the method which I have taken upon me to defend; his expectation I shall endeavour to satisfy by alleging the authority of the greatest commander of later ages, whom neither his friends nor his enemies will deny to have been well versed in these subjects, and whose success is a sufficient proof of the soundness of his principles.

The illustrious duke of Marlborough was of opinion, that the whole force of the French armies consisted in the number of the officers, and that to be always equal to them in the field, it was necessary to form our troops nearly upon the same plan; to this scheme he conformed in his practice of war, and how much his practice confirmed his opinion, let Blenheim and Ramillies attest.

As I pretend not to have determined myself on this question, otherwise than by authority, and as I know not any authority equal to that of the duke of Marlborough, I cannot discharge the trust reposed in me by my country, any otherwise than by proposing, that on this occasion we agree to grant his majesty the sum calculated for raising the new regiments, as I believe that method of augmentation most likely to produce success in our undertakings, and consequently to procure a speedy conclusion of the war.

Mr. PULTENEY spoke next to the following effect:—Sir, I have been so long accustomed to the debates of this house, and have so often attended to the eloquence of the right honourable gentleman, that I am never startled at paradoxes, nor shocked at absurdities; I can now hear with great tranquillity an harangue upon the necessity of placemen in this house, upon the usefulness of standing armies, and the happiness of a general excise.

I am no longer offended with facts quoted in opposition to history, nor with calculations drawn up without regard to the rules of arithmetic; I know that there are persons in this house, who think themselves obliged to speak even when in their own opinion nothing can be said with weight or with propriety, who come hither prepared against the shame of confutation, and determined not to be convinced.

To reason with such men, Sir, is indeed no pleasing task; it is to fight with enchanted heroes upon whom the common weapons of argument

gument have no effect, and who muſt he ſoftened by a counter-
charm before they can be attacked with any proſpect of ſucceſs.

There are ſome, however, of whom I am willing to believe that
they diſpute only for truth, and enquire with the view of attaining a
ſolution of their doubts. For the ſake of theſe, Sir, I think it neceſſary to declare my ſentiments, as I ſhall be deſirous, in my turn,
to hear their ſentiments; but with regard to thoſe whoſe opinion I
know already by their poſts, I ſhould think it of great advantage to
the diſpatch of public affairs, if they would content themſelves with
voting for their pay, without any ambition of other ſervice, or adding the praiſe of volubility to that of ſteadineſs.

Having this opportunity, Sir, of declaring my opinion of the meaſures purſued in regulating our military preparations, I ſhall not confine myſelf entirely to the preſent queſtion, but lay before the houſe
my thoughts upon ſome parts of the eſtabliſhment, which may perhaps require a reform, and which are at leaſt proper objects of conſideration, though not abſolutely neceſſary to the determination of
our opinion upon the preſent motion.

I have long ago, Sir, declared, what therefore it is ſcarely of any
uſe to repeat, that I know not any advantage to be hoped from a
ſtanding army, nor can diſcover why the ableſt and moſt vigorous of
the inhabitants of this kingdom ſhould be ſeduced from the loom,
the anvil, and the plough, only to live at eaſe upon the labour of
induſtry, only to inſult their landlords, and rob the farmers. I
never could find why any body of men ſhould be exempt from the
common labour of ſocial duties, or why they ſhould be ſupported
by a community, who contribute neither to its honour nor its
defence.

I doubt not, Sir, but I ſhall hear, on this occaſion, of the ſervice
of our troops in the ſuppreſſion of riots; we ſhall be told, by the
next pompous orator who ſhall riſe up in defence of the army, that
they have often diſperſed the ſmugglers, that the colliers have been
driven down by the terror of their appearance to their ſubterraneous
fortifications, that the weavers in the midſt of that rage which hunger and oppreſſion excited, fled at their reproach, that they have at
our markets bravely regulated the price of butter, and ſometimes in
the utmoſt exertion of heroic fury, broken thoſe eggs which they
were not ſuffered to purchaſe on their own terms.

Some one perhaps of more penetration, may inform us of the uſe
                                                              which

rhich has been made of them at elections, where the furly burgesses
ave been sometimes blind to the merit of those worthy gentlemen,
rhom the foldiers have known how to esteem according to their
efert; nor indeed do I see how those can refuse their votes in favour
f our troops, who are indebted for the power of giving them,
o their kind interpofition.

To these arguments, Sir, I shall content myself with answering,
hat those, who are versed in the history of Britain, know that we
iave had colliers and weavers for many years before a standing army
vas heard of among us, and that it is nevertheless no where recorded
hat any of our kings were depofed by those formidable bodies of
nen, or that any remarkable changes were made by them in the form
if our government; and, therefore, till some reason shall be al-
eged, why such infurrections are now more dangerous, and our
:ivil magistrates more impotent than in former ages, I humbly con-
:eive that even without the protection of a standing army we might
jet fleep in fecurity, notwithstanding the plots of the colliers and
.he combinations of the weavers.

But I must own, Sir, these are not our only enemies, for there is
'omewhere, yet in exiftence, a person that lays claim to the domi-
:ion of these kingdoms, and pleads an hereditary title to difpofe of
our wealth, to fubvert our liberties, and deftroy our religion.

If any foreigner, Sir, unacquainted with our affairs, were to be
prefent at our debates, and to hear with what ardour we animate
tach other to an obftinate refiftance of this pretender to the throne,
how often he is reprefented as hovering over us, and how often we
have caught a general panic, and imagined ourselves upon the verge
of deftruction, how often our most zealous patriots take opportunities of declaring their refolution to die in defence of their liberties,
and how pathetically our most elegant declaimers have expatiated
on the mifery of that unhappy race whom they should leave behind to
groan under the oppreffion of abfolute power, what would be his
opinion of this pretender, whom he faw fo perpetually dreaded,
against whom fo many alliances were formed, fo many armies were
levied, and fo many navies equipped?

Would he not believe him to be fome formidable tyrant in a neighbouring country, the lord of wide dominions, and the mafter of numerous armies and powerful fleets? Would he not imagine that he
could affemble half the continent at his call, that he was fupported
by

by powerful alliances, and that nothing but a fair wind was required to land him on our coasts at the head of millions? And would he not, even on that supposition, be inclined to censure us as timorous, as somewhat regardless of the honour of our nation, and condemn us for giving way to such suspicions and exclamations as have a natural tendency to heighten the apprehension of danger, and depress the spirits of the people?

But what would be his conclusion, Sir, when he should be told what in reality is true, that this dreadful pretender is an unhappy fugitive, driven in his infancy from this country, and by consequence without any personal interest; that he is supported by the charity of a prince whose name is hated almost by every inhabitant of the kingdom; that he has neither sovereignty, nor money, nor alliances nor reputation in war, nor skill in policy; that all his actions are watched by British spies; and that the few friends that remain to support the farce of a court, are such only as dare not return to their native country, and are therefore without fortune, and without dependants?

What could a wise man conceive of a nation held in continual alarms by an enemy like this; of a nation always watchful against an invasion from a man who has neither dominions to supply, nor money to hire a single regiment; from a man whose title all the neighbouring princes disown, and who is at such a distance from them, that he cannot be assisted by them without open preparations of which we cannot fail of having intelligence, and which may be defeated, without danger, by the vessels regularly stationed on our coasts?

Would not any stranger imagine, Sir, that we were a nation infected with a general frenzy, that cowardice had perverted our imaginations, filled us with apprehensions of impossible invasions, raised phantoms before our eyes, and distracted us with wild ideas of slavery and tyranny, oppression and persecution?

I have dwelt thus long on this point, because I know the pretender is the last refuge of those who defend a standing army; not that I propose to convince any man of the folly of such apprehensions, or to fortify him against such terrors for the time to come; for if any man, in reality, now dreads the pretender, fear must be his distemper; he is doomed to live in terrors, and it is of no importance whether he dreads an invasion or a goblin, whether he is
afraid

afraid to difband the army, or to put out his candle in the night; his imagination is tainted, and he muft be cured, not by argument, but by phyfick.

But the greateft part of thofe who difturb our confultations with the mention of the pretender, are men of a very different cha-racter, men equally unconcerned about his defigns, or his motions, with thofe who are moft defirous of fetting the nation free from the burthen of an army, and very often fuch as we may difcover, from their conduct, to be determined to comply with every government, and fuch as have therefore nothing to fear from a change of mafters.

The men for whofe fake I am now fpeaking, Sir, laugh equally with myfelf at the apprehenfions of thofe whom they contribute to terrify; they know too well the impotence of the pretender to dread an invafion from him, and affect only to continue their outcries, that they may not be deprived of a topic, on which, by long practice, they have attained an uncommon facility of haranguing, which they know how to diverfify with various combinations of circumftances, and how to accommodate to any emergent occafion, without the pain of torturing their inventions.

It may be ufeful, Sir, to inform thefe men, that their difguife ought at laft to be thrown off, becaufe it deceives no longer, and that the nation cannot be cheated but at the expence of more cunning than they are willing, or perhaps able, to difplay. A mafk muft ne-ceffarily be thrown afide, when, inftead of concealing, it difcovers him by whom it is ufed.

Thofe who are attempting, Sir, to deceive others, and whofe character is exalted, in their own opinion, in proportion to the fuc-cefs of their endeavours, have furely a fenfe of fhame, though they have none of virtue, and cannot without pain find their artifices de-tected, and themfelves made the objects of ridicule by thofe ftrata-gems which they employ for the deception of others.

I hope, therefore, Sir, that, for their own fakes, thefe declaimers on the exploded ftory of the pretender, will change their bugbear, that if it be neceffary to frighten thofe whom they want art or eloquence to perfuade, they will find out fome other object of terror, which, after a little practice in private meetings, they may firft produce in the court, and then turn loofe in the fenate.

The world, methinks, allows them a fufficient choice of tyrants more

more formidable than the pretender. Suppose they should revive the history of the Mohocks. The Mohocks are a dreadful race, not to be mentioned without horror, by a true lover of his country, and a steady adherent to the house of Hanover ; they might then very easily encrease our army, or inhance our taxes ; for who would not be urged by his wife and daughter to agree to any measures that might secure them from the Mohocks ?

But as an army is at present likely to be kept up for our defence against an enemy less formidable, it may be more seasonable to propose the regulation than the dismission of our troops, and to mention those evils which arise from the present establishment, rather than those which are inseparable from the expence of a standing force.

If it be necessary, Sir, to support soldiers, I suppose that it will not be denied by the advocates for an army, that we ought to levy such troops as may be of use ; yet in their practice they seem to have paid very little regard to this principle. Our troopers are mounted upon horses which can serve no purpose but that of show, which may indeed wheel about in the park with a formidable air, but can neither advance upon an enemy with impetuosity, nor retreat from him with expedition ; and which, therefore, though purchased by the nation at a very high price, and supported at a large expence, can only grace a review, but are of very little use in an enemy's country, and must perish in the march, or stand unactive in the battle.

Nor is much more service to be expected, Sir, from their riders, than from the horses, for there are very few of them acquainted with the first elements of their profession, or who have ever learned more than a few postures of exercise, and the meaning of a few words of command, but have a number of officers with large appointments.

The French troops, Sir, if they are doubly officered, are officered and maintained at a less expence, and to greater effect ; for the soldiers are better instructed, and the same number of men cost not, perhaps, much more than half the charge of a British regiment.

The guards, Sir, that are maintained about this metropolis, for no other purpose than to keep up the splendour of a modern court, cost the nation yearly such a sum as would be sufficient to support an army of Frenchmen, for the protection of their frontier towns, or the invasion of neighbouring countries.

For my part, I cannot see what injury would be done to the nation by abolishing an establishment at the same time useless and expensive,

penſive, and employing that money which is at preſent ſquandered
upon idlers without effect, upon levies of uſeful ſoldiers for march-
ing regiments, who might be employed, when occaſion ſhould require them, in the ſervice of their country.

It will doubtleſs be objected that the officers of this body of men,
many of whom are perſons of the higheſt merit, and who have generally purchaſed their commiſſions, might very juſtly complain of
being deprived without a crime, of that which they have bought
at its full value, and to which therefore they imagine themſelves intitled, till they ſhall forfeit their right by ſome offence againſt the
laws, or ſome neglect of their duty.

I ſhall not, Sir, at preſent enquire into the juſtice of this plea,
nor examine, whether he who purchaſes an employment, which he
knows to be uſeleſs, and therefore burthenſome to the publick, deſerves that the publick ſhould be ſolicitous to ſupport him in the enjoyment of it : but I ſhall declare, on this occaſion, with confidence,
that I know many of the officers of the guards to be men of honour,
who would gladly exchange their poſts, ſo chargeable to the nation,
for an opportunity of ſerving it, and who are not very anxious for
the increaſe of their pay, ſo they may not be degraded from their
preſent rank.

If theſe gentlemen, Sir, might, in the regiments that ſhould be
raiſed by diſbanding the guards, be advanced to higher commiſſions,
though with ſome diminution of their pay, they would imagine themſelves abundantly compenſated by the happineſs of becoming uſeful
ſubjects, and ſerving that nation by which they have been hitherto
ſupported only to fill up the pomp of levies, and add to the magnificence of drawing-rooms, to loiter in anti-chambers, and to quarrel
at gaming tables.

If this ſcheme ſhould not be approved, the method eligible, in
the next degree, ſeems to be that of incorporating our new levies into the regiments already raiſed, that being aſſociated with men already acquainted with diſcipline, they may learn their duty much
more expeditiouſly than in ſeparate bodies, where one officer will be
obliged to attend to the inſtruction of great numbers, and where no
man will be excited to application, becauſe no man will ſee any degree of excellence which he may be ambitious of attaining.

I have indeed heard no reaſon alleged for the neceſſity of new
levies which appeared likely to convince even thoſe by whom it was

produced. It appears to me that our prefent army is more than fufficient for the publick fervice without an augmentation, and that fome
of our regiments might immediately embark, not only without danger to the nation, but with far greater hopes of fuccefs, as our enemies would have lefs time to ftrengthen their fortifications, and collect their troops, and as difciplined forces are more formidable than
troops newly levied ; for difcipline muft be of great efficacy to the
fuccefs of military undertakings, or all arguments which have been
ufed in the defence of a ftanding army fall to the ground.

In anfwer to this propofal, we fhall probably be once again intimidated with an invafion, whether from the pretender, the Spaniards,
the French, or any other power, it is of no great importance. An
invafion is a formidable found ; the fack of towns, the deftruction
of villages, the captivity of our children, the ruin of our fortunes,
and the defolation of our country, are frightful images, and may
therefore be fuccefsfully produced, on this occafion, to perplex our
thoughts, and embarrafs our enquiries.

To remove therefore this panic, and to diffipate for ever the phantoms of invafion, I will lay before the houfe the opinion of the great
commander whofe name has already been introduced in this debate. In
the late reign, on a day when the great officers of the crown and many
of the council were at a publick feaft in the city, a report was fuddenly fpread that the duke of Ormond had landed in the weft with
two thoufand men. This account was in appearance well attefted,
and univerfally believed ; all jollity was, therefore, at an end, the
company departed, the council was fummoned, and every man offered
fuch expedients as his prefent thoughts, confufed and oppreffed
with the proximity of the danger, fuggefted to him. One propofed that a body of troops fhould be fent to a diftant part of the
kingdom, to reftrain the feditions of the populace ; another apprehended more danger from a different quarter, and advifed that the inhabitants fhould be awed by another detachment fent thither ; the
moft experienced eafily faw the unprofitablenefs of the meafures propofed, but could not fo eafily ftrike out more efficacious expedients,
and therefore fat in great perplexity. Lord Somers particularly
fhook his head, and feemed to confider the kingdom as in the hands
of the invaders, and the dreadful pretender as feated on the throne.

At laft the duke of Marlborough, who had hitherto fat filent,
afked calmly whether they were certain that any forces were really
landed,

landed, and was anfwered, that though it might not be abfolutely certain, yet they were to confult and fend orders upon that fuppofition. Then, fays he, I will lay down this great rule to be obferved invariably, whenever you are invaded. Attend only to one point, nor have any other purpofe in view than that of deftroying the regular forces that fhall be landed in the kingdom, without any regard to petty infurrections, which may be always eafily quelled, and which will probably ceafe of themfelves, when the army by which they were excited is cut off. For this end let it be your rule to keep your army undivided, and to make no motion but towards the enemies; fight them with the utmoft expedition before they can fortify themfelves, or receive re-inforcements from the continent. By the obfervation of this plain method of operation, continued he, I will engage without any other force than the regiments generally ftationed about the capital, to put a ftop to any troops that fhall be landed on the coaft of Britain.

So far was this great officer, who was acquainted with the whole art of war, from finking into aftonifhment at the found of an invafion, and fo far from thinking it neceffary that the nation fhould be harraffed by ftanding troops, to preferve it from being plundered by a foreign army.

But though our troops, Sir, fhould not be neceffary to prevent an invafion, they may be ufeful in fervices of equal importance; the miniftry may think the fuffrages of the officers more ferviceable than their fwords, and may be more afraid of expofing themfelves than the nation by any detachment of their forces.

Such is at prefent, Sir, the ftate of this unhappy country, that neither in peace nor war are any meafures taken, but with a view of increafing or confirming the power of the miniftry; for this purpofe thofe troops whofe officers have feats here, are to be retained at home, and the fate of our American fettlements to be committed to new levied forces without military fkill.

For this reafon is an army to be raifed without neceffity, and raifed in a manner that may furnifh the court with an opportunity of extending its influence, by the difpofal of great numbers of new commiffions. By this plan every family that is burthened with a relation, whofe vices have ruined his fortune, or whofe ftupidity difqualifies him for employment, will have an opportunity of felling for a commiffion its intereft at the approaching election; dependance will be propagated, and the troublefome fpirit of liberty be depreffed.

To

To little purpose will it be objected, that foldiers and officers will be equally ignorant, that difcipline is not infufed inftantaneoufly, that a military drefs will not make a foldier, that men can only know their duty by inftruction, and that nothing is to be hoped from ploughmen, and manufacturers, commanded by fchool-boys. The fuccefs of the expedition is not fo much confidered by thofe who have the direction of the levies, as that of the election, and while they keep their pofts, they are very little concerned about the affairs of America.

In defence of this method it has, indeed, been affirmed, that it was preferred by the duke of Marlborough ; but we are not informed to whom, or upon what occafion he declared his opinion, and therefore are left at liberty to doubt, whether his authority is not produced for a method which he did not approve, or approved only at fome particular time for fome extraordinary fervice.

It is urged that he recommended it by his practice, and that his fuccefs is a fufficient proof that his practice was founded upon right maxims. But if it be remembered what was, in that time, the method of obtaining commiffions, and who it was that had the difpofal of them, it will appear not abfolutely certain, that his practice ought to be produced as a decifive proof of his opinion.

If the fuccefs of troops be properly urged as an argument for the form of their eftablifhment, may not the victories of prince Eugene afford a proof, equally convincing, that a few officers are fufficient ? And if the arguments which arife from fuccefs are equal on both fides, ought not the neceffity of faving the publick money to turn the balance ?

War, Sir, is in its own nature a calamity very grievous to the moft powerful and flourifhing people, and to a trading nation is particularly deftructive, as it at once exhaufts our wealth, and interrupts our commerce, at once drinks up the ftream and choaks up the fountain. In thofe countries, whofe affairs are wholly tranfacted within their own frontiers, where there is either very little money, or where their wealth is dug out of their own mines, they are only weakened by the lofs of men, or by the diminution of their dominions, and in general can only fuffer by being overcome.

But the ftate of Britain is far different, it is not neceffary to our ruin that an enemy fhould be ftronger than ourfelves, that he fhould be able to pour armies into our country, to cover the fea with fleets,

to

to burn our villages by incursions, or destroy our fortresses with bombs ; for he that can secure his own dominions from our attacks, to which nothing but distance and some advantages of situation are necessary, may support a war against us, and he that can fit out privateers to interrupt our trade, may, without obtaining a victory, reduce us to distress.

Our situation, Sir, as it preserves us from the danger of an invasion, except from that powerful monarch the pretender, who is indeed always to be dreaded, has likewise the effect of securing other nations from being invaded by us, for it is very difficult to transport in one fleet, and to land at one time, a number sufficient to force their way into a country where the ports are fortified, and the inhabitants in arms.

Our wars, Sir, are threfore to be determined by naval battles, and those nations have very little to fear from us who have no trade to be disturbed, and no navies to be destroyed ; if they can only fit out cruisers, which may always be done by granting commissions to foreign adventurers, they may ruin our merchants by captures, exhaust the nation by the necessity of convoys, and give neutral traders an opportunity of establishing their credit at those markets which have been hitherto supplied by our manufactures.

This is indeed far from being at present an exact account of the state of Spain, whose wide-extended dominions are liable to insults, and from whom many of her most wealthy provinces may be torn without great hazard or difficulty. The particular state of her commerce, which, being only carried on from one part of her dominions to another, can only be for a time interrupted, but is in no danger of being invaded by any rival, or lost by disuse, at least requires our consideration, and we ought to make war with the utmost frugality against a people whom no hostilities can really impoverish, whose commerce may be said to lie at rest rather than to be shackled, as it will rise into greater vigour at the end of the war, and whose treasures, though the want of them is a present inconvenience, are only piled up for a time of security.

As the only method, Sir, of reducing this nation, must be that of invading its colonies, and dismembering its provinces, by which the chief persons will be deprived of their revenues, and a general discontent be spread over the people, the forces which are levied for this expedition, an expedition on which so much of the honour of

our

our arms and the profperity of our trade muft neceffarily depend, ought to be felected with the greateft care, and difciplined with the exacteft regularity.

On this occafion, therefore, it is furely improper to employ troops newly collected from fhops and villages, and yet more irrational to truft them to the direction of boys called on this occafion from the frolicks of a fchool, or forced from the bofoms of their mothers, and the foft-nefs of the nurfery. It is not without compaffion, compaffion very far extended, that I confider the unhappy ftriplings doomed to a camp, from whom the fun has hitherto been fcreened, and the wind excluded, who have been taught by many tender lectures the unwholefomenefs of the evening mifts and the morning dews, who have been wrapt in furs in winter, and cooled with fans in fummer, who have lived without any fatigue but that of drefs, or any care but that of their complexion.

Who can forbear, Sir, fome degree of fympathy when he fees animals like thefe taking their laft farewel of the maid that has fed them with fweetmeats, and defended them from infects; when he fees them dreft up in the habiliments of foldiers, loaded with a fword, and invefted with a command, not to mount the guard at the pa-lace, nor to difplay their lace at a review, not to protect ladies at the door of an affembly room, nor to fhew their intrepidity at a country fair, but to enter into a kind of fellowfhip with the rugged failor, to hear the tumult of a ftorm, to fuftain the change of climates, and to be fet on fhore in an enemy's dominions?

Surely, he that can fee fuch fpectacles without forrow, muft have hardened his heart beyond the common degrees of cruelty, and it may reafonably be expected, that he who can propofe any method by which fuch hardfhips may be efcaped, will be thought entitled to gratitude and praife.

For my part, I fhould imagine, Sir, that an eafy method might be difcovered of obviating fuch mifery, without leffening that num-ber of officers, which, perhaps, in oppofition to reafon and ex-perience, fome gentlemen will continue to think neceffary, and hope that this may be no improper time to declare my opinion.

I have obferved, that for fome time no private centinel has ever rifen to any rank above that of a ferjeant, and that commiffions have been referved as rewards for other fervices than thofe of the camp. This procedure I cannot but think at once impolitick and unjuft.

It

It is impolitick, Sir, as it has a natural tendency to extinguish in the soldiery all emulation and all industry. Soldiers have an equal genius with other men, and undoubtedly there might be found among them great numbers capable of learning and of improving the military sciences; but they have likewise the same love of ease, and the desire of honour and of profit, and will not condemn themselves to labour without the prospect of reward, nor sacrifice their time to the attainment of that knowledge, which can have no other effect than to make them discover the stupidity of their commanders, and render their obedience more difficult, as it will destroy that reverence which is necessary to subordination.

It is unjust, Sir, because it is not to be doubted, that some soldiers, by the natural force of their faculties, or by a laudable activity of mind, have extended their knowledge beyond the duties of a private station, and he that excels in his profession has an equitable claim to distinction and preferment. To advance any man in the army, because his father is an orator in the senate, or the chief inhabitant of a borough, seems not more rational, than to make another man a judge, because some of his ancestors were skilled in gunnery; nor would the lawyers have juster reasons for complaint in one case, than the soldiers in the other.

It is therefore, Sir, in my opinion, necessary to the advancement of military knowledge, that, as a centinel is, for excelling in his profession, advanced to the degree of a serjeant, the serjeant, who continues his application, and performs his duty, should, in time, be honoured with a commission.

It may be objected indeed, that serjeants, though they are skilful commanders in war, can very seldom arrive at any remarkable skill in politicks, and though they should be so fortunate as to gain estates, could never be of any use as the representatives of a borough; and to what purpose should those men be advanced, who can only serve their country, but can contribute very little to the support of the court?

This is, I own, Sir, an objection, which I despair of answering to the satisfaction of those by whom it will be raised. The hardy serjeant would never cringe gracefully at a levee, would never attain to any successful degree of address in soliciting votes, and if he should by mere bribery be deputed hither, would be unable to defend the conduct of his directors.

E 4

In

In vindication of the prefent fcheme, I believe few of thofe rugged warriors would find many arguments ; they would not recommend to the nation a troop of boys, under the command of boys, as the moft proper forces to be fent to make conquefts in diftant countries, nor would imagine, that unfkilful foldiers could, under the direction of officers equally ignorant with themfelves, attain the knowledge of their duty in the fame time as if they were incorporated with regular troops, in which every man might receive inftructions, and learn his bufinefs from his comrade.

I had lately, Sir, the opportunity of hearing the opinion of one of the greateft generals in the world, on this fubject, who declared with the utmoft confidence of certainty, that raw troops could be difciplined in a fhort time, only by being incorporated with thofe that had been already taught their duty, and afferted, that with an army fo mixed, he fhould think himfelf fufficiently enabled to meet any forces of the fame number, and fhould not fear to acquit himfelf fuccefsfully, either in attacking or defending.

Such are the fentiments of this great man, to whom I know not whether any name can be oppofed that deferves equally to be reverenced. He has had the honour of defending the rights of his country in the fenate as well as in the field, has fignalized himfelf equally in the debate and in the battle, and perhaps deferves lefs regard for having hazarded his life, than for having been divefted of his employments.

Since therefore, it is apparent that great numbers of officers are by no means neceffary to fuccefs in war, fince they are dangerous to our liberty in time of peace, fince they are certainly expenfive, and at beft not certainly ufeful ; and fince the greateft general of the prefent age has declared, that our new levies ought to be mingled with our ftanding forces, I fhall think it my duty to vote againft the prefent fcheme of raifing new regiments, and fhall agree to no other fupplies than fuch as may be fufficient for adding the fame numbers to the prefent army.

General WADE then fpoke as follows:—Sir, though I cannot pretend to purfue the honourable gentleman through the whole compafs of his argument, nor fhall attempt to ftand up as his rival, either in extent of knowledge, or elegance of language, yet as my courfe of life has neceffarily furnifhed me with fome obfervations elating to the queftion before us, and my prefent ftation in the

army

army may, in some measure, be said to make it my duty to declare my opinion, I shall lay before the house a few considerations, with the artless simplicity of a plain soldier, without engaging in a formal debate, or attempting to overthrow the arguments of others.

It is observed, Sir, that for the greatest part, the farther any man has advanced in life, the less confidence he places in speculation, and the more he learns to rest upon experience as the only sure guide in human affairs; and as the transactions in which he is engaged are more important, with the greater anxiety does he enquire after precedents, and the more timorously does he proceed, when he is obliged to regulate his conduct by conjecture or by deliberation.

This remark, Sir, though it may be just with regard to all states of life, is yet more constantly and certainly applicable to that of the soldier; because, as his profession is more hazardous than any other, he must with more caution guard against miscarriages and errors. The old soldier, therefore, very rarely ventures beyond the verge of experience, unless in compliance with particular accidents, which does not make any change in his general scheme, or in situations where nothing can preserve him but some new stratagem or unprecedented effort, which are not to be mentioned as part of his original plan of operation, because they are produced always by unforeseen emergencies, and are to be imputed not to choice but to necessity; for in consequence of my first principle, an old soldier never willingly involves himself in difficulties, or proceeds in such a manner as that he may not expect success by the regular operations of war.

It will not therefore be strange, if I, who, having served in the army in the wars of king William, may justly claim the title of an old soldier, should not easily depart from the methods established in my youth, methods of which their effects have shewn me, that they at least answer the intention for which they were contrived, and which therefore I shall be afraid of rejecting, lest those which it is proposed to substitute in their place, however probable in speculation, should be found defective in practice, and the reasonings, which indeed I cannot answer, should be confuted in the field, where eloquence has very little power.

The troops of Britain, formed according to the present establishment, have been found successful; they have preserved the liberties of Europe, and driven the armies of France before them; they have

appeared

appeared equally formidable in fieges and in battles, and with ftrength equally irrefiftible have preffed forward in the field, and mounted the breach. It may be urged, that this vigour, alacrity, and fuccefs, cannot be proved to have been produced by the number of officers by whom they were commanded ; but fince, on the contrary, it cannot be fhewn that the number of officers did not contribute to their victories, I think it not prudent to try the experiment, which, if it fhould fucceed, as it poffibly may, would produce no great advantage ; and if it fhould fail, and that it may fail no man will deny, mult bring upon us not only the expence which we are fo folicitous to avoid, but difgrace and loffes, a long interruption of our trade, and the flaughter of great numbers of our fellow fubjects.

Thus far, Sir, I have proceeded upon a fuppofition that the balance of argument is equal on both fides, and that nothing could be alleged on one part but experience, or objected to the other but the want of it ; but as I am now called to declare my opinion in a queftion relating to my profeffion, a queftion of great importance to the publick, I fhould think that I had not difcharged my duty to my country with that fidelity which may juftly be exacted from me, if I fhould omit any obfervation that my memory may fuggeft, by which the houfe may be better enabled to proceed in this enquiry.

I think it therefore proper to declare, that we not only, in the laft great war, experienced the ufefulnefs of numerous officers, but that we have likewife felt the want of them on a fignal occafion, and that the only greateft advantage which our enemies obtained, was gained over an army rendered weak by the want of the ufual number of officers. Such were the forces that were defeated at the fatal battle of Almanza, by which almoft all Spain was recovered from us. And it is, Sir, the opinion of very fkilful commanders, that the Germans, only by having fewer officers than the French, did not fucceed in thofe long and obftinate battles of Parma and Guaftalla.

It is indeed natural to imagine, that a greater number of officers muft promote fuccefs, becaufe courage is kindled by example, and it is therefore of ufe to every man to have his leader in his view. Shame at one time and affection at another, may produce the effects of courage where it is wanted, and thofe may follow their commander, who are inclined to defert their duty; for it is feldom known that, while the officers appear confident, the foldiers defpair, or that they think of retreating but after the example of their leaders.

Where

Where there are only few officers, it is apparent that more is left
to chance, in which it becomes not a wife man to place any confidence; for if the officers are killed at the beginning of the action,
the foldiers muft become an ufelefs, defencelefs herd, without order,
without unanimity, and without defign; but by the prefent method,
if an officer happens to fall, his place is immediately fupplied by
another, the action goes forward, and the enemy receives no advantage from confufion or delay.

I am therefore of opinion, that in raifing troops for the expedition
now intended, the eftablifhed method ought to be followed, and that
we ought not to hazard the fuccefs of our attempt by new regulations, of which no human fagacity can foretel the event.

Though it cannot be denied, that fome addition might be made to
our companies without any vifible or certain inconvenience, yet the
augmentation now intended is too numerous to be fo incorporated
without fome neglect of difcipline, as the officers would be charged
with more men than they could properly fuperintend.

There is indeed, Sir, another method of incorporation, by adding new companies to each regiment; but of this method the
advantage would be fmall, becaufe the number of captains and inferiour officers muft be the fame, and the pay of only the field officers
would be faved, and this trifling gain would be far over-balanced by
the inconveniencies which experience has fhewn to arife from it.
There have been regiments formed of thirteen companies inftead of
ten; but it was found, that as the officers of a company may be over-
charged with foldiers, a colonel may likewife have more companies
than he can conveniently infpect, and the antient regulation was re-
ftored, as the leaft liable to difficulties and objections.

Having thus endeavoured to vindicate the manner in which our new
troops are propofed to be levied, it may be expected that I fhould
now make fome obfervations on the fervice in which they are to be
employed, which I cannot think liable to any unanfwerable objection.
It is now, Sir, in our choice whether we will fend the new regiments abroad or keep them at home; and our choice may eafily be
determined by comparing the value of our colonies with that of their
mother country. If it be not neceffary to have any army here to defend us againft infults and invafions, the queftion about the manner of
raifing or employing new regiments is fuperfluous, becaufe none ought
to be raifed, as our old troops are fufficiently numerous for foreign
                                                              fervice.

fervice. But if the fecurity of the nation requires an army, would it not be madnefs to fend thofe troops to a diftant part of the world, in which we can confide moft? Would not thofe, who fpeak with fuch contempt of an expedition undertaken by boys, have a better reafon for their cenfure, if only boys were ftationed on our coafts to repel the veterans of France? Would not fuch meafures animate our enemies and invite an invafion?

It may perhaps be urged farther, that the troops which are fent into America, are more likely to fucceed in their defign, than any regiment of antient eftablifhment. The chief danger to be feared in that part of the world, is not from the enemy but the climate, with which young men are moft able to contend, though they may not be equally qualified for attempts in which fkill is equally neceffary with vigour.

I am convinced, Sir, that this war has hitherto been profecuted with ardour and fidelity, and that no meafures have been taken but fuch as experience and reafon have fupported, and therefore affirm, without fcruple, that if we are not fuccefsful, our mifcarriages muft be imputed to the chance of war, from which no prudence can exempt us.

Lord QUARENDON fpoke next in the following manner, being his firft fpeech :—Sir, having but very lately had the honour of a feat in this affembly, I am confcious how little I am acquainted with either the fubjects or forms of debate, and fhould therefore continue to liften to the fentiments of perfons more experienced, with filent veneration, did I not obferve with how much indulgence they are heard who mean well, however deficient in knowledge, or in eloquence.

As the honourable gentleman who fpoke laft, Sir, profeffes to have formed his opinion rather from facts than arguments, I hope I fhall be indulged by the houfe, in an attempt to examine thofe facts which he has produced, becaufe I think them not fufficient to fupport his pofitions, which muft therefore be eftablifhed by fome other proofs, before a decifion of this queftion can be fixed by them.

With regard to his experience, to which undoubtedly no fmall degree of veneration is due, he confeffes that we have tried only one of the two forms of eftablifhment now in competition, and that therefore, though he has had reafon to approve that with which he is moft acquainted, he has no certain proofs of the inefficacy or imperfection of the other.

But

But experience, Sir, may be extended much farther than our own perfonal tranfactions, and may very juftly comprehend thofe obfervations which we have had opportunities of making upon the conduct and fuccefs of others.   This gentleman, though he has only commanded in the armies of Britain, has feen the forces of other nations, has remarked their regulations, and heard of their actions with our confederates in the laft war; he has probably acted in conjunction, and though it is known that they differ from us in the proportion of foldiers and officers, he has mentioned no difadvantage which might be fuppofed to arife from their eftablifhment, and therefore, I fuppofe, he cannot deny that their behaviour and fuccefs was the fame with that of our own troops.

The battles of Almanza, Parma, and Guaftalla, which he has particularly mentioned, were loft, as he informs us, by armies not officered according to the eftablifhment which he recommends to us : but it is obfervable that his argument is defective in an effential part; for though he affirms that the armies which were defeated had fewer officers than the enemy, he has neither fhewn, nor attempted to fhew, that the want of officers occafioned the defeat, or that the lofs would have been prevented by a greater number.

Thefe inftances, therefore, can be of no effect on the determination of the prefent queftion ; for though it is certain that at Germany, and at other places, armies with few officers have loft the battle, it is not lefs common for thofe troops that are more liberally fupplied, to be overthrown by others which are differently modelled.

With regard, Sir, to the troops of Germany, I have heard them praifed in many parts of Europe, as not inferiour either to thofe of France, or of any other nation, and have been informed, that their ill fuccefs, both at Parma and Guaftalla, may be juftly imputed to other caufes than the want of officers.

There has perhaps, Sir, feldom been an example of firmnefs, difcipline, and refolution, beyond that which was fhewn by the Germans at the action of Parma, where they attacked the trenches of the French, fuftained the fire of the ramparts of the city, and though they loft their commander in chief and two others, towards the beginning of the action, they continued the fight for eleven hours, and at laft retired only at the approach of night.

At

At Guaftalla, Sir, they attacked the French in their trenches, even with forces inferiour in number, fo far were they from any diffidence in the form of their eftablifhment; and after a fight of feven hours, in which their lofs was under all their difadvantages not greater than that of their enemies, they retreated to their former camp unmolefted and unpurfued. The French, Sir, were preferved in both thefe battles, not by the number of their officers, but by their fituation, by woods, caffines, ditches and intrenchments.

Nor do I difcover, Sir, what can be inferred from his obfervation of the influence of example in time of action, but that officers fhould be felected with great care, and not be promoted by favour, or intereft, or caprice; for an example of cowardice in a leader muft be pernicious, in proportion as that of bravery is beneficial; and as, where more officers are fuppofed neceffary, there is lefs room for choice, it muft be allowed that the troops, which have more officers than other forces, are in more danger of being infected with cowardice.

It appears therefore to me that the expence of the prefent eftablifhment is a certain evil, and that the advantages are very doubtful: it appears that the prefent ftate of the nation requires frugality, and therefore I fhall vote for the incorporation of our new levies with the old regiments.

By this incorporation, Sir, our new-levied troops will be no longer diftinguifhed from our veterans; they will be equally acquainted with difcipline, and will learn, from the converfation of their affociates, a fpirit of enterprize, and a contempt of danger; we may then employ forces equally formidable in all parts of the publick fervice, and invade the dominions of our enemies, without leaving our own country defolate.

The arguments which the honourable gentleman has offered in defence of fending our younger troops to America, which may likewife be ufed againft an incorporation, is in my opinion, Sir, far from being conclufive; for it fuppofes, what will not be granted, that a cold climate may be changed for a hotter with more fafety by a young than an old man. I have been told, on the contrary, that fuperabundant heat is the great difeafe of youth, and that the want of it produces moft of the infirmities of age; and every one has known the lives of perfons languifhing with age, prolonged by a removal into warm countries. I am therefore of opinion, that the honourable gentleman's argument is defective in all its parts, and

hope

hope that I fhall not be charged with obltinacy or perverfenefs for dif-
fenting from him.

Mr. Howe fpoke next in fubftance as follows:—Sir, before I engage
in a difcuffion of the queftion, I cannot but think it neceffary to obferve, that the honourable gentleman, who fpoke the fecond in this
debate, has been very far from confulting either policy or juftice in
his declamation, and that he deviated from the fubject only to ridicule his country, to exalt our enemies, and deprefs our efforts.

He has defcribed, Sir, the Britifh youth, the fons of noble families, and the hopes of the nation, in terms too contemptuous to
be heard without indignation ; he has amufed himfelf with difplaying their ignorance and their effeminacy, and has indulged his imagination in a malignant kind of gaiety, which, however it may divert
himfelf, is very far from contributing either to the reformation or
prevention of thofe practices which he cenfures.

I believe, Sir, it will be granted, that nothing ought to pleafe but in
proportion to its propriety and truth ; and, if we try the fatire that
we have lately heard by this teft, it will be found to have very little
claim to applaufe ; for our armies muft be compofed of the youth of
the nation ; and, for my part, I cannot difcover what advantage we
fhall gain over the Spaniards, by informing them how little our troops
are accuftomed to danger, how fhort a time they have been acquainted
with fatigue, how tenderly they have been nurfed, how eafily they
may be frighted, and how certainly they will be conquered, if they
but meet with oppofition.

Nor, Sir, is fuch an account of the youth of Britain more true,
in my opinion, than it is prudent. I am far from difcovering any
fuch remarkable degeneracy in the age, or any great prevalence of
cowardice and unmanly delicacy; nor do I doubt of hearing that our
youth, if they are fent upon any expedition, have fhewn that the Britifh
courage is not yet extinguifhed, and that, if they are ranged on the
plains of America, they will difcover themfelves the fons of thofe
that forced thofe paffes, and thofe trenches, that other troops would
have failed in attempting.

That the degeneracy of the Britifh youth is at leaft not univerfal,
we have juft now, Sir, received an inconteftable proof from the gentleman who fpoke laft, and fpoke with fo much elegance of language,
and juftnefs of reafoning, as fhews, that there are to be found,
among the youth of Britain, perfons very well qualified for the fe-

nate ;

nate; and I have never heard that a post in the army required greater abilities.

The pleasure, however, with which I have attended to his remarks, has not so far prejudiced me in favour of his opinion, as that I shall easily consent to change that method of discipline to which our troops have been accustomed, and of which we know by experience, that it is at least not less efficacious than that of any other nation. Customs, if they are not bad, are not to be changed, because it is an argument in favour of a practice that the people have experienced it, and approved it, and every change is disagreeable to those who judge only by prejudice, of whom I need not say how great is the number.

Many arguments may, Sir, in my opinion, be added to our experience in favour of the present establishment. The number of officers ———but I find myself unable to pursue my design, because I can no longer read my notes, which, being written by another hand, somewhat embarrass me in this decline of the light. I shall therefore only make some observations upon the speech of the gentleman who spoke the second in this debate, and hope that I shall be allowed to deviate from the principal question, since I do it only in pursuit of another.

He has observed, that our troopers are mounted upon horses that are of no use; a remark, Sir, which I never heard from any other person, and for which, I believe, no authority can be produced: they are mounted, indeed, upon horses very different from those which are used by other nations, because scarcely any other country breeds horses of equal size and strength, and, therefore, I am informed that the French have purchased horses from this island, and believe that all the cavalry of Europe would be mounted upon our horses if they could procure them. I have been informed, that their pressure in the shock of battle is such as no forces in the world are able to sustain; and that it was not less by the strength of our horses than the spirit of our soldiers, that the squadrons of France were, in the battle of Blenheim, pushed into the Danube.

Nor do I less disapprove his censure of the choice which has been made of the troops intended for the American service, which, though I ardently desire its success, I cannot think of equal importance with the defence of our own country; for though we may be disgraced by a defeat, we can be endangered only by an invasion; and

and therefore I think it neceſſary to retain thoſe troops on which we may beſt rely for the ſecurity of this iſland, leſt our enemies ſhould take the advantage of their abſence, and ſet the pretender on the throne.

Sir WILLIAM YONGE next roſe, and ſpoke to the effect following: —Sir, it is a ſtanding maxim, both in private life and public tranſactions, that no man can obtain great advantages, who is afraid of petty inconveniencies ; and that he that will hope to obtain his end without expence, will languiſh for ever in fruitleſs wiſhes, and have the mortification of ſeeing the adventurous and the liberal enjoy that felicity, which, though it is within his reach, he is afraid of ſeizing.

When the depredations of the Spaniards became firſt the ſubject of our debates, nothing was heard amongſt us but threats of vengeance, demands of reparation, aſſertions of ſovereignty, and reſolutions to obtain ſecurity : the importance of our commerce, the neceſſity of rigorous meaſures, the danger of puſillanimity, the meanneſs of negotiation, and the diſadvantages of delay, were thundered from every part of the houſe. Every man ſeemed to imagine that there was no mean between victory and ruin, and that not to humble Spain was to betray our country to inſults, ignominy and ſlavery.

Far was I then, Sir, from ſuſpecting, that when the war, thus vehemently urged, ſhould be declared, that the proſecution of it would produce any debates. I doubted not but that every man would be deſirous of ſignalizing his zeal for the proſperity of commerce, by expediting the ſupplies, and forwarding the preparations, and that the only contention among us would be, who ſhould appear the moſt ardent enemy of Spain.

But no ſooner are hoſtilities begun againſt this inſolent and oppreſſive nation, than thoſe who expreſſed moſt reſentment at the prudence and moderation by which they were delayed, thoſe that accuſed every attempt for an accommodation, of cowardice, and charged the miniſtry with conniving at the rapine of pirates, begin to enquire into the neceſſity of the expences occaſioned by the war, to harangue on the advantages of parſimony, and to think it of more importance to eaſe our taxes, than to ſubdue our enemies.

In purſuance of this new doctrine they are now endeavouring to embarraſs the meaſures of his majeſty, that they may ſave, according to their own computation, only thirty thouſand pounds, which in reality I can eaſily ſhew to be no more than fifteen thouſand.

For

For the fake of this important fum, our army is to be modelled by a new regulation, and the fuccefs of the war is to be impeded, the fecurity of our commerce to be hazarded, and our colonies are to be endangered.

Frugality is undoubtedly a virtue, but is, like others, to be practifed on proper occafions: to compute expences with a fcrupulous nicety in time of war, is to prefer money to fafety, and, by a very perverfe kind of policy, to hazard the whole for the prefervation of a part.

The gentlemen, Sir, who have moft endeavoured to diftinguifh themfelves as the conftant opponents of the adminiftration, have charged it, on all occafions, with giving encouragement to the Spaniards, but can charge it with nothing fo likely to raife the confidence and confirm the obftinacy of the enemy, as the objections which they themfelves have made to the prefent fcheme of levying forces; for to how great a degree of poverty muft they believe that nation reduced, of which the warmeft patriots ftruggle to fave a fum fo inconfiderable, by an experiment of fo much uncertainty? And how eafily will the Spaniards promife themfelves, that they fhall gain the victory only by obliging us to continue in a ftate of war, a ftate which, by our own confeffion, we are not able to fupport?

Had any other argument, Sir, been produced than the neceffity of parfimony, it had been lefs dangerous to have agreed to this new fcheme; but to adopt it only for the fake of fparing fifteen thoufand pounds, would be to make ourfelves contemptible, to intimidate our allies, and to unite all thofe againft us, who are inclined to trample on mifery, and to plunder weaknefs.

I am inclined to judge fo favourably, Sir, of the intentions of thofe whom I am now oppofing, that I believe they have only ufed this argument, becaufe they were able to produce no other, and that if either reafon or experience had been on their fide, the poverty of the nation had not been mentioned.

But the honourable gentleman, who has been fo long engaged in military employments, has fhewn that all our fuccefs has been obtained by the prefent eftablifhment, and that the battle in which we fuffered moft, was loft by our unfortunate deficiency of officers.

Nor do his reafons, Sir, however modeftly offered, deferve lefs regard than his experience, for he has fhewn that a greater number of officers naturally contribute to preferve difcipline, and excite courage;

and

and it is not neceſſary that a man ſhould be much a ſoldier to diſcover, that diſcipline and courage united, muſt generally prevail.

To the examples which he has produced in favour of his opinion, it has been objeſted, that victories equally wonderful have been gained with fewer officers, and, by the honourable gentleman that ſpoke the ſecond on this occaſion, the actions of Eugene were op-poſed to thoſe of the duke of Marlborough.

That victories have been gained by troops differently regulated, I cannot deny ; victories have likewiſe been gained, Sir, under every circumſtance of diſadvantage ; victories have been gained by inferiour numbers, and by raw troops, over veteran armies, yet no prudent general ever produced theſe inſtances as arguments againſt the uſe-fulneſs of diſcipline, or as proofs that ſuperiority of numbers was no advantage.

The ſucceſs of prince Eugene in the late war, was far from con-vincing the Britiſh general, that the German eſtabliſhment was pre-ferable to our own ; for he required that the Heſſian troops, which were paid by Britain, ſhould be officered like our national troops. In this he could be influenced only by his own opinion ; for he nei-ther nominated their officers, nor could advance his intereſt at home by creating new poſts to which he did not recommend ; he could therefore only regard the ſucceſs of the war, and changed their model only becauſe he thought it defective.

The Germans themſelves, Sir, are far from imagining that their armies might not be made more formidable by approaching nearer to the Britiſh methods ; for one of their officers, a man of great reputation and experience, has informed me, that they were convinced of their defect, and that nothing hindered them from adding more officers, but the fear of expences ; that they imputed all their defeats to the neceſſity of parſimony, that their men wanted not courage but leaders, and that their enemies gained advantages merely by the ſupe-riority of their opulence.

In the late war it was common for the auxiliary troops, when they were ſent upon any expedition of importance, to be ſupplied with officers either from their other regiments, or by the Britiſh forces ; ſo neceſſary did the duke of Marlborough think a larger number of officers in time of action, that where he could not alter the eſtabliſh-ment, he deviated from the common methods of war, and transfer-

F 2   red

red his officers occafionally into troops over which they had no fettled authority.

It is therefore moft evident, Sir, that the model on which our troops are formed, was, by this great commander, preferred to that which is now fo warmly recommended, and I know not why we fhould recede from his practice, if we are defirous of his fuccefs.

Nor can I difcover, Sir, any better method of felecting officers than that which has of late been followed, however fome may cenfure or ridicule it. To advance gentlemen to command feems to be the moft likely way to unite authority with rank, for no man willingly obeys thofe to whom he has lately feen himfelf equal, or whofe conduct in lower ftations he has perhaps had opportunities of examining too nearly.

The diftinction of birth, however chimerical in itfelf, has been fo long admitted, and fo univerfally received, that it is generally imagined to confer on one man an indelible and evident fuperiority over another, a fuperiority, which thofe who would eafily imagine themfelves equal in merit cannot deny, and which they allow more willingly, becaufe, though it be an advantage to poffefs it, to want it cannot be juftly confidered as a reproach.

For this reafon, Sir, men chearfully obey thofe to whom their birth feems to have fubjected them, without any fcrupulous enquiries into their virtue or abilities; they have been taught from their childhood to confider them as placed in a higher rank than themfelves, and are therefore not difgufted at any tranfient burfts of impatience, or fudden flarts of caprice, which would produce at leaft refentment, and perhaps mutiny, in men newly exalted from a low ftation. The more attentively, Sir, we look upon the world, the more ftrongly fhall we be convinced of the truth of thefe affertions, and the more evidently fhall we difcover the influence which operates, in a degree fcarcely credible, even to thofe who have experienced its power, and which is indeed one of the chief means of fubordination, by which fociety is held together.

Nor are officers of birth, Sir, to be preferred to men who are recommended by nothing but military fervice, only becaufe they are more chearfully obeyed, but for another reafon of equal importance. It has been obferved, that, in reality, they difcharge the duty of commanders in a manner more likely to preferve dignity and encreafe
reverence;

reverence; that they difcover, on all occafions, a fenfe of honour
and dread of difgrace, which are not eafily to be found in a mind
contracted by a mean education, and depreffed by long habits of fub-
jection.

It is not indeed, Sir, univerfally and unvariably certain, that a
man raifed from meannefs and poverty, will be infolent and oppreffive; nor do I doubt but there are many now languifhing in obfcurity, whofe abilities might add new luftre to the higheft honours, and
whofe integrity would very faithfully difcharge the moft important
truft, and in their favour, where-ever they can be difcovered, fome
exceptions ought to be made; but as general rules are generally to
be followed, as well in military regulations as other tranfactions, it
will be found upon the exacteft enquiry, by no means improper to
advance gentlemen to pofts of command rather than private fentinels,
however fkilful or courageous.

It is to be confidered, Sir, that the prefent ftate of the continent, has for many years made it neceffary to fupport an army
even when we are not engaged in an actual war; that this army,
though of late it has, for the eafe of the people, been fometimes
encamped during the fummer, is for the greateft part quartered in
towns, and mingled with the reft of the community, but governed
at the fame time by the officers, and fubject to the martial law. It
has often been obferved by thofe who have argued againft ftanding
forces, that this difference of government makes different focieties,
which do not combine in the fame intereft, nor much favour one
another; and it is indeed certain that feuds are fometimes produced,
that when any private quarrel happens either by drunkennefs,
or accident, or claims really difputable, between a foldier and any
other perfon, each applies for fupport and affiftance to thofe in
the fame condition with himfelf, the caufe becomes general, and the
foldiers and townfmen are not eafily reftrained from blows and bloodfhed.

It is true likewife that the rhetoric of the patriots has been fo efficacious, that their arguments have been fo clamoroufly echoed, and
their weekly productions fo diligently difperfed, that a great part of
the nation, as men always willingly admit what will produce immediate eafe or advantage, believes the army to be an ufelefs burthen
impofed upon the people for the fupport of the miniftry; that the
landlord therefore looks upon the foldier as an intruder forced into

F 3

his

his house, and rioting in sloth at his expence; and the farmer and manufacturer have learned to call the army the vermin of the land, the caterpillars of the nation, the devourers of other men's industry, the enemies of liberty, and the slaves of the court.

It is not to be suppofed, Sir, that the foldiers entertain the fame ideas of their profeffion, or that they do not conceive themfelves injured by fuch reprefentations: they undoubtedly confider themfelves as the bulwark of their country, as men felected for the defence of the reft of the community, as thofe who have engaged at the hazard of their lives to repel invafion and reprefs rebellion, and who contribute more than their part to the general felicity, by fecuring property and preventing danger.

It is not to be doubted, Sir, but fentiments fo widely different, muft produce an equal contrariety of claims, and diverfity of conduct; the trader imagines, that the man who fubfifts upon the taxes which are raifed only from his labour, ought to confider himfelf as his inferior at leaft, if not as his hireling and his fervant; the foldier wonders how he can ever conceive himfelf fufficiently grateful to him that has devoted his life to his defence, and to whom he muft fly for protection whenever danger fhall approach him, and concludes that he has an inconteftible right to the better part of that, of which the prefervation of the whole depends upon him.

Thus does felf-love magnify every man in his own eyes, and fo differently will men determine when each is to judge in his own caufe. Which of thefe competitors thinks moft juftly of his own ftation and character, or whether both are not miftaken in their opinion, I think it by no means neceffary to decide. This at leaft is evident, that to preferve peace and harmony between two bodies of men obliged to live together with fentiments fo oppofite, there is required an uncommon degree of prudence, moderation, and knowledge of mankind, which is chiefly to be exerted on the part of the foldiers, becaufe they are fubject to more rigorous command, and are more eafily governed by the authority of their fuperiors.

Let us fuppofe any difpute of this kind, Sir, to happen where the foldiers were commanded only by private fentinels, difguifed in the drefs of officers, but retaining, what it cannot be expected that they fhould fuddenly be able to lay afide, the prejudices which they had imbibed in the ranks, and all the ardour of trifling competition in which their ftation had once engaged them. What could be expected

pected from their councils and direction? Can it be imagined, that they would enquire impartially into the original cause of the dispute, that they would attend equally to the parties, endeavour by mildness and candour to soften the malevolence of each, and terminate the dispute by some addressful expedient, or decent accommodation? He surely must be very little acquainted with the vulgar notions of bravery and honour, that could form any hopes of such conduct.

The plain soldier, Sir, has not accustomed himself to regulate his motions by reason, nor has learned any more of honour, than that it consists in adhering invariably to his pretensions, even though he should discover that they are false; and in resenting affronts with the utmost rigour, even when they were provoked by himself, he is taught, that it is his business to conquer in whatever cause, and that to desist from any of his attempts, or retract any of his assertions, is unworthy of a man of honour.

Warm with such notions as these, Sir, would such officers, as have been recommended by the honourable gentleman, apply themselves to the termination of differences? Without any knowledge of the laws of society, without any settled ideas of the different rights of different persons, they would have nothing in view but the honour of their profession, nor endeavour to support it by any other method than that of violence. If a soldier was affronted by a farmer, they would probably lay his territories waste, and ravage his plantations like an enemy's country; if another disagreed with his landlord, they would advise him to *make good his quarters*, to invade the magazines of provision without restraint, to force the barricadoes of the cellar, and to forage in the stables without controul.

But gentlemen, Sir, are proper judges of debates between the army and the rest of the community, because they are equally related to both parties, as men who possess or expect estates, or who are allied to those whose influence arises from their property. As men bred in affluence and freedom, and acquainted with the blessings of our constitution, and the necessity of civil government, they cannot willingly contribute to the increase of the military power, and as members of the army they cannot but be desirous to support their own rank, and to hinder their profession from sinking into contempt; it is therefore their care to repress insolence on one part, and to prevent oppression on the other, to stop dissentions in their beginning, and reconcile all the different pretensions of Britons and soldiers.

I am

I am indeed furprized, Sir, to hear the promotion of ferjeants recommended by the honour.ble gentleman who has fo often ftrained his Jungs, and exhaufted his invention, to explain how much our conftitution is endangered by the army, how readily thofe men will concur in the abolition of property who have nothing to lofe, and how eafily they may be perfuaded to deftroy the liberties of their country, who are already cut off from the enjoyment of them, who, therefore, can only behold with envy and malevolence thofe advantages which they cannot hope to poffefs, and which produce in them no other effects than a quicker fenfe of their own mifery.

Upon what principles, Sir, any gentleman can form thofe notions, or with what view he can fo long and fo ftudioufly difperfe them, it is his province to explain, for the only reafon that can be offered by any other perfon for his inceffant declamations, the defire of fecuring his country from the oppreffion of a ftanding army, is now for ever overthrown by this new propofal ; which, if it were to be received, would in a very few years produce an army proper to be employed in the execution of the moft deteftable defigns, an army that could be of no other ufe than to gratify an ambitious prince or a wicked miniftry, as it would be commanded, not by men who had loft their liberty, but by men who never enjoyed it, by men who would abolifh our conftitution without knowing that they were engaged in any criminal undertaking, who have no other fenfe of the enjoyment of authority than that it is the power of acting without controul, who have no knowledge of any other laws than the commands of their fuperiors.

To men like thefe, Sir, to men raifed up from poverty and fervility to rank and power, to ignorance invefted with command, and to meannefs elated with preferment, would any real patriot, any zealous affertor of liberty, any inflexible enemy to the corruptions of the miniftry, confign the protection of his country, and intruft to thefe our happinefs, properties, and our lives ?

Whether the honourable gentleman has changed any of the fentiments, which he has hitherto appeared to admit with regard to the army, whether this new determination is only an inftance of that inconfiftency, which is fcarcely to be avoided in the vindication of a bad caufe, or whether he was betrayed to it only by his hatred of the adminiftration, which would prompt him to recant his own advice, if it fhould happen to be approved, I will not pretend to determine, but

but I muſt lament on this occaſion the entertainment which the houſe
will loſe, by the ʾeternal ceſſation of any harangues on the army,
ſince he cannot now declaim on either part without contradicting
his former declarations.

Nor will the honourable gentleman find leſs difficulty in proving,
that juſtice, rather than policy, requires the promotion of ſerjeants
to commiſſions. Military preferments are always at the diſpoſal of
the crown, nor can any right be pretended to them, but ſuch as ariſes
from the cuſtom which has been generally followed in confering
them, which is not only variable at pleaſure, but has never been at
any time regularly obſerved. The order of rotation has been ſuffered
ſometimes to proceed, becauſe of two perſons otherwiſe equal, he that
has ſerved longeſt may plead the moſt merit; but the plea of ſervice has been always over-ruled by birth or powerful recommendation. And though, Sir, it is natural for men diſappointed to
complain, yet as thoſe officers, whoſe preferment has been delayed,
were not thought in reality to have received any injury, their murmurs have been the leſs regarded.

It might be expected, Sir, from a patriot, a lamenter of the degeneracy of mankind, and an inflexible opponent of corruption,
that he ſhould conſider rather facts than perſons, that he ſhould
regulate his deciſion by the unvariable principles of reaſon and
juſtice, and that therefore he ſhould not applaud at one time what
he condemns at another.

But this gentleman ſeems to have eſtabliſhed ſome new maxims
of conduct, and perhaps upon new notions of morality; for he
ſeems to imagine, that his friends may ſeize as their right, what his
adverſaries cannot touch without robbery, though the claim of both
be the ſame.

It is well known, Sir, to the whole army, that a noble perſon
whoſe abilities are ſo loudly celebrated, whoſe virtues are ſo liberally
praiſed, and whoſe removal from his military employments is ſo
ſolemnly lamented as a publick calamity, obtained his firſt preferments by pretenſions very different from military merit, and that at
the age only of ſeventeen, a time of life in which, whatever might
be his abilities, very little prudence or experience could be expected,
he was advanced to the command of a regiment, and exalted above
many officers whoſe known bravery and frequent hazards entitled
them to favour.

I do

I do not affert that he was undefervedly promoted, or condemn thofe who either folicited or granted his commiffion ; I maintain only, that what was then reafonable and juft, is not now either iniquitous or ridiculous, and different perfons in the fame circumftances have a right to the fame treatment.

In the reign of queen Anne, a reign, Sir, which every Briton recollects with fo much fatisfaction, and which will for ever afford examples of the wifeft councils, and moft fuccefsful wars, when new regiments were to be raifed, it was far from being thought neceffary to obferve this gentleman's favourite method of rotation ; pofts were filled, not with the officers of other regiments, that room might be left for the promotion of ferjeants, but with gentlemen who had never feen a battle, or learned any part of the military difcipline.

But though, Sir, the regulation of our army be thus violently attacked, the greateft crime of the miniftry is, in this gentleman's opinion, that of levying new troops, when we have no employment for our ftanding forces, of laying unneceffary impofitions upon the nation, and alarming with the fears of an invafion, only that the army might be encreafed.

On this head, Sir, a declaration of the duke of Marlborough has been produced, with a great pomp of circumftances, and fuch a feeming accuracy of narration, that the attention of the houfe was engaged, and the account was received with all the folemnity of univerfal filence, and with the veneration due to fo high an authority in a queftion of fo much importance.

The fubject is indeed fo worthy of regard, that I think, Sir, every man ought to contribute to its elucidation, and, therefore, I take the liberty of adding to the honourable gentleman's relation, what I hope will be heard with equal curiofity, the method by which that great commander propofed to put a ftop to an invafion with fo fmall a number.

He was very far, Sir, from imagining that he fhould be able to repel them by open force, he was far from being fo confident of his fuperiority in military fkill, as to imagine that he fhould defeat them by ftratagem, and therefore, he defigned, by burning the villages, and deftroying the country, to deprive them of the means of fubfiftence, and harrafs them with famine ; to hover at a diftance, and cut off thofe parties which neceffity fhould force out to forage,

till

till a body of troops could be assembled sufficient to overthrow them in a battle, or to drive them back to their ships.

Such was the scheme, Sir, as I have been informed, of this great man, nor, perhaps, can any other be struck out by human abilities, where greater numbers are to be opposed by smaller. But this scheme, though preferable in the last extremities to slavery, is such as cannot be mentioned without horror, and of which the execution ought to be avoided by every expedient that can be practised without the danger of our liberties. We ought certainly not to reject a nauseous medicine, by which that health is preserved, which, if lost, can only be restored by the amputation of a limb.

As it was therefore necessary, Sir, to secure our coasts from an invasion, it was necessary to raise new troops for the American expedition ; nor did this method produce any delay, for the regiments were compleated a long time before the ships of war and the transports were ready to convoy and receive them, nor could the utmost ardour and diligence dispatch them sooner from our coasts.

The ships, Sir, were by the violence of a frost, scarcely exampled, retained for a long time in the harbours, without a possibility of being put to sea ; when they were all assembled at the place appointed for their conjunction, they waited for a wind ; all the delay that can be objected, was produced by the seasons, of which the regulation was in no man's power.

But the time, Sir, which was unwillingly spent in the camp, was not however lost or misemployed, for the troops were, by the order of the general, every day exercised, and instructed in the art of war, so that what was lost in time, was more than recompensed by the advantage of better discipline.

Nor did these troops appear an herd so ignorant and contemptible, as they have been represented by malicious invectives and ludicrous descriptions ; there were not indeed among them many grey-headed warriors, nor were their former campaigns and past exploits the subjects of their conversation ; but there was not one amongst them who did not appear ready to suffer, in the cause of his country, all that the most hardened veteran could undergo, or whose alacrity and eagerness did not promise perseverance in the march, and intrepidity in the battle.

Their general, Sir, who saw them pursue their exercises, declared how much he was satisfied with their proficiency, applauded their appearance and expressed his confidence in their courage; nor do I doubt, but our enemies will find, that it is not necessary to send out our most formidable forces to humble them, and that the youth of Britain will compensate their want of experience by their courage.

If I, Sir, have been drawn aside from the present question, it is by following, perhaps, with an exactness too scrupulous, the honourable gentleman, whose propositions I have now shewn to be erroneous, and whose reproaches will, I believe, now appear rather the effects of disappointment than of zeal, and therefore I think it now necessary to return to the business before us, the consideration of the present establishment, from which, as it was approved by the duke of Marlborough, and has been defended with very strong arguments by one of the most experienced officers of this time, I cannot think it safe or prudent to depart.

Mr. GRENVILLE spoke next to the following effect:—Sir, as a noble person has been frequently hinted at in this debate, to whom my relation is well known, and whom, as I know him well, I have the strongest motives to reverence and honour, I cannot forbear to give, on this occasion, an attestation which he will be allowed to deserve by all those whom interest has not blinded, and corruption depraved.

It will be allowed, Sir, that he is one of those who are indebted for their honours only to merit, one whom the malice of a court cannot debate, as its favour cannot exalt; he is one of those whose loss of employments can be a reproach only to those who take them from him, as he cannot forfeit them but by performing his duty, and can only give offence by steady integrity, and a resolution to speak as he thinks, and to act as his conscience dictates.

There are, Sir, men I know, to whom this panegyric will seem romantic and chimerical, men to whom integrity and conscience are idle sounds, men who are content to catch the word of their leader, who have no sense of the obligation of any law but the supreme will of him that pays them, and who know not any virtue but diligence in attendance, and readiness in obedience.

It is surely, Sir, no loss to the noble person to be debarred from any fellowship with men like these. Nothing can be more unpleasing to virtue than such a situation as lays it under a necessity of beholding wickedness that cannot be reformed; as the sight of a pestilence must raise horror, though we should suppose the spectator secure from the contagion.

Mr. Ord spoke next, in substance as follows:—Sir, as I cannot approve the scheme now proposed, for augmenting our forces, I shall endeavour to shew why the arguments, by which it has hitherto been supported, have failed to convince me, and shall lay before the house some reasons against it, to which I shall expect an answer, before I shall think that I can agree to it, without squandering the money of which my constituents have intrusted me with the disposal.

The argument, Sir, with which this motion was introduced, which is indeed the strongest that has yet been offered, was, that this estimate is less expensive than one that was laid before the house in a late reign, and that therefore it could not reasonably be charged with extravagance.

Let us now consider this argument with that care which is required by the importance of the question, let us enquire what consequences will follow from it, and to what previous suppositions it must owe its force.

The argument, Sir, evidently supposes that the estimate in king William's reign was drawn up without any intention to deceive the house, or to raise money for purposes different from those for which it was really expended. But if we suppose that estimate to be fraudulently calculated, this may contain the same fallacies in a lower degree, and the only merit that can be claimed by the authors of it, will be, that they are not the most rapacious plunderers of their country, that however they may be charged with profusion of publick money, they are yet more modest than some of their predecessors.

But it is known, Sir, that in king William's reign, very few estimates were honestly computed; it is known that the rotation of parties, and fluctuation of measures, reduced the ministry to subsist upon artifices, to amuse the senate with exorbitant demands, only that they might obtain the necessary grants, and to pretend expences which never were incurred, that the supplies which the publick affairs really required, might not be with-held; as fraudulent tradesmen fix immoderate prices, that the buyer may make offers proportionate to their demands.

The estimates therefore of that reign are of very little authority, though they might sometimes pass the house without censure; for it is to be considered, that by the frequency of new elections, the greatest part of the members were often unacquainted with the state of

publick

publick accounts, and that an army was so little known to this kingdom, that the true expence of it might easily be concealed.

Nor is this, Sir, the only fallacy of this argument; for it supposes likewise, that the nation is no less wealthy than in the time when that computation was offered, with which this is so triumphantly compared. For every man knows that publick as well as private expences are to be proportioned to the revenue by which they are supplied, and that the charges which are easily supported at one time, may threaten ruin at another.

But unhappily, Sir, it is evident, that, since the days of that sovereign, the nation has been exhausted by a long and wasteful war, and since, by a peace equally destructive, it is embarrassed with an enormous debt, and intangled in treaties, of which the support may call every day for new expences; it has suffered since that time a thousand losses, but gained no advantage, and yet the expences of that time are mentioned as an example to be compared with those which are proposed in this.

The difference of the condition of the British nation at those two periods of time, Sir, is not less than that of the strength of the same man in the vigour of youth and the frigidity of old age, in the flush of health and the languor of disease, of the same man newly risen from rest and plenty, and debilitated with hunger and fatigue.

To make such a comparison, Sir, betrays at least a very criminal insensibility of the publick misery, if it may not be charged with greater malignity. I know not whether those who shall hear of this debate, may not impute such reflections rather to cruelty than negligence, and imagine that those who squander the treasure of the nation, take pleasure in reproaching that poverty which their counsels produce, and indulge their own vanity by contemplating the calamities from which they are themselves secure, and to which they are indebted for opportunities of increasing their own fortunes, and gratifying their ambition. It is evident, that an estimate which requires less than that which has been mentioned, may yet exact more than the nation can now raise, without feeling too great inconveniencies to be compensated by the advantages which can be expected from our new forces. Nor is it sufficient that it is lower than those of former times; for as it ought to be the care of the government to preserve the ease and happiness of the people, it should be reduced in proportion to the diminution of the national wealth.

The

The right honourable gentleman confeffes, Sir, that frugality is a virtue, and his argument fuppofes that to contract expences is an argument of prudent meafures ; why then is he afraid of carrying virtue to a greater height, of making the burthen ftill more light, and preferring the cheapeft eftimate that can be propofed, when it is afferted by thofe whofe authority is moft worthy of regard, that it will produce no weaknefs in our troops, nor give our enemies any fuperiority?

I do not pretend any other fkill in military affairs, than may be gained by cafual converfation with foldiers, and by a curfory obfervation of daily occurrences ; but I fpeak with greater confidence on this occafion, becaufe I do not think any other qualifications neceffary for the determination of this queftion, than a habit of juft reafoning and freedom from the prejudices of intereft.

Every man knows, Sir, without a military education, that it is imprudent to purchafe any thing at a greater price which may be procured at a lefs, and that when the fame fum will buy two things, of which one is evidently preferable to the other, the beft ought to be chofen.

If the application of either of thefe two pofitions will decide this controverfy, there will be no need of recurring to experience, of citing the authority of foreign commanders, of comparing the actions of the German and Britifh generals, or of enquiring how battles have been loft, or to what victories are to be afcribed.

It is evident, Sir, that the fcheme now propofed, is twice as coftly as that which is recommended in oppofition to it, and therefore, unlefs it will produce twice the advantage, it muft be acknowledged to be imprudently chofen. The advantage in war, is to be rated by comparing the ftrength of different numbers in different circumftances, and enquiring what degree of fuperiority will be found.

If we fuppofe, Sir, two bodies of men equally armed and difciplined oppofed to each other without any advantage of fituation, we muft conceive that neither party could be conquered, that the balance of the day muft remain equal, and that the conteft would continue undecided.

It cannot be objected to this fuppofition, Sir, that no fuch event is recorded in hiftory, becaufe in war many caufes really act which cannot be eftimated ; one army may confift of foldiers more courageous, and more confident in the juftice of their caufe ; unforefeen accidents

may

may operate, orders may be mistaken, or leaders may be misinformed; but all these considerations are to be set aside in speculation, because they may equally be alleged on either part.

Two bodies of men, Sir, equally numerous, being therefore supposed equal, it is to be enquired how either may be superior to the other. It is proposed on one part to produce this effect by doubling the number of officers rather than increasing that of the soldiers, on the other to double the soldiers under the same officers, the expence being the same of both methods.

When two armies modelled according to these different schemes enter the field, what event can be expected? Either five thousand men with a double number of officers, must be equal to ten thousand differently regulated, or the publick has paid more for assistance of the officers than its real value, and has chosen of two methods equally expensive that which is least efficacious.

This, Sir, is the state of the question now before us, our present deficiency is not of men but money, and we may procure ten thousand men regulated like the foreign troops, at the same expence as five thousand in the form proposed; but I am afraid that no man will be found to assert, that the addition of officers will be equivalent to a double number of soldiers.

Thus it is evident, Sir, evident to demonstration, that the most expensive method is at the same time the least advantageous, and that the proposal of new regiments is intended to augment the strength of the ministry rather than of the army.

If we suppose, Sir, what is more than any foreigner will grant, that the additional officers raise a body of five thousand men to an equality with six thousand, is not the pay of four thousand men apparently thrown away? And do not the officers receive a reward which their service cannot deserve? Would it not be far more rational to raise seven thousand, by which our army would be stronger by a seventh part, and as the pay of three thousand would be saved, the publick would be richer by almost a third.   •

Surely, Sir, numerical arguments cannot but deserve some consideration, even from those who have learned by long practice to explain away mere probability at pleasure, to select the circumstances of complicated questions, and only to shew those which may be produced in favour of their own opinions.

In the present question, Sir, there is very little room for fallacy;
nor

nor do I fee what remains to the decifion of it, but that thofe gentlemen who have been acquainted with military operations, inform us,
what degree of fuperiority is conferred by any affignable number of officers; that we may compare their fervice with the price, and difcover whether the fame money will not purchafe greater advantages.

The experience of the late war may evince, Sir, that thofe troops
which have the greateft number of officers are not always victorious ;
for our eftablifhment never admitted the fame, or nearly the fame
number with that of the French our enemies ; neverthelefs we ftill
boaft of our victories ; nor is it certain that we might not have been
equally fuccefsful, though the number of our officers had been yet
lefs.

Foreigners, Sir, are very far from difcovering the defect of their
own eftablifhment, or imagining that they fhould become more formidable by imitating our methods. When I travelled, I took opportunities of converfing with the generals of thofe nations which are
moft famous for the valour of their troops, and was informed by
them, that they thought a multitude of officers by no means ufeful,
and that they were fo far from defiring to fee their own regulation
changed, that they fhould make no fcruple of recommending it to
other nations, who in their opinion fquandered their treafure upon
ufelefs commiffions, and increafed the calamities of war by unneceffary burthens.

I hope no man will think it fufficient to reply to thefe arguments
with general affertions, or will deny the neceffity of frugality, and
extol the opulence of the nation, the extent of our commerce, and
the happinefs of our condition. Such indeed, Sir, is the method of
argumentation made ufe of by the hireling fcribblers of the court, who,
becaufe they feel none of the publick calamities, reprefent all complaints as criminal murmurs, and charge thofe with fedition who petition only for relief. Wretches like thefe would celebrate our victories, though our country fhould be over-run by an invader, would
praife the lenity of any government by which themfelves fhould be
fpared, and would boaft of the happinefs of plenty, when half the
people fhould be languifhing with famine.

I do not fuppofe, Sir, that the defpicable fophiftry of proftitutes
like thefe has any effect here, nor fhould I have thought them worthy of the leaft notice, had it not been proper to enquire, whether
thofe may not be juftly fufpected of fome inclination to deceive, even

Vol. I.   G   in

in this affembly, by whom the moſt profligate of mankind are openly paid for the promulgation of falſhood, and the patronage of corruption.

It is indeed, Sir, artful, in thoſe who are daily impairing our honour and influence, to endeavour to conceal from the people their own weaknefs, that weaknefs which is fo well known in foreign countries, that every nation is encouraged to infult us, and by which it may reaſonably be imagined that new enemies will in a ſhort time be raiſed.

The late changes in our military regulations have indeed taken away all the terror of our arms ; thoſe troops are now no longer dreaded, by which the liberties of Europe were recovered, and the French reduced to abandon their ſchemes of univerſal empire, for the defence of their own country, becauſe the officers by whom they were formerly conducted to glory and to victory, are now difmiſſed, and men advanced to their poſts, who are neither feared nor known.

When the duke of Argyle was lately deprived of his command, the Spaniards could not conceal their fatisfaction ; they beſtowed, however unwillingly, the higheſt panegyric upon his bravery and conduct, by ſhewing that he was the only Briton of whom they were afraid. Nor did their allies the French difcover lefs exultation ; for by them it was declared, that the nation was now difarmed, that either no war was intended, or that none could be fuccefsfully profecuted, fince, as they made no fcruple to aſſert, though I know not whether I ought to repeat it, we have no other man capable of commanding armies, or conducting any great defign

I am informed that this illuſtrious warrior, whoſe abilities are fufficiently atteſted by thoſe enemies that have felt their prevalence, is of opinion, that the number of officers now required is not neceſſary, and has declared that he ſhould with equal confidence undertake either invaſion or defence, with forces modelled after the German cuſtom ; and fince I have ſhewn, that, unlefs the troops fo regulated are equivalent to a double number added to the ſtanding regiments, part of the expence of the officers is evidently fquandered, I ſhall vote againſt the motion, unlefs it be proved, which I believe will not be attempted, that the force of a regiment is doubled by doubling the officers.

General WADE then fpoke to the purpoſe following : —Sir, the
learned

learned gentleman who fpoke laft, muft be acknowledged to have difcovered a very fpecious method of reafoning, and to have carried his enquiry as far as fpeculation without experience can hope to proceed, but has in my opinion admitted a falfe principle, by which all his argument has been perplexed.

He fuppofes that the advantages muft be always in proportion to the money expended in procuring them, and that therefore if five thoufand men, raifed at any given coft, will be equal to five thoufand, they ought, if they are regulated according to an eftablifhment of double the charge, to be able to encounter ten thoufand.

But in this fuppofition, Sir, he forgets that the poffibility of lofs is to be thrown into the balance againft the advantage of the expence faved, and that though the ftrength of the troops be not encreafed in proportion to the encreafe of the coft, yet the additional fecurity againft a great lofs may juftly entitle the moft expenfive regulation to the preference.

Suppofe five thoufand men to be brought into the field againft fix thoufand, if they can by multiplying their officers at a double expence be enabled to engage fuccefsfully a body fuperior in number by only a fixth part, the nation may be juftly faid to gain all that would have been loft by fuffering a defeat.

That we ought not to chufe a worfe method when we can difcover a better, is indifputably true, but which method is worfe or better, can be difcovered only by experience. The laft war has taught us, that our troops in their prefent eftablifhment are fuperior to the forces of France, but how much they might fuffer by any alteration it is not poffible to forefee.

Succefs is gained by courage, and courage is produced by an opinion of fuperiority; and it may eafily be imagined, that our foldiers, who judge of their own ftrength only by experience, imagine their own eftablifhment and difcipline advanced to the higheft perfection; nor would they expect any other confequences from an alteration of it, but weaknefs and defeats. It is therefore dangerous to change the model of our forces, becaufe it is dangerous to deprefs the fpirit of our foldiers.

Though it is confeffed, Sir, that the French, whofe officers are ftill more numerous, have been conquered by our troops, it muft be likewife alleged, that they had yielded us far eafier victories had their officers been wanting; for to them are they indebted for their conquests where-ever they have been succesful, and for their resistance where-ever they have been with difficulty defeated ; their soldiers are a spiritless herd, and were they not invigorated by the example of their leaders, and restrained by the fear of instant punishment, would fly at the approach of any enemy, without waiting for the attack.

I cannot therefore, Sir, but be of opinion, that the necessity of a large number of officers may be learned even from the behaviour of those troops which have been unsuccessful, since it is certain, that though they have been often overcome, they have generally resisted with great steadiness, and retired with great order.

If those who are only speculative warriors shall imagine that their arguments are not confuted, I can only repeat what I declared when I first attempted to deliver my sentiments in this debate, that I do not pretend to be very skilful in the arts of disputation. I, who claim no other title than that of an old soldier, cannot hope to prevail much by my oratory ; it is enough for me that I am confident of confuting those arguments in the field, which I oppose in the senate.

Mr. Fox spoke next in this manner :—Sir, I am far from thinking that this question has been hitherto fully explained by those who have either considered it only as a dispute about money, or a question merely speculative concerning the proportions between different degrees of expence, and probability of success. In a war of this kind expence is the last and lowest consideration, and where experience may be consulted, the conjectures of speculation ought to have no weight.

The method, Sir, by which our troops have hitherto been regulated, is well known to have produced success beyond our expectations, to have exalted us to the arbitration of the world, to have reduced the French to change their threats of forcing a monarch upon us into petitions for peace, and to have established the liberties of almost every nation of the world that can call itself free.

Whether this method, Sir, so successful, so easy, and so formidable, shall be changed, whether it shall be changed at a time when the whole continent is in commotion, and every nation calling soldiers to its standard ; when the French, recovered from their defeats, seem to have forgotten the force of that hand that crushed them in the tide of victory ; when they seem to be reviving their former designs,

and

and rekindling their extinguifhed ambition ; whether, at fuch a time, the regulations of our army fhall be changed to fave, upon the higheft computation, only thirty thoufand pounds, is the prefent queftion.

On fuch a queftion, Sir, I cannot obferve, without aftonifhment, any man deliberating for a fingle moment. To fufpend our opinion in this cafe, would be to balance our lives, our liberties, our patrimonies, and our pofterity, againft thirty thoufand pounds.

The effects of our prefent method, Sir, are well known to ourfelves, our confederates, our enemies, to every man that has heard the name of Blenheim and Ramillies; the confequences of the eftablifhment, now contended for, our moft experienced commanders own themfelves unable to forefee, and I am far from believing that theoretical difquifitions can enable any man to make great difcoveries in military affairs.

Our own inexperience of the method which is fo warmly recommended, is not the ftrongeft objection to it, though even this ought, in my opinion, to reftrain us from trying it at this hazardous conjuncture. But fince arguments, merely negative, may be thought over-balanced by the profpect of faving money, I fhall lay before the houfe, what effects the want of officers has produced, with regard to thofe nations whofe poverty has laid them under a neceffity of parfimonious eftablifhments.

When the Germans were defeated by the French, in the late war, I was at the Sardinian court, where the battle was, as it may eafily be fuppofed, the reigning fubject of converfation, and where they did not want opportunities of informing themfelves minutely of all the circumftances which contributed to the event ; it was there, Sir, univerfally determined, that the Germans loft the day merely for want of officers.

It was obferved, alfo, Sir, that fome troops, which were once courted and feared by all the neighbouring potentates, had loft their reputation in later times, of which no reafon could be alleged, but that they had leffened the number of their officers ; fuch is the change in the model of the Walloons, and fuch is the confequence produced by it.

I am very far, Sir, from thinking, that reafon is not to be confulted in military operations as in other affairs, and have no lefs fatisfaction than the learned gentleman who fpoke laft but one, in clear and demonftrative deductions ; but in this queftion, reafon

it felf

itself informs me, that regard ought only to be had to experience, and that authority unsupported by practice, ought to have no prevalence.

I shall therefore, Sir, make no enquiry into the abilities of the generals, by whom these contrary opinions are defended, nor draw any parallel between their actions or their knowledge. It is sufficient for me that the one is proposing a new scheme, and that the opinion of the other can plead the practice of king William, and the duke of Marlborough, and the success of the last war.

Yet, Sir, if parsimony be a virtue at this time so eminently necessary, it may be urged in favour of this estimate, that it will be less expensive than those that have been formerly offered, and that as all changes ought to be gradual, this may be considered as the first step towards a general reduction of the publick charge.

Mr. HEATHCOATE spoke to the following purpose:—Sir, it is not without astonishment, that I heard the honourable gentleman who spoke lately, conclude his remarks with an attempt to renew our apprehensions of the pretender, a chimerical invader, an enemy in the clouds, without spirit, and without forces, without dominions, without money, and without allies; a miserable fugitive that has not a friend in this kingdom, or none but such as are exasperated by those whom the men, that mention him with so much terror, are attempting to vindicate.

The vanity, Sir, of such fears, the folly of admitting them, if they are real, and of counterfeiting them, if they are false, has been sufficiently exposed in this debate, by my honourable friend; but as he thought it unnecessary to employ arguments in proof of what cannot be denied, and believed it sufficient to ridicule a panic which he supposed merely political, I who judge, perhaps, more favourably of the sincerity of some, and more tenderly of the cowardice of others, shall endeavour to shew, that the frequent revolutions which have happened in this nation, afford us no reason for fearing another equally sudden and unforeseen in favour of the pretender.

The government, Sir, is always stronger, as it is complicated with the private interest of more individuals; because, though there are few that have comprehension sufficient to discern the general advantage of the community, almost every man is capable of attending to his own; and though not many have virtue to stand up in opposition to the approach of general calamities, of which every one may

may hope to exempt himfelf from his particular fhare, yet the moft fanguine are alarmed, and the moft indolent awakened at any danger which threatens themfelves, and will exert their utmoft power to obviate or efcape it.

For this reafon, Sir, I have long confidered the publick funds eftablifhed in this nation, as a barrier to the government, which cannot eafily be broken : a foreign prince cannot now be placed upon the throne, but in oppofition almoft to every wealthy man, who having trufted the government with his money, has repofited a pledge of his own fidelity.

But to this gentleman, Sir, whom I am now anfwering, arguments can be of very little importance, becaufe, by his own confeffion, he is retained as a mere machine, to fpeak at the direction of another, and to utter fentiments which he never conceived, and which his hefitation and abrupt conclufion fhews him to admit with very little examination. He had not even allowed himfelf time to know the opinion which he was to affert, or to imprint upon his memory thofe arguments to which he was to add the fanction of his authority. He feems to have boldly promifed to fpeak, and then to have enquired what he was to fay. Yet has this gentleman often declaimed here with all the apparent ardour of integrity, and been heard with that regard which is only due to virtue and independence.

Some of his affertions are fuch, however, as require confutation, which is, perhaps, more neceffary fince he has produced an authority for them, which many of thofe who heard him may think of much greater weight than his own. He affirms, that we can fuffer only by an invafion, and infers from this pofition, that we need only to guard our own coafts. I am of an opinion very different, and having not yet prevailed upon myfelf to receive notes from any other perfon, cannot forbear to fpeak what I think, and what the publick profperity requires to be generally known. We may furely fuffer by many other caufes, by the ignorance or treachery, or cowardice of the miniftry, by the negligence of that perfon to whom this gentleman was probably indebted for his notes. We may fuffer by the lofs of our fugar colonies, which may be juftly valued at ten millions.

Thefe plantations, which afford us almoft all the profitable trade that is now left us, have been expofed to the infults of the enemy, without any other guard than two fhips, almoft unfit for fervice.

G 4

They

They have been left to the protection of chance, with no other security, at a time when the Spaniards had fitted out a squadron, to infest and ravage our American dominions.

The admiral, who was sent into America, was confined for almost a year in the ports, without forces, ships, or amunition, which yet might have been sent in a few months, had not pretences of delay been studiously invented, had not the preparations been obstructed by clandestine expedients, and had not every man been tacitly assured, that he should recomend himself to his superiors, by raising difficulties, rather than by removing them.

Such was the conduct of those, who now stand up in the face of their country, and, without diffidence or shame, boast of their zeal, their assiduity, and their dispatch; who proclaim with an air of triumphant innocence, that no art or diligence could have been more expeditious, and that the embarkation was only impeded by the seasons and the winds.

With assertions equally intrepid, and arguments equally contemptible, has the same person, who boasted his expedition, endeavoured to defend the establishment of new regiments, in opposition to the practice of foreign nations, and to the opinion of the greatest general among us; and, to shew how little he fears confutation, has recommended his scheme on account of its frugality.

It is not to be wondered, Sir, that such an orator should undertake to defend the model of the troops sent to America, that he should prefer boys to veterans, and assert the propriety of intrusting new levies to unexperienced commanders; for he has given us in this debate such proofs of controversial courage, that nothing can be now imagined too arduous for him to attempt.

His strength, Sir, is indeed not equal to his spirit, and he is frequently unsuccessful in his most vigorous efforts, but it must be confessed that he is generally overborne only by the force of truth, by a power which few can resist so resolutely as himself, and which therefore, though it makes no impression upon him, prevails upon others to leave him sometimes alone in the vindication of his positions.

The examples, Sir, of those noble persons who were advanced early to commissions, will be produced by him without effect, because the cases are by no means parallel. They were not invested with command till they had spent some time in the service, and exhibited proofs of their courage and their capacity; and it cannot be
doubted,

doubted, but fome men may difcover at feventeen more merit, than others in the full ftrength of manhood.

But, Sir, there is another confideration of more importance, which will annihilate the parallel, and deftroy the argument founded upon it. At the time in which thefe perfons were preferred, the nation had but newly feen an army, and had therefore very few old officers whofe experience could be trufted, or whofe fervices required to be rewarded, the minifters were obliged to felect thofe, who, though they did not underftand the military fciences, were likely to attain them in a fhort time, and the event has fufficiently proved, that in the choice no greater regard was paid to intereft than to judgment.

It was prudent likewife, Sir, to chufe young perfons, fuppofing their abilities equal with thofe of others, becaufe the nation was likely to poffefs them longer, and would not be reduced by an interval of peace to make war again with raw forces under the direction of ignorant commanders.

But this provifion, however reafonable, the wifdom of this miniftry has found means to defeat, by detaining at home the difciplined troops, and depriving the moft experienced generals of their commands, at a time when they are moft neceffary, at a time when the whole world is in arms, when the ambition of France is reviving its claims, and the Spaniards are preparing to invade our colonies.

But, Sir, though our generals are difcarded, we are fufficiently informed, that it is not becaufe we are imagined to be in a ftate of fafety; for the encreafe of our army betrays our fear, of which, whether it will be difpelled or encreafed by fuch meafures, it is not difficult to determine.

An army thus numerous, Sir, is, in the opinion of every honeft Briton, of every man that reveres the conftitution, or loves his liberty, an evil more to be dreaded, than any from which we can be defended by it. The moft unpopular act of the moft unpopular of our monarchs, was the eftablifhment of a ftanding army, nor do I know any thing to be feared from the exaltation of the dreadful pretender to the throne, but that he will govern the nation with an armed force.

If our troops continue to be encreafed, which we may reafonably expect, fince, if arguments like thefe be admitted, pretences for

augmentations

augmentations can never be wanting, the confequences are eafily forefeen ; they will grow too numerous to be quartered in the towns, and, with an affectation of eafing them of fuch unwelcome guefts, it will be propofed, that after having fpent the fummer in a camp, they fhall retire in winter to barracks. Then will the burthen of a ftanding army be impofed for ever on the nation ; then may our liberties be openly invaded, and thofe who now opprefs us by the power only of money, will then throw afide the mafk, and deliver themfelves from the conftraint of hypocrify ; thofe who now footh us with promifes and proteftations, will then intimidate us with threatenings, and, perhaps, revenge the oppofition of their fchemes by perfecution and fequeftrations.

Mr. GAGE fpoke next, to the following effect :—Sir, if the weaknefs of arguments proved the infincerity of thofe who produce them, I fhould be inclined to fufpect the advocates for the eftablifhment of new regiments, of defigns very different from the defence of their country ; but as their intentions cannot be known, they cannot be cenfured, and I fhall therefore confine myfelf to an examination of the reafons which they have offered, and the authorities which they have cited.

The German general, who has been mentioned on this occafion with fo much regard, is not lefs known to me than to the honourable gentleman, nor have I been lefs diligent to improve the hours in which I enjoyed his friendfhip and converfation. Among other queftions, which my familiarity with him intitled me to propofe, I have afked him to what caufes he imputed the ill fuccefs of the laft war, and he frankly afcribed the mifcarriages of it to the unhappy divifions by which the German counfels were at that time embarraffed.

Faction produces nearly the fame confequence in all countries, and had then influenced the Imperial court, as of late the court of Great Britain, to difmifs the moft able and experienced commanders, and to intruft the conduct of the war to men unequal to the undertaking ; who, when they were defeated for want of fkill, endeavoured to perfuade their patrons and their countrymen, that they loft the victory for want of officers.

They might, perhaps, think of their countrymen, what our minifters feem to imagine of us, that to gain belief among them, it was fufficient to affert boldly, that they had not any memory of paft tranfactions, and that therefore they could not obferve, that the fame

troops

troops were victorious under Eugene, which were defeated under the
direction of his successors; nor could discover that the regulation
was the same, where the effects were different.

Thus, in every place, it is the practice of men in power, to blind
the people by false representations, and to impute the publick calamities rather to any other cause than their own misconduct. It is every
where equally their practice to oppress and obscure those who owe
their greatness to their virtue or abilities, because they can never be
reduced to blind obedience, or taught to be creatures of the ministry,
because men who can discover truth, will sometimes speak it, and
because those are best qualified to deceive others, who can be persuaded that they are contending for the right.

But it is surely time for this nation to rouse from indolence,
and to resolve to put an end to frauds that have been so long
known. It is time to watch with more vigilance the distribution of the publick treasure, and to consider rather how to contract
the national expences, than upon what pretences new offices may
be erected, and new dependencies created. It is time to consider how
our debts may be lessened, and by what expedients our taxes may be
diminished.

Our taxes, Sir, are such at present, as perhaps no nation was ever
loaded with before, such as never were paid to raise forces against an
invader, or imposed by the insolence of victory upon a conquered
people. Every gentleman pays to the government more than two
thirds of his estate by various exactions.—This assertion is received,
I see, with surprize, by some whose ample patrimonies have exempted
them from the necessity of nice computations, and with an affected
appearance of contempt by others, who, instead of paying taxes,
may be said to receive them, and whose interest it is to keep the nation ignorant of the causes of its misery, and to extenuate those calamities by which themselves are enriched.

But, Sir, to endeavour to confute demonstration by a grin, or to
laugh away the deductions of arithmetic, is surely such a degree of
effrontery, as nothing but a post of profit can produce; nor is it for
the sake of these men, that I shall endeavour to elucidate my assertion;
for they cannot but be well informed of the state of our taxes, whose
chief employment is to receive and to squander the money which
arises from them.

It is frequent, Sir, among gentlemen to miſtake the amount of the taxes which are laid upon the nation, by paſſing over in their eſtimates all thoſe which are not paid immediately out of the viſible rents of their lands, and imagining that they are in no degree intereſted in the impoſts upon manufactures or other commodities. They do not conſider that whenever they purchaſe any thing of which the price is enhanced by duties, thoſe duties are levied upon them, and that there is no difference between paying ten ſhillings a year in land taxes, and paying five ſhillings in land taxes, and five ſhillings to manufacturers to be paid by them to the government.

It would be in reality equally rational for a man to pleaſe himſelf with his frugality, by directing half his expences to be paid by his ſteward, and the event is ſuch as might be expected from ſuch a method of oeconomy; for, as the ſteward might probably bring in falſe accounts, the tradeſman commonly adds two pence to the price of his goods for every penny which is laid on them by the government; as it is eaſy to ſhew, particularly in the prices of thoſe two great neceſſaries of life, candles and leather.

Now, Sir, let any gentleman add to the land tax the duties raiſed from the malt, candles, ſalt, ſoap, leather, diſtilled liquors, and other commodities uſed in his houſe; let him add the expences of travelling ſo far as they are increaſed by the burthen laid upon innkeepers, and the extortions of the tradeſmen which the exciſes have occaſioned, and he will eaſily agree with me that he pays more than two thirds of his eſtate for the ſupport of the government.

It cannot therefore be doubted that it is now neceſſary to ſtop in our career of expences, and to enquire how much longer this weight of impoſts can poſſibly be ſupported. It has already, Sir, depreſſed our commerce, and overborne our manufactures, and if it be yet increaſed, if there be no hope of ſeeing it alleviated, every wiſe man will ſeek a milder government, and enliſt himſelf amongſt ſlaves that have maſters more wiſe or more compaſſionate.

We ought to conſider, Sir, whether ſome of our preſent expences are not ſuperfluous or detrimental, whether many of our offices are not merely penſions without employment, and whether multitudes do not receive ſalaries, who ſerve the government only by their intereſt and their votes. Such offices, if they are found, ought immediately to be aboliſhed, and ſuch ſalaries withdrawn, by which a fund might

be

e now eſtabliſhed for maintaining the war, and afterwards for the
payment of our debts.

It is not now, Sir, in my opinion, a queſtion whether we ſhall chuſe
he deareſt or the cheapeſt method of encreaſing our forces, for it
ſeems to me not poſſible to ſupply any new expences. New troops
will require more money to raiſe and to pay them, and more money
can only be obtained by new taxes; but what now remains to be
taxed, or what tax can be encreaſed? The only reſource left us is a
lottery, and whether that will ſucceed is likewiſe a lottery; but
though folly and credulity ſhould once more operate according to our
wiſhes, the nation is in the mean time impoveriſhed, and at laſt lot-
teries muſt certainly fail like other expedients. When the publick
wealth is entirely exhauſted, artifice and violence will be equally vain.
And though the troops may poſſibly be raiſed according to the eſtimate, I know not how we ſhall pay them, or from what fund, yet
unmortgaged, the officers who will be entailed upon us, can hope
to receive their half pay.

For my part, Sir, I think the queſtion ſo eaſy to be decided, that
I am aſtoniſhed to ſee it the ſubject of a debate, and imagine that the
controverſy might be ended only by aſking the gentleman, on whoſe
opinion all his party appear to rely, without any knowledge or conviction of their own, whether, if he were to defend a nation from its
enemies, and could procure only a ſmall ſum for the war, he would
not model his forces by the cheapeſt method.

Mr. SLOPER then ſpoke thus:—Sir, I cannot without the higheſt
ſatisfaction obſerve any advances made in uſeful knowledge, by
my fellow ſubjects, as the glory of ſuch attainments muſt add to
the reputation of the kingdom which gives riſe to ſuch elevated
abilities.

This ſatisfaction I have received from the obſervations of the right
honourable member, whoſe accurate computations cannot but promiſe great improvements of the doctrine of arithmetic; nor can I
forbear to ſolicit him for the ſake of the publick, to take into his conſideration the preſent methods of traffick uſed by our merchants, and
to ſtrike out ſome more commodious method of ſtating the accompts
between thoſe two contending parties debtor and creditor. This he
would doubtleſs execute with great reputation, who has proved from
the ſtate of our taxes, that new forces require new funds, and that
new funds cannot be eſtabliſhed without a lottery.

I am

I am indeed inclined to differ from him in the laft of his pofitions, and believe the nation not yet fo much exhaufted but that it may eafily bear the expence of the war, and fhall therefore vote for that eftablifhment of our troops which will be moft likely to procure fuccefs, without the leaft apprehenfion of being cenfured either by the prefent age, or by pofterity, as a machine of the miniftry, or an oppreffor of my country.

General WADE fpoke again thus:---Sir, fince the right honourable member has been pleafed to infinuate, that by anfwering a plain queftion I may put an end to the debate, I am willing to give a proof of my defire to promote unanimity in our counfels, and difpatch in our affairs, by complying with his propofal.

If I were obliged with a fmall fum to raife an army for the defence of a kingdom, I fhould undoubtedly proceed with the utmoft frugality; but this noble perfon's ideas of frugality would perhaps be very different from mine; he would think thofe expences fuperfluous, which to me would feem indifpenfably neceffary, and though we fhould both intend the prefervation of the country, we fhould provide for its fecurity by different methods.

He would employ the money in fuch a manner as might procure the greateft numbers; I fhould make my firft enquiry after the moft fkilful officers, and fhould imagine myfelf obliged by my fidelity to the nation, that entrufted me with its defence, to procure their affiftance, though at a high price.

It is not eafy for perfons who have never feen a battle or a fiege, whatever may be their natural abilities, or however cultivated by reading and contemplation, to conceive the advantage of difcipline and regularity, which is fuch, that a fmall body of veteran troops will drive before them multitudes of men, perhaps equally bold and refolute with themfelves, if they are unacquainted with the rules of war, and unprovided with leaders to direct their motions.

I fhould therefore, in the cafe which he has mentioned, prefer difcipline to numbers, and rather enter the field with a few troops well governed and well inftructed, than with a confufed multitude unacquainted with their duty, unable to conduct themfelves, and without officers to conduct them.

Mr. VINER fpoke next to the following effect:---Sir, I am not very folicitous what may be the determination of the houfe upon this queftion, becaufe I think it more neceffary to refolve againft an augmentation

mentation of the army, than to enquire, whether it shall be made by one method or another.

Every addition to our troops I consider as some approach towards the establishment of arbitrary power, as it is an alienation of part of the British people, by which they are deprived of the benefits of the constitution, and subjected to rigorous laws, from which every other individual is exempt.

The principal of these laws, which all the rest are intended to inforce, requires from every soldier an unlimited and absolute obedience to the commands of his officers, who hold their commission, and expect advancement by the same compliance with the orders of the ministry.

The danger of adding to the number of men, thus separated from their fellow subjects, and directed by the arbitrary determinations of their officers, has been often explained with great strength and perspicuity; nor should I have taken this occasion of recalling it to the attention of the house, but that I think it a consideration, to which, in all debates on the army, the first regard ought to be paid.

Colonel MORDAUNT spoke to the purpose following :—Sir, the objection which the honourable gentleman has raised, will be most easily removed, by considering the words of the act by which the military authority is established, where it is by no means declared, that either officers or soldiers are obliged indiscriminately to obey all the orders which they shall receive, but that they shall, on pain of the punishments there enacted, obey all the LAWFUL orders of their commanders.

The obedience therefore, Sir, required from a soldier, is an obedience according to law, like that of any other Briton, unless it can be imagined that the word *lawful* is in that place without a meaning. Nor does his condition differ from that of his fellow subjects by an exemption from any law, but by a greater number of duties, and stricter obligations to the performance of them; and I am not able to conceive how our constitution can be endangered by augmenting an army, which, as it can only act in conformity to it, can act only in defence of it.

The question at last was put, that the new-raised troops be incorporated into the standing corps, but it passed in the negative 232 to 166.

HOUSE OF LORDS.

DEBATE ON TAKING THE STATE OF THE ARMY INTO CONSIDERATION.

THE DUKE of ARGYLE rofe firft, and fpoke to the following effect:—My Lords, as the prefent fituation of our affairs may require an augmentation of our forces, and as the fuccefs of our arms, and the prefervation of our liberties, may equally depend upon the manner in which the new forces fhall be raifed, there is, in my opinion, no queftion more worthy the attention of this auguft affembly, than what may be the moft proper method of increafing our army.

On this queftion, my Lords, I fhall offer my own fentiments with greater confidence, as there are few men who have had more opportunities of being acquainted with it in its whole extent, as I have fpent great part of my life in the field and in the camp. I commanded a regiment under king William, and have long been either the fufft, or almoft the firft man in the army.

I hope, my Lords, it will be allowed without difficulty, that I have at leaft been educated in the beft fchool of war, and that nothing but natural incapacity can have hindered me from making fome ufeful obfervations upon the difcipline and government of armies, and the advantages and inconveniences of the various plans upon which other nations regulate their forces.

I have always maintained, my Lords, that it is neceffary, in the prefent ftate of the neighbouring countries, to keep up a body of regular troops, that we may not be lefs able to defend ourfelves, than our enemies to attack us.

It is well known, my Lords, that ftates muft fecure themfelves by different means, as they are threatened by dangers of different kinds: policy muft be oppofed by policy, and force by force; our fleets muft be increafed when our neighbours grow formidable by their naval power, and armies muft be maintained at a time like this, in which every prince on the continent eftimates his greatnefs by the number of his troops.

But an army, my Lords, as it is to be admitted only for the fecurity

rity of the nation, is to be fo regulated, that it may produce the end for which it is eftablifhed ; that it may be ufeful without danger, and protect the people without oppreffing them.

To this purpofe, my Lords, it is indifpenfably neceffary, that the military fubordination be inviolably preferved, and that difcipline be difcreetly exercifed without any partial indulgence, or malicious feverities ; that every man be promoted according to his defert, and that military merit alone give any pretentions to military preferment.

To make the army yet more ufeful, it ought to be under the fole command of one man, exalted to the important truft by his known fkill, courage, juftice, and fidelity, and uncontrouled in the adminiftration of his province by any other authority, a man enabled by his experience to diftinguifh the deferving, and invefted with power to reward them.

Thus, my Lords, ought an army to be regulated, to which the defence of a nation is intrufted, nor can any other fcheme be formed which will not expofe the publick to dangers more formidable than revolutions or invafions. And yet, my Lords, how widely thofe who have affumed the direction of affairs have deviated from this method is well known. It is known equally to the higheft and meaneft officers, that thofe who have moft opportunities of obferving military merit, have no power of rewarding it ; and, therefore, every man endeavours to obtain other recommendations than thofe of his fuperiors in the army, and to diftinguifh himfelf by other fervices than attention to his duty, and obedience to his commanders.

Our generals, my Lords, are only colonels with a higher title, without power, and without command ; they can neither make themfelves loved nor feared in their troops, nor have either reward or punifhment in their power. What difcipline, my Lords, can be eftablifhed by men, whom thofe who fometimes act the farce of obedience, know to be only phantoms of authority, and to be reftrained by an arbitrary minifter from the exercife of thofe commiffions which they are invefted with ? And what is an army without difcipline, fubordination and obedience ? What, but a rabble of licentious vagrants, fet free from the common reftraints of decency, exempted from the neceffity of labour, betrayed by idlenefs to debauchery, and let loofe to prey upon the people ? Such a herd can only awe the villages, and bluster in the streets, but can never be able to oppose an enemy or defend the nation by which they are supported.

They may, indeed, form a camp upon some of the neighbouring heaths, or pass in review with tolerable regularity; they may sometimes seize a smuggler, and sometimes assist a constable with vigour and success. But unhappy would be the people, who had no other force to oppose against an army habituated to discipline, of which every one founds his hopes of honour and reward upon the approbation of the commander.

That no man will labour to no purpose, or undergo the fatigue of military vigilance, without an adequate motive; that no man will endeavour to learn superfluous duties, and neglect the easiest road to honour and to wealth, merely for the sake of encountering difficulties, is easily to be imagined. And, therefore, my Lords, it cannot be conceived, that any man in the army will very sollicitously apply himself to the duties of his profession, of which, when he has learned them, the most accurate practice will avail him nothing, and on which he must lose that time, which might have been employed in gaining an interest in a borough, or in forming an alliance with some orator in the senate.

For nothing, my Lords, is now considered but senatorial interest, nor is any subordination desired but in the supreme council of the empire. For the establishment of this new regulation, the honours of every profession are prostituted, and every commission is become merely nominal. To gratify the leaders of the ministerial party, the most despicable triflers are exalted to an authority, and those whose want of understanding excludes them from any other employment, are selected for military commissions.

No sooner have they taken possession of their new command, and gratified with some act of oppression the wantonness of new authority, but they desert their charge with the formality of demanding a permission to be absent, which their commander dares not deny them. Thus, my Lords, they leave the care of the troops, and the study of the rules of war, to those unhappy men, who have no other claim to elevation than knowledge and bravery, and who, for want of relations in the senate, are condemned to linger out their lives at their quarters, amuse themselves with recounting their actions and sufferings in former wars, and with reading in the papers of
every

every poft, the commiffions which are beftowed on thofe who never faw a battle.

For this reafon, my Lords, preferments in the army, inftead of being confidered as proofs of merit, are looked on only as badges of dependence ; nor can any thing be inferred from the promotion of an officer, but that he is in fome degree or other allied to fome member of the fenate, or the leading voters of a borough.

After this manner, my Lords, has the army been modelled, and on thefe principles has it fubfifted for the laft and the prefent reign ; neither myfelf, nor any other general officer, have been confulted in the diftribution of commands, or any part of military regulations. Our armies have known no other power than that of the fecretary of war, who directs all their motions, and fills up every vacancy without oppofition, and without appeal.

But never, my Lords, was his power more confpicuous, than in raifing the levies of laft year ; never was any authority more defpotically exerted, or more tamely fubmitted to ; never did any man more wantonly fport with his command, or more capricioufly difpofe of pofts and preferments ; never did any tyrant appear to fet cenfure more openly at defiance, treat murmurs and remonftrances with greater contempt, or with more confidence and fecurity diftribute pofts among his flaves, without any other reafon of preference than his own uncontroulable pleafure.

And furely no man, my Lords, could have made choice of fuch wretches for military commands, but to fhew that nothing but his own private inclinations fhould influence his conduct, and that he confidered himfelf as fupreme and unaccountable : for we have feen, my Lords, the fame animals to-day cringing behind a counter, and to-morrow fwelling in a military drefs; we have feen boys fent from fchool in defpair of improvement, and entrufted with military command ; fools that cannot learn their duty, and children that cannot perform it, have been indifcriminately promoted ; the drofs of the nation has been fwept together to compofe our new forces, and every man who was two ftupid or infamous to learn or carry on a trade, has been placed by this great difpofer of honours above the neceffity of application, or the reach of cenfure.

Did not fometimes indignation, and fometimes pity, check the fallies of mirth, it would not be a difagreeable entertainment, my Lords, to obferve, in the Park, the various appearances of thefe raw

H 2   commanders,

commanders, when they are expofing their new fcarlet to view, and ftrutting with the firft raptures of fudden elevation ; to fee the mechanic new modelling his mien, and the ftripling tottering beneath the weight of his cockade ; or to hear the converfation of thefe new adventurers, and the inftructive dialogues of fchool-boys and fhop-keepers.

I take this opportunity, my Lords, of clearing myfelf from any fufpicion of having contributed by my advice to this ftupendous collection. I only once interpofed with the recommendation of a young gentleman who had learned his profeffion in two campaigns among the Mufcovians, and whom yet neither his own defert, nor my patronage could advance to a commiffion. And, I believe, my Lords, all the other general officers were equally unconfulted, and would, if their advice had been afked, equally have difapproved the meafures that have been purfued.

But thus, my Lords, were our new regiments compleated, in which, of two hundred and fifty officers who have fubfifted upon half-pay, only thirty fix have been promoted, though furely they might have pleaded a jufter claim to employment who had learned their profeffion in the fervice of their country, and had long languifhed in penury, than thofe who had neither knowledge nor capacity, who had neither acted nor fuffered any thing, and who might have been deftined to the hammer or the plough, without any difreputation to their families, or difappointment to themfelves.

I have been told, indeed, my Lords, that to fome of thefe officers commiffions were offered, which they refufed, and for this refufal every reafon is alleged but the true : fome, indeed, excufed themfelves as difabled by age and infirmities from military fervice ; nor can any objection be made to fo juft a plea. For how could thofe be refufed in their age the comforts of eafe and repofe, who have ferved their country with their youth and vigour ?

Others there are, my Lords, who refufed commiffions upon motives very different, in which, neverthelefs, fome juftice cannot be denied. They who had long ftudied and long practifed their profeffion ; they, who had tried their courage in the breach, and given proofs of their fkill in the face of the enemy, refufed to obey the command of novices, of tradefmen, and of fchool-boys : they imagined, my Lords, that they ought to govern thofe whom they fhould be obliged to inftruct, and to lead thofe troops whom they muft range

in

in order. But they had forgot that they had out-lived the time when a foldier was formed by ftudy and experience, and had not heard in their retreats, that a colonel or a captain was now formed in a day; and therefore, when they faw and heard their new commanders, they retired back to their half-pay, with furprize and indignation.

But, my Lords, the follies of laft year cannot be eafily rectified, and are only now to be expofed that they may not be repeated. If we are now to make new levies, and encreafe the number of our land-forces, it is, in my opinion, incumbent upon us to confider by what methods we may beft augment our troops, aud how we may be able to refift our foreign enemies, without expofing the nation to inteftine miferies, and leaving our liberties at the mercy of the court.

There are, my Lords, two methods of increafing our forces; the firft is, that of raifing new regiments; the other, of adding new men to thofe which already fubfift.

By raifing new regiments, my Lords, we fhall only gratify the minifter with the diftribution of new commiffions, and the eftablifh-ment of new dependents; we fhall enlarge the influence of the court, and increafe the charge of the nation, which is already loaded with too many taxes to fupport any unneceffary expence.

By the other method, of adding a hundred men to every company, we fhall not only fave the pay of the officers, which is no flight con-fideration, but, what feems, if the reports raifed by the miniftry, of our prefent danger, be true, of far more importance, fhall form the new forces with more expedition into regular troops; for, by diftributing them among thofe who are already inftructed in their duty, we fhall give them an opportunity of hourly improvement, every man's comrade will be his mafter, and every one will be am-bitious of forming himfelf by the example of thofe who have been in the army longer than themfelves.

If it be objected, my Lords, that the number of officers will not then bear a juft proportion to that of the foldiers, it may be anfwered that the foreign troops of the greateft reputation have no greater number of officers, as every one muft know who is acquainted with the conftitution of the moft formidable armies of Europe. Thofe of the Pruffian monarch, or of the various nations by which we were affifted in the late war, either as confederates or mercenaries, have but few officers. And, I very well remember, my Lords, that whenever they were joined by parties of our own nation, the inequality in the number of the officers produced contests and disputes.

The only troops of Europe, my Lords, that swarm with officers are those of France, but even these have fewer officers in proportion to their private men in time of war; for when they disband any part of their forces, they do not like us reduce their officers to half pay, but add them to the regiments not reduced, that the families of their nobility may not be burthened with needy dependents, and that they may never want officers for new levies.

There are many reasons, my Lords, that make this practice in France more reasonable than it would be in our kingdom. It is the chief view of their governors to continue absolute, and therefore their constant endeavour to keep great numbers in dependence; it ought to be our care to hinder the increase of the influence of the court, and to obstruct all measures that may extend the authority of the ministry, and therefore those measures are to be pursued by which independence and liberty will be most supported.

It is likewise to be remembered, my Lords, that a French officer is supported with pay not much larger than that of a private soldier among us, and that therefore the argument which arises from the necessity of frugality is not of the same force in both nations.

There is yet another reason why the French are under the necessity of employing more officers than any other nation: the strength of their armies consists in their gentlemen, who cannot be expected to serve without some command: the common soldiers of the French army are a mean, spiritless, despicable herd, fit only to drudge as pioneers, to raise intrenchments and to dig mines, but without courage to face an enemy, or to proceed with vigour in the face of danger.

Their gentlemen, my Lords, are of a very different character; jealous of their honour, and conscious of their birth, eager of distinction, and ambitious of preferment. They have commonly their education in the army, and have no expectations of acquiring fortunes equal to their desires by any other profession, and are therefore intent upon the improvement of every opportunity which is offered them of increasing their knowledge and exalting their reputation.

To the spirit of these men, my Lords, are the French armies indebted for all their victories, and to them is to be attributed the
present

prefent perfection of the art of war. They have the vigilance and perfeverance of Romans joined with the natural vivacity and expedition of their own nation.

We are therefore not to wonder, my Lords, that there is in the French armies an eftablifhment for more gentlemen than in other countries, where the difparity between the military virtues of the higher and lower claffes of men is lefs confpicuous. In the troops of that nation nothing is expected but from the officers, but in ours the common foldier meets danger with equal intrepidity, and fcorns to fee himfelf excelled by his officer in courage or in zeal.

We are therefore, my Lords, under no neceffity of burthening our country with the expence of new commiffions, which in the army will be fuperfluous, and in the ftate dangerous, as they will fill our fenate with new dependents, and our corporations with new adherents to the minifter, whofe fteady perfeverance in his favourite fcheme of fenatorial fubordination, will be perhaps the only occafion of thefe new levies, or at leaft has hindered the right application of our ftanding troops. For what reafon, my Lords, can invention or imagination affign, why the troops who had been for fome time difciplined were not rather fent to the affiftance of Vernon than the new marines, except that fome of them were commanded by men who had obtained feats in the other houfe, and who by their fettled adherence and avowed fidelity to the minifter had recommended themfelves too powerfully to be rafhly expofed in the fervice of their country to the bullets of the Spaniards.

So great, my Lords, has been the minifter's regard to fenatorial abilities, and fo ftrict his gratitude to his friends, that I know of but one member of the other houfe that has been hazarded in this expedition, and he a hopelefs, abandoned patriot, infenfible of the capacity or integrity of our miniftry, and whom nothing has been able to reconcile to our late meafures. He therefore, who has never exerted himfelf in defence of the miniftry, was in his turn thought unworthy of minifterial protection, and was given up to the chance of war without reluctance.

But I hope your Lordfhips will concur with me in the opinion, that it is not always neceffary to gratify the miniftry, but that our country claims fome part of our regard, and therefore that in eftablifhing our army we fhould purfue that method which may be moft accommodated to our conftitution, and, inftead of imitating the mili-

tary

tary policy of the French, follow the example of those nations by whose troops they have been conquered.

Had this scheme been hitherto followed, had our new levies, instead of being put under the command of boys, been distributed in just proportions among the standing regiments, where they might soon have been qualified for service by the inspection of experienced officers, we might now have seen an army capable of awing the court of Spain into submission, or, if our demands had been still refused, of revenging our injuries, and punishing those who have insulted and despised us.

From an army thus raised and disciplined, detachments, my Lords, ought to have been sent on board of all our fleets, and particularly that which is now stationed in the Mediterranean, which would not then have coasted about from one port to another, without hurting or frighting the enemy, but might by sudden descents have spread terror through a great part of the kingdom, harrassed their troops by continual marches, and by frequent incursions have plundered all the maritime provinces, driven the inhabitants into the inland country, and laid the villages in ashes.

There is yet, my Lords, no appearance of a peace, for our success has not enabled us to prescribe terms, and I hope we are not yet fallen so low as to receive them; it is therefore proper to form such resolutions as may influence the conduct of the war, and enable us to retrieve the errors of our past measures.

The minister, my Lords, is not without panegyrists, who may perhaps endeavour to persuade us, that we ought to resign all our understandings to his superior wisdom, and blindly trust our fortunes and our liberties to his unshaken integrity. They will in proof of his abilities produce the wonderful dexterity and penetration which the late negotiations have discovered, and will confirm the reputation of his integrity by the constant parsimony of all his schemes, and the unwillingness with which he at any time increases the expences of the nation.

But, my Lords, it is the great duty of your high station to watch over the administration, and to warn those, who are more immediately intrusted with the public affairs, against measures which may endanger the safety or happiness of the nation; and, therefore, if I have proved to your Lordships, that to raise new regiments is dangerous to our liberties, that a multitude of officers is of no use in

war,

war, and that an army may be more expeditiously disciplined by adding new men to every company, I hope your Lordships will agree to
this resolution, which I have drawn up with the utmost brevity, and
of which the meaning cannot be mistaken :

" That the augmenting the army by raising regiments, as it is the
most unnecessary and expensive method of augmentation, is also the
most dangerous to the liberties of the nation."

The DUKE of NEWCASTLE next spoke to this effect :—My
Lords, as my education and employments have afforded me no opportunity of acquiring any skill in military affairs, it will not be expected by your Lordships, that I should be able to confute the arguments of the noble duke, whose acknowledged superiority in the
art of war, and the abilities which he has displayed in the administration of every province which he has undertaken, give him a claim to
the highest deference.

But, my Lords, as I cannot assume the province of disputing on
this question, so I cannot without longer consideration form any resolution concerning it ; for arguments may be fallacious which yet I
cannot confute, and to approve without knowledge is no less weak
than to censure.

There is not any present necessity, my Lords, of forming a resolution on this subject ; we are not now called upon particularly to consider it, and certainly it cannot be prudent by so determinate a deci-
sion, pronounced without reflection or deliberation, to preclude a
fuller examination of this important question.

LORD CARTERET rose and spoke in this manner :—my Lords, the
noble duke who made the present motion has supported it by such
strength of argument, and so fully explained the advantages of the
method which it tends to recommend, that not only the present
age but posterity may probably be indebted to him, for juster notions
of a military establishment, than have been yet attained even by
those whose profession obliges them to such enquiries.

Nor, my Lords, could we expect less from his long experience and
extensive capacity, experience gained in the heat of war, and in the
midst of danger ; a capacity not only cultivated by solitary disquisi-
tions in retirement and security, but exercised by difficulties and
quickened by opposition.

Such abilities, my Lords, matured by such an education, have
justly

juftly made the noble duke the oracle of war, and procured him the efteem and reverence of all the powers upon earth.

As I did not receive from my education any military knowledge, I am not able to add much to the arguments which your Lordfhips have already heard ; but neverthelefs, having been under the neceffity of regulating the army when I had the honour to be employed in Ireland, and having made, in thofe countries where I tranfacted the bufinefs of the crown, fome obfervations upon the different forms of military eftablifhments, I hope I fhall be allowed to offer what my experience or my remarks may fuggeft to me, in confirmation of the fentiments of the noble duke.

When I was in Ireland, my Lords, the troops of that kingdom confifted of twenty-one regiments of which ten were, as laft year, brought into Britain, and the Irifh forces were to be filled up by new levies, which were raifed in the manner now propofed, by increafing every regiment from three hundred and forty to fix hundred men, fo that the eleven regiments remaining compofed a body of nearly the fame number with the twenty-one regiments as formerly conftituted.

Of the Swedifh eftablifhment, my Lords, the reputation and fuccefs of their troops are an uncontrovertible vindication, and I have often had an opportunity of comparing the number of officers with that of ours, and found their private men to be far more numerous in proportion to the officers.

In Hanover, my Lords, I have feen his majefty's troops remarkable for the elegance of their appearance, and being once afked by the commander at what expence one of thofe gallant troopers and his horfe was fupported, was told, after confefling my ignorance, that he coft no more than fourteen pounds a year, who could not in this country be maintained for lefs than forty.

I believe, my Lords, that the French forces are not more expenfive than thofe of Hanover, and therefore we are by no means to imitate their eftablifhment, for the price of provifions and habits of life do not admit of any diminution of the pay of either our officers or foldiers, and we can only leffen our expences by reducing their numbers, to which I fhall for my part moft willingly contribute.

But as this, my Lords, is not the proper time for difbanding our forces, of which the prefent ftate of our affairs may perhaps demand

an

an augmentation, it is neceffary to compare the ftate of our forces with that of foreign troops, and fupply by prudent methods the difadvantages to which we are fubject by the peculiar condition of our country. For if the French can fupport an army at a fourth part of our expence; what muft be the confequence of a war, fuppofing the wealth of the two nations nearly equal? It will be to little purpofe that we boaft, however juftly, of the fuperiority of our troops; for though it fhould be granted that the Britifh cannot be refifted by an equal number, yet it can never be expected that they fhould conquer troops four times as numerous as themfelves.

Thus, my Lords, it appears with all the evidence of arithmetical demonftration, that the method now propofed is highly expedient, nor can any objection, in my opinion, be made to the refolution offered to your Lordfhips.

That this is not a proper time for this enquiry has been indeed urged, but furely no time can be more proper than when we may, by a refolution unanimoufly paffed, regulate in fome degree the conduct of the other houfe, and hint to them the opinion of this affembly on a queftion which is perhaps to-morrow to be brought before them.

Lord CHOLMONDELEY then fpoke thus:---My Lords, though I was once honoured with a command in the army, and confequently ought to have attained fome military knowledge, yet I have fo long refigned my commiffion, poffeffed it for fo fhort a time, and have fuffered my attention to be diverted from enquiries on that fubject by employments of fo different a kind, that I cannot prefume to oppofe any knowledge of my own to the reafons which have been offered; but I cannot think that the conclufions drawn by the noble duke, are fo evidently true as to force conviction, and exclude all poffibility of reply; nor can I conceive it confiftent with the dignity of this affembly, to yield implicitly to any man's affertions, or to pafs any refolution without an accurate enquiry.

Some objections, my Lords, arife upon reflection from my narrow obfervation and tranfient reading, and thefe I fhall lay before your lordfhips, with an open acknowledgement of my infufficiency to difcufs the queftion, and a fincere defire of being inftructed where I may be miftaken.

The fubordination of the army, my Lords, appears to me in general to be fufficiently maintained, nor is it ever infringed but by

particular

particular partiality, that can never be prevented, or a casual difference in the circumstances of the officers, which, though not relative
to their military characters, will always produce some degree of influence.

I know not, my Lords, how the general regulation of our forces,
and the distribution of military honours, can be condemned without
extending some degree of censure to a person who ought not to be
mentioned as concurring in any measures injurious to the publick.
Our army, my Lords, is maintained by the parliament, but commanded by the king, who has not either done or directed any thing
of which his people may justly complain.

Here the duke of ARGYLE interrupted him :—My Lords, it is necessary to clear myself from misrepresentations, and to preserve at
the same time the order of this assembly, by reminding the noble
lord, that his majesty is never to be introduced into our debates, because he is never to be charged with wrong, and by declaring to your
lordships, that I impute no part of the errors committed in the regulation of the army to his majesty, but to those ministers, whose
duty it is to advise him, and whom the law condemns to answer for
the consequences of their counsels.

Lord CHOLMONDELEY resumed :—My Lords, if I misrepresented
any assertion of the noble duke, it was by misapprehension, or fai-
lure of memory, and not by malice or design ; and if in any other objections which I shall make, I shall fall into any error of the same
kind, I desire that it may be ascribed to the same cause.

The ignorance and inexperience of our present officers have
been exposed with great gaiety of imagination, and with the true
spirit of satirical rhetoric, nor can I presume to support them
against so formidable censures. But, my Lords, I cannot discover any method of protracting the lives of our old officers beyond
the usual term, nor of supplying the loss of those whom death takes
away from the army, but by substituting others, who, as they have
seen no wars, can have little experience.

With regard to the number of officers in the foreign troops, I have
been informed, that they were by an express stipulation to be constituted in the same manner with the British and Dutch forces.

Then the duke of ARGYLE again interrupted him :—My Lords,
as it was my province in the late war to superintend the payment of
the foreign troops, I may be allowed to have some knowledge of the
establishment,

eſtabliſhment, and hope I ſhall not be imagined to need any information on that ſubject.

Lord CHOLMONDELEY ſaid :--My Lords, I do not preſume to diſpute any aſſertion of the noble duke, for whoſe knowledge I have the
higheſt veneration, but only to offer ſuch hints for enquiry as may be
purſued by other lords of greater abilities, and to ſhew, that as ſome
difficulties may be raiſed, the reſolution ⚫ught not to be agreed to
without farther deliberation; ſince it not only tends to preſcribe the
meaſures which ſhall be hereafter taken, and prohibit a method of
raiſing forces, which, when diligently examined, may perhaps appear
moſt eligible, but to cenſure the methods, which, when they were
put in practice the laſt year, received the approbation of all the
powers of the legiſlature.

Lord WESTMORELAND ſpoke next as follows :--My Lords, I have
for my own ſatisfaction ſtated the difference of the expence between
the two methods of raiſing forces, and find it ſo great that the method propoſed by the noble duke ought undoubtedly to be preferred,
even though it were attended with ſome inconvenience, from which
he has ſhewn it to be free.

Frugality, my Lords, is one of the chief virtues of an adminiſtration; a virtue without which no government can be long ſupported:
the publick expence can never be too accurately computed, or the
firſt tendency to profuſion too rigorouſly oppoſed; for, as in private
life, ſo in political oeconomy, the demands of neceſſity are eaſily
ſupplied; but if once the calls of wantonneſs and caprice are
complied with, no limits can be fixed, nor will any treaſure be
ſufficient.

Whether the burthens under which the people are now toiling
were all impoſed by neceſſity, I will not enquire, but I think, my
Lords, we may readily determine, that whatever is not neceſſary is
cruel and oppreſſive, and that therefore, ſince the expence of raiſing
new regiments appears at leaſt not to be neceſſary, it ought to be
oppoſed; and how can it be oppoſed more properly or effectually than
by the noble duke's reſolution?

Lord HERVEY ſpoke to this effect :---My Lords, I do not claim
any ſuperiority of knowledge in any affairs that relate to the publick,
but have leſs acquaintance with the military eſtabliſhment than with
any other part of the government, and can therefore neither oppoſe
the reſolution now offered to your lordſhips by ſuch arguments as may

deſerve

deſerve your attention, nor agree to it with that degree of conviction which the importance of it ſeems to require.

That the chief argument which has been produced againſt raiſing new regiments, is leſs formidable than it has been repreſented, will, I believe, appear to your Lordſhips, when it is conſidered that the officers are always gentlemen of the firſt families in the empire, who, therefore, cannot be ſuppoſed voluntarily to give up their relations and poſterity to the power of any miniſtry, or, for the ſake of their commiſſions, to betray that conſtitution by which their own properties are ſecured.

Whether every other argument may not with equal juſtice be controverted, is not, without longer conſideration, poſſible to be determined, and therefore it cannot be reaſonably expected that we ſhould agree to the reſolution, which would be only to decide without examination, and to determine what we don't underſtand ; for I am under no apprehenſion of being imagined to reflect unjuſtly on this aſſembly, in ſuppoſing that many of your Lordſhips may be ſtrangers to the queſtion, which, when the laſt levies were made, was neither diſcuſſed nor propoſed.

I therefore move, that the previous queſtion may be put, which may perhaps gain time ſufficient for a more exact enquiry upon this important ſubject.

Lord Talbot replied to this purport:— My Lords, if, in imitation of ſome noble lords, I profeſs my ignorance of the ſubject on which I am to ſpeak, may it not yet be allowed me, after the example of others, to employ the little knowledge which I have in the defence of a reſolution, which appears to have no other tendency than the advantage of the publick, and to ſhew my zeal for the happineſs of my country, though perhaps without the true knowledge of its intereſt ?

The noble Lord, who ſpoke laſt, is too great a maſter of eloquence not to be heard with all the attention which pleaſure naturally produces, and a reaſoner too formidable not to raiſe in his hearers all the anxiety which is produced by the fear of being deceived by partial repreſentations, and artful deductions. I am always afraid, my Lords, leſt error ſhould appear too much like truth in the ornaments which his Lordſhip's imagination may beſtow, and leſt ſophiſtry ſhould dazzle my underſtanding whilſt I imagine myſelf only guided y the light of reaſon,

I ſhall

I shall therefore endeavour, my Lords, to review his ornaments, and try whether they owe their influence to the force of truth, or to that of eloquence.

His Lordship has observed, that the objections which are now made to the method of raising new regiments, were not produced last year upon a like occasion. I know not, indeed, what can be inferred from this assertion ; for surely it will not maintain, that an error once admitted is to become perpetual.

But, my Lords, another reason may be assigned for which the objections that occurred last year might not be produced. The ministry, after a long course of disgraceful negotiations, and artful delays, were, at length, compelled to a war, by the general clamours of the whole nation; but they acted as men unwilling to execute what they did not approve. They proceeded so slowly in their preparations, and were so languid in all their motions, that it was evident how willingly they would have improved every opportunity of retarding the vengeance which they were forced to threaten; and with what artifices they would have protracted any delay, which they could have imputed to those by whom they were opposed. It was, therefore, to the last degree improper to embarrass their measures of themselves sufficiently perplexed, or to lay any obstacle in the way of those who would gladly be stopped.

That the army is filled with gentlemen is so far, my Lords, from proving that there is nothing to be feared from it, that it is the only foundation of all our sollicitude. For none but gentlemen can injure our liberties, and while the posts of the army are bestowed as rewards of senatorial slavery, gentlemen will always be found who will be corrupted themselves, and can corrupt a borough ; who will purchase a vote in the house, and sell it for military preferments. By the posts of the army the senate may be corrupted, and by the corruption of the senate the army be perpetuated.

Those, my Lords, who are the warmest opponents of the army, apprehend not any danger from their swords, but from their votes. As they have been of late regulated without discipline or subordination, I should not feel such anxiety at seeing them led on by their new commanders against a body of honest ploughmen, united in the cause of virtue and of liberty; I should with great alacrity

draw

draw my sword against them, and should not doubt of seeing them in a short time heap'd upon our fields.

But, my Lords, they are employed to ruin us by a more slow and silent method; they are directed to influence their relations in the senate, and to suborn the voters in our small towns; they are dispersed over the nation to instil dependence, and being enslaved themselves, willingly undertake the propagation of slavery.

That the army is instrumental in extending the influence of the ministry to the senate, cannot be denied, when military preferments are held no longer than while he that possesses them gives a sanction by his vote to the measures of the court; when no degree of merit is sufficient to balance a single act of senatorial opposition, and when the nation is rather to be left to the defence of boys, than the minister be suspected of misconduct.

Could either bravery or knowledge, reputation or past services, known fidelity to his majesty, or the most conspicuous capacity for high trust, have secured any man in the enjoyment of his post, the noble duke who made the motion, had carried his command to his grave, nor had the nation now been deprived either of his arms, or of his counsels.

But, as he has now offered his advice to his country, and supported his opinion with proofs from reason and experience, which even those who oppose them have confessed themselves unable to answer; as the justness of his reasoning, and the extent of his knowledge, have silenced those whose prejudices will not suffer them to own themselves convinced; let us not, my Lords, reject what we cannot condemn, nor suffer our country to be defrauded of the advantage of this resolution, by that low senatorial craft, the previous question.

Then the CHANCELLOR spoke to the following purpose:—My Lords, I am far from suspecting, that an open profession of my inability to examine the question before us, in its full extent, will be imputed to an affectation of modesty, since any knowledge of military affairs could not be acquired in those stations in which I have been placed, or by those studies in which the greatest part of my life is known to have been spent.

It will not be expected, my Lords, that I should attempt a formal confutation of the noble Duke's positions, or that I should be able to defend my own opinion against his knowledge and experience;

nor

nor would I, my Lords, expofe myfelf to the cenfure of having harangued upon war in the prefence of Hannibal.

The noble duke has explained his fentiments to your Lordfhips
with the utmoft accuracy of method, and the moft inftructive perfpicuity of language; he has enforced them with a ftrength of reafoning rarely to be found, and with an extent of knowledge peculiar to himfelf. Yet, my Lords, as his arguments, however powerful in themfelves, do not ftrike me with the fame force with which
others may be affected, who are more capable of receiving them, I
hope that your Lordfhips will allow me to mention fuch objections as
occur to me, that in voting on this queftion I may at leaft preferve
my confcience from violation, and neither adopt the opinion of
another, however great, without examination, nor obftinately reject the means of conviction.

Every lord who has fpoken either in fupport of the noble duke's
opinion, or in oppofition to it, has confeffed that he is very little acquainted with the fubject of our debate; and it may not therefore
be an improper or ufelefs attempt, if I endeavour by objections,
however injudicious, or by arguments however inconclufive, to procure fome illuftration of a queftion fo important, and at the fame
time fo little underftood.

The objections, my Lords, which I fhall produce, are fuch as I
have heard in converfation with thofe whofe long acquaintance with
military employments give them a juft claim to authority in all queftions which relate to the art of war; among whom I find no uni-
formity of opinion with regard to the moft proper method of augmenting our forces. And, my Lords, when we obferve thofe to differ
in their fentiments, whofe education, experience, and opportunities of
knowledge have been nearly the fame, and who have all obtained a very
great degree of reputation in their profeffion, what can be inferred,
but that the queftion is in its own nature obfcure and difficult? That it
involves a multitude of relations, and is diffufed through a great
variety of circumftances? And that, therefore, it is prudent for
every man, who can judge only upon the authority of others, to
fufpend his opinion?

The chief argument, or that at leaft which impreffed itfelf moft
ftrongly on my mind, againft any innovation in our military conftitution, was drawn from the fuccefs of our armies in their prefent
form, with that proportion of foldiers and officers, which the prefent motion tends to abolifh. Our forces, fay the advocates for the

present establishment, have afforded us a sufficient testimony of the
propriety of their regulation, by their frequent victories over troops,
whose discipline has been studied with the utmost vigilance, and which
have been trained up to war with a degree of attention not disproportioned to the mighty design for which they were raised, the subjection of the world, and attainment of universal monarchy. These
troops, who have been taught, almost from their infancy, that cowardice and flight are the greatest crimes, and persuaded by national prejudices, and principles studiously instilled, that no foreign forces
could withstand them, have fled before equal numbers of Britons,
and been driven from one province to another, till, instead of grasp-
ing at general dominion, they were reduced to defend their wives
and children.

How much of this success was to be ascribed to that part of the
regulation which this motion proposes to be changed, it is not, my
Lords, within my province to determine ; the great commander whom
I have the honour to oppose, can best explain to your Lordships the
province of every officer in the field, and how far the number of inferiour officers may influence the success of a battle and the fate of a
kingdom.

But to me, my Lords, the establishment of our armies comprising
different views, and connecting various subordinate regulations,
may be compared to a medicine composed of different ingredients,
and found infallibly efficacious in a dangerous disease, in which,
though some of the parts may seem to physicians of the profoundest
learning, superfluous or improper, it would be no less than the folly
of preferring experiments to life, to make any alteration.

The wantonness of innovation, my Lords, is a dangerous disease
of the mind ; in a private station, it prompts men to be always dis-
contented with what they find, and to lose the enjoyment of good
in search of something better ; it incites them to leave the safe and
beaten tracks of life, in search of those which they imagine
nearer, but which are at best less secure, and which generally lead
them to points far different from that to which they originally intended to direct their course.

It is dangerous, my Lords, to admit any alteration which is not
absolutely necessary, for one innovation makes way for another.
The parts of a constitution, like a complicated machine, are fitted
to each other, nor can one be changed without changing that which
corresponds

corresponds to it. This necessity is not always foreseen, but when discovered by experience is generally complied with ; for every man is more inclined to hazard further changes, than to confess himself mistaken by retracting his scheme. Thus, my Lords, one change introduces another, till the original constitution is entirely destroyed.

By the ambition of innovation, my Lords, have almost all those empires been destroyed, of which nothing now is left but the memory. Every human establishment has its advantages and its inconveniencies, and by weak attempts to remedy these defects, which notwithstanding the utmost attention will embarrass the machine of government, alterations have been introduced which have been quickly followed by a total dissolution.

There seem, my Lords, to be few regulations on which it is more dangerous to make experiments than on that of the armies of a nation. We are sufficiently convinced how much of success is the consequence of courage, and that courage is only an opinion of our own superiority, arising from certain circumstances, either imaginary or real.

The courage which at present animates our forces, arises, my Lords, from a very proper ground, their former victories over the enemies which they are now to combat, and will therefore, doubtless, continue while they can consider themselves as enjoying the same advantage with those particular men by whom the victories were obtained. But, my Lords, if any essential part of their establishment be changed, they will be considered, both by themselves and their enemies, as a different army ; they will then charge with less alacrity, and be opposed with less dejection ; they will consider themselves as fighting without that certainty of success which arises from experience, and their enemies will resolve to try, by an obstinate resistance, whether they are now equally formidable as in their former state.

Thus, my Lords, I have attempted, however weakly, to represent the arguments which I have heard for the continuance of the establishment, of which your Lordships will examine the validity, and shall now proceed to consider the noble duke's system of a military subordination in time of peace.

Whether a standing army in time of peace is made necessary to the change of conduct in foreign courts, it is now useless to enquire ; but it will be easily granted by your Lordships, that no motive but necessity, necessity absolute and inevitable, ought to influence us to

support

support a standing body of regular forces, which have always been accounted dangerous, and generally found destructive to a free people.

The chief reason, my Lords, of the danger arising from a standing army, may be ascribed to the circumstances by which men, subject to military laws, are distinguished from other members of the same community ; they are by the nature of martial government exposed to punishment which other men never incur, and tried by forms of a different and more rigorous kind than those which are practised by the civil power. They are, if not exempted from the jurisdiction of a magistrate, yet subject to another authority which they see more frequently and more severely exerted, and which, therefore, they fear and reverence in a higher degree. They, by entering into the army, lay aside for the most part all prospect of advantage from commerce or civil employments, and, in a few years, neither fear nor hope any thing but from the favour or displeasure of their own officers.

For these, my Lords, or for other reasons, the soldiers have always been inclined to consider themselves as a body distinct from the rest of the community, and independent on it, a government regulated by their own laws, without regard to the general constitution of their country ; they have, therefore, been ready to subvert the constitution from which they received little advantage, and to oppress the civil magistrates, for whom they had lost their reverence.

And how soon, my Lords, might such outrages be expected from an army formed after the model of the noble duke, released from the common obligations of society, disunited from the bulk of the nation, directed solely by their own officers, and ultimately commanded by a man who had the right of commanding no other? Would they not soon consider themselves as a separate community, whose interests were no less than their laws peculiar to themselves ? Would they not consider him from whom they received all their rewards, and all their punishments, as the proper object of their supreme regard, and endeavour to exalt him to the same dominion over others, which he enjoyed in regard to themselves, that they might share in his superiority ?

A body of men, my Lords, thus separated from the rest of the people, must consider themselves as either ennobled or degraded by such distinction, and would soon find themselves inclined to use the

power

power of their arms, either in the exertion of their privileges, or
the revenge of their difgrace. Then, my Lords, would they fet at
defiance the laws of the nation, nor would one of thefe noble Lords
be able to difband, nor the other to refift them.

The army, my Lords, is, in time of peace, then beft regulated
when it is kept under the ftricteft fubordination to the civil power,
that power which it is inftituted to protect and to preferve.

Thus, my Lords, have I examined the propofal and reafons of
the noble duke, perhaps not much to the information of your Lordfhips ; but it cannot be expected that any capacity fhould be able, in
an unexpected and fudden debate, to difpute on a fubject, which the
noble duke's education gave him particular opportunities of underftanding far beyond almoft every other man, and which he has had
time to confider with refpect to this prefent motion.

For this reafon, my Lords, I cannot but think the previous queftion highly expedient, but not for this reafon alone ; for as the ftate
of the army, and the proper methods of augmenting it, are foon to
be examined by the other houfe, to prejudice their determinations,
may raife a conteft about privileges, and oblige us either to perfift,
for our own honour, in oppofition to meafures neceffary to the fecurity of the publick, or, in compliance with the prefent exigence, accept their fcheme however oppofite to our own refolution.

Lord CARTERET fpoke in fubftance as follows :—My Lords, the
known abilities of that noble Lord incline me always to hear him
with uncommon expectation and attention, which feldom fail to be
rewarded by fuch pleafure and information as few other men are able
to afford. But his obfervations on the queftion before us, my Lords,
have only convinced me, that the greateft abilities may be fometimes
betrayed into error, and the moft candid difpofition be vitiated by
accidental prejudices. For his own arguments neither appear juft,
nor his reprefentation impartial, of thofe advanced in favour of the
motion.

With regard to the number of officers neceffary in time of war,
his Lordfhip afferted nothing from his own knowledge, nor do I believe that any other lord will imagine himfelf qualified to difpute
with the noble duke upon queftions purely military. His experience
entitles him to the higheft authority, in debates of this kind, and if
every man has a claim to credit in his own profeffion, furely, he
who has given evidence of his proficiency in the art of war in the

I 3

eyes

eyes of the whole world, will not be denied in this house that superiority which would readily be allowed him in any other part of the universe.

And yet less, my Lords, can it be suspected that he intends to deceive us, than that he can be deceived himself: for not only his probity, his love of his country, and his fidelity to the crown, concur to secure him from any temptations to make an ill use of his credit, but his own interest obliges him to offer that scheme for the regulation of our forces, which in his own opinion will most certainly contribute to their success. For, it is not to be doubted, my Lords, that when we shall be engaged in war too far for negociations and conventions, when we shall be surrounded by enemies, and terrified at the near approach of danger, he will be called upon to lead our armies to battle, and attack once more those enemies that have fled so often before him.

Then, my Lords, if he has contributed to form a weak plan of our military constitution, must he atone for it with the loss of his reputation; that reputation, for which he has undergone so many fatigues, and been exposed to so many dangers.

But, my Lords, it is ridiculous to suspect where nothing appears to provoke suspicion, and I am very far from imagining that the dangers of innovation, however artfully magnified, or the apprehensions of the soldiers, however rhetorically represented, will be thought of any weight.

The establishment of the army, my Lords, is an innovation, and, as the noble Lord has justly represented it, an innovation that threatens nothing less than the destruction of our liberties, and the dissolution of our government. Our vigilance ought therefore, to be very anxiously employed in regulating this new part of our government, and adapting it, in such a manner, to the national constitution, that no detriment may arise from it, and that our civil rights may be protected, not oppressed, by the military power.

To this purpose, says the noble Lord, the soldiers are to be restrained by a due subordination to the magistrate, a position undoubtedly true, but now superfluously urged. For it was never controverted by the noble person whose opinion he intended to oppose.

Should any man assert, my Lords, that the army ought to be formed into a distinct and independent society, which should receive laws only from a council of war, and have no other governor than their officers, none should oppose such an assertion with more ardour or constancy than myself, but what was never advanced it is unnecessary to confute.

Yet, my Lords, to obviate those dangers from the army which have been so strongly and justly represented, it is necessary, not only that a legal subordination to the civil authority be firmly established, but that a personal dependence on the ministry be taken away.

How readily men learn to reverence and obey those on whom their fortunes depend, has been already shewn by the noble Lord, and therefore it will follow, that a minister who distributes preferments at his pleasure, may acquire such an influence in the army, as may be employed to secure himself from justice by the destruction of liberty. And unless it can be proved that no such minister can ever exist; that corruption, ambition, and perfidy, have place only in the military race; every argument that shews the danger of an army dependent only on the general, will shew the danger likewise of one dependent only on the minister.

The influence of the minister, my Lords, is known to arise from the number of the officers, and to be proportioned to the value of the preferment, which it is in his power to bestow: it is therefore evident, by adding new officers to our army, we shall throw weight into the scale, which already is, at least, an equal balance to our constitution, and enable the ministry either to employ an army in defence of their measures, or to obtain such an influence in the senate as shall make any other security superfluous.

Such, my Lords, is the danger of a multitude of officers, a danger which surely deserves more attention, than the imaginary prejudice of the soldiers in favour of the present establishment; a prejudice represented so powerful both in our own forces, and those of our enemies, that the future success of our arms may probably depend upon it.

Surely, my Lords, that cause may be allowed indefensible which such a patron defends so weakly. What can be more chimerical than to imagine that men would lay down their arms, and forsake their standards, because there are twenty more in a company than have formerly been ? That such a panic from such a cause was never found, I need not prove, and I scarce think it necessary to assert, that, without supposing a universal depravity of reason, it never can be found.

The establishment proposed by the noble duke, is the same with

J 4

that

that of moſt foreign troops, and particularly with that of his majeſty's forces in his foreign dominions, and, therefore, cannot but
be approved by him, if it ſhould be propoſed by your Lordſhips. For
why ſhould he imagine a greater number of officers neceſſary to the
troops of Britain, than to thoſe of any other nation.

The expediency of the motion, my Lords, is, in my opinion, ſo
obvious and incontenſtible as to require no farther conſideration, and
therefore it is no argument againſt it, that we were not previouſly
informed of the queſtion.

Much leſs, my Lords, can I diſcover the force of the aſſertion,
that by ſuch a reſolution we ſhall excite the diſpleaſure of the other
houſe; we have, my Lords, at leaſt an equal right with them to examine any poſition relating to the publick ſecurity, a right which
we may exert with leſs danger of diſguſting them, while they have
yet formed no determination, and with leſs danger to the nation,
than when their opinion, whatever it may be, cannot be controverted
without retarding the important bill againſt mutiny.

We are never offended, my Lords, at receiving the opinions of
the other houſe, which we often adopt without any alteration, and
often make uſe of for our own inſtruction, and now are become ſo
contemptible as that no regard ſhould be paid by them to our reſolutions.

It is well known, my Lords, that this aſſembly is an eſſential and
conſtituent part of the legiſlature of this kingdom, and that we received from our anceſtors a great extent of power, which it ought
to be our care not to ſuffer to be contracted by degrees, till this
aſſembly ſhall become merely formal, and fit only to ratify implicitly
the determinations of the other houſe.

Several other Lords ſpoke in the debate, and the preſident having
put the previous queſtion, "Whether the queſtion ſhould be then
put?" upon a diviſion, it paſſed in the negative. Content 42.
Not content 59.

HOUSE

HOUSE OF COMMONS.

December 12, 1740.

RESPECTING OFFICERS ON HALF-PAY.

Mr. SANDYS *this day moved for an humble address to his majesty, that, for the future ease of his majesty's subjects, all officers now subsisting upon half-pay, &c. might be employed in the army, and supported it to the following effect:*

SIR, though I have often known motions opposed without any just objections, or at least without any proof of such inconveniencies likely to arise from them, as were equivalent to the advantages which they would have produced, yet I cannot but confess, that any opposition to this will be unexpected and surprizing; for it is, in my opinion, supported by every law of justice and humanity. If we regard the publick in general, it cannot but produce some alleviation of the national expence; and if we consider the particular persons to whom it immediately relates, they have certainly a just claim to that regard which it is the tendency of this motion to procure them.

To burthen with superfluous officers, and unnecessary expences, a people already overwhelmed with taxes, and over-run with the dependents on the crown, is surely to the highest degree cruel and absurd. And to condemn those men to contempt and penury, who have served their country with bravery and fidelity, to prefer unexperienced striplings to those commissions, which would gladly be accepted by men who have already tried their courage in the battle, and borne the fatigues of marches, and the change of climates, is surely not only to oppress the deserving, and scatter promotion without just distinction; but, what is yet more enormous, it is to wanton with the publick safety, and expose us to our enemies.

Nor does it appear to me sufficient, that the veteran officers be restored to the commissions which they formerly enjoyed; they ought, upon an augmentation of our troops, to be recompenced by some advancement for their services and their sufferings; the ensign ought to become a lieutenant, and the lieutenant be exalted to a captain; stations which they will surely fill with more dignity and greater abilities,

lities, than boys newly difcharged from fchool, and entrufted with unexpected authority.

If it be reafonable, Sir, that expence fhould be fpared in a time of general poverty, if it be politic to carry on war in the manner moft likely to produce fuccefs, if it be juft, that thofe who have ferved their country fhould be preferred to thofe who have no merit to boaft, this motion cannot be rejected.

Sir WILLIAM YONGE anfwered to this purpofe :—Sir, to the motion now made, it will not I believe be objected, that it is unrea-fonable, or unjuft, but that it is unneceffary, and that it is not drawn up with fufficient confideration.

It is unneceffary, becaufe his majefty is advifed by it to no other meafures than thofe which he has already determined to purfue; for he has declared to me, Sir, his intention of conferring the new com-miffions upon the officers who receive half-pay, before any other officers fhall be promoted.

The motion appears to me not to be very attentively confidered, or drawn up with great propriety of expreffion ; for it fuppofes all the half-pay officers fit for the fervice, which cannot be imagined by any man, who confiders that there has been peace for almoft thirty years ; a fpace of time, in which many vigorous conftitutions muft have declined, and many who were once well qualified for command, muft be difabled by the infirmities of age. Nor is the promotion of one of thefe gentlemen confidered always by him as an act of favour ; many of them have in this long interval of peace engaged in methods of life very little confiftent with military employments, many of them have families which demand their care, and which they would not forfake for any advantages which a new commiffion could afford them, and therefore it would not be very confiftent with humanity to force them into new dangers and fatigues which they are now unable to fupport.

With regard to thefe men, compaffion and kindnefs feem to require that they fhould be fuffered to fpend their few remaining days with-out interruption, and that the dangers and toils of their youth fhould be requited in their age with eafe and retirement.

There are others who have lefs claim to the regard of the publick, and who may be paffed by in the diftribution of new preferments without the imputation of neglecting merit. Thefe are they who have voluntarily refigned their commiffions for the fake of half-pay, and

and have preferred indolence and retreat to the service of their country.

So that it appears, that of those who subsist upon half-pay, some are unable to execute a commission, some do not desire, and some do not deserve it; and with regard to the remaining part, which can be no great number, I have already the intention of his Majesty, and therefore cannot but conclude that the motion is needless.

Mr. PULTENEY spoke as follows:—Sir, I know not by what fatality it is, that all the motions made by one party are reasonable and necessary, and all that are unhappily offered by the other, are discovered either to be needless, or of pernicious tendency. Whenever a question can be clouded and perplexed, the opponents of the ministry are always mistaken, confuted, and, in consequence of the confutations, defeated by the majority of votes. When truth is too notorious to be denied, and too obvious to be contested, the administration claim the honour of the first discovery, and will never own that they were incited to their duty by the remonstrances of their opponents, though they never before those remonstrances had discovered the least intention of performing it.

But that the motion is allowed to be just and proper, is sufficient; the importance of it will be easily discovered. For my part I shall always consider that motion as important, which tends to contract the expences of the publick, to rescue merit from neglect, and to hinder the increase of the dependents on the ministry.

Sir ROBERT WALPOLE answered:--Sir, there is no temper more opposite to that incessant attention to the welfare of the publick, which is the perpetual boast of those who have signalized themselves by opposing the measures of the administration, than a lust of contradiction, and a disposition to disturb this assembly with superfluous debates.

Whether this disposition is not discovered in the reply made to the declaration of his majesty's intentions, and the confession of the propriety of the motion, let the house determine. It must surely be confessed, that it is not necessary to advise what is already determined.

Nor is it less evident, that many of the officers whose interest is now so warmly solicited, must be incapacitated by their age for service, and unable to receive any benefit from the offer of new commissions.

miffions. To deny this, is to queftion the flux of time, or to imagine that the conftitution of a foldier is exempt from its injuries.

Mr. SANDYS explained himfelf to this effect :—Sir, I am far
from intending by this motion to fill the army with decrepit officers,
or to obftruct in any manner the fervice of the publick ; nor have I
any other intention, than to fecure to thofe whofe years permit, and
whofe inclinations incite them to enter once more into the army, that
preferment to which they have a claim, not only from their paft fervices, but from the ftate of penury and obfcurity in which they have
languifhed.

I defire to preferve thofe, whofe valour has heretofore made our nation the terror of the world, from the mortification of feeing themfelves infulted by chidhood, and commanded by ignorance ; by ignorance exalted to authority by the countenance of fome rhetorician
of the fenate, or fome mayor of a borough.

Whoever has obferved the late diftribution of military honours, will
eafily difcover that they have been attained by qualifications very different from bravery, or knowledge of the art of war ; he will find that
regiments and companies are the rewards of a feafonable vote, and
that no man can preferve his poft in the army, whether given
him as the reward of acknowledged merit, or fold him for the full
value, any longer than he employs all his influence in favour of the
miniftry.

Sir ROBERT WALPOLE then faid:---Sir, it has been already admitted, that the motion can only be objected to as fuperfluous and
therefore all farther debate is mere wafte of time without any profpect of advantage ; nor is any thing now neceffary, but to review the
motion, and correct fuch expreffions as may be thought inaccurate or
improper.

That all the half-pay officers are not able to enter into the fervice,
has been already fhewn, and therefore I fhould imagine, that, inftead
of all the officers, we might very juftly fubftitute officers properly
qualified.

Sir JOHN BARNARD replied :---Sir, though I cannot difcover the
neceffity of any alteration, fince it cannot be conceived that the
fenate can advife impoffibilities, yet fince fo much accuracy is affected,
it may be allowed that the word all fhall be left out, as feeming to
imply more than can be intended.

But

But the honourable gentleman is not, in my opinion, fo happy in his amendment, as in his objection; for the words *properly qualified* convey to me no diftinct idea. He that is *qualified* is, I fuppofe, *properly qualified*, for I never heard of *improper qualifications*; but if the word *properly* be omitted, I have no objection to the amendment.

This motion was agreed to.

HOUSE OF COMMONS.

January 24, 1740-1.

ADDRESS FOR PAPERS.

Mr. WALLER *this day offered the following motion in writing,* That an humble addrefs be prefented to his majefty, that he will be gracioufly pleafed to give directions that there may be laid before this houfe copies of two particular letters written by his majefty's fecretary of ftate to admiral* Haddock, *which had been addreffed for before, and of the letters received from admiral* Ogle *mentioned therein; together with all letters written by admiral* Haddock *to either of his majefty's fecretaries of ftate, concerning the faid letters, and the execution of the orders contained therein.*

This motion he fupported by arguments to the following effect :--- Sir, no man who confiders the prefent fituation of our foreign affairs, the expence and inefficacy of our military preparations, the appearance of negligence in our naval expeditions, and the general difappointment of the hopes which the nation had conceived of victories, vengeance, and reparations, can, in my opinion, doubt the expediency of the motion which I have taken the liberty to make.

When the expectations of the nation are deceived, it certainly becomes thofe who are deputed to watch over the profperity of the publick, to enquire whence the difappointment proceeds, and either to inform their conflituents that their uneafinefs arifes from their own error, and that their hopes are deftroyed becaufe they had no rational foundation; or to detect the weak management of thofe by whom the

publick

publick measures have been ill-conducted, or the national treasure has been misapplied.

With regard, Sir, to the present war, I know not how the nation can be charged with having formed unreasonable expectations. If they considered the speech from the throne, the most authentick declaration of the intentions of the government, they found there the warmest resentments of the injuries which they had sustained, and the strongest assurances of a vigorous prosecution of all those measures which might produce speedy recompence and inviolable security.

If they reflect, Sir, on the preparations for war, on the multitude of ships, the demand of materials for naval equipments, and the high prices at which workmen were retained, they could not but imagine that either some mighty attempt was designed, or some formidable enemy dreaded, and as they know not whom they had to fear, they ascribed the vigour of our proceedings to a resolution of humbling our enemies by one fatal blow, and re-establishing our naval dominion by a single effort.

And justly, Sir, might they indulge this pleasing imagination, with reason might they anticipate a triumph over an enemy whose strength bears no proportion to the force that was fitted out against them, and expect that in a few months they should see the ambassadors of Spain supplicating for peace.

To raise their expectations yet higher, their trade was suspended by an embargo, long continued, and in the strictest manner enforced, and the impresses were let loose upon the sailors; they saw nothing omitted, however grievous to the nation, that could contribute to make it formidable, and bore part of the miseries of war without impatience, in hopes of being rewarded by military glory, and repaid by the plunder of Spain.

But, Sir, when so long a time has elapsed, and no account is brought of either a victory, or a battle, when they hear nothing but that our fleets have visited several neutral ports, and those of the enemy sailed unmolested from coast to coast, and when they are every day told of the losses of our merchants, are insulted in our own channel by the Spanish privateers, and receive no relations of our success upon the shores of our enemies, can it be wondered that they suspect the reality of our designs, or enquire whence it proceeds that their money has been wasted, their trade interrupted, and the liberty of their fellow-subjects invaded to no purpose?

But

But how much more juftly, Sir, are they inflamed when they hear of the lucky ftratagems, or daring enterprizes of thofe enemies, which a juft fenfe of their own fuperiority had induced them to con-fider as vanquifhed before the battle, and of whom they had no ap-prehenfions but that their cowardice would always fecure them from vengeance? How juftly may they murmur when they read, that our fleets leave every part of the enemy's coaft where their prefence is ne-ceffary, and have afforded the Spaniards an opportunity of changing one port for another, as it is moft convenient, and at length of joining the French fquadrons, and failing to the defence of their American dominions?

May they not juftly, Sir, require of their reprefentatives fome rea-fon for fuch inexplicable conduct? May they not reafonably demand an account of the arguments which procured their approbation of meafures, which, fo far as they can be examined by thofe who have no opportunity of perufing the neceffary papers, appear either cow-ardly or treacherous?

And what anfwer, Sir, can we return to fuch remonftrances un-lefs this motion be agreed to? How can we appeafe the difcontents of our conftituents, or difcharge the truft repofed in us, without a very minute and attentive enquiry into queftions thus obfcure and thus important?

Are we to tell our conftituents, that we abfolutely rely upon the prudence and fidelity of the miniftry and admirals, and recommend to them the fame implicit dependence? Are we to confefs that we have now for two feffions voted in the dark, and approved what we were not fuffered to examine and underftand?

Such anfwers, Sir, to queftions fo reafonable, will not contribute to encreafe the veneration of the people either for ourfelves, or our con-ftitution; and yet this anfwer, and this only, they can receive from us, if the papers mentioned in the motion I have made are denied.

Mr. CLUTTERBUCK replied in the following manner:---Sir, this motion, though fo warmly urged, and fo artfully fupported, I can confider only as a repetition of a former motion which was approved by the affembly, fo far as it could properly be complied with, nor was any paper then concealed which it would not have been an injury to the nation to have divulged.

If the defign of this motion be to promote the fuccefs of the prefent war, and the zeal with which it has been preffed, be incited only by
the

the ardour of true patriotiſm, I doubt not but it will eaſily be withdrawn by thoſe who are now moſt inclined to ſupport it, when they
ſhall reflect that it tends to the diſcovery of our ſchemes, and to the
overthrow of our deſigns, that it will expoſe all our conſultations to
our enemies, and inſtruct them how to annoy us with moſt ſucceſs,
and how to ſhelter themſelves from our intended attacks.

It is the firſt care, Sir, of every adminiſtration, that their military deſigns ſhould only be diſcovered by the execution of them, and that their
enemies, by being obliged to guard all parts, ſhould be weak in all.
If by laying our papers before this houſe, the Spaniards ſhould come
to be informed againſt what part of their dominions our expeditions
are deſigned, will they not increaſe their ſtrength, improve their fortifications, and double their vigilance? And if we are thus obliged
to form new ſchemes, muſt we not impute the defeat of the former to
our own imprudent zeal, or unſeaſonable curioſity?

Mr. SANDYS ſpoke to this effect:—Sir, that we ſhould demand
the ſchemes laid for the future conduct of the war with Spain was
never propoſed, nor, as it may reaſonably be concluded, ever imagined; for what is mentioned in the motion but the papers relating
to the tranſactions of the two laſt years.

That it ſhould be neceſſary to remind gentlemen of the difference
between the *future* and the *paſt*, would hardly be ſuſpected by any
man not accuſtomed to ſenatorial controverſies and artifices of ſtate;
and yet in the argument which has been offered againſt the motion,
nothing has been aſſerted but that the orders relating to paſt tranſactions are not to be laid before us, leſt the enemy ſhould thereby
gain intelligence of what we now deſign againſt them.

The neceſſity of ſecrecy in war needs not be urged, becauſe it will
not be denied; but when deſigns have been laid, and miſcarried, the
reaſons of that miſcarriage may ſurely be enquired, without danger of
betraying the counſels of our country.

If the negligence of our counſels, and the miſconduct of our commanders, has been ſuch, that no deſigns have been premeditated; if a
war has been carried on by chance, and nothing has ſucceeded becauſe nothing has been attempted; if our commanders have not done
ill, and have only done nothing; if they have avoided loſs by avoiding
danger; we may ſurely enquire to whom ſuch proceedings are to be
imputed, whether the defeat of our deſigns is to be charged upon the
ſtrength of our enemy, or the cowardice of our officers; or whether
the

the inactivity and apparent neutrality of our forces is occasioned by the negligence of our admirals, or the irresolution of our own ministry.

There have been, Sir, many incidents in these two last years, of which the examination can be of very little advantage to the Spaniards. I do not know what pernicious intelligence they can glean from an enquiry into the reasons for which Haddock's fleet was divided, and Ogle sent to the defence of Minorca, or for which he afterwards returned.

Nor can I conceive that any advantage, except that of merriment and diversion, can be thrown into the hands of our enemies, though we should seriously enquire into what no man has yet pretended to understand, the wonderful escape of the Spanish squadron. A transaction on which we had dwelt long enough with that admiration which ignorance produces, and on which it may not be improper at length to enable us to reason.

This is an affair, perhaps, much better understood by our enemies than by ourselves, and surely we cannot therefore be afraid of informing them of it; at least since the fleet has long since sailed out, and left their coast, we can hardly be restrained in our enquiries by the fear of discovering our *future* designs.

If, therefore, it be the incontestable right of the senate to examine the conduct of publick affairs, which I suppose will scarcely be denied, this motion cannot be rejected as unseasonable, nor can the papers be refused without increasing those suspicions which are already too prevalent throughout the nation.

Nor, indeed, for our own sakes, ought we to delay this enquiry any longer, lest by having long acted without being accountable, the minister should form a prescription against our privilege, and, in time, tell us in plain terms that we are his slaves, and that we are not to presume to carry our examinations, however solemn and important they may continue to appear, further than he shall be pleased to permit; and that whatever may be the opinion of the people that deputes us, or whatever antient claims we may plead to authority, we are now to consider ourselves only as the oppressors of the nation, and the panegyrists of the court.

Mr. WALPOLE next rose and spoke to this purpose:---Sir, it cannot be denied to be reasonable that all those papers should be laid before the senate, which can be communicated without injury to the publick. Of this number we may juftly imagine the orders fent to the admirals, in which the time of their departure is fixed, and many others which may be of ufe to inform the houfe, but cannot enable the enemy to judge either of our force or our defigns.

But it is evident, that there muft be others included in this motion, which our regard for the fuccefs of the war, and the profperity of our country, ought to determine us to conceal, and fuch as are never expofed by any adminiftration; it is therefore proper to limit the addrefs to papers of a certain kind, or a certain date, which may be confidered by the houfe without benefit to our enemies, and for the examination of which a day or two will be more than fufficient.

Mr. Pulteney fpoke in fubftance as follows:---Sir, I know not what number of papers the wifdom of the adminiftration will allow us, but, if we judge by the time propofed to be fpent in examination, we fhall not be diftracted with a great diverfity of fubjects; intelligence will be very penurioufly dealt out, and if we fubmit to their choice of the writings which fhall be laid before us, our enquiry will probably end without any difcoveries made either by our enemies or ourfelves.

But I hope, Sir, we fhall not be fo cheaply fatisfied, nor expofed by the fear of one enemy to the infolence of another. I hope we fhall refolutely continue our demands of information, while a fingle line is concealed, from which any light can be expected.

There may indeed be circumftances in which our demands, however loud, will neceffarily be vain. It is not impoffible that we may fufpect thofe tranfactions of deep art, and fecret contrivance, which have been the confequences of mere indolence, and want of confideration. Our great minifters have been perhaps only doing nothing, while we have imagined that they were working out of fight.

Mifled, Sir, by this notion, we may call for the orders that have been difpatched in thefe two laft years, when perhaps our fecretaries of ftate have been fattening on their falaries without employment, and have flept without care, and without curiofity, while we have been congratulating ourfelves upon their vigilance for our prefervation.

Or if orders have been given, it is to be confidered, that the end of in getting out is to compare them with the conduct of the admirals to whom they were directed: from this comparifon I doubt not that many gentlemen expect uncommon difcoveries; but to check all unreafonable unreasonable hopes before they have taken possession of their hearts, for unreasonable hopes are the parent of disappointment, I think it proper to remind them, that to draw any conclusions from the orders, it is necessary to understand them.

This consideration alone is sufficient to redress the ardour of enquiry, for every man that has had opportunities of knowing the wonderful accomplishments of our ministry, the depth of their designs, the subtilty of their stratagems, and the closeness of their reasoning, will easily conceive it probable that they might send such orders as none but themselves could understand; and what then will be the consequence of our idle curiosity, but that we be led into a labyrinth of endless conjectures? For we have long ago found that no explanations are to be expected, and that our ministry are too wise to discover their secrets to their enemies.

Let us, therefore, examine the naked facts which have fallen within our observation, and endeavour to inform ourselves of the meaning of these secret orders by the execution of them.

Admiral Ogle was dispatched from Haddock's fleet to protect Minorca, and, in his absence, the Spanish squadron sailed away. Perhaps he was ordered to watch Ferrol and Minorca at the same time, and not understanding how that was to be done, neglected one part of his charge by an attention to the other; as a watchman who should be employed to guard at once the bank in London, and the treasury in Westminster.

Admiral Norris, Sir, sailed lately forth, I suppose, in pursuance of orders, with a very formidable fleet, and after having lost sight for some days of the British coast, sailed back again with great precipitation. Whether his orders were only to sail forth, or whether when he examined them farther he could not understand them, I pretend not to determine; but it may reasonably be imagined that his orders were of the same kind with those of our other admirals, because they produced the same consequences.

I have been told, that formerly our commanders were ordered to *burn*, *sink*, and *destroy*; and that in those times it was not uncommon for a British admiral to do much mischief with a strong fleet; but it is evident that the stile is since changed, for our admirals are now very inoffensive, and go out only to come back. I therefore think the motion highly necessary, and such as ought to be complied with.

Admiral Norris here rose up and spoke thus:---Sir, I am not conscious that my conduct in any part of my life has exposed me

to be juftly treated with contempt and ridicule, and what I have not
deferved I will not bear.

If any gentleman in this houfe can accufe me of having neglected
my duty, or deferted it, let him not fpare infults or invectives, let
him now expofe my cowardice or my carelefnefs, let him prove me
unworthy of truft or of command.

But my own confcience acquits me, and I defy any man to produce and fupport his accufation; nor can you, Sir,* who have thus
contemptuouſly treated me, allege any thing againft me that may
juftify your neglect of decency: that you have tranfgreffed the rules
of decency is the fofteſt cenfure that your behaviour admits, and I
think it may with equal propriety be afferted, that you have broken
the laws of juſtice.

Mr. PULTENEY replied in this manner:---Sir, I fhall fubmit to
you, and all who hear me, whether I have treated the honourable
gentleman's name with any contemptuous freedom of fpeech. The
ufual method of mentioning an expedition is that of naming the
commander, who is not thereby neceffarily included in the cenfure of
an unfuccefsful attempt, and I am very far from calling his courage
and capacity into queftion.

Not that I fhall ever think it neceffary to make an apology for expreffing my fentiments with freedom as a member of this houfe, in
which I fhall always fpeak what I think, and in what manner it
fhall appear to me moft proper, nor fhall I fear to repeat without
doors what I fay here.

Sir ROBERT WALPOLE next rofe up and fpoke to this purpofe:--
Sir, as I am not acquainted with any meafures purfued by the adminiftration, which it is their particular intereft to conceal, I am defirous
that all papers fhould be laid before the houfe which will not afford
our enemies any opportunity of obviating our defigns.

What neceffity there is for this addrefs I cannot indeed difcover,
becaufe I know not any foundation for fufpicion of either negligence
or treachery, which have been both infinuated in this debate.

Nor are the miniftry, however ludicroufly their abilities have been
treated, afraid of difcovering their ignorance, by laying before the
houfe the orders which they have given to our admirals; orders of
which they are far from doubting that they will appear upon a candid
examination rational and proper.

* Addreffing himfelf to Mr. Pulteney.

The

The chief objection to this motion arises from its unreasonableness, and the necessity which it will produce of assigning to a fruitless enquiry those hours that may be more usefully employed.

Mr. PITT replied in terms to the effect following:—Sir, it is my opinion, that our time cannot be more usefully employed during a war, than in examining how it has been conducted, and settling the degree of confidence that may be reposed in those to whose care are entrusted our reputations, our fortunes, and our lives.

There is not any enquiry, Sir, of more importance than this, it is not a question about an uncertain privilege, or a law, which if found inconvenient may hereafter be repealed; we are now to examine whether it is probable that we shall preserve our commerce and our independence, or whether we are sinking into subjection to a foreign power.

But this enquiry, Sir, will produce no great information, if those whose conduct is examined are allowed to select the evidence. For what accounts will they exhibit but such as have often already been laid before us, and such as they now offer without concern: accounts obscure and fallacious, imperfect and confused; from which nothing can be learned; and which can never entitle the minister to praise, though they may screen him from punishment.

Mr. PELHAM spoke as follows:—Sir, I am confident that no man engaged in the administration, desires to be *screened* from the most rigorous enquiry, or would defer to exhibit the papers a moment for any other reason than his regard for the publick.

I am confident, that nothing could so much contribute to advance the particular and distinct interest of the ministry as the publication of all the writings that relate to the present war, by which it would incontestably appear, that nothing has been omitted that could promote our success, that our commanders have been sent out with orders to act with the utmost vigour, and that our preparations have been not disproportioned to the importance of our design.

It will appear that no former ministry have given greater proofs of their zeal for the publick interest, or have more steadily pursued the most proper measures by which it might be advanced.

I am not indeed certain that those who now call so loudly for information would be prevailed on by any degree of evidence to suspend their censures. Them, who are now dissatisfied, I shall despair

—spair

fpair of influencing by reafon or teftimony ; for they feem to enquire
only to condemn ; nor is this motion, perhaps, made fo much for
the fake of obtaining information, as of harraffing the miniftry with
delays, and fufpending affairs of greater importance.

This motion was agreed to, and upon another motion made by
Mr. Sandys, it was refolved,

" That an humble addrefs be prefented to his majefty, that he
will be gracioufly pleafed to give directions, that there may be
laid before this houfe a copy of the reafons fent by admiral
Cavendifh, in purfuance of an order from the commiffioners of
the admiralty, which had retarded the failing of admiral
Ogle's fquadron, fo much beyond expectation."

Likewife,

" That an humble addrefs be prefented to his majefty, that he will
be gracioufly pleafed to give directions, that there may be laid
before this houfe a copy of the reafons tranfmitted by admiral Ogle, that did prevent him from failing, purfuant to
his repeated orders for that purpofe, and particularly to thofe
fent him by the commiffioners of the admiralty."

HOUSE OF COMMONS.

February 3, 1740-1.

*Mr. Sandys this day prefented a motion in writing, for petitioning
His majefty to inform them when the regency received intelligence that
the French and Spanifh fquadrons failed, which was feconded as follows by Mr. WALLER :—*

SIR, the information now moved for, appears to me fo neceffary in
our deliberations on the conduct of the war, that without it we can
only conjecture in the dark, and entangle ourfelves in an inextricable
labyrinth.

It is well known, that in war all motions are in a great degree
to be regulated by thofe of the enemy, and that therefore no vigilance is to be fpared by which any knowledge can be gained of their
defigns, nor any methods omitted of communicating them to thofe
who have the direction of the war.

A miniftry may, in conducting military operations, difappoint
the expectations of their country, either by neglecting to procure intelligence,

telligence, or by failing to make use of those opportunities which seasonable information puts into their power, and they may, when their designs fail of success, justify themselves, by proving that they were deceived by intelligence which it was reasonable to believe, or that better intelligence was not attainable, or that they made use, however unsuccessfully, of all the forces that could then be employed, and of all the advantages that were then in their possession.

But how shall we judge of our administration, how shall we know what confidence we ought to repose in their prudence and fidelity, and what miscarriages are to be attributed to the chance of war or superior force of our enemies, if we cannot be informed with what diligence they endeavour at information, and how early they have notice of the motions of the enemy?

The failing, or rather escape of the Ferrol squadron, and departure of the French fleet, are the most important events of the present war; events that threaten very dangerous consequences, no less than descents upon our American colonies, the conquest of our dominions, the slavery of our fellow subjects, and perhaps the destruction of the brave Vernon, who is secure in the imagined vigilance of the other commanders, and may perhaps in a few days see himself surrounded by formidable squadrons of different nations, and exposed to the attack of forces to which his little fleet bears no proportion.

Nothing appears more evident, than that we had opportunities of observing at least all the preparations of the French, and of watching the moment of their departure, and that our force on the coast of Spain was sufficient to have confined their fleets for ever in their harbours, or to have destroyed them at their first entrance into the open seas, of which we may justly enquire, why it was not attempted, but shall enquire to no purpose till we know when they departed, that we may consider the state of our own forces, and whether our enemies escaped by our negligence, cowardice, or weakness.

Mr. WINNINGTON then spoke to the following purpose :—Sir, that we cannot deliberate upon subjects which we do not understand, and that, therefore, no necessary or useful information ought to be denied to the house, I shall readily admit ; but must observe, at the same time, that the reputation of the house would be very little consulted, in demanding information which cannot be given.

To address his majesty to inform us of the time at which the squa-

drons

drons of our enemies failed, is to enquire of him what it ought to be the highest care of those princes to conceal from him, and which he can only know, by having spies in their privy councils.

And of what importance is it to enquire what intelligence was brought him, or when he received it, if it appears that his intelligence must be in its own nature uncertain and dubitable?

That they have left their ports is now certain, because they have been twice discovered in different parts of the world; but, as we can now only form conjectures on their designs and courses, so, before they failed, it was impossible to know when they were fully equipped, or what time was fixed for their departure. It is to be remembered, that they form their measures, and make their preparations in their own dominions, and therefore, have more advantages of concealing their schemes, than we of discovering them.

Mr. Advocate CAMPBELL then spoke thus:—Sir, this motion, which has been represented as unreasonable and absurd, is, in my opinion, not only proper, but important.

It is important, because it will enable us to judge, upon sufficient foundations, of the conduct of the ministry, who are censured by the voice of the nation, for having been either defective in vigilance, or inactivity, for having been either ignorant by their own fault of the designs of the enemy, or perfidiously passive in permitting the execution of them.

I am far from believing that such intelligence, as our ministry is expected to procure, requires any uncommon subtilty, or any other agents than are always employed by every minister, to transmit to them informations from foreign courts. Such, I am afraid, are always hovering about our consultations, and I know not why our ministers should be less diligent or less successful than those of other princes.

If, therefore, such intelligence might have been obtained, it was criminal not to obtain it; and if the departure of the Spanish squadron was foreseen, it ought to be enquired, why it was not prevented; and if it was only known when it was too late to hinder it from failing, why it was not pursued, or why succours were not immediately dispatched to admiral Vernon.

All these questions can only be resolved, in consequence of the information which his majesty shall give us; and for which, it is therefore, in my opinion, necessary to petition.

Mr. HENRY

Mr. HENRY PELHAM spoke next to this purpose:— Sir, how the regency could be informed of the intention of the Spaniards to leave their ports till it appeared by their departure, or by what means it can be expected that his majesty should be now acquainted with their particular course, or farther designs, I confess myself unable to conceive.

With regard, Sir, to the intelligence transmitted from foreign courts by agents and spies, a little consideration will easily discover that it is not to be trusted. For what can be generally expected from them, but that they should catch flying reports, or by chance intercept uncertain whispers, that they should enquire timorously, and therefore, for the greatest part, of those from whom no satisfactory accounts can be received, and that they should often endeavour to deserve their salaries by such information as is rather pleasing than true.

All the knowledge that can be obtained of an enemy's designs, must arise from a diligent comparison of one circumstance with another, and from a general view of his force, his interest, and his opportunities. And that such conjectures will be often erroneous, needs not be told.

Probability, therefore, is, in such enquiries, all that can be attained, and he that sits idle in the time of war, expecting certain intelligence, will see his enemies enjoying the advantages of his folly, and laying hold on a thousand opportunities which he has neglected to improve.

The war in which we are now engaged, has been carried on by the administration with the utmost diligence and vigour; nor have any measures been omitted that could probably produce success, and the success of the wisest measures is only probable.

Should the great admiral, who is now present in the house, have met the French and Spaniards in the open seas, by what art could he arrive at a certain knowledge of their designs? He might by his acquaintance with the situation and state of neighbouring countries, the observation of their course, the periods of particular winds, and other hints of observation, form probable conjectures, but could never reach to certainty or confidence.

It seems to me, therefore, highly improper, to petition his majesty for intelligence which he cannot be imagined to have received, and I cannot agree to any motion for that purpose.

Mr. Sandys

Mr. Sandys then made another motion, to address his majesty, that there may be laid before the house copies of all letters received from, or written to, admiral Vernon since his going to the West Indies. Which being seconded,

Mr. PELHAM spoke to this effect :—Sir, this motion, if the intention of it be limited by proper restrictions, is doubtless reasonable and just ; for the right of this house to examine into the conduct of publick affairs, and consequently for calling for the papers necessary to enlighten their enquiries, is not to be disputed.

But, as the end of all such enquiries is the promotion of the publick welfare, so they are not to be made in a manner by which that end may be defeated. Papers are not to be demanded, which cannot be produced without discovering our own secrets, and acquainting our enemies either with that weakness which we ought carefully to conceal, or that force which will be most effectually employed if it is not known, and therefore no preparations are made to oppose it.

It cannot be imagined, but that many of the papers which have passed between the admiralty, and the commander in America, contain plans for the prosecution of the war, observations on the conditions of our own colonies, and, perhaps, intelligence of the estate of the Spanish fortresses and towns. Many informations of the utmost consequence to our enemies may be collected from those papers, but nothing can be expected from them, that will enable us to prosecute a senatorial enquiry with more success, that will put it in our power to discover frauds, negligence, or treachery.

There are, Sir, other papers which may indeed be laid before us, without any benefit to our enemies, and perhaps with some advantage to ourselves ; the papers which contain the accompts of our preparations and stores, the lists of our forces, and the calculation of our expences, are the proper subjects of senatorial enquiries ; and if the motion be restrained to those, I believe it will not be opposed by any gentleman engaged in the administration of our affairs. I shall beg leave to propose these words may be added, " So far as the same relates to a supply of ships, marines, or land forces."

The motion, thus amended, was agreed to.

H O U S E   O F   L O R D S.

February 13, 1740-1.

DEBATE ON ADDRESSING HIS MAJESTY FOR REMOVING SIR ROBERT WALPOLE.

The oppofition which for a long time had been made in the Commons, to the meafures of the adminiftration, was, on this day pufhed to a crifis, and produced a motion in both houfes. In the houfe of Lords it occafioned the following debate :

LORD CARTERET began in this manner : —My Lords, as the motion which I am about to make is of the higheft importance, and of the moft extenfive confequences ; as it cannot but meet with all the oppofition which the prejudices of fome, and the intereft of others, can raife againft it ; as it muft have the whole force of minifterial influence to encounter without any affiftance but from juftice and reafon ; I hope to be excufed by your Lordfhips for fpending fome time in endeavouring to fhew, that it wants no other fupport, that it is not founded upon doubtful fufpicions, but upon unconteftable facts ; that it is not dictated by private intereft, but by the fincereft regard to publick happinefs ; not abetted by the perfonal malevolence of particular men, but enforced by the voice of the people ; a voice which ought always to be attended to, and generally to be obeyed.

To endeavour, my Lords, to remove from places of publick truft all thofe who appear to want either the virtues or abilities neceffary for executing their offices, is the intereft of every member of a community. And it is not only the intereft but the duty of all thofe who are either by the choice of the people, or by the right of birth, invefted with the power of infpecting publick affairs, and intrufted with the general happinefs of their country. That therefore every motive combines to make it the duty, and every argument concurs to prove it the privilege of your Lordfhips, is too evident to be doubted.

How often this privilege has been exerted by this houfe, and how

often

often it has refcued our country from oppreffion, infolence, and rapine ; how often our conftitution has been re-animated, and impend-
ing ruin been averted by it, a fuperficial acquaintance with hiftory
may inform us.   And we are now called upon by the univerfal cry
of the nation, and urged by the perplexed and uncertain ftate of our
foreign affairs, and declenfion of our wealth and attacks upon our
liberties at home, to recollect thefe precedents of magnanimity and
juftice, and to make another effort for the relief of our country.

This houfe, my Lords, has proceeded againft minifters, whofe
conduct they difapproved, by methods of greater or lefs feverity,
according to the neceffity of affairs, or the fuppofed malignity of
the crimes alleged againft them ; and therefore have fometimes
thought it neceffary to deter pofterity from imitating them by rigorous cenfures, aud exemplary punifhments, and fometimes have
thought it fufficient to fet the nation free from its diftreffes, without
inflicting any penalties on thofe by whofe mifconduct they imagined
them produced.

What were the more violent and vindictive methods of proceeding
it is not neceffary, with regard to this motion, to examine ; fince I
fhall only propofe, that we fhould, in imitation of our predeceffors,
in cafes of this nature, humbly addrefs his majefty to remove the
minifter from his prefence and counfels.

Nothing, my Lords, can be more moderate or tender than fuch
an addrefs, by which no punifhment is inflicted, nor any forfeiture
exacted.   The minifter, if he be innocent, if his mifconduct be
only the confequence of his ignorance or incapacity, may lay down
in peace an office for which nature has not defigned him, enjoy the
vaft profits of long employment in tranquillity, and efcape the refentment of an unhappy people ; who, when irritated to the higheft degree, by a continuation of the fame mifcarriages, may, perhaps, in
the heat of a more malevolent profecution, not fufficiently diftinguifh between inability and guilt.

Thefe, therefore, among your Lordfhips, that think him honeft
but miftaken, muft willingly agree to a motion like this, as the beft
expedient to appeafe the people without the ruin of the minifter.   For
furely no man who has read the hiftory, or is acquainted with the
temper of this nation, can expect that the people will always bear to
fee honours, favours, and preferments, diftributed by the direction
of one univerfally fufpected of corruption, and arbitrary meafures ;
or

or will look only with filent envy upon the affluence of thofe whom they believe to be made great by fraud and plunder, fwelled to in-folence by the profperity of guilt, and advanced to wealth and lux-ury by publick miferies.

Such of your Lordfhips who join with the people in afcribing our pre-fent unhappy ftate not to the errors, but to the crimes of the minifter, and who therefore think a bare removal not fufficient to fatisfy the demands of juftice, muft doubtlefs give their confent to the motion, for the fake of obtaining proper evidence of his wickednefs, which cannot be expected while he ftands exalted in profperity, and dif-tributes the riches of the nation, and the gifts of his fovereign at his own choice ; while he is in poffeffion of every motive that can in-fluence the mind, enforce fecrecy, and confirm fidelity ; while he can bribe the avaricious, and intimidate the fearful; while he can increafe the gratification of luxury, and enlarge the profpects of ambition. For, my Lords, if it be confidered from whom this evi-dence muft be drawn, it will foon appear that no very important dif-coveries can be made, but by thofe whom he has intrufted with his fecrets, men whofe difregard of virtue recommended them to his favour, and who, as they are moved only by intereft, will continue faithful while they can hope for recompence ; but may, perhaps, be willing to buy their own fecurity by facrificing their mafter, when they fhall fee no farther profpect of advantage from ferving him, or any other method of efcaping punifhment.

But, my Lords, all muft allow this motion to be reafonable, whatever they think of the minifter's conduct, who are of opinion that a free people have a right of complaining when they feel op-preffion, and of addreffing the crown to remove a minifter that has incurred their univerfal deteftation.

That fuch is the condition of the prefent minifter, I believe, will fcarcely be denied, or may be difcovered by thofe who find them-felves inclined to doubt it, by afking any man whom they fhall ac-cidentally meet, what are his fentiments on the fituation of national affairs, and of the hands by which they are adminiftered. What anfwer he will receive is well known to moft of your Lordfhips. Let him not be fatisfied with a fingle fuffrage, let him repeat the queftion to ten thoufand perfons, different in their ages, their con-ditions, and religious opinions, in every thing that produces con-trariety of difpofitions and affections, he will yet find them unanimous

ruous in complaining of publick misconduct, and in censuring one gentleman as the author of it.

Let us not imagine, my Lords, that these accusations and murmurs are confined to the lowest class of the people, to men whose constant attention to more immediate distresses, hinder them from making excursions beyond their own employments. For though perhaps it might be made evident from the accounts of past times, that no general dissatisfaction, even among men of this rank, was ever groundless ; though it might be urged that those who see little can only clamour, because they feel themselves oppressed ; and though it might not unseasonably be hinted that they are at least formidable for their numbers, and have sometimes executed that justice which they had not interest to procure, and trampled upon that insolence that has dared to defy them ; yet I shall not insist upon such motives, because it is notorious that discontent is epidemical in all ranks, and that condition and observation are far from appeasing it.

Whether the discontent thus general is groundless, whether it is raised only by the false insinuations of the disappointed, and the wicked arts of the envious, whether it is, in exception to all the maxims of government, the first dislike of an administration that ever overspread a nation without just reasons, deserves to be enquired into.

In this enquiry, my Lords, it will be necessary to consider not only the state of domestick affairs, increase or diminution of our debts, the security or violation of our liberties, the freedom or dependence of our senates, and the prosperity or declension of our trade, but to examine the state of this nation, with regard to foreign powers; to enquire, whether we are equally feared and equally trusted now as in former administrations ; whether our alliances have contributed to secure us from our inveterate and habitual enemies, or to expose us to them ; whether the balance of Europe be still in our hands ; and whether, during this long interval of peace, our power has increased in the same proportion with that of our neighbours.

France, my Lords, is the constant and hereditary enemy of Britons, so much divided from her in religion, government, and interest, that they cannot both be prosperous together; as the influence of one rises, that of the other must by consequence decline. Alliances may form a temporal show of friendship, but it cannot continue ; for their fituation produces a natural rivalfhip, which every accidental circumftance has contributed to increafe. Long wars for many reigns after the conqueft eftablifhed a radical and infuperable hatred between us, nor did thofe wars ceafe till the reformation produced new occafions of jealoufy and averfion. France was by thefe reafons obliged for many ages to employ all her influence and policy in ftrengthening herfelf againft us, by treaties and alliances ; and in our times has given us a new reafon for jealoufy by extending her commerce, and improving her manufactures.

It has been, therefore, my Lords, the fettled principle of every wife adminiftration, of every Briton whofe opinions were not regulated by fome other motives than thofe of reafon, to attend with the higheft degree of vigilence to all the defigns of the French, and oppofe with inceffant diligence every attempt to increafe their force, or extend their influence, and to check their conquefts, obftruct their alliances, and foreftal their trade.

For this great end it has been our conftant endeavour to fupport the Auftrian family, whofe large dominions and numerous forces make a counter-balance on the continent to the power of France. For this end we entered into a long war, of which we ftill languifh under the confequences, fquandered the lives of our countrymen, and mortgaged the polleffions of our pofterity. For failing in the profecution of this purpofe, for leaving France too formidable, and neglecting the interefts of the emperor, was the treaty of Utrecht cenfured, and the authors of it profecuted by the prefent minifter ; but how much he has improved the errors of his predeceffors to his own advantage, how diligent he has been to rectify the mifcarriages of their conduct, and fupply the defect, I fhall endeavour to explain.

It is well known, my Lords, that during the regency of the duke of Orleans, we had nothing to apprehend from French machinations ; his intereft, a tye which that nation is feldom found to break, held him fteady to his engagements with us ; nor is it lefs known how much he diftrufted Spain, and how little by confequence he favoured her. We had at that time no neceffity of anxioufly attending to every whifper of the French court, which was fufficiently engaged in regulating their domeftick affairs, and repairing the ruins of a deftructive war ; but, my Lords, we ought to obferve, that it

had

had been happy for us had our minister laboured with equal address at the same employment.

After the death of this duke, the affairs of France were restored to their former situation, her old schemes were revived, her ancient alliances cultivated, and her general interest pursued. Spain was again considered as the power which had the same views with her, and which could never rival, but might always assist her.

This alliance, my Lords, was intended to have been unalterably confirmed by a marriage, but as no human policy can form measures certain of success, an irreconcileable hatred was nearly produced by the measure intended to confirm a settled and indissoluble friendship. The Infanta was sent back after her arrival in France, an affront which no nation would soon have forgot, but which the general character and habitual sentiments of the Spaniards inclined them to resent beyond any other people. To any one, acquainted with their character in this respect, it will readily appear, that no other insult or injury could so sensibly affect them, or excite so eager a desire of revenge. This, my Lords, the sagacity of our minister should have discovered, this opportunity should have been improved with the utmost care, by which Spain and France might possibly have been disunited for ages, and Britain have gained such advantages as would have made her the sole arbitress of Europe.

The Spaniards were not deficient on their side, nor did they neglect to court our friendship, but gave us the highest proof of their confidence by offering us the sole mediation of their differences with the emperor of Germany; but at this time it was, that the gentleman whose conduct I am examining, obtained the chief influence in our counsels, and by his peculiar penetration discovered, that nothing was to be done which might give the least offence to the French. We therefore refused to mediate, unless French ministers might be associated with ours, which the Spaniards had too much spirit to consent to.

Thus, my Lords, was neglected the first opportunity of forming against the French an alliance by which they might have been awed in all their designs, and by which the peace of Europe might have been long preserved.

The Spaniards, finding that we would not undertake to reconcile their differences with the emperor of Germany, and continuing
their

their abhorrence of French mediators, concluded, without the intervention of any other power, a treaty both of peace and alliance with his Imperial majesty.

This, my Lords, was the famous treaty of Vienna, the source of so many projects and expedients, of so much terror and solicitude, of such immense expences and perplexed negotiations. This treaty, a paper innocent and well-meaning, which related only to the contracting parties, kept for some time this nation in alarms, in apprehensions of conspiracies, and expectations of invasions.

To this treaty, had we singly regarded our own affairs, without applying to France for instructions, we ought to have acceded, by which we should have divided the interest of the house of Bourbon, broken the combination of these pontifical powers, and, by improving one lucky incident, obtained what our arms and our politicks had never hitherto been able to accomplish.

But the French, sensible of their danger, and well acquainted with our minister, contrived an expedient which indeed would not often have succeeded, but which was so well adapted to the intellects of this gentleman that it extricated them from all their difficulties.

They told us, my Lords, and what is yet more wonderful, they prevailed upon us to believe, that in this dreadful treaty of Vienna, it was stipulated between the German emperor and Spain, that they should employ their joint forces against Britain, that they should exalt the pretender to the throne, take immediate possession of Gibraltar, and without mercy debar us for ever from our trade both in Spain and in the Western Indies. This his late majesty was advised to assert in his speech from the throne, which I desire may be read.

Of which the following clauses were read.

" My Lords and Gentlemen,

" The distressed condition of some of our religious brethren abroad, and the negotiations and engagements entered into by some foreign powers, which seem to have laid the foundation of new troubles and disturbances in Europe, and to threaten my subjects with the loss of several of the most advantageous branches of their trade, obliged me, without any loss of time, to concert with other powers such measures as might give a check to the ambitious views of those who are endeavouring to render themselves formidable, and put a stop to the farther progress of such dangerous designs. For these ends I have entered into a defensive alliance with the French king, and the king of Prussia, to which several other powers, and particularly the Dutch, have been invited to accede, and I have not the least reason to doubt of their concurrence. This treaty shall in a short time be laid before you.

" By these means, and by your support and assistance, I trust in God, I shall be able not only to secure to my own subjects the enjoyment of many valuable rights and privileges, long since acquired for them by the most solemn treaties, but effectually to preserve the peace and balance of Europe, the only view and end of all my endeavours.

" It is not to be doubted, but the enemies to my government will conceive hopes, that some favourable opportunity for renewing their attempts may offer, from the prospect of new troubles and commotions : they are already very busy by their instruments and emissaries in those courts, whose measures seem most to favour their purposes, in soliciting and promoting the cause of the pretender ; but I persuade myself, notwithstanding the countenance and encouragement they may have received, or flatter themselves with, the provision you shall make for the safety and defence of the empire, will effectually secure me from any attempts from abroad, and render all such projects vain and abortive.

" When the world shall see that you will not suffer the British crown and nation to be menaced and insulted, those, who most envy the present happiness and tranquillity of this empire, and are endeavouring to make us subservient to their ambition, will consider their own interest and circumstances before they make any attempt upon so brave a people, strengthened and supported by prudent and powerful alliances, and though desirous to preserve the peace, able and ready to defend themselves against the efforts of all aggressors. Such resolutions and such measures timely taken, I am satisfied, are the most effectual means of preventing a war, and continuing to us the blessings of peace, and prosperity."

Who would not have been terrified, my Lords, at a treaty like this? Our religion was to be destroyed, our government subverted, and our trade reduced to nothing. What could a ministry thus intimidated do,

do, but refign themfelves implicitly to the direction of a kind neighbour that promifed to fhelter them from the ftorm?

There have been minifters, my Lords, in former times, who,
upon hearing fuch a reprefentation, would have confidered, that
Britain was an ifland, that the pretender could not be forced upon
us without an army, and that an army could not be tranfported
without fhips, that the emperor of Germany had neither navies nor
ports, that Gibraltar might be eafily fupplied with every thing requifite for its defence, and that any attempt made by Spain to injure
our trade, might eafily be punifhed by intercepting their plate fleets.

They would then have confidered whether attempts fo improbable,
and ftipulations fo abfurd and ridiculous, ought to be credited upon
the information of an ambaffador's fecretary, who, as he propofed
to reveal his mafter's fecrets for a bribe, might as probably take another reward for impofing upon thofe whom he pretended to inform.
Thofe, therefore, who advifed his majefty to affert to the fenate
what they knew from no better authority, thofe whofe daring infolence could make their fovereign inftrumental in alarming the people with falfe terrors, and oppreffing them with unneceffary burthens,
well deferve to feel a fenatorial cenfure.

But our minifters, my Lords, were too much frighted to make
fuch reflections: they imagined that deftruction was hanging over
us, and, in a dread of arbitrary government, oppreffion and perfecution, concluded at Hanover a treaty with the French.

Thus the French gained our confidence, and raifed in us a diftruft
of both the powers with whom it was our intereft to be united : but
the alliance of the emperor of Germany with Spain made them
ftill uneafy ; and therefore they determined once more to make our
credulity inftrumental in procuring a reconciliation between them
and the Spaniards.

To effect this, they kindly gave us intelligence, that when the
Spaniards fhould receive their treafures from the Weftern Indies, they
defigned to employ it in favour of the pretender, and that therefore
it was neceffary to intercept it. This advice was thankfully liftened
to, a fleet was fitted out, and thoufands were facrificed without any
advantage ; for the French not only forbore to affift us in the expedition, but forbade us to feize the treafure when we had found it.

The Spaniards apprehending themfelves attacked, omitted no opportunity of fhewing their refentment ; they feized our fhips, and

L 2   Laid

laid siege to Gibraltar, while our new allies looked quietly on, and
expected the event of their own scheme, which was far from being
defeated by our policy; for the Spaniards, finding the return of their
American revenues insuperably obstructed, and knowing that the
emperor of Germany, that emperor who was to invade Britain, had
not any power even to assist them, were obliged to have recourse to
the nation which they then hated, and to forgive the past affront,
that they might obtain their good offices in this exigence.

But, my Lords, it was not sufficient for the designs of the French,
that they had recovered their antient allies the Spaniards, unless they
could disunite them from the emperor of Germany: this it was likewise our interest to prevent, and yet this likewise we enabled them
to effect; for they prevailed upon us to promise in our stipulations
with the Spaniards, what they had not the least claim to demand,
that Spain, instead of neutral troops, should be introduced into Italy,
to secure certain successions there to a son of the queen of Spain.

With what reluctance the emperor of Germany would consent to
see troops placed in the provinces bordering upon his dominions,
which would certainly on the first occasion be employed to invade
them, it was easy to foresee, and with what degree of good-will he
would regard those by whom they were introduced; yet, my Lords,
such was the influence of France, and so ardent our desire of diverting Spain from setting the pretender upon the throne of Britain, that
we complied at all events, without any prospect or promise of advantage.

Thus were the Spaniards, by being persuaded to make this demand,
and we, by granting it, brought equally to ill terms with the emperor of Germany; and France was, by procuring such agreeable
conditions to the Spaniards, again considered as their most useful
ally.

That nation, my Lords, is in a very unhappy state, which is reduced to admit such terms as mediators are pleased to prescribe. We
durst not refuse the introduction of Spanish troops, nor durst we
introduce them without the emperor of Germany's consent, which,
however, he granted at an easy rate, for he demanded only that we
should become guarantees of the Pragmatic Sanction. This we
gladly agreed to, and thought ourselves so happy in purchasing so
cheaply an opportunity of ingratiating ourselves with Spain, that we
desired no other recompence.

This

This treaty with the emperor of Germany, was, however, by no means improper, nor could we, after the errors which had been committed, do any thing more effectual to preserve the balance of Europe, and re-establish our credit.

But, my Lords, this only treaty, which it was for our interest to make, seems to have been made without any intention of observing it; for about this time all the northern powers were alarmed by the approaching election of Poland, and every nation that had any thing either to hope or fear from the event of it, endeavoured to influence it.

How this election was determined, my Lords, and by what means, it is unnecessary to relate; but it may not be improper to remark, that whatever cause we may have to congratulate ourselves upon the choice, it does not appear that we had any part in promoting it. Nay, as it is not common for ministers to keep the best part of their conduct secret, there is reason for suspecting that they were not altogether without foundation reported to have favoured France.

The emperor of Germany, sensible of his own interest, promoted the election with vigour and resolution, proportioned to the greatness of the danger that might have arisen from neglecting it. By this conduct he drew upon himself the resentment of the French, who had now a pretence for taking measures which might effectually re-unite them to Spain, and, as the event shewed, alienate us from the emperor, and therefore, in vindication of the claim of Stanislaus, declared war upon Germany, in conjunction with Spain.

Now, my Lords, the emperor learned to set the true value upon his alliance with Britain, and all Europe had an opportunity of remarking our spirit, our power, and our vigilance. The troops which we prevailed upon his Imperial majesty to admit into Italy, were now drawn out of the garrisons against him, his dominions were attacked on each side, by formidable enemies, and his British allies looked with tranquillity and unconcern upon the difficulties into which they had betrayed him. The liberties of Europe were endangered by a new combination of the houses of Bourbon; and Britain, the great protectress of the rights of mankind, the great arbitress of the balance of power, either neglected or feared to interpose.

Of the event of the war, my Lords, I need only observe, that it

added

added new ftrength to France, and contributed to fuch an union between her and Spain, as the moft artful politician cannot hope to diffolve.

Thus, my Lords, whether by negligence, ignorance, cowardice, or treachery, it is not eafy to determine, we were made the inftruments of the French policy. Thus was that power enabled by our affiftance to retrieve all that fhe had loft by the ill fuccefs of her arms, and by her indecent and contemptuous treatment of Spain. Thus was the German emperor difpirited and weakened ; thus were we deprived at once of our allies and our reputation.

Our lofs of reputation, the greateft lofs that bad meafures can bring upon a nation, is made evi'ent beyond controverfy, by the infolence with which the Spaniards have treated us while we were flattering, enriching, and fupporting them. While we were fitting out fquadrons to convey their princes to Italy, and increafing their dominions at our own expence, they feem to have confidered our good offices, not as the benefits of friends, but the drudgery of flaves, and, therefore, could fcarcely refrain from infults while they employed us, at leaft when they no longer wanted our immediate affiftance. They renewed their contempt and cruelty, their robberies and oppreffions ; they prefcribed laws to our navigation, and laid claim to our colonies.

To thefe ravages and injuries what did we oppofe ? What but humble intreaties, pacific negotiations, and idle remonftrances ? Inftead of afferting our juft claims, and inconteftable poffeffions, inftead of preventing war by threatening it, and fecuring ourfelves from a fecond injury by punifhing the firft, we amufed ourfelves with enquiries, demands, reprefentations, and difputes, till we became the jeft of that nation, which it was in our power to diftrefs, by intercepting their treafure, and to reduce to terms almoft without bloodfhed.

Thus, my Lords, did we proceed, new queftions ever arofe, and the controverfy became more intricate ; commiffaries were difpatched to Spain, who returned without obtaining either reftitution or fecurity, and in the mean time no opportunity was neglected of plundering our merchants and infulting our flag : accounts of new confifcations and of new cruelties daily arrived, the nation was enraged and the fenate itfelf alarmed, and our minifters, at length awakened from their tranquillity, fent orders to the envoy at the Spanifh court

to

to expedite an accommodation; thefe directions were immediately obeyed, and produced the celebrated convention.

What was given up or what was endangered by this deteftable treaty, your Lordfhips have often had occafion to obferve, and the confequences of it were fo obvious, that the nation was aftonifhed. Every man faw, that we were either treacheroufly betrayed by our own miniftry, or that the minifters were almoft the only men in the kingdom utterly unacquainted with our claims, our injuries, and our danger.

A war could now no longer be avoided, it was not in the power of the miniftry any longer to refufe to fend out our fleets, and make an appearance of hoftile meafures; but they had ftill fome expedients remaining to fhelter the Spaniards from our refentment, and to make their country yet more contemptible: they could contrive fuch orders for their admirals as fhould prevent them from deftroying their enemies with too little mercy; and if any one was fufpected of intentions lefs pacific, there were methods of equipping his fleet in fuch a manner as would effectually fuftrate his fchemes of revenge, reprifals, and deftruction.

Thefe, my Lords, are not the murmurs of the difappointed, nor the infinuations of the factious; it is well known to our countrymen and to our enemies, how ill admiral Vernon was furnifhed with naval and military ftores, and how little his importunate demands of a fupply were regarded. What opportunities were loft, and what advantages neglected, may be conjectured from the fuccefs of his inconfiderable force. A very little reflection on the fituation and ftate of thofe countries will eafily fatisfy your Lordfhips, how far a fmall body of land forces might have penetrated, what treafures they might have gained, and what confternation they might have fpread over the whole Spanifh America.

That our fquadrons in the Mediterranean have been at leaft ufelefs, that they have failed from point to point, and from one coaft to another, only to difplay the bulk of our fhips, and to fhew the opulence of our nation, can require no proof: I wifh, my Lords, there was lefs reafon for fufpecting that they acted in concert with our enemies, that they retired from before their ports only to give them an opportunity of efcaping, and that they in reality connived at fome attempts which they were in appearance fent to prevent.

There are fome mifcarriages in war, my Lords, which every

L 4   reafonable

reasonable man imputes to chance, or to causes of which the influence could not be foreseen; there are others that may justly be termed the consequences of misconduct, but of misconduct involuntary and pardonable, of a disregard perhaps of some circumstances of an affair produced by too close an attention to others. But there are miscarriages too for which candour itself can find no excuses, and of which no other causes can be assigned than cowardice or treachery. From the suspicion of one, the past actions of the admiral who commands our fleet in those seas will secure him, but I know not whether there are now any that will attempt to clear the minister's character from the imputation of the other.

All the insolence of the Spaniards, a nation by no means formidable, is the consequence of the re-union of the houses of Bourbon; a re-union which could not easily have been accomplished, but by the instrumental offices of our ministry, whom, therefore, the nation has a right to charge with the diminution of its honour, and the decay of its trade.

Nor has our trade, my Lords, been only contracted and obstructed by the piracies of Spain, but has been suffered to languish and decline at home, either by criminal negligence, or by their complaisance for France, which has given rise to our other calamities. The state of our woollen manufactures is well known, and those whose indolence or love of pleasure keep them strangers to the other misfortunes of their country, must yet have been acquainted with this, by the daily accounts of riots and insurrections, raised by those who, having been employed in that manufacture, can provide for their families by no other business, and are made desperate by the want of bread.

We are told, my Lords, by all parties, and told with truth, that our manufactures decline, because the French have engrossed most of the foreign markets: and it is not denied even by those whose interest it might be to deny it, that the cloth which they ruin us by vending, is made of our own wool, which they are suffered to procure either by the folly of an unskilful, or the connivance of a treacherous administration.

If our own manufactures, my Lords, had been carefully promoted, if the whole influence of our government had been made to co-operate with the industry of our traders, there had always been such a demand for our wool, that they could not have afforded to
purchase

purchafe it at a price equivalent to the danger of exporting it : and if any means were now fteadily practifed to prevent the exportation, our trade muft confequently revive, becaufe cloth is one of the neceffaries of life, which other nations muft have from Britain, when France can no longer fupply them.

But, my Lords, notwithftanding the decay of trade, our expences have never been contracted ; we have fquandered millions in idle preparations, and oftentatious folly ; we have equipped fleets which never left the harbour, and raifed armies which were never to behold any other enemy than the honeft traders and hufbandmen that fupport them. We have indeed heard many reafons alleged for oppreffing the empire with ftanding troops, which can have little effect upon thofe who have no intereft to promote by admitting them : fometimes we are in danger of invafions, though it is not eafy to imagine for what purpofe any prince fhould invade a nation, which he may plunder at pleafure, without the leaft apprehenfion of refentment, and which will refign any of its rights whenever they fhall be demanded : fometimes, as we have already heard, the pretender is to be fet upon the throne by a fudden defcent of armies from the clouds ; and fometimes the licencioufnefs and difobedience of the common people, requires the reftraint of a ftanding army.

That the people are to the laft degree exafperated and inflamed, I am far from intending to deny, but furely they have yet been guilty of no outrage fo enormous as to juftify fo fevere a punifhment ; they have generally confined themfelves to harmlefs complaints, or at leaft to executions in effigy. The people, my Lords, are enraged becaufe they are impoverifhed, and, to prevent the confequences of their anger, their poverty is encreafed by new burthens, and aggravated by the fight of an ufelefs defpicable herd, fupported by their induftry, for no other purpofe than to infult them.

By thefe ufelefs armaments and military farces, our taxes, my Lords, have been continued without diminifhing our debts, and the nation feems condemned to languifh for ever under its prefent miferies, which, by furnifhing employment to a boundlefs number of commiffioners, officers, and flaves to the court under a thoufand denominations, by diffufing dependence over the whole country, and enlarging the influence of the crown, are too evidently of ufe to the minifter, for us to entertain any hopes of his intention to relieve us.

Let it not be boafted that nine millions are paid, when a new debt
of

of feven millions appears to be contracted ; nothing is more eafy than to clear debts by borrowing, or to borrow when a nation is mortgaged for the payment.

But the weight of the prefent taxes, my Lords, though heavier than was perhaps ever fupported by any nation for fo long a time, taxes greater than ever were paid, to purchafe neither conquefts nor honours, neither to prevent invafions from abroad, nor to quell rebellions at home, is not the moft flagrant charge of this wonderful adminiftration, which, not contented with moft exorbitant exactions, contrives to make them yet more oppreffive by tyrannical methods of collection. With what reafon the author of the excife fcheme dreads the refentment of the nation, is fufficiently obvious; but furely, in a virtuous and benevolent mind, the firft fentiments that would have arifen on that occafion, would not have been motions of anger but of gratitude. A whole nation was condemned to flavery, their remonftrances were neglected, their petitions ridiculed, and their deteftation of tyranny treated as difaffection to the eftablifhed government ; and yet the author of this horrid fcheme riots in affluence, and triumphs in authority, and without fear as without fhame lifts up his head with confidence and fecurity.

How much, my Lords, is the forbearance of that people to be admired, whom fuch attacks as thefe have not provoked to tranfgrefs the bounds of their obedience ; who have continued patiently to hope for legal methods of redrefs, at a time when they faw themfelves threatened with legal flavery, when they faw the legiflative power, eftablifhed only for their protection, influenced by all poffible methods of corruption to betray them to the mercy of the miniftry?

For, that corruption has found its way into one of the houfes of the legiflature, is univerfally believed, and without fcruple maintained by every man in the nation, who is not evidently reftrained from fpeaking as he thinks; and that any man can even be of a different opinion, that any man can even affirm that he thinks otherwife, would be, in any other age, the fubject of aftonifhment. That an immenfe revenue is divided among the members of the other houfe, by known falaries and publick employments, is apparent; that large fums are privately fcattered on preffing exigencies, that fome late tranfactions of the miniftry were not confirmed but at a high price, the prefent condition of the civil lift, a civil lift vaftly fuperior to all the known expences of the crown,

makes

makes highly probable. That the commons themfelves fufpect the determinations of their affembly to be influenced by fome other motives than juftice and truth, is evident from the bill this day fent hither for our concurrence; and furely no aggravation can be added to the crimes of that man who has patronized our enemies, and given up our navigation, funk his country into contempt abroad, and into poverty at home, plundered the people, and corrupted the legiflature.

But, my Lords, the minifter has not only contributed by his wickednefs or his ignorance to the prefent calamities, but has applied all his art and all his intereft to remove from pofts of honour and truft, to banifh from the court, and to exclude from the legiflature, all thofe whofe counfels might contribute to reftore the publick affairs, without any regard to the popularity of their characters, the ufefulnefs of their talents, or the importance of their paft fervices to the crown. Had any of thefe confiderations prevailed, we had not feen the greateft general in Britain difpoffeffed of all his preferments, difpoffeffed at a time when we are at war with one nation, and in expectation of being attacked by another far more powerful, which will doubtlefs be encouraged, by his removal, to more daring contempt, and more vigorous meafures.

What where the motives of this procedure, it is eafy to difcover. As his open defence of the prefent royal family in the late rebellion exempts him from the imputation of being difaffected to the crown, the only crime with which he can be charged is difaffection to the minifter.

Perhaps, my Lords, the minifter may have determined to have no need of generals in his tranfactions with foreign powers; but in proportion as he relies lefs upon the fword, he muft depend more upon the arts of peaceable negotiation, and furely there has been another perfon difmiffed from his employments, whofe counfels it had been no reproach to have afked, and to have followed.

The nature of my motion, my Lords, makes it not neceffary to produce evidence of thefe facts, it is fufficient that any minifter is univerfally fufpected; for when did an innocent man, fupported by power, and furnifhed with every advantage that could contribute to exalt or preferve his character, incur the general hatred of the people? But if it could ever happen by a combination of unlucky accidents, what could be more for the happinefs of himfelf, his mafter,

.   and

and the nation, than that he should retire and enjoy the consciousness of his own virtue.

His own interest in such a retirement I have already considered, and that both of the prince and the people is no less apparent : while a hated minister is employed, the king will always be distrusted by the nation, and surely nothing can so much obstruct the publick happiness, as a want of confidence in those who are intrusted with its preservation.

That common fame is in this case sufficient, will not be questioned, when it is considered that common fame is never without a foundation in facts, that it may spread disquiet and suspicion over all the kingdom, and that the satisfaction of millions is very cheaply purchased by the degradation of one man, who was exalted only for their benefit.

The objection, that there is no sole minister, will create no greater difficulty ; if there be many concerned in these transactions, *respondeat superior* : but it is too apparent that there is in reality one whose influence is greater than that of any other private man, and who is arrived at a height not consistent with the nature of the British government ; it is uncontested that there is one man to whom the people impute their miseries, and by whose removal they will be appeased.

The affairs of Europe, my Lords, will probably be so much embarrassed, and the struggles between the different designs of its princes be so violent, that they will demand all our attention, and employ all our address, and it will be to the highest degree dangerous to be distracted at the same time with apprehensions of domestick troubles ; yet such is the present unhappy state of this nation, and such is the general discontent of the people, that tranquillity, adherence to the government, and submission to the laws, cannot reasonably be hoped, unless the motion I shall now take leave to make your Lordships, be complied with: And I move, " That an humble address be presented to his majesty, most humbly to advise and beseech his majesty, that he will be most graciously pleased to remove the right honourable Sir Robert Walpole, knight of the most noble order of the blue ribband, first commissioner of his majesty's treasury, and chancellor of the exchequer, and one of his majesty's most honourable privy council, from his majesty's presence and councils for ever."

He

He was feconded by Lord ABINGDON in the following manner :--
My Lords, the copioufnefs and perfpicuity with which the noble
lord has laid down the reafons of his motion, make it neither eafy
nor neceffary to enlarge upon them. I fhall therefore only offer to
your Lordfhips a few thoughts upon the authority of common fame,
as the evidence upon which the motion is in part founded.

That all the mifcarriages of our late meafures are by common fame
imputed to one man, I fuppofe, will not be denied, nor can it, in
my opinion, be reafonably required, that in the prefent circumftances
of things any other proof fhould be brought againft him.

Common fame, my Lords, is admitted in courts of law as a
kind of auxiliary or fupplemental evidence, and is allowed to corro-
borate the caufe which it appears to favour. The general regard
which every wife man has for his character, is a proof that in the
eftimation of all mankind, the teftimony of common fame is of too
great importance to be difregarded.

If we confider the nature of popular opinions on publick affairs, it
will be difficult to imagine by what means a perfuafion not founded
on truth fhould univerfally take poffeffion of a people; it will be yet
more difficult to believe that it fhould preferve its empire, and that
in oppofition to every art that can be made ufe of to undeceive them,
they fhould pertinacioufly adhere to an error not imbibed in their
education, nor connected with their intereft. And how has any man
been originally prejudiced againft the prefent minifter? Or what
paffion or intereft can any man gratify, by imagining or declaring his
country on the verge of ruin? The multitude, my Lords, cenfure
and praife without diffimulation, nor were ever accufed of difguifing
their fentiments; their voice is at leaft the voice of honefty, and has
been termed the voice of heaven by that party of which thofe affect to
be thought whom it now condemns.

Let it not be urged, that the people are eafily deceived, that they
think and fpeak merely by caprice, and applaud or condemn without
any calm enquiry or fettled determination; thefe cenfures are applicable only to fudden tumults, and gufts of zeal excited by fallacious appearances, or by the alarms of a falfe report induftrioufly
diffeminated, but have no relation to opinions gradually propagated,
and flowly received.

If the credulity of the people expofes them to fo eafy an admiffion
of every report, why have the writers for the minifter found fo
little credit? Why have all the loud declamations and the labours
argument

arguments, the artful infinuations, and pofitive affertions which have
been for many years circulated round the nation, at the expence of
the government, produced no effect upon the people, nor convinced
any man who was not apparently bribed to refign his private opinion
to that of his patrons? Whence comes it, my Lords, that falfhood
is more fuccefsful than truth, and that the nation is inclined to complain rather than to triumph? It is well known that the people have
been charged in all former ages, with being too much dazzled by the
glitter of fortune, and the fplendour of fuccefs, and beftowing their
applaufes not according to the degrees of merit, but profperity. The
minifter, my Lords, has defeated his opponents in almoft all their
attempts; his friends have founded victory every feffion, and yet the
people declare againft him; his adverfaries have retired into the
country with all the vexation of difappointment, and have been rewarded for their unfuccefsful efforts with general acclamations. What
is it, my Lords, but the power of truth, that can preferve the vanquifhed from ridicule, and influence the nation to believe them the
only patrons of their commerce and liberty, in oppofition to all the
writers and voters for the miniftry?

If we confult hiftory, my Lords, how feldom do we find an innocent minifter overwhelmed with infamy? Innocent men have
fometimes been deftroyed by the hafty fury, but fcarcely ever by the
fettled hatred of the populace. Even that fury has generally been
kindled by real grievances, though imputed to thofe who had no
fhare in producing them; but when the tempeft of their firft rage has
fubfided, they have feldom refufed to hear truth, and to diftinguifh
the patriot from the oppreffor.

But though it fhould be acknowledged, my Lords, that the people
have been blinded by falfe reprefentations, and that fome caufes yet
undifcovered, fome influence which never has been known to operate
in any ftate before, hinder them from beholding their own felicity;
yet as publick happinefs is the end of government, and no man can
be happy that thinks himfelf miferable, it is in my opinion neceffary
to the honour of his majefty, and to the tranquillity of the nation,
that your Lordfhips fhould agree to the prefent motion.

The Duke of NEWCASTLE anfwered to this effect:——My
Lords, it is not without wonder that I hear a motion fo uncommon
and important, a motion which may be reafonably fuppofed to have
been long premeditated, and of which fuch affecting expectations
have

have been raifed, fo weakly fupported by evidence. I cannot think that any other atteftation is needful for the vindication of the right honourable gentleman, whofe conduct is this day to be examined, than the declaration of the noble lord, that there appears no pofitive evidence againft him.

The pretence that no evidence can be expected while he continues in his prefent ftation, is too openly fallacious to impofe upon your Lordfhips; for why fhould his influence be greater, and his power lefs refiftible than that of other minifters, who are well known to have found accufers in the height of their authority, and to have been dragged to punifhment almoft from behind the throne?

It is fufficiently known, that during the continuance of this ad-miniftration, many have been difmiffed from their employments, who appear not altogether unaffected with the lofs, and from whofe refent-ment a difcovery of wicked meafures might be reafonably expected, as their acquaintance with the fecrets of the government muft have given opportunities of detecting them. If, therefore, no particular crimes are charged upon him, if his enemies confine themfelves to obfcure furmifes, and general declamations, we may reafonably con-clude, that his behaviour has been at leaft blamelefs. For what can be a higher encomium than the filence of thofe who have made it the bufinefs of years to difcover fomething that might be alleged againft him on the day of trial.

I fuppofe that no man can queftion the penetration of thofe noble lords who have opened this debate, and I, my Lords, fhall be very far from infinuating that cowardice fuppreffes any of their fentiments. As the higheft reproach that can be thrown upon any man, is to fuggeft that he fpeaks what he does not think, the next degree of meannefs would be to think what he dares not fpeak, when the publick voice of his country calls upon him.

When therefore popular reports are alleged as the foundation of the addrefs, it is probable that it is not founded in reality upon known crimes or attefted facts, and if the fudden blafts of fame may be efteemed equivalent to attefted accufations, what degree of virtue can confer fecurity?

That the clamour is fo loud and fo general as it is reprefented, I can difcover no neceffity of admitting; but however the populace may have been exafperated againft him, we are furely not to be influenced by their complaints, without enquiring into the caufe of them, and

informing

informing ourselves whether they proceed from real hardships, unnecessary severities, and calamities too heavy to be borne, or from
caprice, and inconstancy, idle rumours, and artful representations.

I very readily allow, my Lords, that nothing has been left unattempted that might fill the people with suspicion and discontent.
That inevitable calamities have been imputed to misconduct, or to
treachery, and even the inconstancy of the winds and severity of
the weather charged upon the right honourable gentleman, the daily
libels that are in every man's hand, are a standing evidence; and
tho' I should grant that the people never complain without cause, and
that their burthens are always heavy before they endeavour to shake
them off, yet it will by no means follow, that they do not sometimes
mistake the cause of their miseries, and impute their burthens to the
cruelty of those whose utmost application is employed to lighten
them.

Common fame is therefore, my Lords, no sufficient ground for
such a censure as this, a censure that condemns a man long versed in
high employments, long honoured with the confidence of his sovereign, and distinguished by the friendship of the most illustrious persons in the nation, to infamy and contempt, unheard, and even un-
accused; for he against whom nothing is produced but general
charges, supported by the evidence of common fame, may be justly
esteemed to be free from accusation.

That other evidence will appear against him when he shall be reduced, in consequence of our agreeing to this motion, to the level
with his fellow-subjects, that all informations are now precluded by
the terrors of resentment, or the expectations of favour, has been
insinuated by the noble lord, who made the motion : whether his
insinuation be founded only upon conjecture, whether it be one of
those visions which are raised by hope in a warm imagination, or
upon any private informations communicated to his Lordship, I pretend not to determine ; but if we may judge from the known conduct of the opposition, if we consider their frequent triumphs before
the battle, and their chimerical schemes of discoveries, or prosecu-
tions and punishments, their constant assurance of success upon the
approach of a new contest, and their daily predictions of the ruin
of the administration, we cannot but suspect that men so long accustomed to impose upon themselves, and flatter one another with
fallacious hopes, may now likewise be dreaming of intelligence which
they

they never will receive, and amufing themfelves with fufpicions which they have no reafonable expectation of feeing confirmed.

And to confefs the truth, my Lords, if I may be allowed, in imitation of thefe patrons of their country, to indulge my own imagination, and prefume to look forward to the future conduct of thofe who have exerted fuch unwearied induftry in their attempts upon the adminiftration, and fo long purfued the right honourable gentleman with enquiries, examinations, rhetoric, and ridicule, I cannot but find myfelf inclined to queftion whether, after their motion fhall have been received in this houfe, and their petition granted by his majefty, they will very folicitoufly enquire after evidence, or be equally diligent in the difcovery of truth, as in the perfecution of the minifter.

I am afraid, my Lords, that they will be too deeply engaged in the care of making a dividend of the plunder in juft proportions, to find leifure for purfuit of the enemy, and that the fight of vacant pofts, large falaries, and extenfive power, will revive fome paffions, which the love of their country has not yet wholly extinguifhed, and leave in their attention no room for deep reflections, and intricate enquiries. There have formerly, my Lords, been patriots, who, upon a fudden advancement to a place of profit, have been immediately lulled into tranquillity, learned to repofe an implicit confidence in the minifters, forgotten to harangue, threaten, enquire, and proteft, and fpent the remaining part of their lives in the harmlefs amufement of counting their falaries, perquifites, and gratuities.

How great, my Lords, would be the difappointment of the people, that unhappy people which has been long neglected and oppreffed, which fo juftly detefts the minifter, and calls fo loudly for vengeance, when they fhall fee their defenders remit the vigour of the purfuit, when once the minifter flies before them, and inftead of driving him into exile, contend about his places !

Unhappy then furely, my Lords, would the nation be : the adminiftration, we are told, is already univerfally abhorred, and its hope is only in the oppofition ; but fhould the zeal of the patriots once grow cold, fhould they difcover to the publick, that they have been labouring not for general liberty, but for private advantage ; that they were enemies to power only becaufe it was not in their hands ; and difapproved the meafures of the government only becaufe they were not confulted ; how inevitably muft the people then fink into defpair ; how certain muft they then imagine their deftruction ?

It feems therefore, my Lords, equally prudent and juft to reject this motion, till better proof fhall be brought to fupport it; left by complying with it, we fhould heighten rather than appeafe the difcontent of the people; left we fhould too foon deprive them of their only confolation, and expofe the patriots to cenfure, without vindicating the miniftry.

In my opinion, my Lords, all who have approved the conduct of the prefent miniftry, muft neceffarily join in rejecting the motion, as cruel and unequitable, and incline to fupport a juft, and continue a wife adminiftration; and all thofe whom the reftlefs clamours of the oppofite party have perfuaded to regard them as arbitrary, corrupt, and perfidious, muft, if they are true friends to their country, and fteady exactors of juftice, refolve to defer their compliance, in order to bring to light the evidences neceffary for a legal conviction, and feverer punifhment.

That thefe evidences will never be found, and that therefore no legal punifhment will ever be inflicted, we may reafonably collect from the injuftice of the laboured charge which your Lordfhips have now heard; a charge drawn up with all the affiftance of fenatorial and political knowledge, and difplayed with all the power of eloquence, a collection of every occurrence for many years, of which any circumftance could be fhewn in an unfavourable light, and a recapitulation of all the meafures which have mifcarried by unforefeen events, or which the populace have been perfuaded to diflike.

In the adminiftration of governments, my Lords, many meafures reafonable and juft, plann'd out in purfuance of a very exact knowledge of the ftate of things then prefent, and very probable conjectures concerning future events, have yet failed to produce the fuccefs which was expected; they have been fometimes defeated by the inconftancy or diffhonefty of thofe who are equally engaged in them, and fometimes fruftrated by accidents, of which only Providence has the difpofal. It will even be allowed, my Lords, that the miniftry have been fometimes miftaken in their conjectures, and perhaps deceived by their intelligence, but I will prefume to fay, it never will be difcovered that they willingly betrayed, or heedlefsly neglected their truft, that they ever oppreffed their country with unneceffary burthens, or expofed it to be infulted by foreign powers. Nor will it, perhaps, be found that they ever appeared grofsly ignorant of the

publick

publick intereſt, or failed to diſcover any obvious truth, or foreſee any probable contingencies.

But, my Lords, I am willing to confeſs that they cannot judge of events to come with ſuch unerring and demonſtrative knowledge as their opponents can obtain of them after they have happened; and they are inclined to pay all neceſſary deference to the great ſagacity of thoſe wonderful prognoſticators, who can ſo exactly *foreſee* the *paſt*. They only hope, my Lords, that you will conſider how much harder their taſk is than that of their enemies; they are obliged to determine very often upon doubtful intelligence, and an obſcure view of the deſigns and inclinations of the neighbouring powers; and as their informers may be either treacherous or miſtaken, and the intereſts of other ſtates are ſubject to alterations, they may be ſometimes deceived and diſappointed. But their opponents, my Lords, are exempt by their employment from the laborious taſk of ſearching into futurity, and collecting their reſolutions, from a long compariſon of dark hints and minute circumſtances. Their buſineſs is not to lead or ſhew the way, but to follow at a diſtance, and ridicule the perplexity, and aggravate the miſtakes of their guides. They are only to wait for conſequences, which, if they are proſperous, they miſrepreſent as not intended, or paſs over in ſilence, and are glad to hide them from the notice of mankind. But if any miſcarriages ariſe, their penetration immediately awakes, they ſee at the firſt glance the fatal ſource of all our miſeries, they are aſtoniſhed at ſuch a concatenation of blunders, and alarmed with the moſt diſtracting apprehenſions of the danger of their country.

Accuſation of political meaſures is an eaſy province, eaſy, my Lords, in the ſame proportion as the adminiſtration of affairs is difficult; for where there are difficulties, there will be ſome miſtakes; and where there are miſtakes, there will be occaſions of triumph, to the factious and the diſappointed. But the juſtice of your Lordſhips will certainly diſtinguiſh between errors and crimes, and between errors of weakneſs and inability, and ſuch as are only diſcoverable by conſequences.

I may add, my Lords, that your wiſdom will eaſily find the difference between the degree of capacity requiſite for recollecting the paſt, and foreknowing the future; and expect that thoſe whoſe ambition incites them to endeavour after a ſhare in the government of their country ſhould give better proofs of their qualifications for that high

truſt,

truſt, than mere ſpecimens of their memory, their rhetoric, or their malice.

Even the noble Lord, who muſt be confeſſed to have ſhewn a very extenſive acquaintance with foreign affairs, and to have very accurately conſidered the intereſts and diſpoſitions of the princes of Europe, has yet failed in the order of time, and by one error very much invalidated his charge of miſconduct in foreign affairs.

The treaty of Vienna, my Lords, was not produced by the rejection of the Infanta, unleſs a treaty that was made before it could be the conſequence of it; ſo that there was no ſuch opportunity thrown into our hands as the noble Lord has been pleaſed to repreſent. Spain had diſcovered herſelf our enemy, and our enemy in the higheſt degree, before the French provoked her by that inſult; and therefore, how much ſoever ſhe might be enraged againſt France, there was no proſpect that ſhe would favour us, nor could we have courted her alliance without the loweſt degree of meanneſs and diſhonour.

See then, my Lords, this atrocious accuſation founded upon falſe dates, upon a prepoſterous arrangement of occurrences; behold it vaniſh into ſmoke at the approach of truth, and let this inſtance convince us how eaſy it is to form chimerical blunders, and impute groſs follies to the wiſeſt adminiſtration; how eaſy it is to charge others with miſtakes, and how difficult to avoid them.

But we are told, my Lords, that the dangers of the confederacy at Vienna were merely imaginary, that no contract was made to the diſadvantage of our dominions, or of our commerce, and that if the weakneſs of the Spaniards and Germans had contrived ſuch a ſcheme, it would ſoon have been diſcovered by them to be an airy dream, a plan impoſſible to be reduced to execution.

We have been amuſed, my Lords, on this occaſion with great profuſion of mirth and ridicule, and have received the conſolation of hearing that Britain is an iſland, and that an iſland is not to be invaded without ſhips. We have been informed of the nature of the king's territories, and of the natural ſtrength of the fortreſs of Gibraltar; but the noble Lord forgot that though Britain has no dominions on the continent, yet our ſovereign has there a very extenſive country, which, though we are not to make war for the ſake of ſtrengthening or enlarging it, we are ſurely to defend when we have drawn an invaſion upon it.

The

The weaknefs of the Spaniards, my Lords, has been alſo much enlarged upon, but the ſtrength of the Jacobites at home has been paſſed over in ſilence, though it is apparent how eaſily the pretender might have landed here, and with what warmth his cauſe would have been eſpouſed, not only by thoſe whoſe religion avowed and pro-feſſed makes them the enemies of the preſent royal family, but by many whom proſpects of intereſt, the love of novelty, and rage of diſappointment, might have inclined to a change.

That no ſuch.ſtipulations were made by that treaty, that no injury was intended to our commerce, nor any invaſion propoſed in favour of the pretender, are very bold aſſertions, and though they could be ſupported by all the evidence that negatives admit of, yet will not eaſily be believed by your Lordſhips, in oppoſition to the ſolemn aſ-ſurances of his late majeſty. It is evident from this inſtance how much prejudice prevails over argument; they are ready to condemn the right honourable gentleman to whom they give the title of ſole miniſter, upon the ſuffrage of common fame, yet will not acquit him upon the teſtimony of the king himſelf.

But, my Lords, the arguments alleged to prove the improbability of ſuch a confederacy, are ſo weak in themſelves, that they require no ſuch illuſtrious evidence to overbalance them. For upon what are they founded, but upon the impoſſibility of executing ſuch deſigns ?

It is well known, my Lords, how differently different parties conſider the ſame cauſe, the ſame deſigns, and the ſame ſtate of affairs. Every man is partial in favour of his own equity, ſtrength, and ſagacity. Who can ſhew that the ſame falſe opinion of their own power, and of our inteſtine diviſions, which now prompts the Spaniards to contend with us, might not then incite them to invade us, or at leaſt to countenance the attempts of one, whom they are in-duſtriouſly taught to believe the greateſt part of the nation is ready to receive ?

That they might have injured our trade is too evident from our preſent experience, and that they would have ſupported the Oſtend company, which they eſpouſed in an open manner, is undeniable. Nor is it in the leaſt unlikely, that elated with the certain power of doing much miſchief, and with the imaginary proſpects of far greater effects, they might engage in a confederacy, and farther at-tempts againſt us.

I am far from imagining, my Lords, that it was in the power of

the

the Germans and Spaniards united to force the pretender upon us, though we had stood alone against them ; but the impossibility of succeeding in their design was not then so apparent to them as it is at present to us ; they had many reasons to wish, and therefore would not be long without some to believe it practicable ; and it was not the danger but the insult that determined his late majesty to enter into an alliance with France.

War, my Lords, is always to be avoided, if the possessions and reputation of a people can be preserved without it ; it was therefore more eligible to oblige them to lay aside their scheme while it was yet only in idea, than to defeat it in its execution. And an alliance with France effectually restrained the emperor, as our fleets in America reduced the Spaniards to desire peace.

Why we did not seize the cargo of the galleons, has been often asked, and as often such answers have been returned as ought to satisfy any rational examiner. We did not seize them, my Lords, because a larger part belonged to other nations than to the Spaniards, and because the interests of our trade made it convenient not to exasperate the Spaniards, so far as to render a reconciliation very difficult.

In the terms of this reconciliation, my Lords, it is charged upon the ministry, that they were guilty of contributing to the power of the house of Bourbon, by stipulating that Spain, instead of neutral troops, should be introduced into Italy. That those troops were less agreeable to the emperor cannot be denied, but it has already been shewn how little reason we had to consult his satisfaction ; and with regard to the advantages gained by the French and Spaniards in the late war, a very small part of them can be ascribed to six thousand troops.

With as little reason, my Lords, is the charge advanced of neglecting to preserve the balance of Europe, by declining to assist the emperor against the French ; for the intention of the war seems to have been rather revenge than conquest, and the emperor rather exchanged than lost his dominions.

That we declined engaging too far in the affairs of the continent, proceeded, my Lords, from a regard to the trade of the nation, which is not only suspended and interrupted during the time of war, but often thrown into another channel, out of which it is the business of many years to recover it.

Nor have the ministry, my Lords, deviated from their regard to
trade,

trade, in their tranfactions with Spain, which have been the fubject of fo much clamour, and fuch pathetic declamations; they always knew what the nation now feels, that the merchants would fuffer much more from a war than from piracies and depredations, which, however, they were far from fubmitting to, and for which they conftantly made demands of fatisfaction. To thefe demands they received fuch anfwers, as, if they had been fincere, would have left the nation no room to complain; but when it was difcovered that nothing but verbal fatisfaction was to be expected, the fecurity of our trade, and the honour of our country, demanded that war fhould be declared.

The conduct of the war, my Lords, has been frequently the fubject of cenfure; we are told of the inactivity of one fleet, and the imperfect equipment of another, the efcape of our enemies, and the interception of our trading fhips. War, my Lords, is confeffed to be uncertain, and ill fuccefs is not always the confequence of bad meafures: naval wars are by the nature of the element on which they are to be conducted, more uncertain than any other; fo that, though it cannot but be fufpected that the common people will murmur at any difappointment, call every misfortune a crime, and think themfelves betrayed by the miniftry, if Spain is not reduced in a fingle fummer, it might be reafonably hoped, that men enlightened by a long familiarity with the accounts of paft, and inftructed by perfonal experience in national tranfactions, will produce ftronger arguments than want of fuccefs, when they charge the miniftry with mifconduct in war.

But, my Lords, they have not any misfortunes to complain of; nor is the accufation, that we have been defeated ourfelves, but that we have not enough molefted our enemies. Of this, my Lords, it is not eafy to judge at a diftance from the fcene of action, and without a more accurate knowledge of a thoufand minute circumftances, which may promote or retard a naval expedition. It is undoubtedly true, my Lords, that many of our merchant fhips have been taken by the enemy; but it is not certain that they do not murmur equally that they have been obftructed in their commerce, and have been fo little able to interrupt ours, fince they have fo many advantages from the fituation of their coafts. When we reckon thofe that are loft, let us not forget to number thofe that have efcaped. If admiral Vernon's fleet was ill provided with arms and ammunition, even then, let all

cenfure

cenfure be fufpended till it can he proved that it was ill furnifhed by the fault of the miniftry.

Nothing is more common, my Lords, in all naval wars, than fudden changes of fortune; for on many occafions an accidental guft of wind, or unexpected darknefs of the weather, may deftroy or preferve a fleet from deftruction; or may make the moft formidable armaments abfolutely ufelefs: and in the prefent difpofition of fome people towards the miniftry, I fhould not wonder to hear an alteration of wind charged upon them.

For what objections may they not expect, my Lords, when all the difadvantages which the nation fuffers from the enemies of his majefty, are imputed to them; when daily endeavours are ufed to make them fufpected of favouring arbitrary power, for maintaining an army which nothing has made neceffary but the ftruggles of thofe men, whofe principles have no other tendency than to enflave their country. Let not our domeftic animofities he kept alive and fomented by a conftant oppofition to every defign of the adminiftration, nor our foreign enemies incited by the obfervation of our divifions, to treat us with infolence, interrupt our trade, prefcribe bounds to our dominions, and threaten us with invafions, and the army may fafely be difbanded.

For the miniftry, my Lords, are not confcious of having confulted any thing but the happinefs of the nation, and have therefore no apprehenfions of publick refentment, nor want the protection of an armed force. They defire only the fupport of the laws, and to them they willingly appeal from common fame and unequitable charges.

I mention the miniftry, my Lords, becaufe I am unacquainted with any man who either claims or poffeffes the power or title of fole minifter. I own in my province no fuperior but his majefty, and am willing and ready to anfwer any charge which relates to that part of the publick bufinefs which I have had the honour to tranfact or direct.

A great part of what I have now offered was therefore no otherwife neceffary on the prefent occafion, than becaufe filence might have appeared like a confcioufnefs of mifconduct, and have afforded a new fubject of airy triumph to the enemies of the adminiftration; for very few of the tranfactions which have been fo feverely cenfured, fell under the particular infpection of the right honourable gentleman againft whom the motion is levelled; he was not otherwife concerned in counselling or in ratifying, than as one of his majesty's privy council; and therefore though they should be defective, I do not see how it is reasonable or just, that he should be singled out from the rest for disgrace or punishment.

The motion therefore, my Lords, appears to me neither founded on facts nor law, nor reason, nor any better grounds than popular caprice, and private malevolence.

If it is contrary to law to punish without proof, if it is not agreeable to reason that one should be censured for the offences of another, if it is necessary that some crime should be proved, before any man can suffer as a criminal, then, my Lords, I am convinced that your Lordships will be unanimous in rejecting the motion.

The Duke of ARGYLE spoke next, as follows:—My Lords, if we will obstinately shut our eyes against the light of conviction, if we will resolutely admit every degree of evidence that contributes to support the cause which we are inclined to favour, and to reject the plainest proofs when they are produced against it, to reason and debate is to little purpose: as no innocence can be safe that has incurred the displeasure of partial judges, so no criminal that has the happiness of being favoured by them, can ever be in danger.

That any lord has already determined how to vote on the present occasion, far be it from me to assert: may it never, my Lords, be suspected that private interest, blind adherence to a party, personal kindness or malevolence, or any other motive than a sincere and unmingled regard for the prosperity of our country, influences the decisions of this assembly; for it is well known, my Lords, that authority is founded on opinion; when once we lose the esteem of the publick, our votes, while we shall be allowed to give them, will be only empty sounds, to which no other regard will be paid than a standing army shall enforce.

The veneration of the people, my Lords, will not easily be lost: this house has a kind of hereditary claim to their confidence and respect; the great actions of our ancestors are remembered, and contribute to the reputation of their successors; nor do our countrymen willingly suspect that they can be betrayed by the descendants of those, by whose bravery and counsels they have been rescued from destruction.

But esteem must languish, and confidence decline, unless they are renewed and re-animated by new acts of beneficence; and the higher
expectations

expectations the nation may have formed of our penetration to difcover its real advantages, and of our steadinefs to purfue them, the
more violent will be its refentment, if it fhall appear on this important queition, that we are either ignorant or timorous, that we are
unconcerned at the miferies of the people, or content ourfelves with
pitying what our anceftors never failed to redrefs.

Let us therefore, my Lords, for our own intereft, attend impartially to the voice of the people ; let us hear their complaints with
tendernefs, and if at laft we rejeft them, let it be evident that they
were impartially heard, and that we only differed from them becaufe
we were not convinced.

Even then, my Lords, we fhall fuffer for fome time under the
fufpicion of crimes, from which I hope we fhall always be free, the
people will imagine that we were influenced by thofe whofe intereft it appears to continue their miferies, and, my Lords, all the
confolation that will be left us, muft arife from the confcioufnefs of
having done our duty.

But, my Lords, this is to fuppofe what I believe no hiftory can
furnifh an example of, it is to conceive that we may enquire diligently
after the true ftate of national affairs, and yet not difcover it, or not
be able to prove it by fuch evidence as may fatisfy the people.

The people, my Lords, however they are mifreprefented by thofe
who, from a long practice of treating them with difregard, have
learned to think and fpeak of them with contempt, are far from
being eafily deceived, and yet farther from being eafily deceived into
an opinion of their own unhappinefs : we have fome inftances of
general fatisfaction, and an unfhaken affection to the government, in
times when the publick good has not been very diligently confulted,
but fcarce'y any of perpetual murmurs and univerfal difcontent, where
there have been plain evidences of oppreffion, negligence, or treachery.

Let us not therefore, my Lords, think of the people as of a herd
to be led or driven at pleafure, as wretches whofe opinions are
founded upon the authority of feditious fcribblers, or upon any other
than that of reafon and experience ; let us not fuffer them to be at
once oppreffed and ridiculed, nor encourage by our example the
wretched advocates for thofe whom they confider as their enemies,
nor reprefent them as imputing to the mifconduct of the miniftry the
late contrariety of the winds, and feverity of the winter.

The people, my Lords, if they are miftaken in their charge, are
                                                                miftaken

miftaken with fuch evidence on their fide, as never mifled any nation before; not only their reafon but their fenfes muft have betrayed them, and thofe marks of certainty that have hitherto eftablifhed truth, muft have combined in the fupport of falfhood.

They are perfuaded, my Lords, too firmly perfuaded, to yield up their opinions to rhetoric, or to votes, or any proof but demonftration, that there is a *firft*, or to fpeak in the language of the nation, a *fole* minifter, one that has the poffeffion of his fovereign's confidence, and the power of excluding others from his prefence, one that exalts and degrades at his pleafure, and diftributes for his own purpofes the revenues of his mafter, and the treafure of the nation.

Of this, my Lords, can it be maintained that they have no proof? Can this be termed a chimerical fufpicion, which nothing can be produced to fupport? How can power appear but by the exercife of it? What can prove any degree of influence or authority, but univerfal fubmiffion and acknowledgement? And furely, my Lords, a very tranfient furvey of the court and its dependents, muft afford fufficient conviction, that this man is confidered by all that are engaged in the adminiftration, as the only difpofer of honours, favours, and employments.

Attend to any man, my Lords, who has lately been preferred, rewarded, or careffed, you will hear no expreffions of gratitude but to that *man*; no other benefactor is ever heard of, the royal bounty itfelf is forgotten and unmentioned, nor is any return of loyalty, fidelity, or adherence profeffed, but to the minifter; the minifter! a term, which however lately introduced, is now in ufe in every place in the kingdom, except this houfe.

Preferments, my Lords, whether civil, ecclefiaftical, or military, are either wholly in his hands, or thofe who make it the bufinefs of their lives to difcover the high road to promotion, are univerfally deceived, and are daily offering their adorations to an empty phantom that has nothing to beftow; for, no fooner is any man infefted with avarice or ambition, no fooner is extravagance reduced to beg new fupplies from the publick, or wickednefs obliged to feek for fhelter, than this man is applied to, and honour, confcience, and fortune offered at his feet.

Did either thofe whofe ftudies and ftation give them a claim to advancement in the church, or thofe whofe bravery and long fervice entitle them to more honourable pofts in the army; did either thofe

W.10

who profefs to underftand the laws of their own country, or they who declare themfelves verfed in the interefts and tranfactions of foreign powers, apply to any other man for promotion or employment, he might then indeed be called the *chief*, but not properly the *fole* minifter.

But it is well known, my Lords, many of us know it too well, that whatever be the profeffion or the abilities of any perfon, there is no hope of encouragement or reward by any other method than that of application to this man, that he fhall certainly be difappointed who fhall attempt to rife by any other intereft, and whoever fhall dare to depend on his honefty, bravery, diligence, or capacity, or to boaft any other merit than that of implicit adherence to his meafures, fhall inevitably lie neglected and obfcure.

For this reafon, my Lords, every one whofe calmnefs of temper can enable him to fupport the fight, without ftarts of indignation and fallies of contempt, may daily fee at the levy of this great man, what I am afhamed to mention, a mixture of men of all ranks and all profeffions, of men whofe birth and titles ought to exalt them above the meannefs of cringing to a mere child of fortune, men whofe ftudies ought to have taught them, that true honour is only to be gained by fteady virtue, and that all other arts, all the low applications of flattery and fervility will terminate in contempt, difappointment, and remorfe.

This fcene, my Lords, is daily to be viewed, it is oftentatioufly difplayed to the fight of mankind, the minifter amufes himfelf in publick with the fplendour, and number, and dignity of his flaves; and his flaves with no more fhame pay their proftrations to their mafter in the face of day, and boaft of their refolutions to gratify and fupport him. And yet, my Lords, it is enquired why the people affirm that there is a *fole* minifter?

Thofe who deny, my Lords, that there is a *fole* minifter to whom the mifcarriages of the government may juftly be imputed, may eafily perfuade themfelves to believe that there have been no mifcarriages, that all the meafures were neceffary, and well formed, that there is neither poverty nor oppreffion felt in the nation, that our compliance with France was no weaknefs, and that our dread of the treaty of Vienna was not chimerical.

The treaty of Vienna, my Lords, which has been the parent of fo many terrors, confultations, embaffies, and alliances. is, I find, not yet to be acknowledged what it certainly was, a mere phantom, an empty illufion fent by the arts of the French to terrify our miniftry. His late majefty's teftimony is cited to prove that ftipulations were really entered into by the two powers allied by that treaty, to deftroy our trade, fubvert our conftitution, and fet a new king upon the throne, without confent of the nation.

Such improbabilities, my Lords, ought indeed to be proved by a high teftimony, by a teftimony which no man fhall dare to queftion or contradict; for as any man is at liberty to confult his reafon, it will always remonftrate to him, that it is no lefs abfurd to impute the folly of defigning impoffibilities to any powers not remarkable for weak counfels, than unjuft to fufpect princes of intending injuries, to which they have not been incited by any provocation.

But, my Lords, notwithftanding the folemnity with which his late majefty has been introduced, his teftimoy can prove nothing more than that he believed the treaty to be fuch as he reprefents, that he had been deceived into falfe apprehenfions and unneceffary cautions by his own minifters, as they had been impofed upon by the agents of France.

This is all, my Lords, that can be collected from the royal fpeech, and to infer more from it is to fuppofe that the king was himfelf a party in the defigns formed againft him; for if he was not himfelf engaged in this treaty, he could only be informed, by another, of the ftipulations, and could only report what he had been told upon the credit of the informer, a man, neceffarily of very little credit. Thus, my Lords, all the evidence of his late majefty vanifhes into nothing more than the whifper of a fpy.

But as great ftrefs ought doubtlefs to be laid upon intelligence which the nation is believed to purchafe at a very high price, let it be enquired, what proofs thofe have who dare to fufpect the fagacity of our minifters, to put in the balance againft their intelligence, and it will be difcovered, my Lords, that they have a teftimony no lefs than that of the German emperor himfelf, who could not be miftaken with regard to the meaning of the treaty concluded at his own court, and to whom it will not be very decent to deny fuch a degree of veracity as may fet him at leaft on the level with a traytor and a hireling.

If the treaty of Vienna was an impofture, moft of our misfortunes are evidently produced by the weaknefs of the minifter; but even

suppofing

suppofing it real, as it was only a formidable mockery, as a
threat that could never be executed, it was not neceffary, that a
order to obviate it, we fhould give ourfelves implicitly into the hand
of France.

It was not neceffary, my Lords, that we fhould fuffer them fist
to elude the treaty of Utrecht, by making a port at Mardyke, and
then directly and openly to violate it by repairing Dunkirk. That
this latter is a port contrary to treaty, the bills of entry at the Cu-
tom houfe daily fhew; and as the cuftoms are particularly under the
infpection of the commiffioners of the treafury, this man can-
plead ignorance of this infraction, were no information given him
by other means. If it fhould now be afked, my Lords, what in my
opinion ought to be done, I cannot advife that we fhould attempt to
demolifh it by force, or draw upon ourfelves the whole power of
France by a declaration of war, but what it may be difficult now to
remedy, it was once eafy to obviate.

Had we fhewn the fame contempt of the French power with our
anceftors, and the fame fteadinefs in our councils, the fame firenefs
in our alliances, and the fame fpirit in our treaties, that court would
never have ventured to break a known folemn ftipulation, to have
exafperated a brave and determined adverfary by flagrant injuftice,
and to have expofed themfelves to the hazard of a war, in which it
would have been the intereft of every prince of Europe who regarded juftice or pofterity to wifh their defeat.

Now they fee us engaged in a war, my Lords, they may be animated to a more daring contempt of the faith of treaties, and infult us
with yet greater confidence of fuccefs, as they cannot but remark
the cowardice or the ignorance with which we have hitherto carried
on this war. They cannot but obferve that either our minifter meant
in reality to make war rather upon the Britons than the Spaniards, or
that he is totally unacquainted with military affairs, and too vain to
afk the opinion of others who have greater knowledge than himfelf.

Nothing, my Lords, is more apparent than that the minifter was
forced by the continual clamours of the nation to declare war, contrary to his own inclination, and that he always affected to charge it
upon others, and to exempt himfelf from the imputation of it. It
is therefore probable that he has not acted on this occafion fo well
as even his own experience and penetration might, if they were

A 2

neftly employed, enable him to act, and that he has suffered our
counfels to be embarraffed, that he fees with great tranquillity thofe
fuffering by the war, at whofe requeft it was begun, and imagines it a
proof of the excellence of his own fcheme, that thofe who forced
him to break it, may in time repent of their importunities.

For that in the management of the war, my Lords, no regard
has been had either to the advantages which the courfe of our trade
inevitably gives to our enemies, or to the weaknefs to which the extent of their dominions neceffarily fubjects them, that neither the intereft of the merchant has been confulted, nor the eafe of the nation in general regarded, that the treafure of the publick has been
fquandered, and that our military preparations have intimidated no
nation but our own, is evident beyond contradiction.

It is well known, my Lords, to every man but the Minifter, that
we have nothing to fear from either the fleets or armies of the Spaniards, that they cannot invade us except in America, and that they
can only moleft us by intercepting our traders. This they can only
effect by means of their privateers, whofe veffels being light and
active may be eafily fitted out, nimbly feize their prey, and fpeedily
retire.

The experience of the laft French war, my Lords, might have
taught us how much we have to fear from the activity of men incited
by profpects of private gain, and equipped with that care and vigilance, which, however omitted in national affairs, the intereft of
particular men never fails to dictate. It is well known, my Lords,
how much we loft amidft our victories and triumphs, and how fmall
fecurity the merchants received from our magnificent navies, and celebrated commanders. It was therefore furely the part of wife men,
not to mifcarry twice by the fame omiffion, when they had an opportunity to fupply it.

I need not inform your Lordfhips of what every reader of newf-
papers can tell, and which common fenfe muft eafily difcover, that
privateers are only to be fuppreffed by fhips of the fame kind
with their own, which may fcour the feas with rapidity, purfue
them into fhallow water, where great fhips cannot attack them, feize
them as they leave the harbours, or deftroy them upon their own
coafts.

That this is in its own nature at once obvious to be contrived, and
eafy to be done, muft appear upon the bare mention of it, and yet
that

that it has been either treacherouſly neglected, or ignorantly omitted, the accounts of every day have long informed us. Not a week paſſes in which our ſhips are not ſeized, and our ſailors carried into a ſtate of ſlavery. Nor does this happen only on the wide ocean which is too ſpacious to be garriſoned, or upon our enemies coaſts where they may have ſometimes inſuperable advantages, but on our own ſhores, within ſight of our harbours, and in thoſe ſeas of which we vainly ſtile our nation the ſovereign.

Who is there, my Lords, whoſe indignation is not raiſed at ſuch ignominy ? Who is there by whom ſuch negligence will not be reſented ? It cannot be alleged that we had not time to make better preparations ; we had expected war long before we declared it, and if the miniſter was the only man by whom it was not expected, it will make another head of accuſation.

Nor was his diſregard of our dominions leſs flagrant than that of our trade ; it was publickly declared by Don Geraldino, that his maſter would never give up his claim to part of our American colonies, which yet were neither fortified on the frontiers, nor ſupplied with arms, nor enabled to oppoſe an enemy, nor protected againſt him.

One man there is, my Lords, whoſe natural generoſity, contempt of danger, and regard for the publick, prompted him to obviate the deſigns of the Spaniards, and to attack them in their own territories, a man whom by long acquaintance I can confidently affirm to have been equal to his undertaking, and to have learned the art of war by a regular education, who yet miſcarried in his deſign, only for want of ſupplies neceſſary to a poſſibility of ſucceſs.

Nor is there, my Lords, much probability that the forces ſent lately to Vernon will be more ſucceſsful, for this is not a war to be carried on by boys ; the ſtate of the enemies dominions is ſuch, partly by ſituation, and partly by the neglect of that man whoſe conduct we are examining, that to attack them with any proſpect of advantage, will require the judgment of an experienced commander of one who had learned his trade, not in Hyde-Park, but in the field of battle, of one that has been accuſtomed to ſudden exigencies and unſuſpected difficulties, and has learned cautiouſly to form, and readily to vary his ſchemes.

An officer, my Lords, an officer qualified to invade kingdoms is not formed by bluſtering in his quarters, by drinking on birth-nights,

of

or dancing at affemblies; nor even by the more important fervices of regulating elections, and fuppreffing thofe infurrections which are produced by the decay of our manufactures. Many gallant colonels have led out their forces againft women and children, with the exactest order, and fcattered terror over numerous bodies of colliers and weavers, who would find difficulties not very eafily furmountable, were they to force a pafs, or ftorm a fortrefs.

But, my Lords, thofe whom we have deftined for the conqueft of America, have not even flufhed their arms with fuch fervices, nor have learned what is moft neceffary to be learned, the habit of obedience; they are only fuch as the late froft hindered from the exercife of their trades, and forced to feek for bread in the fervice; they have fcarcely had time to learn the common motions of the exercife, or diftinguifh the words of command.

Nor are their officers, my Lords, extremely well qualified to fupply thofe defects, and eftablifh difcipline and order in a body of new raifed forces; for they are abfolutely ftrangers to fervice, and taken from fchool to receive a commiffion, or if tranfplanted from other regiments, have had time only to learn the art of drefs. We have fent foldiers undifciplined, and officers unable to inftruct them, and fit in expectation of conquefts to be made by one boy acting under the direction of another.

To their commander in chief, my Lords, I object nothing but his inexperience, which is by no means to be imputed to his negligence, but his want of opportunities; though of the reft furely it may be faid that they are fuch a fwarm as were never before fent out on military defigns; and, in my opinion, to the other equipments, the government fhould have added provifions for women to nurfe them.

Had my knowledge of war, my Lords, been thought fufficient to have qualified me for the chief command in this expedition, or had my advice been afked with regard to the conduct of it, I fhould willingly have affifted my country with my perfon or my counfels; but, my Lords, this man who engroffes all authority, feems likewife to believe that he is in poffeffion of all knowledge, and that he is equally capable, as he is equally willing, to ufurp the fupreme and uncontroulable direction both of civil and military affairs.

Why new forces were raifed, my Lords, is very eafy to judge; new forces required new commiffions, and new commiffions pro-

duced new dependencies, which might be of use to the minister at
the approaching election ; but why the new-raised troops were sent
on this expedition rather than those which had been longer disciplined, it is very difficult to assign a reason, unless it was considered
that some who had commands in them had likewise seats in the senate,
and the minister was too grateful to expose his friends to danger,
and too prudent to hazard the loss of a single vote. Besides the
commander in chief, there is but one senator in the expedition, and,
my Lords, he is one of too great integrity to be corrupted, and,
though sensible of the weakness of the troops, too brave to quit his
post. How much our country may suffer by such absurd conduct, I
need not explain to your Lordships ; it may easily be conceived how
much one defeat may dispirit the nation, and to what attempts one
victory may excite our enemies, those enemies, whom under a steady
and wise administration, we should terrify into submission, even
without an army.

I cannot forbear to remark on this occasion, how much the ignorance of this man has exposed a very important part of our foreign
dominions to the attempts of the Spaniards. Gibraltar, my Lords, is
well known to be so situated, as to be naturally in very little danger of
an attack from the land, and to command the country to a great
distance ; but these natural advantages are now taken away, or great-
ly lessened by new fortifications, erected within much less than gun-
shot of the place, erected in the sight of the garrison, and while
one of our admirals was cruizing upon the coast.

The pretence, my Lords, upon which they were erected, was,
that though Gibraltar was granted to Britain, yet there was no dis-
trict appendent to it, nor did the British authority extend beyond
the walls of the town: this poor excuse did the chicanery of the
Spaniards invent, and with this, my Lords, was our minister contented, either not knowing or not appearing to know what, I hope,
the children whom we have dispatched to America, have been
taught, and what no man versed in national affairs can be ignorant
of without a crime, that when a fortress is yielded to another nation,
the treaty always virtually includes, even without mentioning it,
an extent of land as far as the guns of the fortification can reach.

Whether this man, my Lords, was so ignorant as to be deceived
thus easily, or so abandoned as willingly to deceive his country, he
is equally unqualified to support the office of first minister, and al-
                                                        most

most equally deserves to be prosecuted by the indignation and justice of this assembly in the severest manner; for how great must be his wickedness who undertakes a charge above his abilities, when his country may be probably ruined by his errors?

Your Lordships cannot but observe, that I make use rather of the term minister than that of the administration, which others are so desirous to substitute in its place, either to elude all enquiry into the management of our affairs, or to cover their own shameful dependence.

Administration, my Lords, appears to me a term without a meaning, a wild indeterminate word, of which none can tell whom it implies, or how widely it may extend : a charge against the administration may be imagined a general censure of every officer in the whole subordination of government, a general accusation of instruments and agents, of masters and slaves ; my charge, my Lords, is against the minister, against that man who is believed by every one in the nation, and known by great numbers, to have the chief, and whenever he pleases to require it, the sole direction of the publick measures, he, to whom all the other ministers owe their elevation, and by whose smile they hold their power, their salaries, and their dignity.

That this appellation is not without sufficient reason bestowed upon that man, I have already proved to your Lordships ; and as it has already been made appear that common fame is a sufficient ground of accusation, it will easily be shewn that this man has a just claim to the title of minister, for if any man be told of an accusation of the minister, he will not ask the name of the person accused.

But there is in the motion one title conferred upon him, to which he has no pretensions ; for there is no law for styling him the first commissioner of the treasury. The commissioners, my Lords, who discharge in a collective capacity the office of lord high treasurer, are constituted by the same patent, invested with equal power and equal dignity, and I know not why this man should be exalted to any superiority over his associates.

If we take, my Lords, a review of our affairs, and examine the state of the nation in all its relations and all its circumstances, we cannot surely conceive that we are in a state of prosperity, unless discontent at home, and scorn abroad, the neglect of our allies, and insolence of our enemies, the decay of trade, and multitude of our imposts, are to be considered as proofs of a prosperous and flourishing nation.

Will it be alleged, my Lords, has this man one friend adventurous enough to assert in open day, that the people are not starving by
thousands, and murmuring by millions, that universal misery does
not overspread the nation, and that this horrid series of calamities
is not universally among all conditions imputed to the conduct of
this man?

That great evils are felt, my Lords, no Briton, I am certain,
who converses promiscuously with his countrymen, will attempt to
dispute, and until some other cause more proportioned to the effect
shall be assigned, I shall join with the publick in their opinion, and
while I think this man the author of our miseries, shall conclude
it necessary to comply with the motion.

Lord HARDWICK spoke next, to the following effect:—My Lords,
though I very readily admit, that crimes ought to be punished, that
a treacherous administration of publick affairs is in a very high degree criminal, that even ignorance, where it is the consequence of
neglect, deserves the severest animadversion, and that it is the privilege and duty of this house to watch over the state of the nation, and
inform his majesty of any errors committed by his ministers; yet I am
far from being convinced either of the justice or necessity of the motion now under consideration.

The most flagrant and invidious part of the charge against the
right honourable gentleman appears to consist in this, that he has
engrossed an exorbitant degree of power, and usurped an unlimited
influence over the whole system of government, that he disposes of
all honours and preferments, and that he is not only *first* but *sole*
minister.

But of this boundless usurpation, my Lords, what proof has been
laid before you? What beyond loud exaggerations, pompous rhetoric,
and specious appeals to common fame; common fame, which at least
may sometimes err, and which, though it may afford sufficient
ground for suspicion and enquiry, was never yet admitted as con-
clusive evidence, where the immediate necessities of the publick did
not preclude the common forms of examination, where the power
of the offender did not make it dangerous to attack him by a legal prosecution, or where the conduct of the accusers did not plainly
discover that they were more eager of blood than of justice, and more
solicitous to destroy than to convict.

I hope none of these circumstances, my Lords, can at present obstruct

ftruct a candid and deliberate enquiry: with regard to the publick, I am not able to difcover any preffing exigences that demand a more compendious method of proceeding, than the eftablifhed laws of the land, and the wifdom of our anceftors have prefcribed. I know not any calamity that will be aggravated, nor any danger that will become more formidable, by fuffering this queftion to be legally tried.

Nor is there, my Lords, in the circumftances of the perfon accufed, any thing that can incite us to a hafty procefs; for if what is alleged by the noble Lords, is not exaggerated beyond the truth, if he is univerfally detefted by the whole nation, and loaded with execrations by the publick voice, if he is confidered as the author of all our miferies, and the fource of all our corruptions, if he has ruined our trade, and depreffed our power, impoverifhed the people and attempted to enflave them, there is at leaft no danger of an infurrection in his favour, or any probability that his party will grow ftronger by delays. For, my Lords, to find friends in adverfity, and affertors in diftrefs, is only the prerogative of innocence and virtue.

The gentleman againft whom this formidable charge is drawn up, is, I think, not fufpected of any intention to have recourfe either to force or flight, he has always appeared willing to be tried by the laws of his country, and to ftand an impartial examination, he neither oppofes nor eludes enquiry, neither flies from juftice, nor defies it.

And yet lefs, my Lords, can I fufpect that thofe by whom he is accufed, act from any motive that may influence them to defire a fentence not fupported by evidence, or conformable to truth; or that they can wifh the ruin of any man whofe crimes are not notorious and flagrant, that they perfecute from private malice, or endeavour to exalt themfelves by the fall of another.

Let us therefore, my Lords, enquire before we determine, and fuffer evidence to precede our fentence. The charge, if it is juft, muft be by its own nature eafily proved, and that no proof is brought, may perhaps be fufficient to make us fufpect that it is not juft.

For, my Lords, what is the evidence of common fame, which has been fo much exalted, and fo confidently produced? Does not every man fee that on fuch occafions two queftions may be afked of which perhaps neither can eafily be anfwered, and which yet muft

N 3   both

both be refolved before common fame can be admitted as a proof of facts.

It is firft to be enquired, my Lords, whether the reports of fame are neceffarily or even probably true ? A queftion very intricate and diffufive, entangled with a thoufand, and involving a thoufand dif-tinctions ; a queftion of which it may be faid, that a man may very plaufibly maintain either fide, and of which perhaps after months or years wafted in difputation, no other decifion can be obtained than what is obvious at the firft view, that they are often true, and often falfe, and, therefore, can only be grounds of enquiry, not reafons of determination.

But if it appear, my Lords, that this oracle cannot be deceived, we are then to enquire after another difficulty, we are to enquire *what is fame ?*

Is fame, my Lords, that fame which cannot err, a report that flies on a fudden through a nation, of which no man can difcover the original, a fudden blaft of rumour, that inflames or intimidates a people, and obtains without authority a general credit ? No man verfed in hiftory can enquire whether fuch reports may not deceive. Is fame rather a fettled opinion prevailing by degrees, and for fome time eftablifhed ? How long then, my Lords, and in what degree muft it have been eftablifhed to obtain undoubted credit, and when does it commence infallible ? If the people are divided in their opi-nions, as in all publick queftions it has hitherto happened, fame is, I fuppofe, the voice of the majority ; for if the two parties are equal in their numbers, fame will be equal ; then how great muft be the majority before it can lay claim to this powerful auxiliary ? And how fhall that majority be numbered ?

Thefe queftions, my Lords, may be thought, perhaps with juf-tice, too ludicrous in this place, but in my opinion they contribute to fhew the precarious and uncertain nature of the evidence fo much confided in.

Common fame, my Lords, is to every man only what he himfelf commonly hears ; and it is in the power of any man's acquaintance to vitiate the evidence which they report, and to ftun him with cla-mours, and terrify him with apprehenfions of miferies never felt and dangers invifible. But without fuch a combination, we are to re-member that moft men affociate with thofe of their own opinions, and

nd that the rank of thofe that compofe this affembly naturally dif-
pofes fuch as are admitted to their company, to relate, or to invent
fuch reports as may be favourably received, fo that what appears to
one Lord the general voice of common fame, may by another be
thought only the murmur of a petty faction, defpicable with regard
to their numbers, and deteflable if we confider their principles.

So difficult is it, my Lords, to form any folid judgment concerning the extent and prevalence of any particular report, and the degree of credit to be given to it. The induftry of a party may fupply
the defect of numbers, and fome concurrent circumftances may contribute to give credit to a falfe report.

But, my Lords, we are ourfelves appealed to as witneffes of the
truth of facts which prove him to be *fole* minifter, of the number
of his dependents, the advancement of his friends, the difappointments of his opponents, and the declarations made by his followers
of adherence and fidelity.

If it fhould be granted, my Lords, that there is nothing in thefe
reprefentations exaggerated beyond the truth, and that nothing is
reprefented in an improper light, what confequence can we draw,
but that the followers of this gentleman, make ufe of thofe arts
which have always been practifed by the candidates of preferment,
that they endeavour to gain their patron's fmile by flattery and panegyric, and to keep it by affiduity and an appearance of gratitude.
And if fuch applications exalted any man to the authority and title
of firft minifter, the nation has never in my memory been without
fome man in that ftation, for there is always fome one to whom ambition and avarice have paid their court, and whofe regards have
been purchafed at the expence of truth.

Nor is it to be wondered at, my Lords, that pofts of honour and
profit have been beftowed upon the friends of the adminiftration ; for
who enriches or exalts his enemies ? Who will encreafe the influence
that is to be exerted againft him, or add ftrength to the blow that is
levelled at himfelf ?

That the right honourable gentleman is the only difpofer of honours has never yet appeared ; it is not pretended, my Lords, that
he diftributes them without the confent of his majefty, nor even that
his recommendation is abfolutely neceffary to the fuccefs of any
man's applications. If he has gained more of his majefty's confidence and efteem than any other of his fervants, he has done only

what

what every man endeavours, and what therefore is not to be imputed
to him as a crime.

It is impossible, my Lords, that kings, like other men, should
not have particular motions of inclination or dislike ; it is possible,
that they may fix their affection upon objects not in the highest degree worthy of their regard, and overlook others that may boast of
greater excellencies and more shining merit, but this is not to be supposed without proof, and the regard of the king, as of any other
man, is one argument of desert more than he can produce, who has
endeavoured after it without effect.

This imputed usurpation must be proved upon him either by his
own confession, or by the evidence of others ; and it has not been yet
pretended that he assumes the title of *prime minister*, or indeed, that
it is applied to him by any but his enemies, and it may easily be conceived how weakly the most uncorrupted innocence would be supported, if all the aspersions of its enemies were to be received as
proofs against it.

Nor does it appear, my Lords, that any other evidence can be
brought against him on this head, or that any man will stand forth
and affirm that either he has been injured himself by this gentleman,
or known any injury done by him to another by the exertion of authority with which he was not lawfully invested ; such evidence, my
Lords, the laws of our country require to be produced before any
man can be punished, censured, or disgraced.   No man is obliged to
prove his innocence, but may call upon his prosecutors to support
their accusation, and why this honourable gentleman, whatever may
have been his conduct, should be treated in a different manner than
any other criminal, I am by no means able to discover.

Though there has been no evidence offered of his guilt, your
Lordships have heard an attestation of his innocence, from the noble
duke who spoke first against the motion, of whom it cannot be suspected that he would, voluntarily, engage to answer for measures
which he pursued in blind compliance with the direction of another.
The same testimony, my Lords, can I produce, and affirm with
equal truth, that in the administration of my province, I am independent, and left entirely to the decisions of my own judgment.

In every government, my Lords, as in every family, some either
by accident or a natural industry, or a superior capacity, or some
other cause, will be engaged in more business, and treated with more
confidence

confidence than others ; but if every man is willing to anfwer for the
conduct of his own province, there is all the fecurity againft corruption that can poffibly be obtained ; for if every man's regard to his
own fafety and reputation will prevent him from betraying his truft or
abufing his power, much more will it incite him to prevent any mifconduct in another for which he muft himfelf be accountable. Men
are ufually fufficiently tenacious of power, and ready to vindicate their
feparate rights, when nothing but their pride is affected by the ufurpation, but furely no man will patiently fuffer his province to be invaded when he may himfelf be ruined by the conduct of the invader.

Thus, my Lords, it appears to me to be not only without proof,
but without probability, and the firft minifter can, in my opinion,
be nothing more than a formidable illufion, which, when one man
thinks he has feen it, he fhews to another as eafily frighted as himfelf, who joins with him in propagating the notion, and in fpreading
terror and refentment over the nation, till at laft the panic becomes
general, and what was at firft only whifpered by malice or prejudice
in the ears of ignorance or credulity, is adopted by common fame,
and echoed back from the people to the fenate.

I have hitherto, my Lords, confined myfelf to the confideration of
one fingle article of this complicated charge, becaufe it appears to
me to be the only part of it neceffary to be examined; for if once
it be acknowledged that the affairs of the nation are tranfacted not
by the minifter but the adminiftration, by the council in which
every man that fits there has an equal voice and equal authority,
the blame or praife of all the meafures muft be transferred from him
to the council, and every man that has advifed or concurred in
them, will deferve the fame cenfure or the fame applaufe; as it is
unjuft to punifh one man for the crimes of another, it is unjuft to
chufe one man out for punifhment from among many others equally
guilty.

But I doubt not, my Lords, when all thofe meafures are equitably
confidered, there will be no punifhment to be dreaded, becaufe neither negligence nor treachery will be difcovered. For, my Lords,
with regard to the treaty of Vienna, let us fuppofe our minifters
deceived by ignorant or corrupt intelligence, let us admit that they
were cautious where there was no danger, and neglected fome opportunities, which, if they had received better information, they
might have improved to the advantage and fecurity of the nation.

What

What have they done even under all these disadvantageous suppositions, but followed the lights which they judged most clear, and by which they hoped to be conducted to honour and to safety?

Policy, my Lords, is very different from prescience, the utmost that can be attained is probability, and that for the most part in a low degree. It is observed that no man is wise but as you take into consideration the weakness of another; a maxim more eminently true of political wisdom, which consists, very often, only in discovering designs which could never be known but by the folly or treachery of those to whom they are trusted. If our enemies were wife enough to keep their own secrets, neither our ministers nor our patriots would be able to know or prevent their designs, nor would it be any reproach to their sagacity, that they did not know what nobody would tell them.

If therefore, my Lords, the princes, whose interest is contrary to our own, have been at any time served by honest and wise men, there was a time when our ministers could act only by conjecture, and might be mistaken without a crime.

If it was always in our power to penetrate into the intentions of our enemies, they must necessarily have the same means of making themselves acquainted with our projects, and yet when any of them are discovered we think it just to impute it to the negligence of the minister.

Thus, my Lords, every man is inclined to judge with prejudice and partiality. When we suffer by the prudence of our enemies, we charge our ministers with want of vigilance, without considering, that very often nothing is necessary to elude the most penetrating sagacity, but obstinate silence.

If we enquire into the transactions of past times, shall we find any man, however renowned for his abilities, not sometimes imposed upon by falsehoods, and sometimes betrayed by his own reasonings into measures destructive of the purposes which he endeavoured to promote? There is no man of whose penetration higher ideas have been justly formed, or who gave more frequent proofs of an uncommon penetration into futurity than Cromwell; and yet succeeding times have sufficiently discovered the weakness of aggrandizing France by depressing Spain, and we wonder now how so much policy could fall into so gross an error, as not rather to suffer power to remain in the distant enemy, than transfer it to another equally divided

from

from us by interest, and far more formidable by the situation of his dominions.

Cromwell, my Lords, suffered himself to be hurried away by the near prospect of present advantages, and the apprehension of present dangers; and every other man has been, in the same manner, sometimes deluded into a preference of a smaller present advantage, to a greater which was more remote.

Let it not be urged, my Lords, that politics are advanced since the time of Cromwell, and that errors which might then be committed by the wisest administration, are now gross and reproachful; we are to remember that every part of policy has been equally improved, and that if more methods of discovery have been struck out, there have been likewise more arts invented of eluding it.

When, therefore, we enquire into the conduct, or examine the abilities of a minister, we are not to expect that he should appear never to have been deceived, but that he should never be found to have neglected any proper means of information, nor ever to have willingly given up the interest of his country ; but we are not to impute to his weakness what is only to be ascribed to the wisdom of those whom he opposed.

If this plea, my Lords, is reasonable, it will be necessary for those who support the motion, to prove, not only that the treaty of Vienna was never made, but that the falshood of the report either was or might have been known by our ministers, otherwise those who are inclined to retain a favourable opinion of their integrity and abilities, may conclude, that they were either not mistaken, or were led into error by such delusions as would no less easily have imposed on their accusers, and that by exalting their enemies to their stations, they shall not much consult the advantage of their country.

This motion, therefore, my Lords, founded upon no acknowledged, no indisputable facts, nor supported by legal evidence ; this motion, which by appealing to common fame, as the ultimate judge of every man's actions, may bring every man's life, or fortune, into danger ; this motion, which condemns without hearing, and decides without examining, I cannot but reject, and hope your Lordships will concur with me.

Lord CARLISLE spoke next, to the following purport:—My Lords, the state of the question before us has, in my opinion, not been rightly apprehended by the noble Lord who spoke last, nor is

the

the innocence or guilt of the minister the chief question before us, because a minister may possibly mean well, and yet be in some particular circumstances unqualified for his station.

He may not only want the degree of knowledge and ability requisite to make his good intentions effectual, but, my Lords, however skilful, sagacious, or diligent, he may be so unfortunate in some parts of his conduct, as to want the esteem and confidence of the people.

That a very able and honest minister may be misinformed by his intelligence, disappointed by his agents, or baffled by other men of equal capacity and integrity with himself, cannot be controverted ; but it must surely be owned likewise, that when this has happened so often, and in cases of such importance, as to deprive him entirely of the regard and affection of the people ; when he is reduced to intrench himself behind his privileges, to employ all the influence of the crown for his own security, and make it his daily endeavour to create new dependencies, he ought to be pitied and discarded.

That this is the state of the minister whose removal is desired by the motion, cannot be denied ; the exaltation of his adherents to places and preferments, the noble lord has been so far from questioning, that he has endeavoured to justify it, and has in plain terms enquired, who would have acted otherwise ?

Every man, my Lords, would have acted otherwise, whose character had not been blasted by general detestation ; every man would have acted otherwise who preferred the publick good to his own continuance in power ; and every man has acted otherwise who has distinguished himself as a friend to the publick.

It is the interest of the nation, my Lords, that every office should be filled by that man who is most capable of discharging it, whatever may be his sentiments with regard to the minister ; and that his attention should be confined to his employment rather than distracted by various concerns and opposite relations. It is therefore an injury to the publick, to thrust a skilful commissioner into the senate, or to embarrass an industrious senator with a post or commission.

Yet, my Lords, that multitudes have obtained places, who have no acquaintance with the duties of their offices, nor any other pretentions to them, than that they have seats in the other house, and that by distinguishing himself in that assembly, any man may most eafily obtain the preferments of the crown, is too obvious for controverfy.

This practice, my Lords, is a fufficient foundation for the motion ; a practice fo injurious to the nation, fo long continued, and fo openly avowed, requires to be vigoroufly oppofed, left it fhould become eftablifhed by long cuftom, and entangle itfelf with our conftitution.

If the minifter, my Lords, has made it neceffary to employ none but his adherents and blind followers, this neceffity is alone a fufficient proof how little he confides in his own prudence or integrity, how apprehenfive he is of the cenfure of the fenate, and how defirous of continuing his authority, by avoiding it. And furely, my Lords, it is our duty, as well as our right, to addrefs the throne, that a minifter fhould be removed who fears the people, fince few men fear without hating, and nothing fo much contributes to make any man an enemy to his country, as the confcioufnefs that he is univerfally abhorred.

But, my Lords, if this is done by him without neceffity, if the general preference of his friends is only the confequence of miftaken judgment, or corrupt gratitude, this addrefs is equally neceffary, becaufe the effects are equally pernicious.

When a minifter fufpected of ill intentions is continued in employment, difcontent muft naturally fpread over the nation ; and if the end of government be the happinefs of the people ; if fufpicion and jealoufy be contrary to a ftate of happinefs ; and if this fufpicion which generally prevails, this difcontent which fills the whole nation, can only be appeafed by the removal of the minifter ; prudence, juftice, and the examples of our anceftors, ought to influence us to endeavour that the affairs of the nation may be transferred to fuch whofe greater integrity or wifdom has recommended them to the affection of the people.

In this motion, therefore, we need not be fuppofed to imply that the minifter is either ignorant or corrupt, but that he is difliked by the people, difliked to fuch a degree, my Lords, that it is not fafe for his majefty to employ him.

It is doubtlefs our duty, my Lords, to guard both the rights of the people, and the prerogatives of the throne, and with equal ardour to remonftrate to his majefty the diftreffes of his fubjects, and his own danger. We are to hold the balance of the conftitution, and neither to fuffer the regal power to be overborne by a torrent of popular

fury,

fury, nor the people to be oppreffed by an illegal exertion of authority, or the more infupportable hardfhips of unreafonable laws.

By this motion, my Lords, the happinefs of the people, and the fecurity of his majefty, are at once confulted, nor can we fupprefs fo general a clamour, without failing equally in our duty to both.

To what, my Lords, is the untimely end of fo many kings and emperors to be imputed, but to the cowardice or treachery of their counfellors, of thofe to whom they trufted that intercourfe, which is always to be preferved between a monarch and his people ? Were kings honeftly informed of the opinions and difpofitions of their fub-jects, they would never, or at leaft rarely perfift in fuch meafures, as by exafperating the people, tend neceffarily to endanger themfelves.

It is the happinefs of a Britifh monarch, that he has a ftanding and hereditary council, compofed of men who do not owe their ad-vancement to the fmiles of caprice, or the intrigues of a court, who are therefore, neither under the influence of a falfe gratitude, nor of a fervile dependence, and who may convey to the throne the fentiments of the people, without danger, and without fear. But, my Lords, if we are either too negligent, or too timorous to do our duty, how is the condition of our fovereign more fafe, or more happy than that of an emperor of Turkey, who is often ignorant of any complaints made againft the adminiftration, till he hears the people thundering at the gates of his palace.

Let us therefore, my Lords, whatever may be our opinion of the conduct of the minifter, inform his majefty of the difcontent of his fubjects, fince whether it is juft or not, the danger is the fame, and whenever any danger threatens the king, we ought either to enable him to oppofe, or caution him to avoid it.

Lord CHOLMONDELLY fpoke next, to the following effect :— My Lords, I cannot but obferve in this debate an ambition of po-pularity, in my opinion not very confiftent with the freedom of de-bate, and the dignity of this affembly, which ought to be influenced by no other motive than the force of reafon and truth.

It has been a common method of eluding the efficacy of arguments to charge the opponent with blind adherence to intereft, or corrupt compliance with the directions of a court ; nor has it been lefs frequent to prevent enquiries into publick meafures, by reprefenting them as the clamours of faction, the murmurs of difobedience, and the pre-lude to rebellion.

So

So neceſſary, my Lords, has it been always thought to be unin-
fluenced in our examinations by dependence or intereſt, that the moſt
irrefragable reaſons have loſt the power of conviction by the condition and characters of thoſe by whom they were produced, and ſo
much is it expected from innocence and juſtice to deſpiſe all foreign
aſſiſtance, and to ſtand the teſt of enquiry without aſking the ſupport of power, that every man has been concluded guilty that has
fled for ſhelter to the throne.

And ſurely, my Lords, if that man's ſuffrage is of little weight
who appears determined to ſubſcribe to the dictates of a miniſter, no
greater credit can be aſſigned to another who profeſſes himſelf only
the echo of the clamours of the populace. If it be a proof of
a weak cauſe, and conſciouſneſs of miſconduct to apply to the
crown for ſecurity and protection, it may be accounted an acknowledgement of the inſufficiency of arguments, when the people is called in to ſecond them, and they are only to expect ſucceſs
from the violence of multitudes.

That all government is inſtituted for the happineſs of the people,
that their intereſt ought to be the chief care of the legiſlature, that
their complaints ought patiently to be heard, and their grievances
ſpeedily redreſſed, are truths well known, generally acknowledged,
and I hope always predominant in the mind of every Lord in this
aſſembly. But, that the people cannot err, that the voice of fame
is to be regarded as an oracle, and every murmur of diſcontent to
be pacified by a change of meaſures, I have never before heard, or
heard it only to diſregard it.

True tenderneſs for the people, my Lords, is to conſult their advantage, to protect their liberty, and to preſerve their virtue ; and
perhaps examples may be found ſufficient to inform us that all theſe
effects are often to be produced by means not generally agreeable to
the publick.

It is poſſible, my Lords, for a very ſmall part of the people to
form juſt ideas of the motives of tranſactions and the tendency of
laws. All negotiations with foreign powers are neceſſarily complicated with many different intereſts, and varied by innumerable
circumſtances, influenced by ſudden exigencies, and defeated by
unavoidable accidents. Laws have reſpect to remote conſequences,
and involve a multitude of relations which it requires long ſtudy to
diſcover. And how difficult it is to judge of political conduct, or

legiſlative

legiſlative proceedings, may be eaſily diſcovered by obſerving how often the moſt ſkilful ſtateſmen are miſtaken, and how frequently the laws require to be amended.

If then, my Lords, the people judge for themſelves on theſe ſubjects, they muſt neceſſarily determine without knowledge of the queſtions, and their deciſions are then of ſmall authority. If they receive implicitly the dictates of others, and blindly adopt the opinions of thoſe who have gained their favour and eſteem, their applauſes and complaints are with reſpect to themſelves empty ſounds, which they utter as the organs of their leaders. Nor are the deſires of the people gratified, when their petitions are granted ; nor their grievances overlooked, when their murmurs are neglected.

As it is no reproach to the people, that they cannot be the proper judges of the conduct of the government, ſo neither are they to be cenſured when they complain of injuries not real, and tremble at the apprehenſion of ſeverities unintended. Unjuſt complaints, my Lords, and unreaſonable apprehenſions, are to be imputed to thoſe who court their regard only to deceive them, and exalt themſelves to reputation by reſcuing them from grievances that were never felt, and averting dangers that were never near.

He only who makes the happineſs of the people his endeavour, loves them with a true affection and a rational tenderneſs, and he certainly conſults their happineſs who contributes to ſtill all groundleſs clamours, and appeaſe all uſeleſs apprehenſions, who employs his care not only to preſerve their quiet and their liberty, but to ſecure them from the fear of loſing it, who not only promotes the means of happineſs, but enables them to enjoy it.

Thus it appears, my Lords, that it is poſſible to be a friend at the ſame time to the people and the adminiſtration, and that no man can more deſerve their confidence and applauſe, than he that diſſipates their uſeleſs terrors, and contributes to reconcile them to a good government.

That moſt of the clamours againſt the preſent government ariſe from calumnies and miſrepreſentations, is apparent from the ſanction of the ſenate, which has been given to all the meaſures that are charged as crimes upon the adminiſtration.

That the army is ſupported by the conſent of the ſenate, that the ſenate has approved the convention, and that our taxes are all impoſed and continued by the ſenate, cannot be denied. What then is
demanded

demanded by thofe that cenfure the conduct of publick affairs, but that their opinion fhould be confidered as an overbalance to the wifdom of the fenate, that no man fhould be allowed to fpeak but as they dictate, nor to vote but as they fhall influence them by their rhetoric or example?

To repeat the particular topicks of accufation, and recapitulate the arguments which have been produced to confute it, would be a tedious and unneceffary labour; unneceffary becaufe it is well known that they once had the power of convincing this houfe, and that nothing has fince happened to leffen their force, and becaufe many of them now have been already repeated by the noble lords that have oppofed the motion.

To fearch far backward for paft errors, and to take advantage of later difcoveries in cenfuring the conduct of any minifter, is in a high degree difingenuous and cruel; it is an art which may be eafily practifed, of perplexing any queftion, by connecting diftant facts, and entangling one period of time with another.

The only candid method of enquiry is to recur back to the ftate of affairs, as it then appeared, to confider what was openly declared, and what was kept impenetrably fecret, what was difcoverable by human fagacity, and what was beyond the reach of the moft piercing politician.

With regard to the Hanover treaty, it is not, my Lords, requifite that we fhould engage ourfelves in a very minute examination; for it was not only not tranfacted by the right honourable gentleman whofe behaviour is the fubject of this debate, but cannot be proved to have been known by him till it was formally ratified. If he afterwards approved it either in the council or the fenate, he cannot juftly, how deftructive or ridiculous foever that treaty may be thought, be charged with more than his fhare of the guilt, the bare guilt of a fingle vote.

But there is one accufation yet more malicious, an accufation not only of crimes which this gentleman did not commit, but which have not yet been committed, an accufation formed by prying into futurity, and exaggerating misfortunes which are yet to come, and which may probably be prevented. Well may any man, my Lords, think himfelf in danger, when he hears himfelf charged not with high crimes and mifdemeanors, not with accumulative treafon, but with mifconduct of publick affairs, paft, prefent, and future.

The only charge against this gentleman, which seems to relate more to him than to any other man engaged in the administration, is the continuance of the harbour of Dunkirk, which, says the noble duke, he must be acquainted with as commissioner of the treasury; but if the title of first commissioner be denied, if his authority be but the same with that of his associates, whence comes it, my Lords, that he is more particularly accused than they? Why is his guilt supposed greater if his power is only equal?

But, my Lords, I believe it will appear, that no guilt has been contracted on this account, and that Dunkirk was always intended, even by those that demanded the demolition of it, to continue a harbour for small trading vessels, and that if larger ever arrived from thence, they lay at a distance from the shore, and were loaded by small vessels from the town.

With regard to other affairs, my Lords, they were all transacted by the council, not by his direction, but with his concurrence, and how it is consistent with justice to single him out for censure, I must desire the noble Lords to shew who approve the motion.

If the people, my Lords, have been, by misrepresentations industriously propagated, exasperated against him, if the general voice of the nation condemns him, we ought more cautiously to examine his conduct, lest we should add strength to prejudice too powerful already, and instead of reforming the errors, and regulating the heat of the people, inflame their discontent and propagate sedition.

The utmost claim of the people is to be admitted as accusers, and sometimes as evidence, but they have no right to sit as judges, and to make us the executioners of their sentence; and as this gentleman has yet been only condemned by those who have not the opportunities of examining his conduct, nor the right of judging him, I cannot agree to give him up to punishment.

Lord HALIFAX spoke next in substance as follows :—My Lords, though I do not conceive the people infallible, yet I believe that in questions like this they are seldom in the wrong, for this is a question not of argument but of fact; of fact discoverable, not by long deductions and accurate ratiocinations, but by the common powers of seeing and feeling.

That it is difficult to know the motives of negotiations, and the effects of laws, and that it requires long study and intense meditation to discover remote consequences, is indubitably true. And, with re-

gard

gard to the people in general, it cannot be denied, that neither their education qualifies them, nor their employments allow them to be much verfed in fuch enquiries.

But, my Lords, to refer effects to their proper caufes, and to obferve, when confequences break forth, from whence they proceed, is no fuch arduous tafk. The people of the loweft clafs may eafily feel that they are more miferable this year than the laft, and may enquire and difcover the reafon of the aggravation of their mifery; they may know that the army is encreafed, or our trade diminifhed, that the taxes are heavier, and penal laws become more grievous.

Nor is it lefs eafy for them to difcover that thefe calamities are not brought upon them by the immediate hand of heaven, or the irrefiftible force of natural caufes: that their towns are not ruined by an invafion, nor their trade confined by a peftilence; they may then eafily collect that they are only unhappy by the mifconduct of their governors, they may affign their infelicity to that caufe, as the only remaining caufe that is adequate to the effect.

If it be granted, my Lords, that they may be miftaken in their reafoning, it muft be owned that they are not miftaken without probabilities on their fide: it is probable that the miniftry muft injure the publick intereft when it decays without any other vifible caufe; it is ftill more probable, when it appears that among thofe whofe ftation enables them to enter into national enquiries, every man imputes their calamities to the minifter, who is not vifibly dependent on his favour. It becomes more probable yet when it appears that it is the great bufinefs of the minifter to multiply dependencies, to lift accomplices, and to corrupt his judges.

At leaft, my Lords, if it be granted, which furely cannot be denied, that the people may be fenfible of their own miferies, it is their part to declare their fufferings, and to apply to this houfe for relief, and it is our bufinefs to difcover the authors of them, and bring them to punifhment.

That the people are very loud and importunate in their complaints, is daily evident, nor is it lefs apparent that their complaints are juft; if therefore their miferies muft have an author, let the defenders of this gentleman point out the man whom they may more properly accufe.

But,

But, my Lords, nothing is more evident, than that the crimes and the criminal are equally known, that there is one man predominant in his majesty's councils, and that it has long been the practice of that man at once to oppress and ridicule the people, to plunder them, and set them at defiance.

Nothing is more known than that this man pretends to a superior knowledge, and exerts a superior power in the management of the publick revenues, and that they have been so ill managed for many years, that the expences of peace have been almost equal to those of a most vigorous and extensive war.

Nothing is more probable than that most of the foreign negotiations are conducted by his direction, nor more certain than that they have generally tended only to make us contemptible.

That the excise was projected in his own head, that it was recommended by him upon his own conviction, and pressed upon the legislature by his influence, cannot be questioned; and if this were his only crime, if this were the only scheme of oppression that ever he planned out, it is such a declaration of war upon the publick liberty, such an attack of our natural and constitutional rights as was never perhaps pardoned by any nation.

Nor is it less notorious that the late infamous convention was transacted by one of his own dependents, that he palliated or concealed the losses of our merchants, that he opposed the declaration of war, and has since obstructed its operations.

On this occasion, my Lords, it may be useful to remark the apparent partiality of this gentleman's vindicators, who declare that measures are not to be censured as imprudent, only because they are unsuccessful, and yet when other instances of his conduct fall under our examination, think it a sufficient defence to exclaim against the unreasonableness of judging before the event.

To deny that in the conduct both of civil and military affairs he has obtained, I know not by what means, an authority superior to that of any other man, an authority irresistible, uncontroulable, and regal, is to oppose not only common fame, but daily experience. If as commissioner of the treasury he has no more power than any of his associates, whence is it, that to oppose or censure him, to doubt of his infallibility, to suspect his integrity, or to obstruct his influence, is a crime punished with no lighter penalty than forfeiture of employ-

ment,

ment, as appears, my Lords, from the late difmiffion of a gentleman, againft whom nothing can be alleged but an obftinate independence and open difregard of this arbitrary minifter.

But happy would it be, my Lords, for this nation, if he endeavoured not to extend his authority beyond the treafury or the court;
if he would content himfelf with tyrannizing over thofe whofe ac-
ceptance of falaries and preferments has already fubjected them to his
command, without attempting to influence elections, or to direct the
members of the other houfe.

How much the influence of the crown has operated upon all publick councils fince the advancement of this gentleman, how zealoufly
it has been fupported, and how induftrioufly extended, is unneceffary
to explain, fince what is feen or felt by almoft every man in
the kingdom cannot reafonably be fuppofed unknown to your
Lordfhips.

Nothing can be more contrary to the true notion of the Britifh conftitution, than to imagine, that by fuch meafures his majefty's real
intereft is advanced. The true intereft, my Lords, of every monarch, is to pleafe the people, and the only way of pleafing Britons, is to preferve their liberties, their reputation, and their commerce. Every attempt to extend the power of the crown beyond
the limits prefcribed by our laws, muft in effect make it weaker,
by diverting the only fource of its ftrength, the affection of his
fubjects.

It is, therefore, my opinion, my Lords, that we ought to agree to
this motion, as a ftanding memorial not only of our regard for the
nation, but of our adherence to our fovereign; that his councils may
be no longer influenced by that man whofe pernicious advice, and
unjuftifiable conduct, has added new hopes and new ftrength to his
enemies, impoverifhed and exafperated his fubjects, inflamed the
difcontent of the feditious, and almoft alienated the affection of the
loyal.

The Bifhop of SALISBURY fpoke next, to the following purport:
—My Lords, after all the exaggerations of the errors, and all the
reprefentations of the mal-conduct of the right honourable gentleman, after the moft affecting rhetoric, and the moft acute enquiries,
nothing has appeared of weight fufficient to prevail with me to agree
to the prefent motion, a motion, if not of an unprecedented, yet
or a very extraordinary kind, which may extend in its confe-

quences to futurity, and be perhaps more dangerous to innocence than guilt.

I cannot yet difcover any proof fufficient to convict him of having ufurped the authority of *firſt* miniſter, or any other power than that accidental influence which every man has, whofe addrefs or fervices have procured him the favour of his fovereign.

The ufurpation, my Lords, of regal power muſt be made evident by fomewhat more than general aſſertions, muſt appear from fome publick act like that of one of the prelates left regent of the kingdom by Richard the firſt, who as foon as the king was gone too far to return, in the firſt elevations of his heart, began his new authority by imprifoning his colleague.

To charge this gentleman with the difmiſſion of any of his colleagues, can, after the ſtrongeſt aggravations, rife no higher than to an accufation of having adviſed his majeſty to difmifs him, and even that, my Lords, ſtands at prefent unfupported by evidence, nor could it, however uncontellably proved, difcover either wickednefs or weaknefs, or ſhew any other authority than every man would exercife, if he were able to attain it.

If he had difcharged this gentleman by his own authority, if he had tranfacted fingly any great affair to the difadvantage of the publick, if he had impofed either upon the king or the fenate by falfe reprefentations, if he had fet the laws at defiance, and openly trampled on our conftitution, and if by thefe practices he had exalted himſelf above the reach of a legal profecution, it had been worthy of the dignity of this houfe, to have over-leaped the common boundaries of cuftom, to have neglected the ſtanding rules of procedure, and to have brought fo contemptuous and powerful an offender to a level with the reſt of his fellow-fubjects by expeditious and vigorous methods, to have repreffed his arrogance, broken his power, and overwhelmed him at once by the refiftlefs weight of an unanimous cenfure.

But, my Lords, we have in the prefent cafe no provocations from crimes either openly avowed, or evidently proved ; and certainly no incitement from neceffity to exert the power of the houfe in any extraordinary method of profecution. We may punish whenever we can convict, and convict whenever we can obtain evidence; let us not therefore condemn any man unheard, nor punish any man uncondemned.

The Duke of BEDFORD fpoke next, in fubſtance as follows:—

My

My Lords, it is eafy to charge the moft blamelefs and gentle proce-dure with injuftice and feverity, but it is not eafy to fupport fuch an accufation without confounding meafures widely different and dif-guifing the nature of things with fallacious mifreprefentations.

Nothing is more evident than that neither condemnation nor pu-nifhment is intended by the motion before us, which is only to re-move from power a man who has no other claim to it than the will of his mafter, and who, as he had not been injured by never obtain-ing it, cannot juftly complain that it is taken from him.

The motion, my Lords, is fo far from inflicting punifhment, that it confers rewards, it leaves him in the poffeffion of immenfe wealth, however accumulated, and enables him to leave that office in fe-curity, from which moft of his predeceffors have been precipitated by national refentment, or fenatorial profecution.

There is no cenfure, my Lords, made of his conduct, no charge of weaknefs or fufpicion of difhonefty, nor can any thing be equitably inferred from it, than that in the opinion of this houfe his majefty may probably be ferved by fome other perfon, more to the fatisfaction of the Britifh nation.

Though it is not juft to punifh any man without examination, or to cenfure his conduct merely becaufe it has been unpleafing or un-fuccefsful; though it is not reafonable that any man fhould forfeit what he poffeffes in his own right, without a crime, yet it is juft to withdraw favours only to confer them on another more deferving; it is juft in any man to withhold his own, only to preferve his right, or obviate an injurious prefcription, and it is therefore juft to advife fuch a conduct whenever it appears neceffary to thofe who have the right of offering advice.

To advife his majefty, my Lords, is not only our right but our duty; we are not only juftifiable in practifing, but criminal in neglecting it. That we fhould declare our apprehenfions of any impending danger, and our difapprobation of publick mifconduct, is expected both by our fovereign and the people, and let us not by omitting fuch warnings lull the nation and our fovereign into a dangerous fecurity, and from tendernefs to one man prolong or en-creafe the miferies of our country, and endanger or deftroy the ho-nour of our fovereign.

Lord HERVEY fpoke next, in effect as follows:—My Lords, this is furely a day deftined by the noble Lords who defend the motion,

for

for the fupport of paradoxical affertions, for the exercife of their penetration, and oftentation of their rhetoric; they have attempted to maintain the certainty of common fame in oppofition to daily obfervation; the exiftence of a fole minifter in contradiction to the ftrongeft evidence; and having by thefe gradations arrived at the higheft degree of controverfial temerity, are endeavouring to make it appear, that the publick cenfure of the houfe of Lords is no punifhment.

If we take the liberty, my Lords, of ufing known words in a new fenfe, in a meaning referved to ourfelves only, it will indeed be difficult to confute, as it will be impoffible to underftand us; but if punifhment be now to be underftood as implying the fame idea which has hitherto been conveyed by it, it will not be eafy to fhew that a man thus publickly cenfured is not feverely punifhed, and, if his crimes are not clearly proved, punifhed in oppofition to law, to reafon, and to juftice.

It has been hitherto imagined, my Lords, that no punifhment is heavier than that of infamy, and fhame has, by generous minds, been avoided at the hazard of every other mifery. That fuch a cenfure as is propofed by the motion, muft irreparably deftroy the reputation of the perfon againft whom it is directed, that it muft confirm the reports of his enemies, impair the efteem of his friends, mark him out to all Europe as unworthy of his fovereign's favour, and reprefent him to lateft pofterity as an enemy to his country, is indifputably certain.

Thefe, my Lords, are the evident confequences of the addrefs moved for by the noble lord; and, if fuch confequences are not proved, it will be no longer in our power to enforce our laws by fanctions of terror.

To condemn a man unheard is an open and flagrant violation of the firft law of juftice, but it is ftill a wider deviation from it to punifh a man unaccufed; no crime has been charged upon this gentleman proportioned to the penalty propofed by the motion, and the charge that has been produced is deftitute of proof.

Let us therefore, my Lords, reverence the great laws of reafon and juftice, let us preferve our high character and prerogative of judges, without defcending to the low province of accufers and executioners; let us fo far regard our reputation, our liberty, and our pofterity, as to reject the motion.

Several

Several other lords fpoke in this debate, which lafted eleven hours; at length the queftion was put, and on a divifion carried in the negative. Content 59. Not content 108.

After the determination of the foregoing queftion, the duke of MARLBOROUGH rofe up and fpoke as follows :—

My Lords, though your patience muft undoubtedly be wearied by the unufual length of this day's debate, a debate protracted in my opinion, not by the difficulty of the queftion, but by the obftinacy of prejudice, the ardour of paffion, and the defire of victory ; yet I doubt not but the regard which this affembly has always paid to the fafety and happinefs of the ftate, will incline you to fupport the fatigue of attention a little longer, and to hear with your ufual impartiality another motion.

The propofition which I am about to lay down, my Lords, is not fuch as can admit of controverfy ; it is fuch a ftanding principle as was always acknowledged even by thofe who have deviated from it. Such a known truth as never was denied, though it appears fometimes to have been forgotten.

But, my Lords, as it never can be forgotten without injury to particular perfons, and danger to the ftate in general, it cannot be too frequently recollected, or too firmly eftablifhed ; it ought not only to be tacitly admitted, but publickly declared, fince no man's fortune, liberty, or life, can be fafe, where his judges fhall think themfelves at liberty to act upon any other principle. I therefore move, " That any attempt to inflict any kind of punifhment on any perfon without allowing him an opportunity to make his defence, or without any proof of any crime or mifdemeanor committed by him, is contrary to natural juftice, the fundamental laws of this realm, and the ancient eftablifhed ufage of fenate, and is a high infringement of liberties of the fubject."

He was feconded by the Duke of DEVONSHIRE :—My Lords, though the motion made by the noble duke is of fuch a kind, that no oppofition can be expected or feared, yet I rife up to fecond it, left it fhould be imagined that what cannot be rejected, is yet unwillingly admitted.

That where this maxim is not allowed and adhered to, rights and liberties are empty founds, is uncontestably evident ; if this principle be forfaken, guilt and innocence are equally fecure, all caution is vain, and all teftimony ufelefs. Caprice will in our courts

fupply

supply the place of reason, and all evidence must give way to malice, or to favour.

I hope, therefore, my Lords, that your regard to justice, to truth, and to your own safety, will influence you to confirm this great and self-evident principle by a standing resolution, that may not only restrain oppression in the present age, but direct the judiciary proceedings of our successors.

Lord LOVEL rose next, and spoke as follows :—My Lords, liberty and justice must always support each other, they can never long flourish apart, every temporary expedient that can be contrived to preserve or enlarge liberty by means arbitrary and oppressive, forms a precedent which may in time be made use of to violate or destroy it. Liberty is in effect suspended, whenever injustice is practised, for what is liberty, my Lords, but the power of doing right without fear, without controul, and without danger.

But, my Lords, if any man may be condemned unheard, if judgment may precede evidence, what safety, or what confidence can integrity afford? It is in vain that any man means well, and acts prudently, it is even in vain that he can prove the justice and prudence of his conduct.

By liberty, my Lords, can never be meant the privilege of doing wrong without being accountable, because liberty is always spoken of as happiness, or one of the means to happiness, and happiness and virtue cannot be separated. The great use of liberty must therefore be to preserve justice from violation, justice the great publick virtue, by which a kind of equality is diffused over the whole society, by which wealth is restrained from oppression, and inferiority preserved from servitude.

Liberty, general liberty, must imply general justice; for wherever any part of a state can be unjust with impunity, the rest are slaves. That to condemn any man unheard is oppressive and unjust, is beyond controversy demonstrable, and that no such power is claimed by your Lordships will, I hope, appear from your resolutions.

Lord GOWER spoke next :—My Lords, to the principle laid down by these noble lords, I have no objection, and concur with them in hoping that all our proceedings will contribute to establish it ; but why it should be confirmed by a formal resolution, why the house should solemnly declare their assent to a maxim which it

would

would be madnefs to deny, it is beyond my penetration to difcover.

Though the noble lord's pofition cannot be controverted, yet his
motion, if it is defigned to imply any cenfure of the proceedings
of this day, may reafonably be rejected, and that fome cenfure
is intended, we may conjecture, becaufe no other reafon can be
given why it was not made at fome other time.

Lord HALIFAX then rofe:—My Lords, that a cenfure is intended,
will, I fuppofe, not be denied, and that fuch a cenfure is unjuft
muft doubtlefs be the opinion of all thofe who are fuppofed to have
incurred it, and it will therefore not be wondered that the motion
is oppofed by them, as indecent and calumnious: late as it is, my
Lords, I will not for my part fuffer fuch an indignity without oppofition, and fhall think my confcience and my honour require, that
I fhould not be overborne by perfeverance or by numbers, but that I
fhould, if I cannot convince the noble lords by argument, of the
impropriety of the motion, record my reafons againft it, which
may perhaps be more candidly received by pofterity.

Lord TALBOT fpoke to this effect:—My Lords, it is not without
indignation that I hear a motion fo injurious to my own honour,
and to that of the noble lords who have concurred with me in the
laft debate, nor without contempt that I obferved the motion confounded with the pofitions contained in it, the low fubtility of fuch
conduct is no lefs to be defpifed than the malice to be abhorred.

Fifty nine lords are here branded as ftrangers or enemies to the
firft principle of judicial equity, for doing what will entitle them to
the general applaufe of every man in the kingdom that has the full
poffeffion of his underftanding or the free ufe of his fenfes, of every
man that can diftinguifh truth or feel oppreffion.

They have endeavoured to refcue their country from the rapine of
penfioners and the tyranny of an army, from perpetual taxes, and
ufelefs expences; they have attempted to expofe the errors of arrogant ignorance, and to deprefs the power of greatnefs founded on
corruption and fwelling beyond legal reftraints.

That for fuch attempts they are vilified and reproached, is not
to be obferved without indignation and aftonifhment; aftonifhment
which nothing could abate but the recollection of the fituation of
thofe lords who have united to promote fo unjuft a cenfure.

Let us, my Lords, confider the circumftances of the three noble
lords

lords by whom this motion has been made and supported, let us take a view of their conduct, and confider the vifible motives to which it may be afcribed, their places, their dependence——

Lord CHOLMONDELEY fpoke next in fubftance as follows :—My Lords, I rife thus abruptly to preferve that order and decency which is effential to publick councils, and particularly fuitable to the dignity of this affembly, which can only become a fcene of tumult and confufion by fuch methods of debate, and lofe that refpect which it has hitherto preferved, not only by the juftice of its determinations, but by the folemn grandeur of its procedure.

The motion, my Lords, is allowed to contain nothing but what every man avows in fpeculation, and obferves, or ought to obferve, in publick tranfactions, and yet thofe that offer and fupport it are reprefented as abettors of oppreffion, and inftruments of tyranny.

It is furely wonderful, my Lords, that thofe who are follicitous for the prefervation of their own honour, and fo diligent to obviate the moft remote reflection that may glance upon it, fhould not remember, that the fame delicacy may raife in others the fame refentment, when their reputation is openly attacked; and that while they are afferting the right of the minority to an exemption from cenfure, they fhall not allow the greater number at leaft an equal claim to the fame privilege.

Lord TALBOT then refumed :—My Lords, whether any thing has efcaped from me that deferves fuch fevere animadverfions, your Lordfhips muft decide. For what I might intend to fay, fince by the laft eruption of that noble lord I was hindered from proceeding, I hope I fhall not be accountable.

Not that I acknowledge myfelf to have afferted any thing either contrary to law, or to the privileges of the houfe, or inconfiftent with the character of an independent lord, a character which I fhall always endeavour to preferve, and which I will not forfeit for the fmiles of a court, the dignity of high employment, or the affluence of a penfion.

Nor, my Lords, whenever the neceffities of my country require that I fhould fpeak my fentiments with freedom, will I be awed into filence and fubmiffion, but will fet any power at defiance that fhall dare to reftrain me.

I pretend not, my Lords, to be always in the right, I claim no other merit than that of meaning well, and when I am convinced,

after

after proper examination, that I am engaged on the side of truth, I will trample on that insolence that shall command me to suppress my sentiments.

When I reflect, my Lords, on the distresses of my country, when I observe the security and arrogance of those whom I consider as the authors of the publick miseries, I cannot always contain my resentment; I may perhaps sometimes start out into unbecoming transports, and speak in terms not very ceremonious of such abandoned, such detestable ———But as this is, perhaps, not the language of the house, I shall endeavour to repress it, and hope that the bounds of decency have never been so far transgressed by me that I should be exposed to the censure of your Lordships.

Lord ABINGDON next rose and said: —My Lords, the present motion is undoubtedly just, but by no means necessary, or particularly adapted to the present time. It contains a general principle, uncontested, and established; a principle which this assembly has never denied, and from which I know not that it has ever departed.

As there is therefore no particular necessity of confirming it by a new resolution, and as the present time seems less proper than any other, I cannot but declare my opinion, that to resume it at some other time will be more prudent, than to give the lords who think their conduct censured any occasion of resentment or discontent.

Lord CARTERET spoke to the following effect:—My Lords, the maxim laid down in the present motion, is in itself incontestable, and so far from any inconsistency with the former, that as there was no reason for making, there is in my opinion none for opposing it; as it may at any time be made, it may at any time be properly passed. And I hope that our unanimity on this occasion will shew that truth, however unseasonably advanced, will in this house, be always received.

But, lest the noble lords who have opposed the motion should think their honour engaged in continuing the opposition, I take the liberty, my Lords, to move that the previous question may be put.

Other lords spoke on each side; at last the previous question was put by the president, who demanded, ' Is it your Lordships pleasure, that the question be now put? Those lords who are for it, say Content: those who are against it say, Not content.' There was accordingly a cry of both; after which the president

, dent

dent declared, ' the contents have it ; and some lords replying
' the non contents have it,' his lordship said ' the non contents must go below the bar ;' which is the manner of dividing
the house.   Those who remained being told in their seats, and
those who went out being told at coming in again, there were
Content 81,   Not content 54 :
So that the resolution moved for, passed without a division.

HOUSE   OF   COMMONS.

February 24, 1740-1.

Lord TYRCONNELL *made a motion for bringing in a bill for the better
cleansing and paving the streets of Westminster, and the liberties
thereof : in support of which motion he spoke to the following purpose :* —

SIR, though the grievance which I am about to lay before the house
is not of the most formidable or dangerous kind, yet as it is such as
grows every day greater, and such as every day endangers the lives of
thousands, I hope it will not be thought useless or improper to propose it to the consideration of this assembly, to offer my thoughts on
the methods by which it may be most easily removed, and to endeavour to incite others to the same considerations.

It is impossible, Sir, to come to this assembly, or to return from it without observations on the present condition of the streets of Westminster ;
observations forced upon every man, however inattentive, or however engrossed by reflections of a different kind.

The warmest zeal for publick happiness, the most anxious vigilance
against general dangers, must I believe sometimes give way to objects
immediate, though of less importance, nor will the most public spirited
senators deny, that they have often been in the streets alarmed with
obstructions, or shocked with nuisances.

The filth, Sir, of some parts of the town, and the inequality and
ruggedness of others, cannot but in the eyes of foreigners disgrace
our nation, and incline them to imagine us a people, not only without delicacy, but without government, a herd of barbarians, or a
colony of hottentots.

The

The moft difgufting part of the character given by travellers, of the moft favage nations, is their neglect or cleanlinefs, of which perhaps no part of the world affords more proofs, than the ftreets of the Britifh capital ; a city famous for wealth, and commerce, and plenty, and for every other kind of civility and politenefs, but which abounds with fuch heaps of filth, as a favage would look on with amazement.

If that be allowed which is generally believed, that putrefaction and ftench are the caufes of peftilential diftempers ; the removal of this grievance may be preffed from motives of far greater weight than thofe of delicacy and pleafure, and I might folicit the timely care of this affembly for the prefervation of innumerable multitudes, and intreat thofe, who are watching againft flight misfortunes, to unite their endeavours with mine, to avert the greateft and moft dreadful of calamities.

Not to dwell, Sir, upon dangers, which may perhaps be thought only imaginary, I hope that it will be at leaft confidered, how much the prefent neglect of the pavement is detrimental to every carriage, whether of trade or pleafure, or convenience, and that thofe who have allowed fo much of their attention to petitions, relating to the roads of the kingdom, the repair of fome of which is almoft every feffion thought of importance fufficient to produce debates in this houfe, will not think the ftreets of the capital alone unworthy of their regard.

That the prefent neglect of cleanfing and paving the ftreets is fuch as ought not to be borne, that the paffenger is every where either furprifed and endangered by unexpected chafms, or offended or obftructed by mountains of filth, is well known to every one that has paffed a fingle day in this great city ; and that this grievance is without remedy is a fufficient proof that no magiftrate has at prefent power to remove it ; for every man's private regard to his own eafe and fafety, would incite him to exert his authority on this occafion.

I humbly propofe, therefore, that a bill may be brought into the houfe, to enable his majefty's juftices of peace for the liberties of Weftminfter, to infpect the publick ways of this city; and punifh the neglect of cleanfing and paving them ; or that a new officer be appointed, and vefted with full authority for the fame purpofe.

Mr.

Mr. SANDYS spoke next to this effect:——Sir, I believe the grievance, so much complained of by the right honourable member, is not difficult to be removed without a new act of the legislature, being perhaps more properly to be imputed to the negligence of the justices, than a defect of their authority; for they have already sufficient power to regulate this disorder: and I may be allowed to hope, Sir, that they do not want leisure to observe it, for their number is so great, that if we suppose them to be wholly engaged by the common business of their office, a foreigner would have occasion of reproaching us with defects more important than want of delicacy, and might justly censure us as a people corrupt beyond the common rate of human wickedness, a nation divided only into two classes, magistrates and criminals.

But they in reality abound so much among us, that most of them are only nominal magistrates, vested with authority which they never exert, or exert to bad purposes, and which it were well if they were obliged to employ in the real service of their country, by superintending the paviours and the scavengers.

For this reason it is unnecessary to erect a new officer, as an inspector of our streets, since every office that is not necessary is pernicious. Were the consequences of this grievance such as they have been represented I should perhaps willingly erect a new office, though I should not be surprised to hear the wisest man declare rather for a pestilence than an increase of officers.

As I neither think the grievance insupportable, nor the methods proposed for removing it necessary or proper, I declare myself against the motion.

Lord GAGE spoke in the following manner:—Sir, as the grievance cannot be denied to be real, and the motion therefore may reasonably be imagined to have been made without any other intention than of benefiting the publick by an useful law, I cannot discover any sufficient reason for a rejection so peremptory and contemptuous.

That every man is disgusted, and almost every man daily endangered in our streets, has not been denied; nor will any man, I suppose, question what, if he has not yet experienced it, he may perhaps be fully convinced of, in his next visit or excursion.

Those evils, which every man feels, though slight, are worthy of the attention of the legislature, and that danger that threatens multitudes,

titudes, though diftant, ought to be averted ; for a fmall diforder, like a fmall expence, when it extends to multitudes, becomes a national affair.

But though this motion may perhaps be liable to fome objections, there is certainly no fuch abfurdity to be found in it, as may juftify us in rejecting it without examination : to reject a motion when it is firft offered, is a proof of prejudice, next to that of rejecting it unheard ; it is to determine a queftion, before it is difcuffed or can be fully underftood.

Mr. SANDYS replied in fubftance as follows :—Sir, I cannot but differ very widely in opinion from the right honourable member that fpoke laft, with regard to the propriety of oppofing a motion when it is firft made ; a practice, which I can by no means think inconfiftent with either decency or prudence, and which would perhaps be of ufe to the publick, if it was more frequent.

When any motion is made, it is fubjected to the confideration of this affembly, and every member is at full liberty to examine and difcufs it. If it appears to deferve farther attention, it may be admitted, but if the fubject be either improper or unfeafonable, or the meafures propofed injudicious or dangerous, it is then to be rejected, and if it is at laft to be rejected, it is apparent that no time ought to be thrown away upon it.

The hours, and days, and weeks, that have been unprofitably fpent upon bills which after all our endeavours could not be paffed ; the delays of real benefits to the publick, which have been produced by long purfuits of fhadowy advantages, have inclined me to a more expeditious method of proceeding, and determined me fpeedily to reject what I cannot hope to amend.

The queftion being put, paffed in the negative, 142 againft 109.

HOUSE OF COMMONS.

February 27, 1740-1.

THE bill being read, Sir JOHN BARNARD spoke thus:—Sir, there
cannot be brought before this house any questions more difficult in
themselves, more entangled with a multiplicity of relations, or more
perplexed with an endless diversity of circumstances, than those
which relate to commercial affairs; affairs on which the most experienced often disagree, and on which the most sagacious may deceive
themselves with erroneous conjectures.

There are no questions, Sir, which require so much personal knowledge of the subject to which they relate, nor is there any subject
with which so few gentlemen in this house have had opportunities of
being acquainted. There are no questions, Sir, which their variety
of relations to different persons exposes to be so easily misrepresented
without detection, nor any in which the opposition of particular interests so much incites a false representation. In all these cases, deceit is easy, and there is a strong temptation to deceive.

Nor are these questions, Sir, always perplexed by intentional
fraud, or false assertions, of which they that utter them are themselves
conscious.

Those who deceive us, do not always suppress any truth of which
they are convinced, or set facts before us in any other light, than that
in which themselves behold them; they for the most part err with an
honest intention, and propagate no mistakes but those which they
have themselves admitted.

Of this kind, Sir, are doubtless the measures proposed in the bill
before us, which those by whom they are promoted may easily
think to be of benefit to the publick, but which, I believe, will
appear the result of imperfect views, and partial consideration.

The great and fundamental error, Sir, of the patrons of this bill,
seems to be an opinion that the practice of insuring is not known to
other nations, nor can be carried on in any other place, and from
this principle they deduce consequences, which, if they were inevitably

tably certain, might eafily influence us to an immediate approbation of the bill, as neceffary to fecure our commerce, and diftrefs our enemies.

They conclude, Sir, with fufficient juftnefs, that very few merchants would hazard their fortunes in long voyages or diftant commerce, or expofe themfelves to the dangers of war, without fecurity which infurances afford them, and having perfuaded themfelves that fuch fecurity is to be obtained from no other nation, they imagine that we might, by prohibiting it, confine all the foreign veffels in their ports, and deftroy by one refolution the trade of both our rivals and our enemies.

That our Eaft India company may defire the ratification of this bill, I cannot deny, becaufe they might perhaps receive from it fome temporary advantage by the fhort inconveniencies which thofe whom they confider as the enemies of their commerce would feel from it. They may defire it, becaufe the experiment, if it fails, as it muft, cannot injure them ; and if it fucceeds, may produce great advantages to them: they may wifh it, becaufe they will feel the immediate benefit, and the detriment will fall upon others.

I fhall not enquire whether our merchants are inclined to look with malevolence on all thofe who cultivate the fame branches of commerce with themfelves, though they have neither the violation of natural rights, nor the infringement of national treaties, to complain of. I fhould be unwilling to fufpect a Britifh merchant, whofe acquaintance with the conftitution of his own country ought to fhew him the value of liberty, who ought to be above narrow fchemes, by the knowledge which his profeffion enables him to gain, of a defire to encroach upon the rights of others, or to engrofs the general benefits of nature; and fhall only obferve, that feveral other nations can plead a claim to the Eaft India trade, a claim of equal validity with our own; that the Danes have their fettlement there, and that the Portuguefe difcovered the way to thofe regions of wealth, from which fome perhaps are inclined to exclude them.

But nothing is more vain than to attempt to exclude them by refufing to enfure their fhips, becaufe the opinion that they can be infured by no other nation is entirely without foundation. There are at this time offices of infurance along the whole coafts of the Midland fea, among the Dutch, and even among the French. Nothing can debar any nation from the trade of infurance but the want

of

of money, and that money is not wanted by foreigners for this purpose, appears from the great sums which they have depofited in our funds.

That this trade is now carried on chiefly by this nation, though not folely, is inconteftible, but what can be inferred from that, but that we ought not to obftruct our own gain; that we ought not to make a law to deprive ourfelves of that advantage of which either favourable accidents or our own fagacity have put us in poffeffion.

For this reafon it appears that it would not contribute to the wealth of the publick to debar us from infuring the fhips even of thofe with whom we are at war, for it is always to be remembered that they will receive no detriment from fuch prohibitions, nor will feel any other confequence from them than a neceffity of transferring to fome other nation the profit which we receive from it.

What the profit is which arifes to the nation from the trade of infurance it is not poffible exactly to determine, but that the trade is really advantageous may be reafonably conceived, becaufe after many years experience it is diligently followed, and a law was never neceffary to prohibit the purfuit of a bufinefs by which nothing was to be gained. But could the gain of the infurer be a doubtful point, there is a certain advantage to the nation by the money paid for commiffion, brokerage, ftamps, and the credit of the premium depofited here.

I might add, Sir, another confiderable fum yearly arifing to the government from the additional letters, occafioned by this trade, which encreafe the revenues of the poft-office, without any deduction for additional charge.

That the lofs of this profit, and the gain of infuring, will enfue upon the ratification of this bill, cannot be denied; nor does it appear, that this lofs will be counterbalanced by any advantage that will be gained over our rivals or our enemies.

Whether this bill, Sir, would produce to the merchants of that city by which it is promoted, the advantages which they expect from it, or remove any of the grievances of which they complain, I am not able pofitively to determine; but know, that it is not uncommon for merchants, as well as other men, to confound private with publick grievances, and to imagine their own intereft the intereft of the nation.

With regard, Sir, to the practice of infuring, *intereft or no intereft*, as the term is, when an imaginary value is put upon the fhip or cargo,

cargo, often much above its real worth, it cannot be denied, that some opportunities may be given by it for wicked practices. But there will always be circumstances in which there can be no security against frauds, but common faith; nor do I see how we can secure the insurers against the possibility of being defrauded.

I cannot indeed discover, Sir, how this method of insuring can be prevented; for how can the value of a cargo be estimated, which is to be collected in a long voyage, at different ports, and where the success of the adventurers often depends upon lucky accidents, which are indeed always hoped for, but seldom happen. An imaginary value must therefore be fixed upon, when the ship leaves the port; because the success of that voyage cannot be foreknown, and the contracting parties may be safely trusted to set that value, without any law to direct or restrain them.

If the merchants are oppressed by any peculiar inconveniences, and can find means of redressing them without injuring the publick commerce, any proposal for that purpose ought to be favourably received; but as the bill now before us proposes general restraints, and proposes to remove grievances, which are not felt, by remedies, which those, upon whom they are to operate, do not approve, I think it ought not to be referred to a committee, but rejected.

Mr. SOUTHWELL spoke next in terms to this purpose':—Sir, when I first proposed this bill to the house, I lamented the absence of that honourable gentleman, from whose discussions and arguments I expected great information; and for whose judgment, in all commercial questions, I have the highest esteem, as his penetration not only enables him to discover the consequences of methods which have not yet been tried, but as his extensive acquaintance with many branches of trade, cannot but have informed him of the success of many expedients tried, as well in other nations as our own, for the advancement of it.

Trade, Sir, is a subject, of which it has been justly observed, that very few gentlemen have attained knowledge sufficient to qualify themselves to judge of the propriety of any new regulation; and I cannot but confess, that I have no uncommon skill in these questions. What I have to offer on this occasion, has been suggested to me, not so much by my own observations, as by the intelligence which I have very industriously sought, and by which, as I endea-

voured

voured to enquire of thofe whofe opinion was leaft likely to be perverted by their intereft, I hope I have not been mifled.

The merchants, Sir, to whom it has been my fortune to apply,
have generally concurred in the opinion that the prefent practice of
infuring is prejudicial to our commerce, nor have I found any
difagreement between my conftituents and the traders of this great
metropolis.

I am unwilling to imagine that there can be any evil, for which
the wifdom of this affembly cannot difcover a remedy, and am therefore of opinion, that if the grievance is real, fome expedient may
be difcovered for removing it ; and that it is real, I cannot but be
convinced by the declarations of fo many men, who can have no intereft in complaining when they fuffer nothing, and whofe known
abilities exempt them from the fufpicion of imputing any part of
their uneafinefs to a caufe which cannot produce it.

The bill before us, Sir, requires, in my opinion, fome amendments, and in its prefent ftate might, perhaps, produce more detriment than advantage ; but fince it is neceffary at leaft to attempt
fomething for the relief of men fo ufeful to this nation, it appears
to me neceffary to form a committee, and to deliberate on this fubject with more attention.

Mr. LOCKWOOD fpoke next to the following effect:—Sir, though
I am not of opinion that the bill in its prefent ftate ought to be
paffed into a law, yet I am far from thinking it fo imperfect as not
eafily to be amended, and, therefore, am defirous that it fhould be
confidered in a committee.

I have not, indeed, Sir, often obferved, that bills injudicioufly
drawn up at firft have received great improvements from a fecond confideration, and have found it more eafy to form a new bill, than to
make alterations in one that is laid before us, for fome original error
will commonly remain, and the fentiments of different men purfuing different views, can feldom be modelled into one confiftent
fcheme. But I am far from confidering this bill as one of thofe
that cannot be amended, for I can difcover but few objections to
the regulations propofed in it, and thofe not relating to any of the
effential parts, but flight and circumftantial, fuch as will eafily be
removed, or perhaps anfwered.

The grievance, Sir, for which this bill propofes a remedy, is fo
generally known, and fo univerfally lamented, that, I believe,
                                                         there

there is not any thing more worthy of the attention of the legiſlature than an enquiry into the cauſe of it, and the proper method of redreſſing it.

In our enquiry into the cauſes of this obſtruction of trade, I am of opinion, Sir, that the practice of inſuring, *intereſt or no intereſt*, will appear to be the foundation of this general uneaſineſs, it will be found a practice of ſo natural a tendency to fraud, and ſo eaſily ſuſceptible of diſhoneſt artifices, that I believe, every member of this houſe will deſire its ſuppreſſion.

To confirm my aſſertion, Sir, and illuſtrate the queſtion before us, I ſhall mention ſome particular inſtances of fraud to which this cuſtom has given occaſion, of fraud ſo evident and ſo deteſtable that it cannot be related without indignation.

The Royal George was a large ſhip belonging to the South-ſea company, which having been a voyage to Vera Cruz, put in at Jamaica in her return; and being there refitted to proceed on her voyage homewards, ſet ſail, and came within a week's ſailing of the port, when upon a ſudden the officers entered into a conſultation, and determined to go back a month's voyage to Antigua, for what reaſon, Sir, may eaſily be gueſſed, when it was told that a ſhip was inſured upon a ſuppoſed value of ſixty thouſand pounds.

This reſolution, Sir, was no ſooner formed, than orders were given to change the courſe and ſteer to Antigua, in oppoſition to all the remonſtrances of the carpenter, who is the proper judge of the condition of a veſſel, and who declared with honeſty and reſolution againſt their whole procedure. But they purſued their new ſcheme without any regard to his murmurs or aſſertions, and when they arrived at Antigua, found ſome method of influencing the officers of that iſland to declare the ſhip unfit for the proſecution of the voyage.

Their deſign, Sir, was now happily compleated. To confirm the determination which had been pronounced in their favour, they ſtranded the ſhip upon a bank of ſand, forced out the iron that grapples the timber together, and having firſt taken away the maſts and rigging, and whatever elſe could be uſed or ſold, threw the ballaſt to each end, and ſo broke the veſſel in the middle.

By this well-contrived ſhipwreck, having as they imagined raiſed their fortunes, they came home triumphantly from their proſperous voyage, and claimed the money for which the ſhip was inſured.

The

The infurers ftartled at a demand fo unexpected, enquired into the affair with all the induftry which its importance might naturally incite, and after fome confultation determined to try whether the fhip might not be refitted and brought to Britain.

In purfuance of this refolution, they fent workmen and materials, and without much expence, or any difficulty, brought it hither.

I believe, Sir, this relation is fufficient at once to prove the practice, and explain the nature of the frauds to which this method of infurance gives occafion; but as the frequency of them is fuch, that many inftances may be produced, I fhall offer another fhort narrative of the fame kind.

A fhip that belonged to the Eaft India company, infured after this method, was run afhore by the captain, in fuch a manner that he imagined none but himfelf able to recover it, and therefore, though it coft five thoufand pounds, fold it for five hundred, but the purchafer, no lefs expert than the captain, found means very fpeedily to difengage it, to reftore it to a proper condition with little expence, and was much enriched by his fortunate bargain.

I cannot but obferve, Sir, that this kind of fraud is more formidable, as it may be practifed without a poffibility of detection: had the captain, inftead of ftranding, deftroyed his veffel, how could his wickednefs ever have been difcovered; or how could the South-fea company's fhip have been brought home, had it been funk in fome diftant corner of the world.

This practice, Sir, and the frauds which it has occafioned, and the fufpicions which the eafy practice of frauds always creates, have produced fo many trials, and filled the courts of juftice with fuch intricate contentions, that the judges, who know perhaps nothing of this practice but from its effects, have often declared it to be fo pregnant with contefts and cheats, that it ought not to be fuffered, and that a law for fuppreffing it would much contribute to the eftablifhment of peace, and the fecurity of property.

I am not infenfible, Sir, of the force of the argument made ufe of by the honourable gentleman who fpoke in favour of this practice, and cannot but allow it that regard which his reafonings always deferve; it is the ftrongeft, and perhaps the only argument, that can be produced. His affertion of the impoffibility of eftimating the real value of a fhip, or of foreknowing the fuccefs of a voyage, is inconteftible; but perhaps it will follow from thence, not that an imagi-

nary

nary value ought to be admitted, but that no infurance ought to be allowed, where there is no rational method of afcertaining it; or at leaft that all fuch infurance ought to be rather below the probable value, than above it.

If the grievance complained of has been proved not to be imaginary, we ought doubtlefs to confult how it may be remedied; nor do I believe that our confultations will be ineffectual, if we engage in them, not with an intention to perplex, but to inform each other. I am of opinion, Sir, that the importance of the queftion requires a committee; nor can I difcover any effential defect in the bill, which fhould hinder it from paffing into a law.

Mr. BURRELL fpoke to this effect:—Sir, I am convinced by experience, as well as reafon, that fo many inconveniencies arife from this method of infurance, that it affords fo many opportunities of fraud, and gives fuch encouragement to negligence, that I fhall willingly concur in any meafures that may effectually fupprefs it.

It is, Sir, too well known to require proof, that intereft is the parent of diligence, and that men attend to the performance of their duty, in proportion as they muft fuffer by the neglect of it; and therefore every practice that deprives honefty of its reward, is injurious to the publick.

But that this is the confequence of eftimating fhips at an imaginary value in the offices of infurance, is to the higheft degree evident. When a fhip is eftimated above its real value, how will the commander fuffer by a wreck, or what fhall reftrain him from deftroying his veffel, when it may be done with fecurity to himfelf, except that integrity which indeed ought to be generally diffufed, but which is not always to be found, and to which few men think it fafe to truft upon occafions of far lefs importance.

To fhew, Sir, that I do not indulge groundlefs fufpicions, or magnify the bare poffibility of fraud into reality; that I do not blacken human nature, or propofe laws againft wickednefs that has not yet exifted; it may be proper to mention fome letters, in which I have been informed by my correfpondent at Leghorn, of the ftate of the fhips which have arrived there; fhips fo weakly mann'd, and fo penurioufly or negligently ftored, fo much decayed in the bottoms and fo ill fitted with rigging, that he declares his aftonifhment at their arrival.

It may deferve our confideration, Sir, whether the fuccefs of the
Spanifh

Spanish privateers may not be in great part attributed to this pernicious practice; whether captains, when their vessels are insured for more than their value, do not rashly venture into known danger? Whether they do not wilfully miss the security of convoys? Whether they do not direct their courses where privateers may most securely cruize? Whether they do not surrender with less resistance than interest would excite? And whether they do not raise clamours against the government for their ill success, to avoid the suspicion of negligence or fraud?

That other frauds are committed in the practice of insuring, is well known to the honourable gentleman: it is a common practice to take money upon bottomree, by way of pledge, for the captain's fidelity, and to destroy this security by insuring above the real value; so that the captain may gain by neglecting the care of his vessel, or at least secure himself from loss, and indulge his ease or his pleasure without any interruption from the fear of diminishing his fortune.

The whole practice of insurance, Sir, is in its present state, I believe, so perplexed with frauds, and of such manifest tendency to the obstruction of commerce, that it absolutely requires some legal regulations.

Sir JOHN BARNARD then spoke to this purpose:—Of frauds in the practice of insurance, with regard to which the honourable gentleman has appealed to me, I can confidently affirm that I am totally ignorant: I know not of any fraudulent practices openly carried on, or established by custom, which I suppose are meant: for with regard to single acts of fraud, committed by particular men, it is not to be supposed but that they have been detected in this, as in all other branches of traffic: nor can I conceive that any argument can be drawn from them against the practice; for if every part of commerce is to be prohibited, which has furnished villains with opportunities of deceit, we shall contract trade into a narrow compass.

With regard, Sir, to the instance of the Royal George, though the proceedings of the officers are not wholly to be vindicated, yet part of their conduct is less inexplicable than it has been represented. Their return to Antigua when they were bound for Britain, and were within a week's sailing of their port, is easily to be defended, if the wind was contrary to their intended course; for it is not difficult to conceive that they might reach a distant port with a favourable
able

able wind, much fooner than one much nearer, with the wind againſt them.

I have always obſerved, Sir, that the gentlemen engaged in the trade to the Eaſt-Indies, aſſume an air of ſuperiority, to which I know not what claim they can produce, and ſeem to imagine, that their charter gives them more extenſive knowledge, and more acute ſagacity, than falls to the lot of men not combined in their aſſociation.

But however theſe gentlemen may diſapprove my arguments, and however they may miſrepreſent them, I ſhall be ſatisfied, that they will have with the diſintereſted and impartial their juſt weight, and that this affair will not be haſtily determined upon an imperfect examination.

Sir ROBERT WALPOLE replied to this effect:—Whether the merchants are ſatisfied with the preſent methods of inſuring, or what is the opinion of any ſeparate body of men, I think it abſolutely unneceſſary to enquire. We are conſtituted for the publick advantage, and are engaged by our ſenatorial character to conſider, not the private intereſt of particular men, but the general advantage of our country.

In our purſuit, Sir, of national intereſt, we ſhall be obliged frequently to oppoſe the ſchemes which private men or ſeparate fraternities have formed for their own advantage, and which they may be expected to defend with all their art ; both becauſe every man is unwilling to imagine that the publick intereſt and his own are oppoſite, and becauſe it is to be feared, that many may conſider the publick only in ſubordination to themſelves, and be very little ſollicitous about the general proſperity of their country, provided none of the calamities which afflict it extend their influence to themſelves.

We are in the diſcuſſion of this queſtion, Sir, to conſider that we are engaged in a war againſt a nation from which inſults, depredations, oppreſſions, and cruelties, have been long complained of, and againſt which we are therefore to act with a reſolution proportioned to the injuries which we have ſuffered, and to our deſire of vengeance. We are to practiſe every method of diſtreſſing them, and to promote the ſucceſs of our arms even at the expence of preſent gain, and the intereſt of private men.

It is well known, Sir, to all who have either heard or read of the Spaniards, that they live in careleſſneſs and indolence, neglect all

the

the natural advantages of their own country, defpife the gain of foreign commerce, and depend wholly on their American fettlements, for all the conveniencies, and perhaps for moft of the neceffaries of life.

This is the particular circumftance that makes a war with Britain fo much to be dreaded by them. A nation fuperior to them by fea holds them befieged, like a garrifon furrounded by an army, precludes them from fupplies, intercepts their fuccours, and if it cannot force their walls by attack, can at leaft by a blockade ftarve them to a capitulation.

Thus, Sir, by a naval war with an enemy of fuperior ftrength, they muft at length be fubdued, and fubdued perhaps without a battle, and without the poffibility of refiftance ; againft fuch an enemy their courage or their difcipline is of no ufe ; they may form armies indeed, but which can only ftand upon the fhore, to defend what their enemies have no intention of invading, and fee thofe fhips feized in which their pay is treafured, or their provifions are ftored.

Such, Sir, is our natural fuperiority over the Spaniards, a fpecies of fuperiority that muft inevitably prevail, if it be not defeated by our own folly, and furely a more effectual method of defeating it, the Spaniards themfelves could not have difcovered, than that of infuring their fhips among our merchants.

When a fhip thus infured is taken, which notwithftanding all precautions muft fometimes happen, we examine the cargo, find it extremely valuable, and triumph in our fuccefs ; we not only count the gain to ourfelves, but the lofs to our enemies, and determine that a fmall number of fuch captures will reduce them to offer us peace upon our own terms.

Such are the conclufions which are made, and made with reafon, by men unacquainted with the fecret practices of our merchants, and who do not fufpect us to be ftupid enough to fecure our enemies againft ourfelves ; but it is often found upon a more clofe examination, that our fhips of war have only plundered our merchants, and that our privateers may indeed have enriched themfelves, but impoverifhed their country. It is difcovered that the lofs of the Spaniards is to be repaid, and perhaps fometimes with intereft, by the Britifh infurers.

If it be urged, that we ought not to enact any laws which may obftruct the gain of our fellow fubjects, may it not be afked, why all trade with Spain is prohibited, may not the trade be equally gain-

ful with the infurance, and may not the gain be more generally diftributed, and therefore be more properly national ?

But this trade was prohibited, becaufe it was more neceffary to
our enemies than to ourfelves ; it was prohibited, becaufe the laws
of war require, that a lefs evil fhould be fuffered to inflict a greater ;
it is upon this principle that every battle is fought, aud that we fire
our own fhips to confume the navies of the enemy.

For this reafon, Sir, it appears to me evident beyond contradiction,
that the infurance of Spanifh fhips ought to be prohibited : we
fhall indeed lofe the profit of the infurance, but we fhall be reim-
burfed by the captures, which is an argument that cannot be produced for the prohibition of commerce.

It is urged, Sir, that they may infure their fhips in other countries,
an affertion of which, whether it be true or not, I am not able to
decide ; but it is acknowledged, that the neceffity of eftablifhing
new correfpondence will be at leaft a temporary obftruction of their
trade, and an obftruction of even a fhort continuance may lay them
at our mercy.

But let us, Sir, reflect upon the weaknefs of this argument, *they
muft be allowed to infure here, becaufe they may infure in other places;*
will it not be equally juft to urge, that *they muft trade with us,
becaufe they may trade with other nations ?* And may it not be
anfwered, that though we cannot wholly fufpend their commerce, it
is yet our bufinefs to obftruct it as far as we are able ?

May it not, Sir, be farther affirmed, that by infuring in other nations, they may injure their allies by falling into our hands, but do
not the lefs benefit us ? that if they do not grow weaker, we at leaft
are ftrengthened ; but that by infuring among us, whatever fteps are
taken, the equilibrium of the war is preferved always the fame ?

It is afferted, and.I fuppofe with truth, that we infure at a lower
rate than others, and it will therefore follow, that the Spaniards,
whenever their fhips fhall efcape us, will fuffer more by having infured
amongft foreigners, than if they had contracted with our merchants.

Thus it appears, Sir, that there are ftronger reafons for prohibiting the infurance of Spanifh fhips, than for putting a ftop to our
commerce with them; and that whether their fhips are taken by us,
or efcape us, it is the general intereft of the nation, that they fhall be
infured by foreign merchants.

With refpect, Sir, to the Eaft India company, I have no regard to their interest, considered as distinct from that of the rest of the nation; nor have received any solicitations from them to promote this bill, or to espouse their interest, but cannot, without concealing my real sentiments, deny that as they have the grant of an exclusive trade to the East Indies, to ensure the ships that are sent thither without their permission, is to invade their rights, and to infringe their charter, and that the practice, if the validity of their charter be admitted, is illegal and ought to be discountenanced.

The practice, Sir, of insuring, *interest or no interest*, or of assigning to ships an imaginary value, is nothing more than a particular game, a mere solemn species of *hazard*, and ought therefore to be prohibited, for every reason that can be urged against games of chance.

With regard to this bill in general, it is in my opinion highly necessary, nor can I discover any important objection that can be made against it. Some law of this kind, and to this purpose, I have long intended to offer to the consideration of this assembly, and since it is now before us, I think we ought to consider it with the attention which may be justly expected from us.

Lord BALTIMORE spoke thus:---Sir, I know not how properly the practice of insuring may be termed a species of hazard, nor do I think any thing more is to be considered, than whether the game be gainful to the nation, or not, for I cannot discover that there is any absurdity in enriching ourselves at the expence of other nations, whether enemies or allies. That we ought to prefer the general good to the advantage of individuals, is undoubted, but I cannot conceive that in this case there can be any opposition between private and publick interest. If our insurers gain by securing the ships of our enemies, the nation is benefited, for all national gain must circulate through the hands of individuals.

No man will assert that we ought to assist our enemies, nor will any man imagine that we assist them by impoverishing them, and if our insurers gain by their practice, the Spaniards must undoubtedly be losers.

Mr. WILLIMOT spoke next, to the following purpose :---Sir, I have conversed on the question to which this bill relates, with men engaged in various kinds of traffick, and who have no common interest but that of their country. I have dispersed among the merchants, most eminent for their acquaintance with the whole extent of commerce, and for their knowledge of the true interest of the nation, copies of this bill, and cannot find any of them so sensible of the grievance of which we have so loud complaints, as to desire that it should be redressed by the measures now proposed.

That frauds are practised on every side, in this, as well as in other trades, the general corruption of our age gives us sufficient reason to suspect, but what is common to every sort of traffick, cannot be produced as an argument for the prohibition of any.

That the practice of insuring an imaginary value may give opportunity for greater frauds than can be practised in common dealings, is likewise evident, but I cannot discover such frauds to require the interposition of the legislature.

If they are practised only by those of our own nation, the publick does not suffer; for property is only transferred from one subject to another: the fraud ought indeed to be severely punished in the courts of criminal justice, but the custom which gave the opportunity of practising it, ought not to be restrained, any more than any other profession not criminal in itself, but liable to accidental abuses.

If our insurers are defrauded by foreigners, the nation is then, indeed, more nearly affected, but even in that case, it is to be remembered, that the private interest of the insurers, who must be immediately ruined, is a sufficient security for the publick. For it cannot, Sir, be conceived that any man will obstinately carry on a business, by which he becomes every day poorer, or, that when he defists he will be succeeded by another, who cannot but know that he engages in that traffick to his certain ruin.

The true state of this affair is, that frauds are, indeed, often committed, and are for that reason always suspected, and that the insurers, when they insure the ship and cargo against accidents, reckon among other chances the probability of being cheated, and proportion their demands, not only to the length and danger of the voyage, but to the character likewise of the man with whom they contract.

This, Sir, is always the practice of those whom experience has made acquainted with the danger of implicit confidence and unsuspecting credulity, nor do any but the young and unskilful suffer themselves to be so exposed to frauds, as that their fortunes should be injured, or the general gain of their business over-balanced, by a few deceits.

Thus it appears, that notwithstanding the ease and safety with
which

which the prefent methods of infurance admit fraud to be practifed, the infurers by a proportionate degree of caution, fecure themfelves from being injured, and by confequence the nation.

The infurance of foreign fhips is now to be confidered, by which great profit arifes to the nation. We infure, Sir, as it has been obferved, at lower rates than other nations, becaufe we have more bufnefs of this kind, and the fmallnefs of our profit is compenfated by the frequency; the cheapnefs of infurances, and eagernefs of foreigners to infure here, reciprocally contribute to each other; we are often applied to, becaufe we infure at an eafy rate, and we can infure at an eafy rate, becaufe we are often applied to.

Nor is the cheapnefs of Britifh infurance the only motive to the preference which it preferves among foreigners, who are induced to apply to this nation, by the reputation which our merchants have defervedly gained for probity and punctuality fuperior to that of any other traders. Our merchants, Sir, bargain without artifice, pay without fubterfuges, and are ready on all occafions to preferve their character at the hazard of their profit.

From thefe two confiderations we may draw unanfwerable arguments againft any reftraints upon the practice of infuring: if foreigners are once difappointed in their applications to us, our bufinefs will in a great part ceafe, and as we fhall not then be able to infure at lower rates than other nations, we fhall never recover that branch of our trade. And as the character of the Britifh merchants exempts them from any fufpicion of practices pernicious to the publick, why fhould they be reftrained? Why, Sir, fhould they appear to be fufpected by the legiflature of their own country, whom foreigners truft without hefitation?

It has been objected to them with great warmth, and urged with much rhetorical exaggeration, that they affift the enemies of their country, that they prolong the war, and defeat thofe advantages which our fituation and commerce have given us; imputations fufficiently atrocious, if they were founded upon truth.

But let us, Sir, examine the arguments by which this accufation has been fupported, and enquire whether this triumph of eloquence has been occafioned by any real fuperiority of evidence or reafon; it is urged, that we have already prohibited commerce with the Spaniards, and that therefore we ought likewife to prohibit the infurance of their fhips.

It will not require, Sir, an imagination very fertile, or a know-ledge very extensive, to supply arguments sufficient to refute the sup-posed demonstration ; in opposition to which it may be urged, that this kind of commerce is of a peculiar nature, that it subsists upon opinion, and is preserved by the reputation of our insurers ; a repu-tation that the insurers of other nations may obtain by the same means, and from whom we shall therefore never recover it.

It may be observed, Sir, that other commodities are the peculiar product of different countries, and that there is no danger of losing our other trade by suspending it, because it depends upon the ex-cellence of our manufactures ; but that insurance may be the com-modity of any country, where money and common honesty are to be found.

This argument may perhaps be yet more effectually invalidated, or perhaps entirely subverted by denying the expedience of that pro-hibition which is produced as a precedent for another restraint.   Nor indeed does it appear why we should preclude ourselves from a gain-ful trade, because the money is drawn by it out of the hands of our enemies ; or why the product of our lands should lie unconsumed, or our manufactures stand unemployed, rather than we should sell to our enemies what they will purchase at another place, or by the inter-vention of a neutral power.

To sell to an enemy that which may enable him to injure us, that which he must necessarily obtain, and which he could buy from no other, would indeed be, to the last degree, absurd ; but that may surely be sold them without any breach of morality or policy, which they can want with less inconvenience than we can keep.   If we were besieging a town, I should not advise our soldiers to sell to the inhabitants ammunition or provisions, but cannot discover the folly of admitting them to purchase ornaments for their houses, or bro-cades for their ladies.

But, without examining with the utmost accuracy, whether the late prohibition was rational or not, I have, I hope, suggested ob-jections sufficient to make the question doubtful, and to incline us to try the success of one experiment before we venture upon another more hazardous.

I am never willing, Sir, to load trade with restraints ; trade is in its own nature so fugitive and variable, that no constant course can

be preſcribed to it; and thoſe regulations which were proper when
they were made, may in a few months become difficulties and ob-
ſtructions. We well know, that many of the meaſures which our
anceſtors purſued for the encouragement of commerce, have been
found of pernicious conſequence; and even in this age, which perhaps experience more than wiſdom has enlightened, I have known
few attempts of that kind which have not defeated the end for which
they were made.

It is more prudent to leave the merchants at liberty to purſue thoſe
meaſures which experience ſhall dictate upon every occaſion, and
ſuffer them to ſnatch the preſent opportunity of honeſt gain whenever
it ſhall happen; they will never injure their own intereſt by the uſe
of this liberty, and by preſerving themſelves they will preſerve the
nation from detriment; nor will they need to be reſtrained by a law
propoſed without their ſolicitation, and of which they cannot diſcover any beneficial conſequences.

Mr. HORACE WALPOLE ſpoke next to this purpoſe:—Sir, for the
bill now before us I have no particular fondneſs, nor deſire that it
ſhould be promoted by any other means than rational arguments and
the repreſentation of indubitable facts.

I have no regard, Sir, in this enquiry, to any private intereſt, or
any other deſire than that of ſecuring the intereſt of my country,
which, in my opinion, evidently requires that we ſhould give no
aſſiſtance to our enemies, that our merchants ſhould co-operate with
our navies, and that we ſhould endeavour to with-hold every thing
that may make the war leſs burthenſome to them, and conſequently
of longer continuance.

It was obſerved, Sir, in the beginning of the debate, by a gentleman eminently ſkilled in mercantile affairs, that inſurance was
practiſed by many nations; but he did not inform us of what one of
the clauſes makes it proper to enquire, whether they allowed the
method of inſuring *intereſt or no intereſt*, and rating ſhips at an imaginary value. This is, I know, prohibited by the Dutch, a nation
whoſe authority on commercial queſtions will not be diſputed, nor
do they allow their Eaſt Indian ſhips to be inſured at all.

The difficulty of eſtimating the value of any cargo has been urged
in defence of this practice, nor is the defence wholly without weight,
becauſe the cargo in many voyages cannot be aſcertained. I ſhall,
however,

however, take this opportunity of obferving, though I may fomewhat digrefs from the prefent argument, how neceffary it is that fome of our exported cargoes fhould be exactly fpecified.

I have been lately informed, Sir, that fix fhips laden with Britifh wool, have entered at one time into a port of France; nor do I know how this practice, which is juftly complained of as pernicious to our trade, and threatening the ruin of our country, can be prevented but by a conftant and regular particularization of every cargo carried to France.

I admit, Sir, that fome cargoes which are imported cannot be particularly regiftered; fuch is the gold with which we are daily fupplied by our commerce with the Portuguefe in oppofition to their laws, and which our merchants are therefore under the neceffity of concealing.

It is not indeed eafy to forefee all the inconveniences that may arife from new regulations of commerce, but the difficulty is not fo great as has been reprefented, nor can I conceive why all our confultations on trade fhould be without effect. Gentlemen may obtain fome knowledge of commerce from their own obfervation, which they may enlarge by an unconfined and indifferent converfation with traders of various claffes, and by enquiries into the different branches of commerce; enquiries, Sir, which are generally neglected by thofe whofe employments confine their attention to particular parts of commerce, or whofe application to bufinefs hinders them from attending to any opinions but thofe which their own perfonal experience enables them to form.

From thefe informations impartially collected, and diligently compared, a man not engaged in the profeffion of a merchant may form general principles, and draw confequences more certain, and more extenfive in their relations, than thofe which are ftruck out only from the obfervation of one fubdivided fpecies of commerce.

A member of this houfe, Sir, thus enlightened by enquiry, and whofe judgment is not diverted from its natural rectitude by the impulfe of any private confideration, may judge of any commercial debate with lefs danger of error or partiality than the merchants, of whom neverthelefs I have the higheft efteem, and whofe knowledge or probity I do not intend to depreciate, when I declare my fears that they may fometimes confound general maxims of trade with the opinions of particular branches, and fometimes miftake their own gain for the intereft of the publick.

Q 2

The

The interest of the merchants ought indeed always to be considered in this house; but then it ought to be regarded only in subordination to that of the whole community, a subordination which the gentleman who spoke last seems to have forgotten. He may perhaps not intend long to retain his senatorial character, and therefore delivered his opinion only as a merchant.

He has distinguished between the conduct of experienced and unskilful insurers, with how much justice I shall not determine. I am afraid that a vigorous enquiry would discover, that neither age nor youth has been able to resist strong temptations to some practices, which neither law nor justice can support, and that those, whose experience has made them cautious, have not been always equally honest.

But this is a subject upon which I am not inclined to dwell, and only mention as the reason which convinces me of the propriety of the bill before us.

Sir WILLIAM YONGE spoke to this effect:—Sir, there appears no probability that the different opinions which have been formed of this bill will be reconciled by this debate; nor indeed is there any reason for wondering at this contrariety of sentiments.

The several clauses of the bill have relations and consequences so different, that scarce any one man can approve them all; and in our present deliberation an objection to a particular clause is considered as an argument against the whole bill.

It is therefore necessary, to prevent an unprofitable expence of time, to resolve the house into a committee, in which the bill may be considered by single clauses, and that part which cannot be defended may be rejected, and that only retained which deserves our approbation. In the committee, when we have considered the first clause, and heard the objections against it, we may mend it; or, if it cannot be amended, reject or postpone it, and so proceed though the whole bill with much greater expedition, and at the same time with a more diligent view of every clause, than while we are obliged to take the whole at once into our consideration.

I shall for my part approve some clauses, and make objections to others; but think it proper to reserve my objections, and the reasons of my approbation, for the committee into which we ought to go on this occasion.

The bill was referred to a committee, but not forty members staying in the house, it was dropped.

HOUSE

HOUSE OF COMMONS.

March 2, 1740-1.

*The bill was ordered to be read the second time, and to be printed for the
use of the members, that it might be thoroughly examined and understood.*

*On the 44th day the second reading of the bill was postponed to the 50th;
but the grand motion being debated on that day, nothing else was
heard.*

On the 51st it was again put off; but

*On the 56th day, being read a second time, it was, after some opposition,
referred to a committee of the whole house to sit five days after. In
the mean while,*

*On the 57th it was ordered that the proper officers do lay before this
house an account of what persons were authorized by virtue of the act
in the 4th of queen Anne, for "the encouragement and encrease of
seamen, and for the better and speedier manning her fleet," to conduct
seamen or seafaring men taken upon privy searches made by applications to justices, and what number of seamen or seafaring men were
returned, also the charge attending the same.*

*On the 61st day, moved that the said account should be read; which
being done, the house resolved itself into a grand committee on the present bill; and the first clause being read, proposing the blanks to
be filled thus, that every voluntier seaman, after five years service,
be entitled to six pounds per year, during life,*

SIR JOHN BARNARD rose, and spoke as follows :—Sir, as it is
our duty to provide laws, by which all frauds and oppressions may
be punished, when they are detected, we are no less obliged to
obviate such practices as shall make punishments necessary ; nor are
we only to facilitate the detection, but take away, as far as it is
possible, the opportunities of guilt. It is to no purpose that punish-

Q 3   ments

ments are threatened, if they can be evaded, or that rewards are offered, if they may by any mean artifices be withheld.

For this reason, Sir, I think it neceſſary to obſerve, that the intent of this clauſe, the moſt favourable and alluring clauſe in the bill, may loſe its effect by a practice not uncommon, by which any man, however inclined to ſerve his country, may be defrauded of the right of a voluntier.

Many men have voluntarily applied to the officers of ſhips of war, and after having been rejected by them as unfit for the ſervice, have been dragged on board within a few days, perhaps within a few hours afterwards, to undergo all the hardſhips, without the merit of voluntiers.

When any man, Sir, has been rejected by the ſea-officers, he ought to have a certificate given him which ſhall be an exemption from an impreſs, that if any other commander ſhall judge more favourably of his qualifications, he may always have the privilege of a voluntier, and be entitled to the reward which he deſerved, by his readineſs to enter the ſervice.

If ſuch proviſions are not made, this hateful practice, a practice, Sir, common and notorious, and very diſcouraging to ſuch as would enter the ſervice of the publick, may ſo far prevail, that no man ſhall be able to denominate himſelf a voluntier, or claim the reward propoſed by the bill.

Admiral WAGER ſpoke next to the following effect :—Sir, it is not common for men to receive injuries without applying for redreſs, when it may certainly be obtained. If any proceedings like thoſe which are now complained of, had been mentioned at the board of admiralty, they had been immediately cenſured and redreſſed ; but as no ſuch accuſations were offered, I think it may probably be concluded, that no ſuch crimes have been committed.

For what purpoſe oppreſſions of this kind ſhould be practiſed, it is not eaſy to conceive ; for the officers are not at all rewarded for impreſſing ſailors. As therefore it is not probable that any man acts wickedly or cruelly without temptation : as I have never heard any ſuch injury complained of by thoſe that ſuffered it, I cannot but imagine, that it is one of thoſe reports, which ariſe from miſtake, or are forged by malice, to injure the officers, and obſtruct the ſervice.

Lord BALTIMORE roſe next, and ſpoke to the following effect :—
                                                                    That

That the practice now complained of, Sir, is very frequent, and, whatever may be the temptation to it, such as every day produces some instances of, I have reasons for asserting with great confidence.

have within these few days, as I was accidentally upon the river, informed myself of two watermen ignominiously dragged by force into the service to which they had voluntarily offered themselves a few days before. The reasons of such oppression, it is the business of those gentlemen to enquire, whom his majesty entrusts with the care of his fleet; but to interrupt the course of wickedness, to hinder it from frustrating the rewards offered by the publick, is the province of the representatives of the people. And I hope, Sir, some proviso will be made in this case,

Admiral NORRIS rose and said:—Sir, if any such practices had been frequent, to what can it be imputed, that those who employ their lives in maritime business should be strangers to them? Why have no complaints been made by those that have been injured? Or why should officers expose themselves to the hazard of censure, without advantage? I cannot discover why these hardships should be inflicted, nor how they could have been concealed, and therefore think the officers of the navy may be cleared from the imputation, without further enquiry.

Sir JOHN BARNARD spoke again to the following purpose:— Sir, it is in vain that objections are made, if the facts upon which they are founded may be denied at pleasure: nothing is more easy than to deny, because proofs are not required of a negative. But as negatives require no proof, so they have no authority, nor can any consequence be deduced from them. I might therefore suffer the facts to remain in their present state, asserted on one side by those that have reasons to believe them, and doubted on the other without reasons; for surely he cannot be said to reason, who questions an assertion only because he does not know it to be true.

But as every question by which the liberty of a Briton may be affected, is of importance sufficient to require that no evidence should be suppressed by which it may be cleared, I cannot but think it proper that a committee should be formed to examine the conduct of the officers in this particular; and in confidence of the veracity of those from whom I received my information, I here promise to produce such evidence as shall put an end to controversy and doubt.

If this is not granted, Sir, the fact must stand recorded and
Q 4   allowed;

allowed; for to doubt, and refuse evidence, is a degree of prejudice and obstinacy without example. Nor is this the only objection to the clause before us, which appears very imperfect with regard to the qualifications specified as a title to the reward. The reward ought not to be confined to those who shall hereafter be invited by the promise of it to engage in the service, while those who entered into it without any such prospect, are condemned to dangers and fatigues without a recompence. Where merit is equal, the reward ought to be equal; and surely where there is greater merit, the reward proposed by the senate, as an encouragement to bravery, ought not to be less. To be excluded from the advantages which others have obtained only by avoiding the service, cannot but depress the spirit of those whose zeal and courage incited them at the beginning of the war to enter into the fleet; and to deject those from whom we expect defence and honour, is neither prudent nor just.

Nor is it, in my opinion, proper to offer the same reward indiscriminately to all that shall accept it; rewards ought to be proportioned to desert, and no man can justly be paid for what he cannot perform; there ought therefore to be some distinction made between a seaman by profession, one that has learned his art at the expence of long experience, labour, and hazard, and a man who only enters the ship because he is useless on land, and who can only incommode the sailors till he has been instructed by them.

It appears, Sir, to me a considerable defect in our naval regulations, that wages are not proportioned to ability; and I think it may not be now unseasonably proposed, that sailors should be paid according to the skill which they have acquired; a provision by which an emulation would be raised among them, and that industry excited, which now languishes for want of encouragement, and those capacities awakened which now slumber in ignorance and sloth, from the despair of obtaining any advantage by superiority of knowledge.

Sir Robert Walpole then rose, and spoke as follows:---That this charge, Sir, however positively urged, is generally unjust, the declarations of these honourable gentlemen are sufficient to evince, since it is not probable that the injured persons would not have found some friend to have represented their hardships to the admiralty, and no such representation could have been made without their knowledge.

Yet, Sir, I am far from doubting that by accident, or perhaps by malice, some men have been treated in this manner; for it is not in the

the power of any adminiftration to make all thofe honeft or wife whom they are obliged to employ; and when great affairs are depending, minute circumftances cannot always be attended to. If the vigilance of thofe who are intrufted with the chief direction of great numbers of fubordinate officers be fuch, that corrupt practices are not frequent, and their juftice fuch, that they are never unpunifhed when legally detected, the moft ftrict enquirer can expect no more. Power will fometimes be abufed, and punifhment fometimes be efcaped.

It is, Sir, eafy to be conceived that a report may become general though the practice be very rare. The fact is multiplied as often as it is related, and every man who hears the fame ftory twice, imagines that it is told of different perfons, and exclaims againft the tyranny of the officers of the navy.

But thefe, in my opinion, Sir, are queftions, if not remote from the prefent affair, yet by no means effential to it. The queftion now before us is, not what illegalities have been committed in the execution of impreffes, but how impreffes themfelves may become lefs neceffary? how the nation may be fecured without injury to indviduals? and how the fleet may be manned with lefs detriment to commerce?

Sir, the reward now propofed is intended to excite men to enter the fervice without compulfion; and if this expedient be not approved, another ought to be fuggefted: For I hope gentlemen are united in their endeavours to find out fome method of fecurity to the publick, and do not obftruct the proceedings of the committee, that when the fleets lie inactive and ufelefs, they may have an opportunity to reproach the miniftry.

Admiral NORRIS fpoke next, in fubftance:—Sir, though it is not neceffary to enter into an accurate examination of the gentleman's propofal, yet I cannot but obferve, that by making it he difcovers himfelf unacquainted with the difpofition of feamen, among whom nothing raifes fo much difcontent as the fufpicion of partiality. Should one man, in the fame rank, receive larger wages than another, he who thought himfelf injured, as he who is paid lefs will always think, would be fo far from exerting his abilities to attain an equality with his affociate, that he would probably never be prevailed on to lay his hand upon the tackling, but would fit fullen, or work perverfely, though the fhip were labouring in a ftorm, or finking in a battle.

Mr. GORE then fpoke as follows:—Sir, the danger of introducing diftinction.

distinctions among men in the same rank, where every man that imagines his merit neglected may have an opportunity of resenting the injury, is doubtless such as no prudent commander will venture to incur.

Every man in this case becomes the judge of his own merit; and as he will always discover some reason for the preference of another very different from superiority of desert, he will, by consequence, be either enraged or dispirited, will either resolve to desert his commander, or betray him to the enemies, or not oppose them.

I remember, Sir, though imperfectly, a story which I heard in my travels, of an army in which some troops received a penny a day less than the rest; a parsimony which cost dear in the day of battle; for the disgusted troops laid down their arms before the enemy, and suffered their general to be cut in pieces.

General WADE then spoke to this effect:—Sir, I cannot but concur with the honourable gentleman in his opinion, that those who are already engaged in the service, who have borne the fatigues of a long voyage, and perhaps are at this hour exposing their lives in battle to defend the rights of their country, ought to have the same claim to the reward proposed with those who shall hereafter offer themselves. Nor in my opinion ought those who have hitherto been pressed into our fleets to be discouraged from their duty by an exclusion from the same advantage. For if they were compelled to serve in the fleet, they were compelled when there was not this encouragement for volunteers which, perhaps, they would have accepted if it had been then proposed. Every man at least will allege, that he would have accepted it, and complain he suffers only by the fault of the government; a government which he will not be very zealous to defend, while he is considered with less regard than others from whom no greater services are expected.

A prospect of new rewards, Sir, will add new alacrity to all the forces, and an equal distribution of favour will secure an unshaken and inviolable fidelity. Nothing but union can produce success, and nothing can secure union but impartiality and justice.

Mr. SANDYS rose, and spoke as follows:—Sir, the efficacy of rewards, and the necessity of an impartial distribution, are no unfruitful subjects for rhetoric; but it may perhaps be more useful at present to consider, with such a degree of attention as the question must nuſt be acknowledged to deſerve, to whom theſe rewards are to be paid, and from what fund they are expected to ariſe.

With regard to thoſe who are to claim the reward, Sir, they ſeem very negligently ſpecified; for they are diſtinguiſhed only by the character of having ſerved five years; a diſtinction unintelligible, without explanation.

It is, I ſuppoſe, Sir, the intent of the bill, that no man ſhall miſs the reward but by his own fault, and therefore it may be enquired, what is to be the fate of him who ſhall be diſabled in his firſt adventure, whom in the firſt year or month of his ſervice, an unlucky ſhot ſhall confine for the remaining part of his life to inactivity: as the bill is now formed, he muſt be miſerable without a recompenſe; and his wounds, which make him unable to ſupport himſelf, will, though received in defence of his country, entitle him to no ſupport from the publick.

Nor is this the only difficulty that may ariſe from the ſpecifying of ſo long a ſervice; for how can any man that ſhall enter on board the fleet be informed that the war will continue for five years? May we not all juſtly hope that alacrity, unanimity, and prudence, may in a much ſhorter time reduce our enemies to beg for peace? And ſhall our ſailors loſe the reward of their hazards and their labours, only becauſe they have been ſucceſsful? What will this be leſs than making their bravery a crime or folly, and puniſhing them for not protracting the war by cowardice or treachery?

But let us ſuppoſe, Sir, thoſe defects ſupplied by a more explicit and determinate ſpecification, there will yet ariſe an objection far more formidable; an objection which the preſent ſtate of our revenues will not ſuffer to be anſwered. The conſideration of the greatneſs of the annual payment which this propoſal requires, ought to incite every man to employ all his ſagacity in ſearch of ſome other method equally efficacious and leſs expenſive.

We have already, Sir, forty thouſand ſeamen in our pay, to whom eight thouſand more are ſpeedily to be added: when each of theſe ſhall demand his ſtipend, a new burthen of two hundred and eighty eight thouſand pounds muſt be laid upon the nation; upon a nation, whoſe lands are mortgaged, whoſe revenues are anticipated, and whoſe taxes cannot be borne without murmurs, nor encreaſed without ſedition.

The nation has found by experience, that taxes once impoſed for juſt reaſons, and continued upon plauſible pretences, till they are be-

come

come familiar, are afterwards continued upon motives lefs laudable, are too productive of influence, and too inftrumental towards faci-litating the meafures of the miniftry, to be ever willingly remitted.

Mr. BLADEN fpoke next, as follows:—Sir, it is obvious that when the balance is unequal, it may be reduced to an equilibrium, as well by taking weight out of one fcale, as adding it to the other. The wages offered by the merchants overbalance at prefent thofe which are propofed by the crown; to raife the allowance in the fhips of war, will be to lay new loads upon the publick, and will incommode the merchants, whofe wages muft always bear the fame proportion to the king's. The only method then that remains, is to lighten the oppofite fcale, by reftraining the merchants from giving wages in time of war beyond a certain value; for as the fervice of the crown is then more immediately neceffary to the general advantage, than that of the merchants, it ought to be made more gainful. Sai-lors, Sir, are not generally men of very extenfive views; and there-fore we cannot expect that they fhould prefer the general good of their country before their own prefent intereft, a motive of fuch power, that even in men of curious refearches, refined fentiments, and generous education, we fee too often that it furmounts every other confideration.

Lord BALTIMORE then fpoke again:—Sir, to the expedient which the honourable gentleman who fpoke laft has fuggefted, and which he muft be confefs'd to have placed in the ftrongeft light, many ob-jections may be raifed, which I am afraid will not eafily be removed.

The firft, Sir, which occurs to me on this fhort reflection is not lefs than the impoffibility of putting his fcheme in execution. The prefcription of wages which he propofes, may be eluded by a thou-fand artifices, by advanced money, by gratuitous acknowledgments, the payment of money for pretended fervices, or by fecret contracts, which it will be the intereft of both parties to conceal.

But if this objection could be furmounted by feverity and vigilance, would not this expedient help to defeat the general intention of the bill? A bill not defigned as an immediate refource, a mere tempo-rary project to fupply our fleets for the prefent year, but as a method for removing the only obftruction of the British power, the difficulty of manning our fhips of war.

It is, I think, Sir, the intention of every man who has offered his fentiments on this occafion, to contrive fome general encouragement

for

for feamen, which fhall not only invite them to affift their country
at the firft fummons, but fhail allure others to qualify themfelves for
the publick fervice, by engaging in the fame profeffion.

This is only to be done by making the condition of failors lefs
miferable, by entitling them to privileges and honouring them with
diftinctions. But by limiting the merchants wages, if fuch limita-
tions are indeed poffible, though we may palliate the prefent diftrefs,
we fhall diminifh the number of failors, and thereby not only contract our commerce but endanger our country.

Mr. TRACEY fpoke next to the following effect :—Sir, I know
not for what reafons the prefent method of advancing rewards at entrance is practifed, of which, however fpecious it might appear,
the fuccefs by no means encourages the continuance. The failors,
though not a generation of men much difpofed to reflection, or qualified for ratiocination, are not yet fo void of thought as not eafily
to perceive that a fmall encreafe of conftant wages is of more value
than feveral pounds to be paid only at once, and which are fquandered
as foon as they are received.

Inftead therefore of reftraining the wages of the merchants, it
feems probable that by raifing thofe of the king, we may man the
fleet with moft expedition ; and one method of raifing the wages
will be to fupprefs the advanced money.

The ATTORNEY-GENERAL fpoke next :—Sir, if the fum of
money now paid by way of advance can be fuppofed to have any
effect, if it can be imagined that any number of feamen, however
inconfiderable, are allured by it into the fleet, it is more ufefully employed than it can be fuppofed to be when funk into the current
wages, and divided into fmall payments.

The advance money is only paid to thofe that enter : if no voluntiers prefent themfelves, no money is paid, and the nation doth not
fuffer by the offer : but if the wages are raifed, the expence will be
certain, without the certainty of advantage ; for thofe that enter voluntarily into the fleet, will receive no more than thofe that are
forced into it by an imprefs ; and therefore there will be no incitement to enter without compulfion. Thus every other inconvenience
will remain, with the addition of a new burthen to the nation ; our
forces will be maintained at a greater expence, and not raifed with
lefs difficulty.

Lord BALTIMORE faid :—Sir, I cannot but concur in opinion
with

with the honourable gentleman who fpoke laft, from my own acquaintance with the fentiments and habits that unalterably prevail
among thofe who have been accuftomed to the fea, a race of men to
the laft degree negligent of any future events, and carelefs about any
provifion againft diftant evils; men who have no thoughts at fea,
but how to reach the land, nor at land, but how to fquander what
they have gained at fea. To men like thefe, it may eafily be imagined
that no encouragement is equal to the temptation of prefent gain,
and the opportunity of prefent pleafure.

Of this any man, Sir, may convince himfelf, who fhall talk to a
crew but half an hour; for he fhall find few among them, who will
not, for a fmall fum of prefent money, fell any diftant profpect of
affluence or happinefs.

Whether I am miftaken in my opinion, the honourable members
who have long commanded in the naval fervice, can eafily determine,
and I doubt not but they will agree, that no motive can be propofed
to a failor equivalent to immediate reward.

Sir WILLIAM YONGE fpoke next:—Sir, that fome diftinction
ought to be made to the advantage of voluntiers, if we intend to man
our fleet without compulfion, is obvious and inconteftable; and to
avoid the neceffity of compulfion ought to be the chief end of this
bill; for nothing can be lefs to the advantage of the nation, than to
continue the ufe of fuch ungrateful methods, and yet increafe the
publick expence.

We ought therefore, in my opinion, to determine upon fome
peculiar reward, either to be advanced upon their entrance into the
fervice, or paid at their difmiffion from it.

But as I fee, Sir, no reafon for hoping that all the encouragement
which can be offered, will raife voluntiers in a fufficient number to
fecure our navigation, and affert our fovereignty, it feems not proper
to confine our confultations to this part of the bill; for fince compulfion is on many occafions apparently neceffary, fome method requires
to be confidered, in which it may be legal.

What new power ought to be placed in the magiftrate, for what
time, and with what reftrictions, I am far from affuming the province of determining; but that fome meafures muft be taken for
compelling thofe who cannot be perfuaded, and difcovering thofe
that will not offer themfelves, cannot admit of doubt; and as the magiftrate is at prefent without any authority for this purpofe, it is evident

dent that his power muſt be extended, for the ſame reaſon as it was given in its preſent degree, the general benefit of the whole community.

Sir JOHN BARNARD then ſpoke to the following effect:—Sir, if the intent of this bill be to enable one part of the nation to enſlave the other ; if the plauſible and inviting profeſſions of encouraging and increaſing ſeamen, are to terminate in violence, conſtraint, and oppreſſion ; it is unneceſſary to dwell longer upon particular clauſes. The intention of the bill is deteſtable, and deſerves not the ceremony of debate, or the forms of common regard.

If a man, Sir, is liable to be forced from the care of his own private affairs, from his favourite ſchemes of life, from the engagements of domeſtic tenderneſs, or the proſpects of near advantage, and ſubjected without his conſent to the command of one whom he hates, or dreads, or perhaps deſpiſes, it requires no long argument to ſhew, that by whatever authority he is thus treated, he is reduced to the condition of a ſlave, to that abject, to that hateful ſtate, which every *Engliſhman* has been taught to avoid at the hazard of his life.

It is therefore evident, that a law which tends to confer ſuch a power, ſubverts our conſtitution as far as its effects extend ; a conſtitution, which was originally formed as a barrier againſt ſlavery, and which one age after another has endeavoured to ſtrengthen.

Such a power, therefore, in whatever hands it may be lodged, I ſhall always oppoſe. It is dangerous, Sir, to intruſt any man with abſolute dominion, which is ſeldom known to be impartially exerciſed, and which often makes thoſe corrupt and inſolent, whom it finds benevolent and honeſt.

The bill propoſes only encouragement, and encouragement may be given by his majeſty, without a new law; let us therefore draw up an addreſs, and ceaſe to debate, where there is no proſpect of agreement.

Mr. WINNINGTON ſpoke as follows:—Sir, the payment of an annual ſalary will, in my opinion, be to the laſt degree inconvenient and dangerous. The yearly expence has been already eſtimated, and ariſes to a ſum very formidable in our preſent ſtate. Nor is the neceſſity of adding to the public burthen, a burthen which already is hard to be borne, the only objection to this propoſal.

Nothing can more contribute to diſpirit the nation, than to protract the conſequences of a war, and to make the calamity felt,

when

when the pleasures of victory and triumph have been forgotten ; we
shall be inclined rather to bear oppression and insult than endeavour
after redress, if we subject ourselves and our posterity to endless
exactions.

The expences of the present provision for superannuated and dis-
abled sailors, is no inconsiderable tax upon the public, which is not
less burthened by it for the manner of collecting it by a deduction
from the sailors wages ; for whoever pays it immediately, it is the
ultimate gift of the nation, and the utmost that can be allowed for
this purpose.

It must be confessed, Sir, the persons entitled to the pension are
not sufficiently distinguished in the bill ; by which, as it now stands,
any of the worthless superfluities of a ship, even the servants of the
captains, may, after five years, put in their demand, and plunder
that nation which they never served.

Nor do I think, Sir, the efficacy of this method will bear any proportion to the expence of it ; for I am of opinion, that few of the
sailors will be much affected by the prospect of a future pension. I
am therefore for dazzling them with five pounds to be given them at
their entrance, which will be but a single payment, and probably fill
our fleets with greater expedition, than methods which appear more
refined, and the effects of deeper meditation.

Lord GAGE spoke in the following manner :—Sir, nothing is
more clear than that an yearly pension will burthen the nation, without any advantage ; and as it will give occasion to innumerable
frauds, it is a method which ought to be rejected.

As to the new power, Sir, which is proposed to be placed in the
hands of the magistrates, it undoubtedly reduces every sailor to a
state of slavery, and is inconsistent with that natural right to liberty,
which is confirmed and secured by our constitution. The bill therefore is, in my opinion, defective in all its parts, of a tendency generally pernicious, and cannot be amended but by rejecting it.

Mr. HENRY PELHAM spoke next, to this effect :—Sir, I cannot
but think it necessary, that on this occasion at least gentlemen
should remit the ardour of disputation, and lay the arts of rhetoric
aside, that they should reserve their wit and their satire for questions
of less importance, and unite, for once, their endeavours, that this
affair may meet with no obstructions but from its natural difficulty.

We

We are now, Sir, engaged in a war with a nation, if not of the first rank in power, yet by no means contemptible in itself; and, by its alliances, extremely formidable. We are expofed, by the courfe of our trade, and the fituation of our enemies, to many inevitable loffes, and have no means of preventing our merchants from being feized, without any danger or expence to the Spaniards, but by covering the fea with our fquadrons.

Nor are we, Sir, to fatisfy ourfelves with barely defeating the defigns of the Spaniards; our honour demands that we fhould force them to peace upon advantageous terms; that we fhould not repulfe, but attack them; not only preferve our own trade and poffeffions, but endanger theirs.

It is by no means certain, Sir, that in the profecution of thefe defigns we fhall not be interrupted by the intereft or jealoufy of a nation far more powerful, whofe forces we ought therefore to be able to refift.

A vigorous exertion of our ftrength will probably either intimidate any other power that may be inclined to attack us, or enable us to repel the injuries that fhall be offered: difcord and delay can only confirm our open enemies in their obftinacy, and animate thofe that have hitherto concealed their malignity to declare againft us.

It is therefore, Sir, in no degree prudent to aggravate the inconveniencies of the meafures propofed for accomplifhing what every man feems equally to defire; to declaim againft the expedients offered in the bill as pernicious, unjuft, and oppreffive, contributes very little to the production of better means. That our affairs will not admit of long fufpence, and that the prefent methods of raifing feamen are not effectual, is univerfally allowed; it therefore evidently follows, Sir, that fome other muft be fpeedily ftruck out.

I think it neceffary to propofe, that the houfe be refolved into a committee to-morrow morning; and hope all that fhall affemble on this occafion, will bring with them no other paffion than zeal for their country.

[The fpeaker having taken the chair, the chairman of the committee reported, that they had made fome progrefs; and defiring leave to fit again, it was refolved to go into the committee again on the morrow.]

On the 62d day the affair was put off; but on the 63d, the house re-solving itself into a committee, a clause was offered, by which five pounds were proposed to be advanced to an able seaman, and three pounds to every other man that should enter voluntarily into his ma-jesty's service, after 20 days, and within 60.

After which, Mr. WINNINGTON spoke as follows :—Sir, this is a clause in which no opposition can be apprehended, as those gentlemen who declared their disapprobation of the former, were almost unanimous in proposing this expedient, as the least expensive, and the most likely to succeed.

The time for the reception of volunteers upon this condition, is, Sir, in my opinion, judiciously determined. If it was extended to a greater length, or left uncertain, the reward would lose its efficacy, the sailors would neglect that which they might accept at any time, and would only have recourse to the ships of war, when they could find no other employment.

Yet I cannot conceal my apprehensions, that this bounty will not alone be sufficient to man our fleets with proper expedition ; and that as allurements may be useful on one hand, force will be found necessary on the other ; that the sailors may not only be incited to engage in the service by the hopes of a reward, but by the fear of having their negligence to accept it punished, by being compelled into the same service, and forfeiting their claim by staying to be compelled.

Lord BALTIMORE then spoke to the following effect :—Sir, to the reward proposed in this clause, I have declared in the former conference on this bill, that I have no objection, and therefore have no amendment to propose, except with regard to the time limited for the payment.

As our need of seamen, Sir, is immediate, why should not a law for their encouragement immediately operate ? What advantage can arise from delays ? Or why is not that proper to be advanced now, that will be proper in twenty days ? That all the time between the enaction and operation of this law must be lost, is evident ; for who will enter for two pounds, that may gain five by withholding himself from the service twenty days longer ?

Nor do I think the time now limited sufficient ; many sailors who

are

are now in the fervice of the merchants, may not return foon enough
to lay claim to the bounty, who would gladly accept it, and who
will either not ferve the crown without it, or will ferve with difguft
and complaints ; as the lofs of it cannot be imputed to their back-
wardnefs, but to an accident againft which they could not provide.

Mr. Winnington replied :—Sir, though I think the time now
fixed by the bill fufficient, as I hope that our prefent exigency will be
but of fhort continuance, and that we fhall foon be able to raife naval
forces at a cheaper rate, yet as the reafons alleged for an alteration of
the time may appear to others of more weight than to me, I fhall not
oppofe the amendment.

Sir John Barnard next rofe, and faid :—Sir, with regard to the
duration of the time fixed for the advancement of this bounty, we
may have leifure to deliberate ; but furely it muft be readily granted
by thofe who have expatiated fo copioufly upon the prefent exigencies
of our affairs, that it ought immediately to commence. And if this
be the general determination of the houfe, nothing can be more proper than to addrefs his majefty to offer, by proclamation, an advance
of five pounds, inftead of two which have been hitherto given; that
while we are concerting other meafures for the advantage of our
country, thofe in which we have already concurred may be put in
execution.

Mr. Pulteney rofe up next, and fpoke as follows : —Sir, I take
this opportunity to lay before the houfe a grievance which very much
retards the equipment of our fleets, and which muft be redreffed before any meafures for reconciling the failors to the publick fervice can
be purfued with the leaft probability of fuccefs.

Obfervation, Sir, has informed me, that to remove the deteftation
of the king's fervice, it is not neceffary to raife the wages of the
feamen; it is neceffary only to fecure them; it is neceffary to deftroy
thofe hateful infects that fatten in idlenefs and debauchery upon
the gains of the induftrious and honeft.

When a failor, Sir, after the fatigues and hazards of a long
voyage, brings his ticket to the pay-office, and demands his wages,
the defpicable wretch to whom he is obliged to apply, looks upon
his ticket with an air of importance, acknowledges his right, and
demands a reward for prefent payment ; with this demand, however
exorbitant, the neceffities of his family oblige him to comply.

In this manner, Sir, are the wives of the failors alfo treated when they come to receive the pay of their husbands; women, distressed, friendless, and unsupported; they are obliged to endure every insult, and to yield to every oppression. And to such a height do these merciless exactors raise their extortions, that sometimes a third part of the wages is deducted.

Thus, Sir, do the vilest, the meanest of mankind, plunder those who have the highest claim to the esteem, the gratitude, and the protection of their country. This is the hardship which withholds the sailors from our navies, and forces them to seek for kinder treatment in other countries. This hardship, Sir, both justice and prudence call upon us to remedy; and while we neglect it, all our deliberations will be ineffectual.

Mr. Southwell then spoke to this effect:—Sir, of the hardships mentioned by the honourable gentleman who spoke last, I have myself known an instance too remarkable not to be mentioned. A sailor in Ireland, after his voyage, met with so much difficulty in obtaining his wages, that he was at length reduced to the necessity of submitting to the reduction of near a sixth part. Such are the grievances with which those are oppressed, upon whom the power, security, and happiness of the nation are acknowledged to depend.

Sir Robert Walpole, the prime minister, then rose, and spoke as follows:—Sir, it is not without surprize that I hear the disgust of the sailors ascribed to any irregularity in the payment of their wages, which were never in any former reign so punctually discharged. They receive, at present, twelve months pay in eighteen months, without deduction; so that there are never more than six months for which any demand remains unsatisfied.

But, Sir, the punctuality of the payment has produced of late great inconveniencies; for there has been frequently a necessity of removing men from one ship to another; and it is the stated rule of the pay-office, to assign every man so removed his full pay. These men, when the government is no longer indebted to them, take the first opportunity of deserting the service, and engaging in business to which they are more inclined.

This is not a chimerical complaint, founded upon rare instances, and produced only to counterbalance an objection; the fact and the consequences are well known; so well, that near fourteen hundre sailors are computed to have been lost by this practice.

The president of the commons, who always in a committee take^{is}

seat

feat as another member, rose here, and spoke to the following effect, his honour being pay-master of the navy :—Mr. Chairman, the nature of the employment with which I am entrusted makes it my duty to endeavour that this question may be clearly understood, and the condition of the seamen, with regard to the reception of their pay, justly represented.

I have not been able to discover that any sailor, upon producing his ticket, was ever obliged to submit to the deduction of any part of his wages, nor should any clerk or officer under my inspection, escape for such oppression, the severest punishment and most publick censure; I would give him up to the law without reserve, and mark him as infamous and unworthy of any trust or employment.

But there are extortions, Sir, by which those unhappy men, after having served their country with honesty and courage, are deprived of the lawful gains of diligence and labour. There are men to whom it is usual amongst the sailors to mortgage their pay before it becomes due, who never advance their money but upon such terms as cannot be mentioned without indignation. These men advance the sum which is stipulated, and by virtue of a letter of attorney are reimbursed at the pay-office.

This corruption is, I fear, not confined to particular places, but has spread even to America, where, as in his own country, the poor sailor is seduced, by the temptation of present money, to sell his labour to extortioners and usurers.

I appeal to the gentleman whether the instance which he mentioned was not of this kind. I appeal to him without apprehension of receiving an answer that can tend to invalidate what I have asserted.

This, Sir, is indeed a grievance pernicious and oppressive, which no endeavours of mine shall be deficient in attempting to remove; for by this the sailor is condemned, notwithstanding his industry and success, to perpetual poverty, and to labour only for the benefit of his plunderer.

[The clauses were then read, "empowering the justices of the peace, &c. to issue warrants to the constables, &c. to make general privy searches, by day or night, for finding out and securing such seamen and seafaring men as lie hid or conceal themselves; and making it lawful for the officers appointed to make such searches, to force open the doors of any house, where they

shall

shall *suspect* such seamen to be concealed, if entrance be not readily admitted ; and for punishing those who shall harbour or conceal any seaman."]

Sir JOHN BARNARD upon this rose up, and spoke to the following effect :—Mr. Chairman, we have been hitherto deliberating upon questions, in which diversity of opinions might naturally be expected, and in which every man might indulge his own opinion, whatever it might be, without any dangerous consequences to the publick. But the clauses now before us are of a different kind ; clauses which cannot be read without astonishment and indignation, nor defended without betraying the liberty of the best, the bravest, and most useful of our fellow subjects.

If these clauses, Sir, should pass into a law, a sailor and a slave will become terms of the same signification. Every man who has devoted himself to the most useful profession, and most dangerous service of his country, will see himself deprived of every advantage which he has laboured to obtain, and made the mere passive property of those who live in security by his valour, and owe to his labour that affluence which hardens them to insensibility, and that pride that swells them to ingratitude.

Why must the sailors alone, Sir, be marked out from all the other orders of men for ignominy and misery ? Why must they be ranked with the enemies of society, stopped like vagabonds, and pursued like the thief and the murderer by publick officers ? How or when have they forfeited the common privilege of human nature, or the general protection of the laws of their country ? If it is a just maxim, Sir, that he who contributes most to the welfare of the publick, deserves most to be protected in the enjoyment of his private right or fortune ; a principle which surely will not be controverted ; where is the man that dares stand forth and assert, that he has juster claims than the brave, the honest, the diligent sailor ?

I am extremely unwilling, Sir, to engage in so invidious an undertaking as the comparison of the harmless, inoffensive, resolute sailor, with those who think themselves entitled to treat him with contempt, to overlook his merit, invade his liberty, and laugh at his remonstrances.

Nor is it, Sir, necessary to dwell upon the peculiar merit of this body of men ; it is sufficient that they have the same claims, found-

ed

ed upon the fame reafons with our own, that they have never
forfeited them by any crime, and therefore, that they cannot be taken
away without the moſt flagrant violation of the laws of nature, of reafon, and of our country.

Let us confider the prefent condition of a failor, let us reflect a
little upon the calamities to which cuſtom, though not law, has already made him fubject, and it will furely not be thought that his
unhappineſs needs any aggravation.

He is already expofed to be forced, upon his return from a tedious
voyage, into new hardſhips, without the intermiſſion of a day, and
without the fight of his family; he is liable, after a contract for a
pleafing and gainful voyage, to be hurried away from his profpects of
intereſt, and condemned amidſt oppreſſion and infolence, to labour
and to danger almoſt without the poſſibility of a recompenfe. He
has neither the privilege of chufing his commander, nor of leaving
him when he is defrauded and oppreſſed.

Thefe, Sir, I fay, are the calamities to which he is now fubject,
but there is now a poſſibility of efcaping them. He is not yet deprived of the right of refiſtance, or the power of flight; he may
now retire to his friend, and be protected by him, he may take ſhelter in his own cottage, and treat any man as a robber, that ſhall attempt to force his doors.

When any crews are returning home in time of war, they are acquainted with the dangers of an imprefs, but they comfort themfelves with contriving ſtratagems to elude it, or with the profpect of
obtaining an exemption from it by the favour of their friends; profpects which are often deceitful, and ſtratagems frequently defeated,
but which yet fupport their fpirits, and animate their induſtry.

But if this bill, Sir, ſhould become a law, the failor, inſtead of
amuſing himfelf on his return with the profpects of eafe, or of pleafure, will confider his country as a place of ſlavery, a refidence lefs
to be defired than any other part of the world. He will probably
feek in the fervice of fome foreign prince a kinder treatment, and
will not fail in any country but his own to fee himfelf at leaſt on a
level with other men.

Nor will this bill, Sir, only give the feamen new reafons of dif-
guſt, but it will tend likewife to aggravate thofe grievances, which
already have produced a deteſtation of the publick fervice, fcarcely
to be conquered.

The officers of the navy, Sir, will hardly be made lefs infolent by

an increaſe of power ; they whoſe tyranny has already alienated their
fellow-ſubjects from the king's ſervice, though they could only
depend upon the character of probity and moderation for the proſpect of manning their ſhips in ſucceeding expeditions, will probably,
when they are animated by a law like this, and made abſolute both
by land and ſea, indulge themſelves in the enjoyment of their new
authority, contrive new hardſhips and oppreſſions, and tyrannize
without fear and without mercy. Thus, Sir, will the bill not only
be tyrannical in itſelf, but the parent of tyranny ; it will give ſecurity to the cruel, and confidence to the arrogant.

That any man, at leaſt any man bred from his infancy to change
his reſidence, and accuſtomed to different climates and to foreign
nations, will fix by choice in that country where he finds the worſt
reception, is hardly to be imagined. We ſee indeed, that men unqualified to ſupport themſelves in other countries, or who have, by
long cuſtom, contracted a fondneſs for particular methods of life, will
bear very uncomfortable circumſtances, without endeavouring to
improve their conditions by a change of their habitations. But the
temper of a ſailor, acquainted with all parts, and indifferent to all,
is of another kind. Such, Sir, is his love of change, ariſing either
from wantonneſs or curioſity, that he is hard to be retained by the
kindeſt treatment and moſt liberal rewards ; and will therefore never
ſtruggle with his habitual diſpoſitions, only to continue in a ſtate
of ſlavery.

I think it therefore, Sir, very evident that this new method of *encou-*
raging ſailors will be ſo far from *increaſing* them, that it may probably
drive them out of the empire, and at once ruin our trade and our
navy ; at once beggar and diſarm us.

Let me now ſuppoſe, Sir, for a moment the bill leſs pernicious in
its conſequences, and conſider only the difficulties of executing it.
Every ſeafaring man is to be ſeized at pleaſure by the magiſtrate ; but
what definition is given of a ſeafaring man ? Or by what character-
iſtic is the magiſtrate to diſtinguiſh him ? I have never been able to
diſcover any peculiarities in the form of a ſeaman that mark him out
from the reſt of the ſpecies. There is, indeed, leſs ſervility in his
air, and leſs effeminacy in his face, than in thoſe that are commonly
to be ſeen in drawing rooms, in brothels, and at reviews ; but I
know not that a ſeaman can be diſtinguiſhed from any other man of
equal induſtry or uſe, who has never enervated himſelf by vice, nor
poliſhed himſelf into corruption. So that this bill, Sir, if it ſhall
paſs

>afs into a law, will put it at once in the power of the magiftrate to dif-
>ofe of feamen at his pleafure, and to term whom he pleafes a fea-
man.

Another expedient, Sir, has been offered on this occafion not
equally tyrannical, but equally inadequate to the end in view. It is propofed to reftrain the merchants from giving wages beyond a certain
rate, on the fuppofition that the failors have no motive but that of
larger wages, to prefer the fervice of the merchants to that of the
crown.

This, Sir, is a miftake which might eafily arife from a partial and
imperfect knowledge of the affair, with which very few gentlemen
have opportunities of being well acquainted. The wages, Sir, are
the fmalleft inducements which fix the feamen in their choice. The
profpect of kinder treatment, the certainty of returning home in a
fixed time, and the power of chufing what voyages they will undertake, cannot but be acknowledged very reafonable motives of preference.

On the contrary, Sir, when they are once engaged in a fhip of
war, they know neither whither they are going, what dangers they
fhall encounter, what hardfhips they fhall fuffer, nor when they fhall
de difmiffed.

Befides, Sir, I do not think it poffible by any law to limit the
wages to be paid by merchants, fince they will change the term of
wages into that of a prefent, or admit the failors to a fmall fhare in
the freight, and fo all the precaution we can take will become ineffectual.

In the mean time, Sir, how much fhall we embarrafs our own commerce and impair our natural ftrength, the power of our fleets? We
fhall terrify our failors on the one hand, and endeavour to ftarve
them on the other; we fhall not only drive them from us by unheard
of feverities, but take away every motive that can induce them to
expofe themfelves to the danger of fuffering them.

If we confider, Sir, with what effect methods nearly approaching
thefe were practifed in the reign of the late queen, we fhall find that
not more than 1500 feamen were raifed, and thofe at the expence of
more than four thoufand pounds; fo that the effects bore no proportion to the means; our laws were infringed and our conftitution
violated to no purpofe.

But

But what reafon, Sir, can be affigned for which it muft be more difficult to fupply the fleet now with failors than at any other time? This war, Sir, was demanded by the publick voice, in purfuance of the particular remonftrances of the merchants, and it is not to be fuppofed that the failors or any other body of men engage in it with a particular reluctance.

I am therefore inclined to believe that the fufpicion of great numbers hid in the country, at a diftance from the coaft, is merely chimerical; and that if we fhould pafs this bill, we fhould do nothing more than grant an oppreffive and unconftitutional power of fearch for what in reality is not to be found.

How oppreffive this power may become in the hands of a corrupt or infolent magiftrate, any man may difcover who remembers that the magiftrate is made judge without appeal, of his own right to denominate any man a failor, and that he may break open any man's doors at any time, without alleging any other reafon than his own fufpicion; fo that no man can fecure his houfe from being fearched, or, perhaps, his perfon from being feized.

It may indeed be alleged, Sir, that this will be only a temporary law, and is to ceafe with the exigence that made it neceffary: but long experience has informed us, that fevere laws are enacted more readily than they are repealed; and that moft men are too fond of power to fuffer willingly the diminution of it.

But, Sir, though this law fhould not be perpetuated, every precedent of an infringement of our conftitution makes way for its diffolution; and the very ceffation of an oppreffive law may be a plea hereafter for the revival of it.

This bill, therefore, muft be confeffed to be at once violent and ineffectual; to be a tranfgreffion of the laws of juftice to particular men, without any profpect of real benefit to the community; and therefore cannot be paffed without deviating at once from prudence and our conftitution.

Captain CORNWALL then rofe, and fpoke to this effect:—I have obferved, Sir, that every man is apt to think himfelf ill treated, who is not treated according to his own opinion of his deferts, and will endeavour to diffufe his own notion of the partiality and tyranny of the naval officers; general clamours therefore are little to be regarded.

I have had, from my early years, a command in the fea fervice,

and

and can affert, that I never knew more than one inftance of injuftice, and that was punifhed with the feverity which it deferved.

The Prime Minister rofe next, and fpoke to this effect :—Mr. Chairman, it is with uncommon fatisfaction that I fee every claufe of this bill regularly debated, without unbecoming impatience, or paffionate exclamations. I am willing to collect from this conduct, that the difpofition of every gentleman is, on this occafion, the fame with my own ; and that every expedient here propofed will be diligently examined, and either be ferioufly approved, or be calmly rejected.

Such coolnefs and impartiality, Sir, is certainly required by the importance of the prefent queftion ; a queftion which cannot but influence the profperity of the nation for many years.

It is not neceffary to remind any gentleman of the importance of our trade, of the power of the enemy againft whom we have declared war in defence of it, or of the neceffity of fhewing the world that our declarations of war are not empty noifes, or farces of refentment. But it may be proper, Sir, to remark, that this is not the only enemy, nor the moft powerful, whofe attempts we have reafon to provide againft, and who may oblige us to exert our whole power, and practife every expedient to increafe our forces.

The war has been hitherto profecuted with the utmoft vigour, with all the attention that its importance requires, and with fuccefs not difproportioned to our preparations ; nor will it ever be fuffered to languifh, if the powers neceffary for carrying it on are not denied.

Nothing is more evident, Sir, than that the natural power of the nation confifts in its fleets, which are now, by the care of the government, fo numerous, that the united power of many nations cannot equal them. But what are fleets unfurnifhed with men ? How will they maintain the dominion of the fea, by lying unactive in our harbours?

That no methods hitherto ufed have been fufficient to man our navies, and that our preparations have therefore been little more than an expenfive fhow of war, the whole nation is fufficiently informed ; it is therefore not doubtful that fome new meafures muft be taken ; whether any better can be fuggefted than are offered in this bill, muft be enquired.

With regard, Sir, to the claufe now under our confideration, it is to be remembered, that little more is propofed by it than to add the fanction of legality to a power which has long been exercifed by the admiralty,

admiralty, without any other authority than that of long prescription, the power of issuing warrants of impress upon emergent occasions, by which sailors are forced into the publick service.

This power, in its present state, must be allowed to have no foundation in any law, and by consequence, to be unlimited, arbitrary, and easily abused, and upon the whole, to be justifiable only by necessity : but that necessity is so frequent, that it is often exercised, and therefore ought to be regulated by the legislature ; and by making such regulations, we may rather be said to remove than introduce a grievance.

The power of searching for sailors, however it has been represented, is far from setting them on a level with felons, murderers, or vagabonds ; or indeed from distinguishing them, to their disadvantage, from the rest of the community, of which every individual is obliged to support the government.

Those that possess estates, or carry on trades, transfer part of their property to the publick ; and these ought, by parity of reason, to serve the publick in person, that have no property to transfer. Every man is secured by the constitution in the enjoyment of his life, his liberty, or his fortune ; and therefore every man ought reciprocally to defend the constitution to which he is himself indebted for safety and protection.

I am therefore, Sir, unable to discover in what consists the hardship of a law by which no new duties are enjoined, nor any thing required, which is not already every man's duty. Every man, indeed, who is desirous of evading the performance of any of the duties of society, will consider every compulsion as a hardship, by which he is obliged to contribute to the general happiness ; but his murmurs will prove nothing but his own folly and ingratitude, and will certainly deserve no regard from the legislative power.

There is in the bill before us, Sir, encouragement sufficient for voluntiers, and an offer of greater rewards than some gentlemen think consistent with the present state of the national revenues ; and what remains to be done with respect to those who are deaf to all invitations, and blind to all offers of advantage ? Are they to sit at ease only because they are idle, or to be distinguished with indulgence only for want of deserving it ?

It seems generally granted, Sir, that such drones are the proper objects of an impress. Let us then suppose that every man who is

willing

illing to ferve his country, has laid hold of the reward propofed, and
itered a voluntier.   The fleets are not yet fufficiently manned, and
ore failors muft be procured. Warrants are iffued out in the common
irm.   The negligent, the imprudent, the neceffitous are taken.
'he vigilant, the cunning, and thofe that have more money, find
ichter and efcape.   Can it be faid, that thofe whofe circumftances,
r good fortune, enable them to fecure themfelves from the officers
f the imprefs, deferve any exemption from the publick fervice, or
rom the hardfhips to which their companions are expofed ? Have
hey difcharged their debt of gratitude to the publick fo effectually by
unning away from its fervice, that no fearch ought to be made after
hem ? It feems evident, that if it was right to feize the one, it is
ikewife right to purfue the other, and if it be right to purfue him,
it is likewife right to hinder him from efcaping the purfuers.   It is
then right to veft fome perfons with the power of apprehending him,
and in whom is that power to be lodged, but in the civil magiftrate ?

Every man, Sir, is obliged by compulfive methods to ferve his
country, if he can be prevailed upon by no other.   If any man fhall
refufe to pay his rates or his taxes, will not his goods be feized by
force, and fold before his face ? If any particular methods are propofed for obliging feamen to contribute to the publick fafety, it is
only becaufe their fervice is neceffary upon more preffing occafions
than that of others ; upon occafions which do not admit of delay,
without the hazard of the whole community.

I muft confefs, Sir, there are inftances in which the hardfhips of
the feafaring part of the nation are peculiar, and truly calamitous.
A failor, after the dangers and toils of a long voyage, when he is
now in the fight of the port, where he hopes to enjoy that quiet.
which he has deferved by fo long a feries of fatigues, to repair the injuries which his health has fuffered, by change of climate, and the
diet of the fhips, and to recover that ftrength which inceffant vigilance has worn away ; when he is in expectation of being received by his family with thofe careffes, which the fuccours that he
brings them naturally produce, and defigns to reft awhile from danger and from care; in the midft of thefe pleafing views, he is on the
fudden feized by an imprefs, and forced into a repetition of all his
miferies, without any interval of refrefhment.

Let no man who can think without compaffion on fuch a fcene
as this, boaft his zeal for freedom, his regard for bravery, or his
gratitude

gratitude to thofe who contribute to the wealth and power of their
country; let every man who declares himfelf touched with the pity
which the flighteft reflection upon fuch a difappointment muft naturally produce, fincerely endeavour to obviate the neceffity of fuch
oppreffive meafures, which may at leaft in part be prevented, by
affigning to magiftrates the power of hunting out of their retreats,
thofe who neglect the bufinefs of their callings, and linger at once in
lazinefs and want.

There are great numbers who retire not from wearinefs but idlenefs, or an unreafonable prepoffeffion againft the publick fervice; and
furely nothing is more unreafonable, than that bad difpofitions
fhould be gratified, and that induftry fhould expofe any man to
penalties.

Upon the whole, Sir, I am not able to difcover, that any man
fhould be exempted from an imprefs merely becaufe he finds means to
efcape it, or becaufe idlenefs or difinclination to the publick fervice
prompts him to abfcond.

If any men deferve indulgence, in oppofition to the demands of the
publick, they are rather thofe who have already in fome degree difcharged their duty to it, by contributing to bring in that wealth
which is the confequence of a profperous and well-regulated commerce, and without which war cannot be fupported.

It is not without grief and regret, that I am obliged to reprefent on
this occafion the obftructions which the war has fuffered from thofe
at whofe requeft it was undertaken; and to declare that the conduct of
the merchants has afforded proof that fome law of this tendency is
abfolutely neceffary.

The merchants, Sir, who have fo loudly complained of the decline
of trade, the interruption of navigation, and the infolence, rapacity,
and cruelty of the Spaniards; the merchants who filled the nation
with reprefentations of their hardfhips, difcouragements, and miferies,
and lamented in the moft publick manner, that they were the only
body for whom the legiflature had no regard, who were abandoned
to the caprice of other nations, were plundered abroad and neglected
at home; the merchants, after having at length by their importunities engaged the ftate in a war, of which they have themfelves
certainly not the leaft pretenfions to queftion either the juftice or
neceffity, now, when by the natural confequences of a naval armament, failors become lefs numerous, and fhips more difficult to be
equipped,

equipped, contract in private with such sailors as they are inclined
to employ, and conceal them in garrets hired for that purpose, till
the freight is ready, or the danger of an impress is past, and thus
secure their own private affairs at the hazard of the publick,
and hinder the operations of a war, which they, and they only,
solicited.

The danger of having other enemies than the Spaniards, enemies,
Sir, more active, more powerful, and more ambitious, has already
been mentioned, a danger so near, and so formidable, that he will not
be thought very sollicitous for his country, whom the bare mention of
it does not alarm. This danger we are therefore to obviate by vigorous preparations, and unanimous resolutions; nor do I doubt but
both our enemies, if they find us united, will repent of attacking us.

Sir, the most efficacious method of manning our fleets, which law
or custom has yet put into our hands, is that of suspending our commerce by an embargo, and yet the whole nation knows how much
and by what means it has been eluded: no sooner was it known that
an embargo was laid, than the sailors flew away into the country, or
hid themselves in corners of this great city, as from the most formidable danger; and no sooner did the embargo cease, than the banks
of the river were again crowded with sailors, and all the trading vessels
were immediately supplied.

As I cannot doubt, Sir, that every gentleman is equally zealous
for the success of the war, and the prosperity of his country; and as
the insufficiency of the present methods of providing for them is apparent, I hope, that either the regulations proposed by this bill, to
which I see no important objections, or some other of equal use, will
be established by a general concurrence.

Lord BALTIMORE spoke next:—Though no gentleman in this assembly, Sir, can more ardently wish the success of the British arms, or
shall more willingly concur in any measure that may promote it, yet
I cannot agree to the clause now under our consideration; I disapprove
it both from moral and political motives; I disapprove it as neither
just nor prudent.

The injustice of so flagrant an invasion of the liberty of particular
men has been already exposed; nor is it, in my opinion, less easy to
discover the imprudence of exhausting all our supplies at once, and
sweeping away all our sailors, to supply a single exigency.

It

It has often been remarked, Sir, in favour of a standing army, that it is requisite to have a number of regular forces, who, though too weak to oppose an invasion, might be able to establish discipline in a larger body. An observation which may, with much greater justness, be applied to the seamen, whose art is much more difficult to be attained, and who are equally necessary in war and peace.

If our stock of seamen, Sir, be destroyed, if there is not left in our trading vessels a sufficient number of experienced artists to initiate novices, and propagate the profession, not only our ships of war must lie useless, but our commerce sink to nothing.

Nor have I reason to believe the naval power of France so formidable, as that we ought to be terrified by the apprehensions of into any extraordinary methods of procedure. I am informed that they have now very few ships of force left in their harbours ; and that they have exerted their whole strength in the American fleet.

I am not therefore, Sir, for providing against present dangers, without regard to our future security ; and think nothing more worthy of the consideration of this assembly, than the means of encouraging and increasing our seamen, which will not be effected by the bill before us.

Land forces may be hired upon emergencies ; but sailors are our own peculiar strength, and the growth of our own soil ; we are therefore above all other regards to attend, if I may use the term, to the preservation of the species.

Mr. VYNER next spoke :—Mr. Chairman, as there can be no stronger objection to any law than ambiguity, or indeterminate latitude of meaning, I think it necessary to propose, that some word of known and limited import, be substituted in the place of *seafaring men*; an expression which, if I was asked the meaning of it, I should find it difficult to explain.

Are *seafaring* men those only who navigate in the *sea ?* The term is then superfluous, for all such are evidently comprised in the word *seamen*. Are they bargemen or watermen who ply on rivers, and transport provision or commodities from one inland town to another ? In that sense no body will affirm that it is a proper word ; and impropriety in the expression of laws, produces uncertainty in the execution of them.

Captain CORNWALL rose up :—Sir, the term *seafaring men*, of which an explication is desired, is intended to include all those who live

live by conveying goods or passengers upon the water, whether the sea or inland rivers : nor can we restrain it to a narrower sense, without exempting from the publick service great numbers, whose manner of life has qualified them for it, and from whom their country may with equal justice expect assistance, as from those who are engaged in foreign traffick.

Mr. Vyner replied :—Sir, I am far from concurring with the honourable gentleman in his opinion, that the inland watermen are by their profession in any degree qualified for sea service, or can properly be called *seafaring men.*

All qualifications for the service must consist either in some knowledge of the arts of navigation, or in some familiarity with the dangers of the sea. With regard to any previous knowledge of naval business, it is well known that they have no advantage over any common labourer ; for the manner of navigating a ship and a barge have for the most part nothing in common.

Nor are these watermen, Sir, more able to stand firm in the terrors of the storm, or the noise of a battle, than those who follow any other occupation. Many of them never saw the sea, nor have less dread of its danger than the other inhabitants of the inland counties. They are therefore neither *seafaring* men, nor peculiarly capable of being made *seamen.*

But the hardship upon particular men is not the strongest objection to this clause, which by obstructing our inland navigation, may make our rivers useless, and set the whole trade of the nation at a stand. For who will bring up his son a waterman, who knows him exposed by that profession to be impressed for a seaman ?

It seems therefore necessary, Sir, either to omit the term * *seafaring men,* or to explain it in such a manner, that inland watermen may not be included.

Lord Gage spoke next :—Sir, so much has been urged against the compulsive methods proposed in this clause, and so little produced in favour of them, that it may seem superfluous to add any thing, or to endeavour, by a multiplicity of arguments, to prove what common reason must immediately discover. But there is one consequence of this clause which has not yet been observed, and which is yet too important not to be obviated by a particular proviso.

* Agreed to be omitted.

It is well known, Sir, that many of those to whom this act will extend are freeholders and voters for electing the representatives of the nation; and it is therefore apparent, that elections may be influenced by an ill-timed or partial execution of it. How easy will it be when an election approaches to raise a false alarm, to propose some secret expedition, or threaten us with an invasion from some unknown country, and to seize on all the seafaring voters whose affections are suspected, and confine them at Spithead till the contest is over.

I cannot therefore, Sir, but think it necessary, that if this clause be suffered to pass, some part of its hateful consequences should be prevented by an exception in favour of freeholders and voters, which surely is no less than what every man owes to his own security, to the welfare of his country, and to those by whom he has been honoured with the care of their liberties.

Mr. HENRY PELHAM then said as follows:—Sir, I do not rise in opposition to the proposal made by that right honourable member, nor do I think this the proper time either for opposing or approving it. Method is of the highest importance in enquiries like these; and if the order of the debate be interrupted by foreign questions or incidental objections, no man will be able to consider the clauses before us with the attention necessary to his own satisfaction, or to the conviction of others; the mind will be dissipated by a multiplicity of views, and nothing can follow but perplexity and confusion.

The great end, Sir, for which we are now assembled, is to strike out methods of manning the fleet with expedition and certainty. It is therefore proper in the first place to agree upon some general measures, to each of which there may undoubtedly be particular objections raised, that may be afterwards removed by exceptions or provisions; but these provisions should, for the sake of order, be inserted in particular clauses, to be separately considered.

Of this kind is the exception now offered, to which I have no objection but its present impropriety, and the interruption of the debate which it may now occasion; for I see at present no reason against admitting it in a particular clause.

When it is considered how much the success of the war may depend upon the determinations of this day, and how much our future happiness and security may depend upon the success of our present undertakings, I hope my sollicitude for regularity and expedition will be easily excused.

                                                        Sir,

Sir HIND COTTON answered:—I am not able, Sir, to discover ny imminent danger to the nation in suspending our attention to the clause before us for a few moments; nor indeed do we cease to attend to it, while we are endeavouring to mollify it, and adapt it to our constitution.

The exception proposed is, in the opinion of the honourable gentleman, so reasonable, that he declares himself ready to approve it in another place; and to me, no place seems more proper of its making part of this bill than this. As a connection between the clause and exception appears necessary and immediate, I cannot see why it should be postponed, unless it is hoped that it may be forgotten.

Mr. PULTENEY then spoke:—Sir, that this exception should be forgotten there is no danger; for how long soever it be delayed, I will never agree to the act till I see it inserted. If we suffer the liberty of the freeholders to be infringed, what can we expect but to be charged with betraying our trust, and giving up to servitude and oppression those who deputed us to this assembly, as the guardians of their privileges, and the asserters of their birthright; a charge too just to be denied, and too atrocious to be borne.

Sir, the right of a freeholder is independent on every other circumstance, and is neither made more or less by wealth or poverty: the estate, however small, which gives a right of voting, ought to exempt the owner from every restraint that may hinder the exertion of his right; a right on which our constitution is founded, and which cannot be taken away without subverting our whole establishment.

To overlook the distinctions which the fundamental laws of our country have made in respect to different orders of men, and to regard only the accidents of affluence and necessity, is surely unjust in itself, and unworthy of this assembly; an assembly, Sir, instituted principally to protect the weak against the strong, and deputed to represent those in a collective state, who are not considerable enough to appear singly, and claim a voice in the legislature.

To expose an honest, a laborious, and an useful man, to be seized by the hands of an insolent officer, and dragged from the enjoyment of his right, only because he will not violate his conscience, and add his voice to those of sycophants, dependants, and prostitutes, the slaves of power, the drudges of a court, and the hirelings of a faction, is the highest degree of injustice and cruelty. Let us rather, Sir, sweep away with an impress, the drones of large fortunes, the

tyrants of villages, and the oppreffors of the poor ; let us oblige thofe
to ferve their country by force, whofe fortunes have bad no other
effect than to make them infolent and worthlefs ; but let fuch who,
by contributing to commerce, make every day fome addition to the
publick wealth, be left in the full enjoyment of the rights which they
deferve: let thofe by whofe labour the expences of the war are
furnifhed, be excufed from contributing to it by perfonal fervice.

It is neceffary, Sir, to have our laws eftablifhed by the reprefentatives of the people ; it is neceffary that thofe reprefentatives fhould
be freely elected ; and therefore every law that obftructs the liberty of
voters, is contrary to the fundamental laws of our conftitution ; and
what multitudes may by this law be either hindered from giving their
votes, or be terrified into fuch a choice as by no means correfponds
with their judgments or inclinations, it is eafy to forefee.

I am indeed of opinion, Sir, that this claufe cannot be adapted to
our conftitution, nor modified by any expedient into a law, which
will not lay infupportable hardfhips upon the nation, and make way
for abfolute power. But as it is neceffary that a conftant fupply of
feamen fhould be provided, I think it not improper to obferve, that
there is one expedient yet remaining, by which, though it will not
much affift us in our prefent exigence, the fleets of this nation may
hereafter be conftantly fupported.

We have at prefent great numbers of charity fchools eftablifhed in
this nation, where the children of the poor receive an education difproportioned to their birth. This has often no other confequences
than to make them unfit for their ftations by placing them in their
own opinion above the drudgery of daily labour, a notion which is
too much indulged, as idlenefs co-operating with vanity, can hardly
fail to gain the attendant, and which fometimes prompts them to fupport themfelves by practices not only ufelefs but pernicious to fociety.
This evil, Sir, cannot be better obviated than by allotting a reafonable proportion out of every fchool to the fervice of the fea, in
which by entering early they cannot fail to become proficients, and
where their attainments, which at prefent too frequently produce
lazinefs and difhonefty, might enable them to excel, and entitle
them to promotion.

Mr. WINNINGTON replied:—Sir, notwithftanding the confidence
with which fome gentlemen have propofed this amendment, and the
eafinefs with which others have confented to it, I declare without hefitation,

fication, that I oppofe it now, and intend to oppofe it whenever it
fhall be offered, becaufe it will defeat all the other provifions which
fhall be made in the bill.

I will venture to fay, Sir, that if every man, who has by whatever tenure the right of voting, fhall be exempted from the neceffity
of contributing to the publick fafety by his perfonal fervice, every
man qualified for the fea will by fome means acquire a vote.

Sir, a very fmall part of thofe who give their votes in this nation
for reprefentatives in fenate, enjoy that right as the appendage of a
freehold; to live in fome towns, and to be born only in others,
gives the unalienable privilege of voting. Any gentleman, to fecure
his own intereft, or obftruct the publick fervice, may, by dividing a
fmall piece of barren ground among a hundred failors, exalt them
all to freeholders, and exempt them from the influence of this law.

However, Sir, I am not lefs a friend to the freeholders than thofe
who propofe the exception in their favour; but in my opinion the
great intereft of the freeholders is the prefervation of their freeholds,
which can only be fecured by a vigorous exertion of the power of the
nation, in the war which is now declared againft the Spaniards.

Mr. BARRINGTON fpoke next:—Sir, by the obfervations which
I have opportunities of making at the place which I have the honour
to reprefent, I am convinced of the influence that this law will have
upon all the boroughs along the coafts. There moft of the voters
are, in one fenfe or other, Sir, feafaring men, being almoft all of
them owners of veffels, and in fome degree acquainted with navigation; they may therefore be hurried away at the choice of an officious
or oppreffive magiftrate, who may by partiality and injuftice obtain a
majority, contrary to the general inclination of the people, and determine the election by his own authority.

Sir WILLIAM YONGE then faid:—Sir, if every freeholder and
voter is to be exempted from the influence of the law, the bill that we
are with fo much ardour endeavouring to draw up and rectify, and of
which the neceffity is fo generally acknowledged, will be no other
than an empty found, and a determination without an object; for
while we are empowering the government to call feamen into the fervice, we are exempting almoft all that are able to ferve from the denomination of feamen: what is this but to difpute without a fubject?
to raife with one hand and demolifh with the other?

In

In the weſtern parts of the nation, Sir, where I reſide, many who vote at elections claim their privilege by no other title than that of boiling a pot; a title which he who has it not, may eaſily obtain, when it will either gratify his lazineſs or his cowardice, and which, though not occaſionally obtained, ſeems not ſufficient to ſet any man out of the reach of a juſt and neceſſary law.

It is therefore, Sir, undoubtedly requiſite that the terms of the exception ſhould be explicit and definitive, and that only thoſe ſhould be exempted who have ſuch poſſeſſions or qualifications as this aſſembly ſhall think a juſt title to exemption. For on the weſtern coaſt, from whence great ſupplies may be expected, almoſt every ſailor has a vote, to which nothing is there required but to hire a lodging and boil a pot; after which, if this exception be admitted in all its latitude, he may ſit at eaſe amidſt the diſtreſſes of his country, ridicule the law which he has eluded, and ſet the magiſtrate at open defiance.

The PRIME MINISTER ſpoke next :—As I think, Sir, ſome exception may be juſt and proper, ſo I ſuppoſe every gentleman will concur with me in rejecting one of ſuch extent as ſhall leave no object for the operation of the law.

It is in my opinion proper to reſtrain the exemption to thoſe freeholders who are poſſeſſed of ſuch an eſtate as gives a vote for the repreſentative of the county, by which thoſe whoſe privilege ariſes from their property will be ſecured; and it ſeems reaſonable that thoſe who have privileges without property, ſhould purchaſe them by their ſervices.

Counſellor BROWN ſpoke next :—Sir, the exception propoſed will not only defeat the end of the bill, by leaving it few objects, but will obſtruct the execution of it on proper occaſions, and involve the magiſtrate in difficulties which will either intimidate him in the exertion of his authority, or, if he perſiſts in diſcharging his duty with firmneſs and ſpirit, will perhaps oblige him ſometimes to repent of his fidelity.

It is the neceſſary conſequence, Sir, of a ſeaman's profeſſion, that he is often at a great diſtance from the place of his legal ſettlement, or patrimonial poſſeſſions; and he may therefore aſſert of his own circumſtances what is moſt convenient without danger of detection. Diſtance is a ſecurity that prompts many men to falſhoods by which
only

nly vanity is gratified, and few men will tell truth in oppofition to their intereft, when they may lie without apprehenfion of being onvicted.

When therefore a magiftrate receives directions to imprefs all the feamen within his diftrict, how few will he find who will not declare themfelves freeholders in fome diftant county, or freemen of fome obfcure borough. It is to no purpofe, Sir, that the magiftrate difbelieves what he cannot confute ; and if in one inftance in a hundred he fhould be miftaken, and, acting in confequence of his error, force a freeman into the fervice, what reparation may not be demanded ?

I therefore propofe it to the confideration of the committee, whether any man ought to claim exemption from this law by a title, that may fo readily be procured, or fo fafely ufurped.

The ATTORNEY-GENERAL fpoke next :—Sir, the practice of impreffing, which has been declaimed againft with fuch vehement exaggerations, is not only founded on immemorial cuftom, which makes it part of the common law, but is likewife eftablifhed by our ftatutes; for I remember to have found it in the ftatutes of queen Mary, and therefore cannot allow that it ought to be treated as illegal, and anti-conftitutional.

That it is not inconfiftent with our conftitution may be proved from the practice of erecting the royal ftandard, upon great emergencies, to which every man was obliged immediately to repair; this practice is as old as our conftitution, and as it may be revived at pleafure, may be properly mentioned as equivalent to an imprefs.

Mr. VINER anfwered :—This word, Sir, which the learned member has by his wonderful diligence difcovered in the ftatutes, may perhaps be there, but in a fignification far different from that which it bears at prefent. The word was, without doubt, originally French, prêt, and implied what is now expreffed by the term ready; and to imprefs any man was in thofe days only to make him ready, or engage him to hold himfelf in readinefs, which was brought about not by compulfion, purfuit, and violence, but by the allurements of a pecuniary reward, or the obligation of fome antient tenure.

S 4   HOUSE

HOUSE OF COMMONS.

March 9, 1740-1.

On the 66th day, the consideration of the bill for raising seamen was resumed, and a clause read, by which every constable, headborough, tythingman, or other person, was liable to be examined upon oath by the justices of peace, who were empowered to lay a fine upon them for any neglect, offence, or connivance.

SIR JOHN BARNARD rose up and spoke to the following effect:—
Mr. Chairman, it is the peculiar happiness of the Britons, that no law can be made without the consent of their representatives, and I hope no such infatuation can ever fall upon them as may influence them to chuse a representative capable of concurring in absurdities like this.

The folly, the iniquity, the stupidity of this clause, can only be conceived by hearing it repeated; it is too flagrant to be extenuated, and too gross to admit exaggerations: to oblige a man to make oath against himself, to subject himself by his own voice to penalties and hardships, is at once cruel and ridiculous, a wild complication of tyranny and folly.

To call upon any man to accuse himself, is only to call upon him to commit perjury, and has therefore been always accounted irrational and wicked: in those countries where it is practised, the confession is extorted by the rack, which indeed is so necessary on such occasions, that I should not wonder to hear the promoters of this clause openly declaring for the expediency of tortures.

Nothing is more evident than that this bill, however the importance of the occasion may be magnified, was drawn up without reflection, and that the clauses were never understood by those that offered them: errors like these must arise only from precipitation and neglect, for they are too gross to be committed either by ignorance or design.

To expose such absurdities is indeed easy, but not pleasing; for what end is answered by pointing at folly, or how is the publick service advanced by shewing that the methods proposed are totally to be rejected? Where a proposition is of a mixed kind, and only erroneous

neous in part, it is an ufeful and no difagreeable tafk to feparate truth from error, and difentangle from ill confequences fuch meafures as may be purfued with advantage to the publick; but mere ftupidity can only produce compaffion, and afford no opportunities for enquiry or difpute.

Admiral WAGER replied:—Sir, This claufe, however contemptuoufly treated, has been already paffed into a law by a fenate which brought no difhonour upon the Britifh nation, by a fenate which was courted and dreaded by the greateft part of the univerfe, and was drawn up by a miniftry that have given their pofterity no reafon to treat them with derifion and contumely.

In the reign of the late great queen, this method of proceeding was approved and eftablifhed, and we may judge of the propriety of the meafures followed in that war by the fuccefs which they procured.

Thofe therefore by whom this bill was drawn up have committed no new abfurdities, nor have propofed any thing which was not enacted by the wifeft of our predeceffors, in one of the moft illuftrious periods of our hiftory.

Mr. GYBBON anfwered,—Sir, I am far from thinking a propofition fufficiently defended by an affertion that it was admitted by our predeceffors, for though I have no inclination to vilify their memory, I may without fcruple affirm that they had no pretenfions to infallibility, and that there are in many of our ftatutes inftances of fuch ignorance, credulity, weaknefs, and error, as cannot be confidered without aftonifhment.

In queftions of an abftrufe and complicated nature, it is certain, Sir, that experience has taught us what could never have been difcovered previoufly by the wifdom of our anceftors, and we have found by their confequences the impropriety of many practices which they approved, and which we fhould have equally applauded in the fame circumftances.

But to what purpofe is obfervation, if we muft fhut our eyes againft it, and appeal for ever to the wifdom of our anceftors?—if we muft fall into error, merely becaufe they were miftaken, and rufh upon rocks out of veneration to thofe who were wreck'd againft them?

In queftions eafily to be examined, and determinations which comprized no perplexing contrarieties of intereft, or multiplicity of circumftances, they were equally liable with ourfelves to be fupine and negligent,

negligent, to sink into security, or be surprized by haste. That the clause now before us was enacted by them, must be ascribed merely to the hurry of the sessions in which it was brought before them; a time in which so many enquiries of the highest importance were to be made, and great diversity of views to be regarded, that it is no wonder that some absurdities should escape without detection.

In the fourth of the reign of the queen, this bill was brought in, as now, at the latter end of a session, when the attention of the senate was fatigued and distracted, and it was hurried through both houses, and ratified by the queen, with very little consideration.

But then, as this circumstance may be justly termed an extenuation of their error, it ought to be a lesson of caution to us, that we may not be in the like manner betrayed into the same weakness.

Mr. HENRY PELHAM next rose up:—Sir, the conduct of our predecessors seems not to stand in need of any excuse; for it might be easy to vindicate it by arguments, but that it is more proper to approve it by imitation.

Whenever the bill was passed, or how hastily soever the law was enacted, it was, I believe, rather the effect of necessity than of inadvertency; of the same necessity which now presses, and which is very ill consulted by tedious debates.

They were then involved in a war, and were not so distracted by private interests as not to unite in the most vigorous opposition of their enemies. They knew that the publick good is often promoted by the temporary inconveniencies of individuals; and when affairs of the highest importance demanded their attention, when the security of the whole nation and the happiness of their posterity were the subject of their enquiries, they wisely suffered less considerations to pass without superfluous and unseasonable sollicitude

How justly they reasoned, Sir, and what vigour their resolutions gave to the military operations, our victories are a sufficient proof: and if experience be the surest guide, it cannot be improper to imitate those who, in the same circumstances with ourselves, found means to raise the honour, and improve the commerce of their country.

That our circumstances are the same with those of the senate by which this law was made, is obvious beyond dispute; or where they vary, the difference is perhaps to our disadvantage. We have, Sir, the same enemies, or, at least, have reason to apprehend the same; but have little hope of the same allies. The present war is to be

                                                            carried

arried on at a greater diftance, and in more places at the fame in-
ſtant; we cannot therefore fupply our fhips occafionally, but muſt
raiſe great numbers in a fhort time.

If therefore it was then concluded, that the method under our examination was ufeful; if meafures, not eligible in themfelves, may
be authorized by neceffity, why may not we, in compliance with
the fame exigencies, have recourfe to the fame expedients?

Sir WILLIAM YONGE then fpoke:—Sir, how much weight is
added to the determinations of the fenate, by the dignity of their
procedure, and the decency of their difputations, a flight knowledge
of mankind is fufficient to evince. It is well known that government is fupported by opinion; and that he who deftroys the reputa-
tation, deftroys the authority of the legiflative power. Nor is it leſs
apparent, that he who degrades debate into fcurrility, and deftroys
the folemnity of confultation, endeavours to fink the fenate into contempt.

It was therefore, Sir, with indignation and furprize that I heard
the claufe before us cenfured with fuch indecency of language, and
the authors of it treated with contumelies and reproaches that
mere error does not deferve, however apparent, but which were now
vented before any error was detected.

I know not, Sir, why the gentlemen who are thus indecently attacked have fuffered fuch reproaches without cenfure and without reply. I
know not why they have omitted to put the honourable gentleman
in mind of the refpect due to this affembly, or to the characters of
thofe whom he oppofes; gentlemen equally fkilled with himfelf in the
fubject of our enquiries, and whom his own attainments, however
large, or his abilities, however comprehenfive, cannot give him a
right to charge with ignorance or folly.

To reproach men with incapacity is a cheap method of anfwering
their arguments, but a method which the rules of this houfe ought to
exclude from our debates, as the general civility of the world has
banifhed it from every other place of concourfe or converfation.

I, for my part, Sir, fhall always endeavour to confine my attention to the queftion before us, without fuffering my reafon to be
biaffed, or my enquiries diverted by low altercations, or perfonal
animofities; nor when any other man deviates into reproachful and
contemptuous language, fhall I be induced to think more highly of
either his arguments or capacity.

Sir,

Sir JOHN BARNARD replied :—Sir, I have always heard it reprefented as an inftance of integrity, when the tongue and heart move
in concert, when the words are reprefentations of the fentiments ;
and have therefore hitherto endeavoured to explain my arguments
with perfpicuity, and imprefs my fentiments with force ; I have
thought it hypocrify to treat ftupidity with reverence, or to honour
nonfenfe with the ceremony of a confutation. As knavery fo folly
that is not reclaimable, is to be fpeedily difpatched, bufinefs is to be
freed from obftruction, and fociety from a nuifance.

Nor, Sir, when I am cenfured by thofe whom I may offend by the
ufe of terms correfpondent with my ideas, will I by a tame and
filent fubmiffion give reafon to fufpect that I am confcjous of a fault,
but will treat the accufation with open contempt, and fhew no
greater regard to the abettors, than to the authors of abfurdity.

That decency is of great ufe in publick debates, I fhall readily
allow; it may fometimes fhelter folly from ridicule, and preferve villainy from publick detection ; nor is it ever more carefully fupported,
than when meafures are promoted that nothing can preferve from
contempt, but the folemnity with which they are eftablifhed.

Decency is a proper circumftance ; but liberty is the effence of
fenatorial difquifitions : liberty is the parent of truth ; but truth and
decency are fometimes at variance : all men and all propofitions are
to be treated here as they deferve ; and there are many who have no
claim either to refpect or decency.

Mr. WINNINGTON then rofe :—Sir, that it is improper in its own
nature, and inconfiftent with our conftitution, to lay any man under
an obligation to accufe himfelf, cannot be denied ; it is therefore
evident, that fome amendment is neceffary to the claufe before us.

I have for this reafon drawn up an amendment, Sir, which, if approved by the committee, will, in my opinion, remove all the objections to this part of the bill, and by reconciling it with our natural
and legal rights, I hope, induce thofe to approve it, who have hitherto
oppofed it.

I therefore propofe that thefe words fhould be fubftituted inftead of
thofe which are the fubject of the debate, or fome other to this purpofe ; *That no perfon fhall be liable to be fined by virtue of this act, unlefs
a witnefs being examined, fhall make oath of the mifdemeanour or neglect.*

Thus the neceffity of examining men upon oath in their own
caufe will be entirely taken away, and as the claufe will then ftand,
there

there will remain no fufpicion of injuftice, or oppreffion, becaufe
none can be practifed without the concurrence of many perfons of
different interefts.

[This claufe, though agreed to in the committee, was at laft rejected.]

Mr. HORACE WALPOLE fpoke next to this effect :—Mr. Chairman,
It does not yet appear that the gentlemen who have engaged in this
debate have fufficiently attended to the exigence of our affairs, and the
importance of the queftion. They have lavifhed their oratory in declaiming upon the abfurdity of the methods propofed, and difcovered
their fagacity, by fhewing how future navies may be fupplied from
charity fchools, but have fubftituted no expedients in the place of thofe
which they fo warmly condemn, nor have condefcended to inform us,
how we may now guard our coafts, or man our fleets for immediate
fervice.

There are fome circumftances, Sir, of the prefent war, which make
our neceffity of raifing fea forces greater than in thofe of William and
Anne that fucceeded him. The chief advantages that we gained over the
French in their wars were the confequences of our victories by land.

At fea, Sir, the balance was almoft equal, though the Dutch fleet
and ours were united ; nor did they quit the fea becaufe their fleets
were deftroyed, but becaufe they were obliged to recruit their land
forces with their failors. Should they now declare war againft us,
they would be under no fuch neceffity of defrauding the fea fervice,
for they have now on foot an army of 160,000 men, which are maintained at no greater expence than 40,000 by the Britifh government ;
as they are therefore, Sir, fo formidable by land, we have no way of
oppofing them but by our fea forces.

Nor is their navy fo contemptible as fome have either by conjecture
or mifinformation reprefented it. The fleet which they have difpatched to America, confifts not of fewer than twenty fhips, of which
the leaft carry fixty guns, and they are fitting out now an equal number in their own ports ; befides, their Eaft India company is obliged to
furnifh ten fhips of the line, at the demand of the government.

Thus it appears that we have neighbours fufficiently powerful to
alarm us with the fenfe of immediate danger ; danger which is made
more imminent by the expeditious methods by which the French man
their fleets, and which we muft imitate if we hope to oppofe them
with fuccefs.

I need not say how little we can depend upon any professions of neutrality, which will be best observed when they cannot be securely violated ; or upon the pacific inclination of their minister, which interest, persuasion, or caprice, may alter, and to which it is not very honourable to trust for safety. How can that nation sink lower, which is only free because it is not invaded by its neighbours, and retains its possessions only because no other has leisure or inclination to take them away ?

If it be asked what can provoke the French to interrupt us in the prosecution of our designs, and in the punishment of those who have plundered and insulted us, it is not only easy to urge the strict alliance between the two crowns, the ties of blood, the conformity of interests, and their equal hatred of the Britons, but another more immediate reason may be added. It is suspected that under pretence of vindicating our own rights, we are endeavouring to gain the possession of the Spanish dominions, and engross the wealth of the new world ; and that therefore it is the interest of every power whose subjects traffic to those countries to oppose us.

Thus, whether we succeed or fail in our attempts on America, we have the French power to apprehend. If we make conquests, they may probably think it necessary to obviate the torrent of our victories, and to hinder the increase of our dominions, that they may secure their own trade, and maintain their own influence.

If we should be defeated, of which no man, Sir, can deny the possibility, the inclination of all to insult the depressed, and to push down the falling is well known ; nor can it be expected that our hereditary enemies would neglect so fair an opportunity of attacking us.

How they might ravage our coasts, and obstruct our trade, how they might triumph in the channel, and block us up in our own ports, bombard our towns, and threaten us with invasions, I hope I need but barely mention, to incite this assembly to such dispatch in manning our fleets, as may secure us at once from insults and from terror.

It is undoubtedly, Sir, in our power to raise a naval force sufficient to awe the ocean, and restrain the most daring of our enemies from any attempts against us, but this cannot be effected by harangues objections, and disputations.

There is nothing, Sir, more frequently the subject of raillery or declamation than the usefulness or danger of a standing army, to which I declare myself no otherwise inclined than by my concern for the common safety; I willingly allow that not one soldier ought to
be

e supported by the public, whose service is not necessary ; but surely
one of those who declare so warmly for the honour and privileges of
their country, would expose it to the insults of foreign powers without defence. If therefore they think the danger of land forces more
than equivalent to the benefit, they ought unanimously to concur in the
increase of our naval strength, by which they may be protected, but
cannot be oppressed : they ought willingly to give their assistance to
any propositions for making the fleet formidable, that their declarations
against the army may not be thought to proceed from a resolution to
obstruct the measures of the government, rather than from zeal for
the constitution. For he that equally opposes the establishment of the
army, and the improvement of the navy, declares in effect against the
security of the nation ; and though, perhaps, without design, exposes
his countrymen to the mercy of their enemies. ·

Mr. PULTENEY spoke next :—Sir, I cannot discover for what reason the bill before us is so vigorously supported, but must observe that
I have seldom known such vehement and continued efforts produced by
mere publick spirit, and unmingled regard for the happiness of the
nation. Nothing, Sir, that can be urged in favour of the measures
now proposed has been omitted. When arguments are confuted,
precedents are cited ; when precedents fail, the advocates for the bill
have recourse to terror and necessity, and endeavour to frighten those
whom they cannot convince.

But perhaps, Sir, these formidable phantoms may soon be put to
flight, and, like the other illusions of cowardice, disappear before the
light. Perhaps this necessity will be found only chimerical ; and
these dangers appear only the visions of credulity, or the bugbears
of imposture.

To arrive at a clear view of our present condition, it will be necessary, Sir, not to amuse ourselves with general assertions, or over-
whelm our reason by terrifying exaggerations : let us consider distinctly the power and the conduct of our enemies, and enquire whether they do not affright us more than they are able to hurt us.

That the force of Spain alone, Sir, is much to be dreaded, no man
will assert ; for that empire, it is well known, has long been seized
with all the symptoms of declining power, and has been supported,
not by its own strength, but by the interests of its neighbours. The
vast dominions of the Spaniards are only an empty show ; they are
lands without inhabitants, and by consequence without defence ; they

are

are rather excrefcences than members of the monarchy, and receive fupport rather than communicate. In the diftant branches of their empire
the government languifhes, as the vital motion in an expiring body ;
and the ftruggles which they now make, may be termed rather ago-
nies than efforts.

From Spain, therefore, unaffifted, we have nothing to apprehend,
and yet from thence we have been threatened with infults and invafions.

That the condition of the French is far different, cannot be denied; their commerce flourifhes, their dominions are connected, their
wealth increafes, and their government operates with full vigour:
their influence is great, and their name formidable. But I cannot
allow, Sir, that they have yet attained fuch a height of power as
fhould alarm us with conftant apprehenfions, or that we ought to fecure ourfelves againft them by the violation of our liberties. Not
to urge that the lofs of freedom, and the deftruction of our conftitution, are the worft confequences that can be apprehended from a conqueft, and that to a flave the change of his mafter is of no great importance, it is evident, that the power of the French is of fuch
kind as can only affect us remotely, and confequentially. They may
fill the continent with alarms, and ravage the territories of Germany
by their numerous armies, but can only injure us by means of their
fleets. We may wait, Sir, without a pannick terror, though not
without fome degree of anxiety, the event of their attempts upon the
neighbouring princes, and cannot be reduced to fight for our
altars and our houfes, but by a fecond armada, which, even then, the
winds muft favour, and a thoufand circumftances concur to expedite.

But that no fuch fleet can be fitted out by the united endeavours of
the whole world ; that our navy, in its prefent ftate, is fuperior
to any that can be brought againft us, our minifters ought not to be
ignorant : and therefore to difpirit the nation with apprehenfions of
armies hovering in the air, and of conquerors to be wafted over by
fupernatural means, is to deftroy that happinefs which government
was ordained to preferve ; to fink us to tamenefs and cowardice ; and
to betray us to infults and to robberies.

If our danger, Sir, be fuch as has been reprefented, to whom muft
we impute it ? Upon whom are our weaknefs, our poverty, and our
miferies to be charged? Upon whom, but thofe who have ufurped
the direction of affairs which they did not underftand, or which their

follicitude

ollicitude for the prefervation of their own power hindered them from attending?

That the Spaniards, Sir, are now enabled to make refiftance, and perhaps to infult and depopulate our colonies; that the French have difpatched a fleet into the American feas to obftruct, as may be conjectured, the progrefs of our arms, and that we are in danger of meeting oppofition which we did not expect, is too evident to be concealed.

But, Sir, is not the fpirit of our enemies the confequence rather of our cowardice than of their own ftrength? Does not the oppofition to our defigns, by whatever nation it fhall be made, arife from the contempt which has been brought upon us by our irrefolution, for-bearance, and delays? Had we refented the firft infult, and repaired our earlieft loffes by vigorous reprizals, our merchants had long ago carried on their traffick with fecurity, our enemies would have courted us with refpect, and our allies fupported us with confidence.

Our negotiations, treaties, propofals, and conceffions, not only afforded them leifure to collect their forces, equip their fleets, and fortify their coafts; but gave them likewife fpirit to refift thofe who could not be conquered but by their own cowardice and folly. By our ill-timed patience, and lingering preparations, we encouraged thofe to unite againft us, who would otherwife have only hated us in fecret; and deterred thofe from declaring in our favour, whom intereft or gratitude might have inclined to affift us. For who will fupport thofe from whom no mutual fupport can be expected? And who will expect that thofe will defend their allies, who defert themfelves?

But, Sir, however late our refentment was awakened, had the war been profecuted vigoroufly after it was declared, we might have been now fecure from danger, and freed from fufpence, nor would any thing have remained but to give laws to our enemies.

From the fuccefs of Vernon with fo inconfiderable forces, we may conjecture what would have been performed with an armament proportioned to his undertaking; and why he was not better fupplied, no reafon has yet been given; nor can it be eafily difcovered why we either did not begin the war before our enemies had concerted their meafures, or delay it till we had formed our own.

Notwithftanding fome opportunities have been neglected, and all the advantages of a fudden attack have been irrecoverably loft; notwithstanding our friends, Sir, have learned to despise and neglect us, and our enemies are animated to confidence and obstinacy, yet our real and intrinsick strength continues the same ; nor are there yet any preparations made against us by the enemy, with views beyond their own security and defence. It does not yet appear, Sir, that our enemies, however insolent, look upon us as the proper objects of a conquest, or that they imagine it possible to besiege us in our own ports, or to confine us to the defence of our own country. We are not therefore to have recourse to measures, which, if they are ever to be admitted, can be justified by nothing but the utmost distress, and can only become proper, as the last and desperate expedient. The enemy, Sir, ought to appear not only in our seas, but in our ports, before it can be necessary that one part of the nation should be enslaved for the preservation of the rest.

To destroy any part of the community, while it is in our power to preserve the whole, is certainly absurd, and inconsistent with the equity and tenderness of a good government : and what is slavery less than destruction ? What greater calamity has that man to expect, who has been already deprived of his liberty, and reduced to the level with thieves and murderers ? With what spirit, Sir, will he draw his sword upon his invaders, who has nothing to defend ? Or why should he repel the injuries which will make no addition to his misery, and will fall only on those to whom he is enslaved ?

It is well known that gratitude is the foundation of our duty to our country, and to our superiors, whom we are obliged to protect upon some occasions, because upon others we receive protection from them, and are maintained in the quiet possession of our fortunes, and the security of our lives. But what gratitude is due to his country from a man distinguished without a crime by the legislature, from the rest of the people, and marked out for hardships and oppressions ? From a man who is condemned to labour and to danger, only that others may fatten with indolence, and slumber without anxiety ? From a man who is doomed to misery without reward, and hunted from his retreat, as the property of his master ?

Where gratitude, Sir, is not the motive of action, which may easily happen in minds not accustomed to observe the ends of government and relations of society, interest never fails to preside, which may be distinguished from gratitude, as it regards the immediate consequences of action, and confines the view to present advantages.

But

But what interest can be gratified by a man who is not master of his own actions, nor secure in the enjoyment of his acquisitions ? Why should he be sollicitous to increase his property, who may be torn from the possession of it in a moment ? Or upon what motive can he act who will not become more happy by doing his duty ?

Many of those to whom this bill is proposed to extend, have raised fortunes at the expence of their ease, and at the hazard of their lives ; and now sit at rest, enjoying the memory of their past hardships, and inciting others to the prosecution of the same adventures : how will it be more reasonable to drag these men from their houses, than to seize any other gentleman upon his own estate ? And how negligently will our navigation and our commerce be promoted, when it is discovered that either wealth cannot be gained by them ; or, if so gained, cannot be enjoyed.

But it is still urged, Sir, that there is a necessity of manning the fleet ; a necessity which indeed cannot totally be denied, though a short delay would produce no frightful consequences, would expose us to no invasions, nor disable us from prosecuting the war. Yet, as the necessity at least deserves the regard of the legislature, let us consider what motives have hitherto gained men over to the publick service ; let us examine how our land forces are raised, and how our merchants equip their ships. How is all this effected without murmurs, mutinies, or discontent, but by the natural and easy method of offering rewards ?

It may be objected, Sir, that rewards have been already proposed without effect ; but, not to mention the corrupt arts which have been made use of to elude that promise, by rejecting those that came to claim them, we can infer from their inefficacy only, that they were too small ; that they were not sufficient to dazzle the attention, and withdraw it from the prospect of the distant advantages which may arise from the service of the merchants. Let the reward therefore be doubled, and if it be not then sufficient, doubled anew. There is nothing but may be bought, if an adequate price is offered ; and we are therefore to raise the reward till it shall be adjudged by the sailors equivalent to the inconveniencies of the service.

Let no man urge that this is profusion ; that it is a breach of our trust, and a prodigality of the publick money. Sir, the money thus paid is the price of liberty ; it is disbursed to hinder slavery from encroaching, to preserve our natural rights from infraction, and the constitution of our country from violation. If we vote away the privilege of one clafs among us, thofe of another may quickly be demanded ; and flavery will advance by degrees, till the laft remains of freedom fhall be loft.

But perhaps, Sir, it will appear upon reflection, that even this method needs not to be practifed. It is well known, that it is not neceffary for the whole crew of a fhip to be expert failors ; there muft be fome novices, and many whofe employment has more of labour than of art. We have now a numerous army which burthens our country, without defending it, and from whom we may therefore draw fupplies for the fleet, and diftribute them amongft the fhips in juft proportions ; they may immediately affift the feamen, and will become able in a fhort time to train up others.

It will doubtlefs, Sir, be objected to this propofal, that the continent is in confufion, and that we ought to continue fuch a force as may enable us to affift our allies, maintain our influence, and turn the fcale of affairs in the neighbouring countries. I know not how we are indebted to our allies, or by what ties we are obliged to affift thofe who never affifted us ; nor can I, upon mature confideration, think it neceffary to be always gazing on the continent, watching the motions of every potentate, and anxioufly attentive to every revolution. There is no end, Sir, of obviating contingencies, of attempting to fecure ourfelves from every poffibility of danger. I am indeed defirous that our friends, if any there be that deferve that name, fhould fucceed in their defigns, and be protected in their claims ; but think it ought always to be remembered, that our own affairs affect us immediately, theirs only by confequence ; and that the neareft danger is to be firft regarded.

With refpect to the amendment offered to this claufe, I cannot fee that it will produce any advantage, nor think any evidence fufficient to juftify the breach of our conftitution, or fubject any man to the hardfhip of having his dwelling entered by force.

And, Sir, I am not entirely fatisfied of the impartiality and equity with which it is promifed that this law will be put in execution, or what new influence is to co operate with this law, by which corruption and oppreffion will be prevented.

It is well known, Sir, that many other laws are made ineffectual by partiality or negligence, which remarkably appears by the immenfe quantities of corn that are daily carried into foreign countries, by illegal exportations, by which traffic I am informed that we obtain moft of our foreign gold, which in reality is paid us for corn by
the

uffer any diminution by a comparifon with thofe who vilify and tra-
luce them.

Thofe, Sir, that treat others with fuch licentious contempt, ought
furely to give fome illuftrious proof of their own abilities; and yet
if we examine what has been produced on this queftion, we fhall
find no reafon to admire their fagacity or their knowledge.

We have been told, Sir, that the fleet might properly be manned
by a detachment from the army, but it has not been proved that we
have any fuperfluous forces in the kingdom, nor, indeed, will our
army be found fufficiently numerous, if by neglecting to equip our
fleet, we give our enemies an opportunity of entering our country.

If it be enquired what neceffity there is for our prefent forces? What
expeditions are defigned? Or what dangers are feared? I fhall not
think it my duty to return any anfwer. It is, Sir, the great unhappinefs of our conftitution, that our determinations cannot be kept
fecret, and that our enemies may always form conjectures of our
defigns, by knowing our preparations; but furely more is not to be
publifhed than neceffity extorts, and the government has a right to
conceal what it would injure the nation to difcover.

Nor can I, Sir, approve the method of levying failors by the incitement of an exorbitant reward, a reward to be augmented at the
pleafure of thofe who are to receive it. For what can be the confequence of fuch prodigality, but that thofe to whom the largeft fum
is offered, will yet refufe their fervice in expectation of a greater.
The reward already propofed is, in my opinion, the utmoft ftretch
of liberality; and all beyond may be cenfured as profufion.

It is not to be imagined, Sir, that all thefe objections were not
made, and anfwered, in the reign of the late queen, when a bill of
the fame nature was propofed; they were anfwered at leaft by the
neceffity of thofe times, which neceffity has now returned upon us.

We do not find that it produced any confequences fo formidable
and deftructive, that they fhould for ever difcourage us from attempting to raife forces by the fame means; it was then readily enacted,
and executed without oppofition, and without complaints; nor do I
believe that any meafures can be propofed of equal efficacy, and lefs
feverity.

Mr. SANDYS replied in fubftance as follows:—Sir, whether the
precedents produced in defence of this bill, will have more weight
than the arguments, muft be fhewn by a careful examination,

which

which will perhaps discover that the order sent to the magistrates of Bristol conveyed no new power, nor such as is in any respect parallel to that which this bill is intended to confer.

They were only enjoined to enquire with more than usual strictness, after strollers and vagabonds, such as the law has always subjected to punishment, and send them to the fleet, instead of any other place of correction; a method which may now be pursued without danger, opposition, or complaint.

But for my part, I am not able, upon the closest attention to the present scene of affairs, to find out the necessity of extraordinary methods of any kind. The fears of an invasion from France, are, in my opinion, Sir, merely chimerical ; from their fleet in America the coasts of Britain have nothing to fear, and after the numerous levies of seamen by which it was fitted out, it is not yet probable that they can speedily send out another. We know, Sir, that the number of seamen depends upon the extent of commerce, and surely there is as yet no such disproportion between their trade and ours, as that they should be able to furnish out a naval armament with much greater expedition than ourselves.

In America our forces are at least equal to theirs, so that it is not very probable, that after the total destruction of our fleet by them, they should be so little injured, as to be able immediately to set sail for the channel, and insult us in our own ports; to effect this, Sir, they must not only conquer us, but conquer us without resistance.

If they do not interrupt us in our attempts, nor expose themselves to an engagement, they may indeed return without suffering great damages, but I know not how they can leave the shores of America unobserved, or pour an unexpected invasion upon us. If they continue there, Sir, they cannot hurt us, and when they return, we may prepare for their reception.

There are men, I know, Sir, who have reason to think highly of the French policy, and whose ideas may be exalted to a belief that they can perform impossibilities; but I have not yet prevailed upon myself to conceive that they can act invisibly, or that they can equip a fleet by sorcery, collect an army in a moment, and defy us on our own coast, without any perceptible preparations.

Then Admiral WAGER spoke thus :—The calamities produced by discord and contention, need not to be pointed out, but it may be

proper

proper to reflect upon the confequences of a houfe divided againft it-felf, that we may endeavour to avoid them.

Unanimity is produced by nothing more powerful than by impend-ing danger, and therefore it may be ufeful to fhew thofe who feem at prefent in profound fecurity that the power of France is more formi-dable than they are willing to allow.

My age, Sir, enables me to remember many tranfactions of the wars in the late reigns, to which many gentlemen are ftrangers, or of which they have only imperfect ideas from hiftory and tra-dition.

In the fecond year of the reign of William, the French gained a victory over the united fleets of the maritime powers, which gave them for the fummer following the dominion of the channel, ena-bled them to fhut up our merchants in their ports, and produced a total fufpenfion of our commerce.

Thofe, Sir, to whom the importance of trade is fo well known, will eafily apprehend the weight of this calamity, and will, I hope, reject no meafures that have a manifeft tendency to prevent it.

Our fhips, Sir, do not lie ufelefs becaufe there is any want of feamen in the nation, but becaufe any fervice is preferred to that of the publick.

There are now, to my knowledge, in one town on the weft coaft, no fewer than twelve hundred failors, of which furely a third part may be juftly claimed by the publick intereft; nor do I know why they who obftinately refufe to ferve their country, fhould be treated with fo much tendernefs. It is more reafonable that they fhould fuffer by their refufal, than that the general happinefs fhould be endangered.

Mr. SOUTHWELL fpoke next, to the following purpofe:—Sir, when any authority fhall be lodged in my hands to be exercifed for the publick benefit, I fhall always endeavour to exert it with honefty and diligence; but will never be made the inftrument of oppreffion, nor execute any commiffion of tyranny or injuftice.

As therefore the power of fearching is to be placed in the hands of juftices of the peace, I think it neceffary to declare that I will never perform fo hateful a part of the office, and that if this bill be-comes a law, I will retire from the place to which my authority s limited, rather than contribute to the miferies of my fellow-fub-jects.

Mr. LITTLETON fpoke as follows:—Sir, all the arguments which have

have been offered in support of this bill, are reduced at last to one constant assertion of the necessity of passing it.

We have been told, Sir, with great acuteness, that a war cannot be carried on without men, and that ships are useless without sailors; and from thence it is inferred that the bill is necessary.

That forces are by some means necessary to be raised, the warmest opponents of the bill will not deny, but they cannot therefore allow the inference, that the methods now proposed are necessary.

They are of opinion, Sir, that cruel and oppressive measures can never be justified, till all others have been tried without effect; they think that the law, when it was formerly passed, was unjust, and are convinced by observing that it never was revived, and that it was by experience discovered to be useless.

Necessity, absolute necessity, is a formidable found, and may terrify the weak and timorous into silence and compliance; but it will be found upon reflection, to be often nothing but an idle feint, to amuse and to delude us, and that what is represented as necessary to the publick, is only something convenient to men in power.

Necessity, Sir, has heretofore been produced as a plea for that which could be no otherwise defended. In the days of Charles the First, ship-money was declared to be legal, because it was necessary. Such was the reasoning of the lawyers, and the determination of the judges; but the senate, a senate of patriots! without fear, and without corruption, and influenced only by a sincere regard for the public, were of a different opinion, and neither admitted the lawfulness nor necessity.

It will become us on this occasion to act with equal vigour, and convince our countrymen, that we proceed upon the same principles, and that the liberties of the people are our chief care.

I hope we shall unite in defeating any attempts that may impair the rights which every Briton boasts as his birth-right, and reject a law which will be equally dreaded and detested with the inquisition of Spain.

Sir WILLIAM YONGE spoke next, to this effect:—Sir, though many particular clauses of this bill have been disapproved and opposed, some with more, and some with less reason, yet the committee has hitherto agreed that a bill for this purpose is necessary in the present state of our affairs; upon this principle we have proceeded thus far, several gentlemen have proposed their opinions, contributed their

their obfervations, and laboured as in an affair univerfally admitted to be of high importance to the general profperity.

But now, Sir, when fome of the difficulties are furmounted, fome expedients luckily ftruck out, fome objections removed, and the great defign brought nearer to execution, we are on a fudden informed, that all our labour is fuperfluous, that we are amufing ourfelves with ufelefs confultations, providing againft calamities that can never happen, and raifing bulwarks without an enemy; that therefore the queftion before us is of no importance, and the bill ought without farther examination to be totally rejected.

I fuppofe, Sir, I fhall be readily believed, when I declare that I fhall willingly admit any arguments that may evince our fafety; but in proportion as real freedom from danger is to be defired, a fupine and indolent neglect of it is to be dreaded and avoided; and I cannot but fear that our enemies are more formidable, and more malicious, than the gentlemen that oppofe this bill have reprefented them.

This bill can only be oppofed upon the fuppofition that it gives a fanction to feverities more rigorous than our prefent circumftances require; for nothing can be more fallacious or invidious than a comparifon of this law with the demand of fhip-money, a demand contrary to all law, and enforced by the manifeft exertion of arbitrary power.

How has the conduct of his prefent majefty any refemblance with that of Charles the Firft? Is any money levied by order of the council? Are the determinations of the judges fet in oppofition to the decrees of the fenate? Is any man injured in his property by an unlimited extenfion of the prerogative? or any tribunal eftablifhed fuperior to the laws of the nation?

To draw parallels, Sir, where there is no refemblance, and to accufe by infinuations where there is no fhadow of a crime, to raife outcries when no injury is attempted, and to deny a real neceffity becaufe it was once pretended for a bad purpofe, is furely not to advance the publick fervice, which can only be promoted by juft reafonings and calm reflections, not by fophiftry and fatire, by infinuations without ground, and by inftances befide the purpofe.

Mr. LITTLETON anfwered:—Sir, true zeal for the fervice of the publick is never difcovered by collufive fubterfuges and malicious reprefentations: a mind attentive to the common good, would hardly on an occafion like this, have been at leifure to pervert an harmlefs illuftration, and extract difaffection from a cafual remark.

It

It is, indeed, not impossible, Sir, that I might express myself obscurely, and it may be therefore necessary to declare that I intended no disrespectful reflection on the conduct of his majesty, but must observe at the same time that obscure or inaccurate expressions ought always to be interpreted in the most inoffensive meaning, and that to be too sagacious in discovering concealed insinuations, is no great proof of superior integrity.

Wisdom, Sir, is seldom captious, and honesty seldom suspicious; a man capable of comprehending the whole extent of a question, disdains to divert his attention by trifling observations, and he that is above the practice of little arts, or the motions of petty malice, does not easily imagine them incident to another.

That in the question of ship-money necessity was pretended, cannot be denied; and therefore all that I asserted, which was only that the nation had been once terrified without reason, by the formidable sound of necessity, is evident and uncontested.

When a fraud has once been practised, it is of use to remember it, that we may not twice be deceived by the same artifice, and therefore I mentioned the plea of necessity, that it may be enquired whether it is now more true than before.

That the senate, Sir, and not the judges, is now applied to, is no proof of the validity of the arguments which have been produced; for in the days of ship-money, the consent of the senate had been asked had there been any prospect of obtaining it; but the court had been convinced by frequent experiments, of the inflexibility of the senate, and despaired of influencing them by prospects of advantage, or intimidating them by frowns or menaces.

May this and every future senate imitate their conduct, and, like them, distinguish between real and pretended necessity; and let not us be terrified by idle clamours into the establishment of a law at once useless and oppressive.

Sir WM. YONGE replied:--Sir, that I did not intend to misrepresent the meaning of the honourable gentleman, I hope it is not necessary to declare; and that I have in reality been guilty of any misrepresentation, I am not yet convinced. If he did not intend a parallel between ship-money and the present bill, to what purpose was his observation? And if he did intend it, was it not proper to shew there was no resemblance, and that all which could be inferred from it was therefore fallacious and inconclusive?

Nor

Nor do I only differ, Sir, in opinion with the honourable gentleman with relation to his comparison of measures, which have nothing
in common with each other ; but will venture to declare, that he is
not more accurate in his citations from history. The king did not
apply to the judges, because the senate would not have granted him
the money that he demanded, but because his chief ambition was to
govern the nation by the prerogative alone, and to free himself and
his defcendants from fenatorial enquiries.

That this account, Sir, is just, I am confident the histories of
those times will discover ; and therefore any invidious comparison between that senate and any other, is without foundation in reason or
in truth.

Mr. BATHURST spoke as follows :—Sir, that this law will easily
admit, in the execution of it, such abuses as will over-balance the
benefits, may readily be proved ; and it will not be consistent with
that regard to the publick expected from us by those whom we represent, to enact a law which may probably become an instrument of oppression.

The servant by whom I am now attended, may be termed, according to the determination of the vindicators of this bill, a seafaring
man, having been once in the West-Indies, and he may therefore be
forced from my service and dragged into a ship by the authority of a
justice of the peace, perhaps of some abandoned prostitute, dignified
with a commission only to influence elections, and awe those whom
excises and riot acts cannot subdue.

I think it, Sir, not improper to declare, that I would by force oppose the execution of a law like this ; that I would bar my doors and
defend them ; that I would call my neighbours to my assistance ; and
treat those who should attempt to enter without my consent, as
thieves, ruffians, and murderers.

Lord GAGE spoke to this effect :—Sir, it is well known that by
the laws of this nation poverty is in some degree considered as a
crime, and that the debtor has only this advantage over the felon, that
he cannot be pursued into his dwelling, nor be forced from the shelter of his own house.

I think it is universally agreed, that the condition of a man in debt is
already sufficiently miserable, and that it would be more worthy of the
legislative power to contrive alleviations of his hardships than additions
to them ; and it seems therefore no inconsiderable objection to this
bill,

bill, that by conferring the power of entering houses by force, it may give the harpies of the law an opportunity of entering, in the tumult of an imprefs, and of dragging a debtor to a noifome prifon, under pretence of forcing failors into the fervice of the crown.

Mr. TRACEY then faid :—Sir, that fome law for the ends propo-f.d by the bill before us is neceffary, I don't fee how we can doubt, after the declarations of the admirals, who are fully acquainted with the fervice for which provifion is to be made, and of the miniftry, whofe knowledge of the prefent ftate of our own ftrength, and the defigns of our enemies, is doubtlefs more exact than they can acquire who are not engaged in publick employments.

If therefore the meafures now propofed are neceffary, though they may not be agreeable to the prefent difpofitions of the people, for whofe prefervation they are intended, I fhall think it my duty to concur in them, that the publick fervice may not be retarded, nor the fafe-ty of a whole nation hazarded, by a fcrupulous attention to minute objections.

Mr. CAMPBELL fpoke as follows :—Sir, I have often amidft my elogies on Britifh liberty, and my declarations of the excellence of our conftitution, the impartiality of our government, and the effi-cacy of our law, been reproached by foreigners with the practice of imprefis, as an hardfhip which would raife a rebellion in abfo-lute monarchies, and kindle thofe nations into madnefs, that have for many ages known no other law than the will of their princes. A hardfhip which includes imprifonment and flavery, and to which therefore no aggravations ought to be added.

But if juftice and reafon, Sir, are to be overborne by neceffity; if neceffity is to flop our ears againft the complaints of the oppreffed, and harden our hearts at the fight of their mifery, let it at leaft not cloud our memories, nor deprive us of the advantages of experience.

Let us enquire, Sir, what were the effects of this hateful authority when it was formerly configned to the magiftrates. Were our fleets mann'd in an inftant ? Were our harbours immediately crouded with failors ? Did we furprize our enemies by our expedition, and make our paths before an invafion could be fufpected ? I have heard, Sir, of no fuch confequences, nor of any advantages which deferved to be purchafed by tyranny and oppreffion. We have found that very few were procured by the magiftrates, and the charge of feizing and conveying was very confiderable, and therefore cannot but conclude

that

that illegal meafures which have been once tried without fuccefs, fhould, for a double reafon, never be revived.

Sir JOHN BARNARD fpoke to this effect :—Sir, it is not without egret that I rife fo often on this occafion : for to difpute with thofe whofe determinations are not influenced by reafon, is a ridiculous tafk, a tirefome labour, without profpect of reward.

But as an honourable gentleman has lately remarked, that by denying the neceffity of the bill, inftead of making objections to particular claufes, the whole defign of finding expedients to fupply the fea fervice is at once defeated ; I think it neceffary to remind him, that I have made many objections to this bill, and fupported them by reafons which have not yet been anfwered. But I fhall now no longer confine my remarks to fingle errors, but obferve that there is one general defect, by which the whole bill is made abfurd and ufelefs.

For the foundation of a law like this, Sir, the defcription of a feaman ought to be accurately laid down, it ought to be declared what acts fhall fubject him to that denomination, and by what means, after having once inlifted himfelf in this unhappy clafs of men, he may withdraw into a more fecure and happy ftate of life.

Is a man, who has once only loft fight of the fhore, to be for ever hunted as a feaman ? Is a man, who by traffic has enriched a family, to be forced from his poffeffions by the authority of an imprefs ? Is a man, who has purchafed an eftate, and built a feat, to folicit the admiralty for a protection from the neighbouring conftable ? Such queftions as thefe, Sir, may be afked, which the bill before us will enable no man to anfwer.

If a bill for this purpofe be truly neceffary, let it at leaft be freed from fuch offenfive abfurdities, let it be drawn up in a form as different as is poffible from that of the bill before us, and at laft I am far from imagining that a law will be contrived not injurious to individuals, nor detrimental to the publick ; not contrary to the firft principles of our eftablifhment, and not loaded with folly and abfurdities.

Mr. VYNER then fpoke ;—Sir, a definition of a feaman is fo neceffary in a bill for this purpofe, that the omiffion of it will defeat all the methods that can be fuggefted. How fhall a law be executed, or a penalty inflicted, when the magiftrate has no certain marks whereby he may diftinguifh a criminal? and when even the man that is profecuted may not be confcious of guilt, or know that

the

the law extended to him, which he is charged with having offended.

If, in defining a feaman on the prefent occafion, it be thought proper to have any regard to the example of our predeceffors, whofe wifdom has in this debate been fo much magnified; it may be obferved that a feaman has been formerly defined, *a man who haunts the feas*, a definition which feems to imply habit, and continuance, and not to comprehend a man who has perhaps never gone more than a fingle voyage.

But though this definition, Sir, fhould be added to the amendments already propofed, and the bill thereby be brought fomewhat nearer to the conflitutional principles of our government; I cannot yet think it fo much rectified, as that the hardfhips will not outweigh the benefits, and therefore fhall continue to oppofe the bill, though to fome particular claufes I have no objection.

The term feafaring man was left out, and the feveral amendments were admitted in the committee, but the claufes themfelves, to the number of eleven, were given up on the report.

HOUSE OF COMMONS.

March 10, 1740-1.

The commons refolved their houfe into a committee, to confider the bill for the encouragement of failors, when admiral WAGER offered a claufe by which it was to be enacted, " That no merchants, or bodies corporate or politic, fhall hire failors at higher wages than thirty-five fhillings for one month, on pain of forfeiting the treble value of the fums paid contrary; which law was to commence after fifteen days, and continue for a time to be agreed on by the houfe:" and then fpoke to the following purpofe :—

Sir, the neceffity of this claufe muft be fo apparent to every gentleman acquainted with naval and commercial affairs, that as no oppofition need be apprehended, very few arguments will be requifite to inforce it.

How

How much the publick calamities of war are improved by the failors to their own private advantage, how generally they fhun the publick fervice, in hopes of receiving exorbitant wages from the merchants, and how much they extort from the merchants, by threatening to leave their fervice for that of the crown, is univerfally known to every officer of the navy, and every commander of a trading veffel.

A law therefore, Sir, to reftrain them in time of war from fuch exorbitant demands, to deprive them of thofe profpects which have often no other effect than to lull them in idlenefs, while they fkulk about in expectation of higher wages, and to hinder them from deceiving themfelves, embarraffing the merchants, and neglecting the general intereft of their country, is undoubtedly juft. It is juft, Sir, becaufe in regard to the publick it is neceffary to prevent the greateft calamity that can fall upon a people, to preferve us from receiving laws from the moft implacable of our enemies ; and it is juft, becaufe with refpect to particular men it has no tendency but to fupprefs idlenefs, fraud, and extortion.

Mr. HENRY Fox fpoke next :—Sir, I have no objection to any part of this claufe, except the day propofed for the commencement ; to make a law againft any pernicious practice, to which there are ftrong temptations, and to give thofe whofe intereft may incite them to it, time to effect their fchemes, before the law fhall begin to operate, feems not very confiftent with wifdom or vigilance.

It is not denied, Sir, that the merchants are betrayed by that regard to private intereft which prevails too frequently over nobler views, to bribe away from the fervice of the crown, by large rewards, thofe failors whofe affiftance is now fo neceffary to the publick, and therefore it is not to be imagined that they will not employ their utmoft diligence to improve the interval which the bill allows in making contracts for the enfuing year, and that the failors will not eagerly engage themfelves before this law fhall preclude their profpects of advantage.

As therefore to make no law, and to make a law that will not be obferved, is in confequence the fame, and the time allowed by the claufe, as it now ftands, may make the whole provifion ineffectual, it is my opinion, that either it ought to begin to operate to-morrow, or that we ought to leave the whole affair in its prefent ftate.

Then

Then Sir ROBERT WALPOLE spoke as follows:—Sir, nothing has a greater appearance of injustice, than to punish men by virtue of laws with which they were not acquainted; the law therefore is always supposed to be known by those who have offended it, because it is the duty of every man to know it; and certainly it ought to be the care of the legislature, that those whom a law will affect, may have a possibility of knowing it, and that those may not be punished for failing in their duty, whom nothing but inevitable ignorance has betrayed into offence.

But if the operation of this law should commence to-morrow, what numbers may break it, and suffer by the breach of it involuntarily, and without design; and how shall we vindicate ourselves from having been accessary to the crime which we censure and punish?

Mr. Fox replied:—Sir, I shall not urge in defence of my motion what is generally known and has been frequently inculcated in all debates upon this bill, that private considerations ought always to give way to the necessities of the publick; for I think it sufficient to observe, that there is a distinction to be made between punishments and restraints, and that we never can be too early in the prevention of pernicious practices, though we may sometimes delay to punish them.

The law will be known to-morrow to far the greatest number of those who may be tempted to defeat it, and if there be others that break it ignorantly, how will they find themselves injured by being only obliged to pay less than they promised, which is all that I should propose without longer warning. The debate upon this particular will be at length reduced to a question, whether a law for this purpose is just and expedient? If a law be necessary, it is necessary that it should be executed, and it can be executed only by commencing to-morrow.

Lord BALTIMORE spoke thus:—Sir, it appears to me of no great importance how soon the operation of the law commences, or how long it is delayed, because I see no reason for imagining that it will at any time produce the effects proposed by it.

It has been the amusement, Sir, of a great part of my life, to converse with men whose inclinations or employments have made them well acquainted with maritime affairs, and amidst innumerable other schemes for the promotion of trade, have heard some for the regulation of wages in trading ships; schemes, at the first appearance

plausible

plaufible and likely to fucceed, but upon a nearer enquiry evidently entangled with infuperable difficulties, and never to be executed without danger of injuring the commerce of the nation.

The claufe, Sir, now before us contains, in my opinion, one of thofe vifionary provifions, which however infallible they may appear, will be eafily defeated, and will have no other effect than to promote cunning and fraud, and to teach men thofe acts of collufion, with which they would otherwife never have been acquainted.

Mr. LODWICK fpoke to this effect :—Sir, I agree with the honourable gentleman by whom this claufe has been offered, that the end for which it is propofed, is worthy of the clofeft attention of the legiflative power, and that the evils, of which the prevention is now endeavoured, may in fome meafure not only obftruct our traffick, but endanger our country ; and fhall therefore very readily concur in any meafures for this purpofe, that fhall not appear either unjuft or ineffectual.

Whether this claufe will be fufficient to reftrain all elufive contracts, and whether all the little artifices of intereft are fufficiently obviated, I am yet unable to determine ; but by a reflection upon the multiplicity of relations to be confidered, and the variety of circumftances to be adjufted in a provifion of this kind, I am inclined to think that it is not the bufinefs of a tranfient enquiry, or of a fingle claufe, but that it will demand a feparate law, and engage the deliberation and regard of this whole affembly.

Sir JOHN BARNARD faid :—Sir, notwithftanding the impatience and refentment with which fome men fee their miftakes and ignorance detected, notwithftanding the reverence which negligence and hafte are faid to be intitled to from this affembly, I fhall declare once more, without the apprehenfion of being confuted, that this bill was drawn up without confideration, and is defended without being underftood ; that after all the amendments which have been admitted, and all the additions propofed, it will be oppreffive and ineffectual, a chaos of abfurdities, and a monument of ignorance.

Sir ROBERT WALPOLE replied :—Sir, the prefent bufinefs of this affembly is to examine the claufe before us ; but to deviate from fo neceffary an enquiry into loud exclamations againft the whole bill, is to obftruct the courfe of the debate, to perplex our attention, and interrupt the fenate in its deliberation upon queftions, in the determination of which the security of the publick is nearly concerned.

The war, Sir, in which we are now engaged, and, I may add, engaged by the general request of the whole nation, can be prosecuted only by the assistance of the seamen, from whom it is not to be expected that they will sacrifice their immediate advantage to the security of their country. Publick spirit, where it is to be found, is the result of reflection, refined by study and exalted by education, and is not to be hoped for among those whom low fortune has condemned to perpetual drudgery. It must be therefore necessary to supply the defects of education, and to produce by salutary coercions those effects which it is vain to expect from other causes.

That the service of the sailors will be set up to sale by auction, and that the merchants will bid against the government, is incontestable; nor is there any doubt that they will be able to offer the highest price, because they will take care to repay themselves by raising the value of their goods. Thus, without some restraint upon the merchants, our enemies, who are not debarred by their form of government from any method which policy can invent, or absolute power put in execution, will preclude all our designs, and set at defiance a nation superior to themselves.

Sir JOHN BARNARD then said:—Sir, I think myself obliged by my duty to my country, and by my gratitude to those by whose industry we are enriched, and by whose courage we are defended, to make once more a declaration, not against particular clauses, not against single circumstances, but against the whole bill; a bill unjust and oppressive, absurd and ridiculous; a bill to harrass the industrious and distress the honest, to puzzle the wise and add power to the cruel; a bill which cannot be read without astonishment, nor passed without the violation of our constitution, and an equal disregard of policy and humanity.

All these assertions will need to be proved only by a bare perusal of this hateful bill, by which the meanest, the most worthless reptile, exalted to a petty office by serving a wretch only superior to him in fortune, is enabled to such his authority by tyrannizing over those who every hour deserve the public acknowledgements of the community; to intrude upon the retreats of brave men, fatigued and exhausted by honest industry, to drag them out with all the wantonness
of

of groveling authority, and chain them to the oar without a moment's
refpite, or perhaps oblige them to purchafe, with the gains of a dangerous voyage, or the plunder of an enemy lately conquered, a
fhort interval to fettle their affairs, or bid their children farewel.

Let any gentleman in this houfe, let thofe, Sir, who now fit at eafe,
projecting laws of oppreffion, and conferring upon their own flaves fuch
licentious authority, paufe a few moments, and imagine themfelves
expofed to the fame hardfhips by a power fuperior to their own; let
them conceive themfelves torn from the tendernefs and careffes of their
families by midnight irruptions, dragged in triumph through the
ftreets by a defpicable officer, and placed under the command of thofe
by whom they have perhaps been already oppreffed and infulted.
Why fhould we imagine that the race of men for whom thefe
cruelties are preparing, have lefs fenfibility than ourfelves? Why
fhould we believe that they will fuffer without complaint, and be injured without refentment? Why fhould we conceive that they will
not at once deliver themfelves, and punifh their oppreffors, by defert-
ing that country where they are confidered as felons, and laying hold
on thofe rewards and privileges which no other government will deny
them?

This is indeed the only tendency, whatever may have been the intention of the bill before us; for I know not whether the moft refined fagacity can difcover any other method of difcouraging navigation than thofe which are drawn together in the bill before us.
We firft give our conftables an authority to hunt the failors like
thieves, and drive them by inceffant purfuit out of the nation; but
left any man fhould by friendfhip, good fortune, or the power of
money, find means of ftaying behind, we have with equal wifdom
condemned him to poverty and mifery; and left the natural courage
of his profeffion fhould incite him to affift his country in the war,
have contrived a method of precluding him from any advantage
that he might have the weaknefs to hope from his fortitude and
diligence. What more can be done, unlefs we at once prohibit
to feamen the ufe of the common elements, or doom them to a general profcription.

It is juft that advantage, Sir, fhould be proportioned to the hazard
by which it is to be obtained, and therefore a failor has an honeft
claim to an advance of wages in time of war; it is neceffary to ex-

cite

cite expectation, and to fire ambition by the prospect of great acquisitions, and by this prospect it is that such numbers are daily allured
to naval business, and that our privateers are filled with adventurers.
The large wages which war makes necessary, are more powerful in-
centives to those whom impatience of poverty determines to change
their state of life, than the secure gains of peaceful commerce, for
the danger is overlooked by a mind intent upon the profit.

War is the harvest of a sailor, in which he is to store provisions for
the winter of old age, and if we blast this hope, he will inevitably
sink into indolence and cowardice.

Many of the sailors are bred up to trades, or capable of any laborious employment upon land ; nor is there any reason for which they
expose themselves to the dangers of a seafaring life, but the hope of
sudden wealth, and some lucky season in which they may improve
their fortunes by a single effort. Is it reasonable to believe that all
these will not rather have recourse to their former callings, and live
in security, though not in plenty, than encounter danger and
poverty at once, and face an enemy without any prospect of recompence ?

Let any man recollect the ideas that arose in his mind upon hearing of a bill for encouraging and increasing sailors, and examine
whether he had any expectation of expedients like these. I suppose
it was never known before that men were to be encouraged by sub-
jecting them to peculiar penalties, or that to take away the gains of
a profession, was a method of recommending it more generally to
the people.

But it is not of very great importance to dwell longer upon the impropriety of this clause, which there is no possibility of putting in
execution. That the merchants will try every method of eluding
a law so prejudicial to their interest, may be easily imagined, and a
mind not very fruitful of evasions, will discover that this law may be
eluded by a thousand artifices. If the merchants are restrained from
allowing men their wages beyond a certain sum, they will make contracts for the voyage, of which the time may very easily be computed,
they may offer a reward for expedition and fidelity, they may pay a
large sum by way of advance, they may allow the sailors part of the
profits, or may offer money by a third hand. To fix the price of
any commodity, of which the quantity and the use may vary their
proportions,

proportions, is the moſt exceſſive degree of ignorance. No man can determine the price of corn, unleſs he can regulate the harveſt, and keep the number of the people for ever at a ſtand.

But let us ſuppoſe theſe methods as efficacious as their moſt ſanguine vindicators are deſirous of repreſenting them, it does not yet appear that they are neceſſary, and to inflict hardſhips without neceſſity, is by no means the practice of either wiſdom or benevolence. To tyrannize and compel is the low pleaſure of petty capacities, of narrow minds, ſwelled with the pride of uncontrolable authority, the wantonneſs of wretches who are inſenſible of the conſequences of their own actions, and of whom candour may perhaps determine, that they are only cruel becauſe they are ſtupid. Let us not exalt into a precedent the moſt unjuſt and rigorous law of our predeceſſors, of which they themſelves declared their repentance, or confeſſed the inefficacy, by never reviving it; let us rather endeavour to gain the ſailors by lenity and moderation, and reconcile them to the ſervice of the crown by real encouragements; for it is rational to imagine, that in proportion as men are diſguſted by injuries, they will be won by kindneſs.

There is one expedient, Sir, which deſerves to be tried, and from which at leaſt more ſucceſs may be hoped than from cruelty, hunger, and perſecution. The ſhips that are now to be fitted out for ſervice, are thoſe of the firſt magnitude, which it is uſual to bring back into the ports in winter. Let us therefore promiſe to all ſeamen that ſhall voluntarily engage in them, beſides the reward already propoſed, a diſcharge from the ſervice at the end of ſix or ſeven months. By this they will be releaſed from their preſent dread of perpetual ſlavery, and be certain, as they are when in the ſervice of the merchants, of a reſpite from their fatigues. The trade of the nation will be only interrupted for a time, and may be carried on in the winter months, and large ſums will be ſaved by diſmiſſing the ſeamen when they cannot be employed.

By adding this to the other methods of encouragement, and throwing aſide all rigorous and oppreſſive ſchemes, the navy may eaſily be manned, our country protected, our commerce re-eſtabliſhed, and our enemies ſubdued; but to paſs the bill as it now ſtands, is to determine that trade ſhall ceaſe, and that no ſhip ſhall ſail out of river.

Mr. PITT ſpoke to the following purport:—Sir, it is ce

thofe to have the greateſt regard to their own intereſt who diſcover the leaſt for that of others. I do not, therefore, deſpair of recalling the advocates of this bill from the profecution of their favourite meaſures, by arguments of greater efficacy than thoſe which are founded on reaſon and juſtice.

Nothing, Sir, is more evident, than that ſome degree of reputation is abſolutely neceſſary to men who have any concern in the adminiſtration of a government like ours ; they muſt either ſecure the fidelity of their adherents by the aſſiſtance of wiſdom, or of virtue ; their enemies muſt either be awed by their honeſty, or terrified by their cunning. Mere artleſs bribery will never gain a ſufficient majority to ſet them entirely free from apprehenſions of cenſure. To different tempers different motives muſt be applied : ſome, who place their felicity in being accounted wiſe, are in very little care to preſerve the character of honeſty ; others may be perſuaded to join in meaſures which they eaſily diſcover to be weak and ill-concerted, becauſe they are convinced that the authors of them are not corrupt but miſtaken, and are unwilling that any man ſhould be puniſhed for natural defects or caſual ignorance.

I cannot ſay, Sir, which of theſe motives influence the advocates for the bill before us ; a bill in which ſuch cruelties are propoſed as are yet unknown among the moſt ſavage nations, ſuch as ſlavery has not yet borne, or tyranny invented, ſuch as cannot be heard without reſentment, nor thought of without horror.

It is, Sir, perhaps, not unfortunate, that one more expedient has been added rather ridiculous than ſhocking, and that theſe tyrants of the adminiſtration, who amuſe themſelves with oppreſſing their fellow ſubjects, who add without reluctance one hardſhip to another, invade the liberty of thoſe whom they have already overborne with taxes, firſt plunder and then impriſon, who take all opportunities of heightening the publick diſtreſſes, and make the miſeries of war the inſtruments of new oppreſſions, are too ignorant to be formidable, and owe their power not to their abilities, but to caſual proſperity, or to the influence of money.

The other clauſes of this bill, complicated at once with cruelty and folly, have been treated with becoming indignation ; but this may be conſidered with leſs ardour of reſentment, and fewer emotions of zeal, becauſe, though perhaps equally iniquitous, it will do no harm ; for a law that can never be executed can never be felt.

That

That it will confume the manufacture of paper, and fwell the books of ftatutes, is all the good or hurt that can be hoped or feared from a faw like this; a law which fixes what is in its own nature mutable, which prefcribes rules to the feafons and limits to the wind. I am too well acquainted, Sir, with the difpofition of its two chief fupporters, to mention the contempt with which this law will be treated by pofterity, for they have already fhewn abundantly their difregard of fucceeding generations; but I will remind them, that they are now venturing their whole intereft at once, and hope they will recollect, before it is too late, that thofe who believe them to intend the happinefs of their country, will never be confirmed in their opinion by open cruelty and notorious oppreffion; and that thofe who have only their own intereft in view, will be afraid of adhering to thofe leaders, however old and practifed in expedients, however ftrengthened by corruption, or elated with power, who have no reafon to hope for fuccefs from either their virtue or abilities.

Mr. BATHURST next fpoke to this effect:—Sir, the claufe now under our confideration is fo inconfiderately drawn up, that it is impoffible to read it in the moft curfory manner, without difcovering the neceffity of numerous amendments: no malicious fubtilties or artful deductions are required in raifing objections to this part of the bill, they croud upon us without being fought, and, inftead of exercifing our fagacity, weary our attention.

The firft error, or rather one part of a general and complicated error, is the computation of time not by days but by kalendar months, which, as they are not equal one to another, may embarrafs the account between the failors and thofe that employ them. In all contracts of a fhort duration, the time is to be reckoned by weeks and days, by certain and regular periods, which has been fo conftantly the practice of the feafaring men, that perhaps many of them do not know the meaning of a kalendar month: this indeed is a neglect of no great importance, becaufe no man can be deprived by it of more than the wages due for the labour of a few days; but the other part of this claufe is more ferioufly to be confidered, as it threatens the failors with greater injuries: for it is to be enacted, that all contracts made for more wages than are here allowed fhall be totally void.

It cannot be denied to be poffible, and in my opinion it is very likely, that many contracts will be made without the knowledge of
this

this law, and confequently without any defign of violating it; but
ignorance, inevitable ignorance, though it is a valid excufe for every
other man, is no plea for the unhappy failor; he muft fuffer, though
innocent, the penalty of a crime; muft undergo danger, hardfhips,
and labour, without a recompenfe, and at the end of a fuccefsful
voyage, after having enriched his country by his induftry, return
home to a neceffitous family without being able to relieve them.

It is fcarcely neceffary, Sir, to raife any more objections to a claufe
in which nothing is right; but, to fhew how its imperfections multiply upon the flighteft confideration, I take the opportunity to obferve that there is no provifion made for regulating the voyages performed in lefs time than a month, fo that the greateft part of the
abufes, which have been reprefented as the occafion of this claufe,
are yet without remedy, and only thofe failors who venture far, and
are expofed to the greateft dangers, are reftrained from receiving an
adequate reward.

Thus much, Sir, I have faid upon the fuppofition that a regulation of the failors wages is either neceffary or juft, a fuppofition of
which I am very far from difcovering the truth. That it is juft to
opprefs the moft ufeful of our fellow fubjects, to load thofe men with
peculiar hardfhips to whom we owe the plenty that we enjoy, the
power that yet remains in the nation, and which neither the folly nor
the cowardice of minifters have yet been able to deftroy, and the
fecurity in which we now fit and hold our confultations; that it is
juft to leffen our payments at a time when we increafe the labour
of thofe who are hired, and to expofe men to danger without recompenfe, will not eafily be proved even by thofe who are moft accuftomed to paradoxes, and are ready to undertake the proof of any
pofition which it is their intereft to find true.

Nor is it much more eafy to fhew the neceffity of this expedient
in our prefent ftate, in which it appears from the title of the bill, that
our chief endeavour fhould be the increafe and encouragement of
failors, and, I fuppofe, it has not often been difcovered, that by
taking away the profits of a profeffion greater numbers have been
allured to it.

The high wages, Sir, paid by merchants are the chief incitements
that prevail upon the ambitious, the neceffitous, or the avaricious,
to forfake the eafe and fecurity of the land, to leave eafy trades, and
healthful employments, and expofe themfelves to an element where
they

they are not certain of an hour's fafety. The fervice of the merchants is the nurfery in which feamen are trained up for his majefty's navies, and from thence we muft, in time of danger, expect thofe forces by which alone we can be protected.

If, therefore, it is neceffary to encourage failors, it is neceffary to reject all meafures that may terrify or difguft them ; and as their numbers muft depend upon our trade, let us not embarrafs the merchants with any other difficulties than thofe which are infeparable from war, and which very little care has been hitherto taken to alleviate.

Mr. HAY replied :—Sir, the objections which have been urged with fo much ardour, and difplayed with fuch power of eloquence, are not, in my opinion, formidable enough to difcourage us from profecuting our meafures ; fome of them may be perhaps readily anfwered, and the reft eafily removed.

The computation of time, as it now ftands, is allowed not to produce any formidable evil, and therefore did not require fo rhetorical a cenfure : the inconveniency of kalendar months may eafily be removed by a little candour in the contracting parties, or that the objection may not be repeated to the interruption of the debate, weeks or days may be fubftituted, and the ufual reckoning of the failors be ftill continued.

That fome contracts may be annulled, and inconveniencies or delays of payment arife, is too evident to be queftioned ; but in that cafe the failor may have his remedy provided, and be enabled to obtain, by an eafy procefs, what he fhall be judged to *have deferved*; for it muft be allowed reafonable, that every man who labours in honeft and ufeful employments, fhould receive the reward of his diligence and fidelity.

Thus, Sir, may the claufe, however loudly cenfured and violently oppofed, be made ufeful and equitable, and the publick fervice advanced without injury to individuals.

Sir ROBERT WALPOLE next rofe and fpoke as follows :—Sir, every law which extends its influence to great numbers in various relations and circumftances, muft produce fome confequences that were never forefeen or intended, and is to be cenfured or applauded as the general advantages or inconveniencies are found to preponderate. Of this kind is the law before us, a law enforced by the neceffity of our affairs, and drawn up with no other intention than to fecure the

publick

publick happinefs, and produce that fuccefs which every man's intereft muft prompt him to defire.

If in the execution of this law, Sir, fome inconveniencies fhould arife, they are to be remedied as faft as they are difcovered, or if not capable of a remedy, to be patiently borne in confideration of the general advantage.

That fome temporary difturbances may be produced is not improbable ; the difcontent of the failors may for a fhort time rife high, and our trade be fufpended by their obftinacy ; but obftinacy however determined muft yield to hunger, and when no higher wages can be obtained they will cheerfully accept of thofe which are here allowed them. Short voyages indeed are not comprehended in the claufe, and therefore the failors will engage in them upon their own terms, but this objection can be of no weight with thofe that oppofe the claufe, becaufe, if it is unjuft to limit the wages of the failors, it is juft to leave thofe voyages without reftriction ; and thofe that think the expedient here propofed equitable and rational, may perhaps be willing to make fome conceffions to thofe who are of a different opinion.

That the bill will not remove every obftacle to fuccefs, nor add weight to one part of the balance without making the other lighter ; that it will not fupply the navy without incommoding the merchants in fome degree ; that it may be fometimes evaded by cunning, and fometimes abufed by malice ; and that at laft it will be lefs efficacious than is defired, may perhaps be proved ; but it has not yet been proved that any other meafures are more eligible, or that we are not to promote the publick fervice as far as we are able, though our endeavours may not produce effects equal to our wifhes.

Sir JOHN BARNARD then fpoke to this effect :—Sir, I know not by what fatality it is that nothing can be urged in defence of the claufe before us which does not tend to difcover its weaknefs and inefficacy. The warmeft patrons of this expedient are impelled by the mere force of conviction to fuch conceffions as invalidate all their arguments, and leave their opponents no neceffity of replying.

If fhort voyages are not comprehended in this provifion, what are we now controverting ? What but the expedience of a law that will never be executed ? The failors, however they are contemned by thofe who think them only worthy to be treated like beafts of burthen, are not yet fo ftupid but that they can eafily find out, that
to

to ferve a fortnight for greater wages is more eligible than to toil a
month for lefs; and as the numerous equipments that have been
lately made have not left many more failors in the fervice of the merchants than may be employed in the coafting trade, thofe who traffic
to remoter parts, muft fhut up their books and waittill the expiration
of this act, for an opportunity of renewing their commerce.

To regulate the wages for one voyage, and to leave another without limitation in time of fcarcity of feamen, is abfolutely to prohibit
that trade which is fo reftrained, and is doubtlefs a more effectual
embargo than has been yet invented.

Let any man but fuppofe that the Eaft India company were obliged
to give only half the wages that other traders allow, and confider how that part of our commerce could be carried on; would not
their goods rot in their warehoufes, and their fhips lie for ever in
the harbour? Would not the failors refufe to contract with them? Or
defert them after a contract, upon the firft profpect of more advantageous employment?

But it is not requifite to multiply arguments in a queftion which
may not only be decided without long examination, but in which
we may determine our conclufions by the experience of our anceftors.
Scarcely any right or wrong meafures are without a precedent, and
amongft others this expedient has been tried by the wifdom of former
times; a law was once made for limiting the wages of taylors, and
that it is totally ineffectual we are all convinced. Experience is a
very fafe guide in political enquiries, and often difcovers what the
moft enlightened reafon failed to forefee.

Let us therefore improve the errors of our anceftors to our own
advantage, and whilft we neglect to imitate their virtues, let us
at leaft forbear to repeat their follies.

Mr. PERRY fpoke to this purpofe:—Sir, there is one objection
more which my acquaintance with foreign trade impreffes too ftrongly
upon my mind to fuffer me to conceal it.

It is well known that the condition of a feaman fubjects him to
the neceffity of fpending a great part of his life at a diftance from
his native country, in places where he can neither hear of our defigns
nor be inftructed in our laws, and therefore it is evident that no law
ought to affect him before a certain period of time in which he may
reafonably be fuppofed to have been informed of it. For every man
ought

ought to have it in his power to avoid punishment, and to suffer only for negligence or obstinacy.

It is quite unnecessary, Sir, to observe to this assembly, that there are now, as at all times, great numbers of sailors in every part of the world, and that they at least equally deserve our regard with those who are under the more immediate influence of the government.

These seamen have already contracted for the price of their labour, and the recompense of their hazards, nor can we, in my opinion, without manifest injustice, dissolve a contract founded upon equity, and confirmed by law.

It is, Sir, an undisputed principle of government, that no person should be punished without a crime ; but is it no punishment to deprive a man of what is due to him by a legal stipulation, the condition of which is on his part honestly fulfilled ?

Nothing, Sir, can be imagined more calamitous than the disappointment to which this law subjects the unhappy men who are now promoting the interest of their country in distant places amidst dangers and hardships, in unhealthy climates and barbarous nations, where they comfort themselves under the fatigues of labour and the miseries of sickness, with the prospect of the sum which they shall gain for the relief of their families, and the respite which their wages will enable them to enjoy ; but upon their return they find their hopes blasted, and their contracts dissolved by a law made in their absence.

No human being, I think, can coolly and deliberately inflict a hardship like this, and therefore I doubt not but those who have by inadvertency given room for this objection will either remove it by an amendment, or what is, in my opinion, more eligible, reject the clause as inexpedient, useless, and unjust.

Sir WILLIAM YONGE spoke next to this effect :—Sir, this debate has been protracted, not by any difficulties arising from the nature of the questions which have been the subject of it, but by a neglect with which almost all the opponents of the bill may be justly charged, the neglect of distinguishing between measures eligible in themselves, and measures preferable to consequences which are apprehended from particular conjunctures ; between laws made only to advance the publick happiness, and expedients of which the benefit is merely occasional, and of which the sole intention is to avert some national

calamity,

calamity, and which are to ceafe with the neceffity that produced them.

Such are the meafures, Sir, which are now intended ; meafures, which in days of eafe, fecurity, and profperity, it would be the higheft degree of weaknefs to propofe, but of which I cannot fee the abfurdity in times of danger and diftrefs. Such laws are the medicines of a ftate, ufelefs and naufeous in health, but preferable to a lingering difeafe, or to a miferable death.

Even thofe meafures, Sir, which have been mentioned as moft grofsly abfurd, and reprefented as parallel to the provifion made in this claufe only to expofe it to contempt and ridicule, may in particular circumftances be rational and juft. To fettle the price of corn in the time of a famine, may become the wifeft ftate, and multitudes might in time of publick mifery, by the benefit of temporary laws, be preferved from deftruction. Even thofe mafts, to which, with a profperous gale, the fhip owes its ufefulnefs and its fpeed, are often cut down by the failors in the fury of a ftorm.

With regard to the fhips which are now in diftant places, whither no knowledge of this law can poffibly be conveyed, it cannot be denied that their crews ought to be fecured from injury by fome particular exception ; for though it is evident in competitions between publick and private intereft, which ought to be preferred, yet we ought to remember that no unneceffary injury is to be done to individuals, even while we are providing for the fafety of the nation.

Mr. FAZAKERLY fpoke to this effect :—Sir, though I cannot be fuppofed to have much acquaintance with naval affairs, and therefore may not perhaps difcover the full force of the arguments that have been urged in favour of the claufe now under confideration, yet I cannot but think myfelf under an indifpenfable obligation to examine it as far as I am able, and to make ufe of the knowledge which I have acquired, however imferior to that of others.

The argument, Sir, the only real argument, which has been produced in favour of the reftraint of wages now propofed, appears to me by no means conclufive; nor can I believe that the meaneft and moft ignorant feaman would, if it were propofed to him, hefitate a moment for an anfwer to it. Let me fuppofe, Sir, a merchant urging it as a charge againft a feaman, that he raifes his demand of wages in time of war, would not the failor readily reply, that harder labour required larger pay ? Would he not afk, why the general practice of

mankind

mankind is charged as a crime upon him only? Enquire, says he, of the workmen in the docks, have they not double wages for double labour? and is not their lot safe and easy in comparison with mine, who at once encounter danger and support fatigue, carry on war and commerce at the same time, conduct the ship and oppose the enemy, and am equally exposed to captivity and shipwreck?

That this is in reality the state of a sailor in time of war, I think, Sir, too evident to require proof; nor do I see what reply can be made to the sailor's artless expostulation.

I know not why the sailors alone should serve their country to their disadvantage, and be expected to encounter danger without the incitement of a reward.

Nor will any part of the hardships of this clause be alleviated by the expedient suggested by an honourable member, who spoke some time ago, of granting, or allowing, to a sailor, whose contract shall be void, what our courts of law should adjudge him to deserve, a *quantum meruit*: for, according to the general interpretation of our statutes, it will be determined that he has forfeited his whole claim by illegal contract. To instance, Sir, the statute of usury. He that stipulates for higher interest than is allowed, is not able to recover his legal demand, but irrecoverably forfeits the whole.

Thus, Sir, an unhappy sailor, who shall innocently transgress this law, must lose all the profit of his voyage, and have nothing to relieve him after his fatigues; but when he has by his courage repelled the enemy, and by his skill escaped storms and rocks, must suffer yet severer hardships, in being subject to a forfeiture where he expected applause, comfort, and recompense.

The ATTORNEY GENERAL spoke next to this purport:—Sir, the clause before us cannot, in my opinion, produce any such dreadful consequences as the learned gentleman appears to imagine: however, to remove all difficulties, I have drawn up an amendment, which I shall beg leave to propose, that the contracts which may be affected as the clause now stands, *shall be void only as to so much of the wages as shall exceed the sum to which the house shall agree to reduce the seamen's pay*; and as to the forfeitures, they are not to be levied upon the sailors, but upon the merchants, or trading companies, who employ them, and who are able to pay greater sums without being involved in poverty and distress.

With regard, Sir, to the reasons for introducing this clause, they are,

are, in my judgment, valid and equitable. We have found it neceffary to fix the rate of money at intereft, and the rate of labour in
feveral cafes, and if we do not in this cafe, what will be the confequence? A fecond embargo on commerce, and perhaps a total ftop to
all military preparations. Is it reafonable that any man fhould rate
his labour according to the immediate neceffities of thofe that employ
him? Or that he fhould raife his own fortune by the publick calamities? If this has hitherto been a practice, it is a practice contrary
to the general happinefs of fociety, and ought to prevail no longer.

If the failor, Sir, is expofed to greater dangers in time of war, is
not the merchant's trade carried on likewife at greater hazard? Is not
the freight equally with the failors threatened at once by the ocean and
the enemy? And is not the owner's fortune equally impaired, whether
the fhip is dafhed upon a rock, or feized by a privateer?

The merchant, therefore, has as much reafon for paying lefs wages
in time of war, as the failor for demanding more, and nothing remains but that the legiflative power determine a medium between
their different interefts, with juftice, if poffible, at leaft with impartiality.

Mr. HORACE WALPOLE, who had ftood up feveral times, but
was prevented by other members, fpoke next, to this purport:—Sir,
I was unwilling to interrupt the courfe of this debate while it was
carried on with calmnefs and decency, by men who do not fuffer
the ardour of oppofition to cloud their reafon, or tranfport them to
fuch expreffions as the dignity of this affembly does not admit. I
have hitherto deferred to anfwer the gentleman who declaimed againft
the bill with fuch fluency of rhetoric, and fuch vehemence of gefture,
who charged the advocates for the expedients now propofed, with
having no regard to any intereft but their own, and with making
laws only to confume paper, and threatened them with the defection
of their adherence, and the lofs of their influence, upon this new
difcovery of their folly and their ignorance.

Nor, Sir, do I now anfwer him for any other purpofe than to remind him how little the clamours of rage and petulancy of invectives
contribute to the purpofes for which this affembly is called together; how little the difcovery of truth is promoted, and the fecurity of the nation eftablifhed by pompous diction and theatrical
emotions.

Formidable founds, and furious declamations, confident affertions, and lofty periods, may affect the young and unexperienced, and perhaps the gentleman may have contracted his habits of oratory by converfing more with thofe of his own age, than with fuch as have had more opportunities of acquiring knowledge, and more fuccefsful methods of communicating their fentiments.

If the heat of his temper, Sir, would fuffer him to attend to thofe whofe age and long acquaintance with bufinefs give them an indifputable right to deference and fuperiority, he would learn, in time, to reafon rather than declaim, and to prefer juftnefs of argument, and an accurate knowledge of facts, to founding epithets and fplendid fuperlatives, which may difturb the imagination for a moment, but leave no lafting impreffion on the mind.

He will learn, Sir, that to accufe and prove are very different, and that reproaches unfupported by evidence, affect only the character of him that utters them. Excurfions of fancy, and flights of oratory, are indeed pardonable in young men, but in no other; and it would furely contribute more, even to the purpofe for which fome gentlemen appear to fpeak, that of deprecisting the conduct of the adminiftration, to prove the inconveniencies and injuftice of this bill, than barely to affert them, with whatever magnificence of language, or appearance of zeal, honefty, or compaffion.

Mr. PITT replied:—Sir, the atrocious crime of being a young man, which the honourable gentleman has with fuch fpirit and decency charged upon me, I fhall neither attempt to palliate nor deny, but content myfelf with wifhing that I may be one of thofe whofe folHes may ceafe with their youth, and not of that number, who are ignorant in fpite of experience.

Whether youth can be imputed to any man as a reproach, I will not, Sir, affume the province of determining; but furely age may become juftly contemptible, if the opportunities which it brings have paffed away without improvement, and vice appears to prevail when the paffions have fubfided. The wretch that, after having feen the confequences of a thoufand errors, continues ftill to blunder, and whofe age has only added obftinacy to ftupidity, is furely the object of either abhorrence or contempt, and deferves not that his grey head fhould fecure him from infults.

Much more, Sir, is he to be abhorred, who, as he has advanced in

age,

age, has receded from virtue, and becomes more wicked with less temptation; who prostitutes himself for money which he cannot enjoy, and spends the remains of his life in the ruin of his country.

But youth, Sir, is not my only crime; I have been accused of acting a theatrical part—A theatrical part may either imply some peculiarities of gesture, or a dissimulation of my real sentiments, and an adoption of the opinions and language of another man.

In the first sense, Sir, the charge is too trifling to be confuted, and deserves only to be mentioned, that it may be despised. I am at liberty, like every other man, to use my own language; and though I may perhaps have some ambition to please this gentleman, I shall not lay myself under any restraint, nor very solicitously copy his diction, or his mien, however matured by age, or modelled by experience.

If any man shall, by charging me with theatrical behaviour, imply that I utter any sentiments but my own, I shall treat him as a calumniator and a villain; nor shall any protection shelter him from the treatment which he deserves. I shall, on such an occasion, without scruple, trample upon all those forms, with which wealth and dignity intrench themselves, nor shall any thing but age restrain my resentment; age, which always brings one privilege, that of being insolent and supercilious without punishment.

But, with regard, Sir, to those whom I have offended, I am of opinion, that if I had acted a borrowed part, I should have avoided their censure; the heat that offended them is the ardour of conviction, and that zeal for the service of my country, which neither hope nor fear shall influence me to suppress. I will not sit unconcerned while my liberty is invaded, nor look in silence upon publick robbery.---I will exert my endeavours at whatever hazard, to repel the aggressor, and drag the thief to justice, whoever may protect them in their villainy, and whoever may partake of their plunder.---And if the honourable gentleman——

Here Mr. WINNINGTON called to order, and Mr. PITT sitting down, he spoke thus :---It is necessary, Sir, that the order of this assembly be observed, and the debate resumed without personal altercations. Such expressions as have been vented on this occasion become not an assembly entrusted with the liberty and welfare of their country. To interrupt the debate on a subject so important as that before us, is, in some measure, to obstruct the publick happiness, and violate our truft: but much more heinous is the crime of expofing our determinations to contempt, and inciting the people to fufpicion or mutiny, by indecent reflections, or unjuft infinuations.

I do not, Sir, undertake to decide the controverfy between the two gentlemen, but muft be allowed to obferve, that no diverfity of opinion can juftify the violation of decency, and the ufe of rude and virulent expreffions; expreffions dictated only by refentment, and uttered without regard to——

Mr. PITT called to order, and faid:—Sir, if this be to preferve order, there is no danger of indecency from the moft licentious tongue; for what calumny can be more atrocious, or what reproach more fevere, than that of fpeaking with regard to any thing but truth. Order may fometimes be broken by paffion, or inadvertency, but will hardly be re-eftablifhed by monitors like this, who cannot govern his own paffion, whilft he is reftraining the impetuofity of others.

Happy, Sir, would it be for mankind, if every one knew his own province; we fhould not then fee the fame man at once a criminal and a judge. Nor would this gentleman affume the right of dictating to others what he has not learned himfelf.

That I may return in fome degree the favour which he intends me, I will advife him never hereafter to exert himfelf on the fubject of order; but, whenever he finds himfelf inclined to fpeak on fuch occafions, to remember how he has now fucceeded, and condemn in filence what his cenfures will never reform.

Mr. WINNINGTON replied:—Sir, as I was hindered by the gentleman's ardour and impetuofity from concluding my fentence, none but myfelf can know the equity or partiality of my intentions, and therefore as I cannot juftly be condemned, I ought to be fuppofed innocent; nor ought he to cenfure a fault of which he cannot be certain that it would ever have been committed.

He has indeed exalted himfelf to a degree of authority never yet affumed by any member of this houfe, that of condemning others to filence. I am henceforward, by his inviolable decree, to fit and hear his harangues without daring to oppofe him. How wide he may extend his authority, or whom he will proceed to include in the fame fentence, I fhall not determine; having not yet arrived at the fame degree of fagacity with himfelf, nor being able to foreknow what another is going to pronounce.

If I had given offence by any improper fallies of paffion, I ought

to

to have been censured by the concurrent voice of the assembly, or have received a reprimand, Sir, from you, to which I should have submitted without opposition; but I will not be doomed to silence by one who has no pretensions to authority, and whose arbitrary decisions can only tend to introduce uproar, discord, and confusion.

Mr. HENRY PELHAM next rose up and spoke to this effect:—Sir, when, in the ardour of controversy upon interesting questions, the zeal of the disputants hinders them from a nice observation of decency and regularity, there is some indulgence due to the common weakness of our nature; nor ought any gentleman to affix to a negligent expression a more offensive sense than is necessarily implied by it.

To search deep, Sir, for calumnies and reproaches is no laudable nor beneficial curiosity; it must always be troublesome to ourselves by alarming us with imaginary injuries, and may often be unjust to others by charging them with invectives which they never intended. General candour and mutual tenderness will best preserve our own quiet, and support that dignity which has always been accounted essential to national debates, and seldom infringed without dangerous consequences.

Mr. LYTTLETON spoke as follows:—Sir, no man can be more zealous for decency than myself, or more convinced of the necessity of a methodical prosecution of the question before us. I am well convinced how near indecency and faction are to one another, and how inevitably confusion produces obscurity; but I hope it will always be remembered, that he who first infringes decency, or deviates from method, is to answer for all the consequences that may arise from the neglect of senatorial customs: for it is not to be expected that any man will bear reproaches without reply, or that he who wanders from the question will not be followed in his digressions and hunted through his labyrinths.

It cannot, Sir, be denied, that some insinuations were uttered injurious to those whose zeal may sometimes happen to prompt them to warm declarations, or incite them to passionate emotions. Whether I am of importance enough to be included in the censure, I despise it too much to enquire or consider, but cannot forbear to observe, that zeal for the right can never become reproachful, and that no man can fall into contempt but those who deserve it.

The clause was amended, and agreed to.

HOUSE OF COMMONS.

March 13, 1740-1.

The 7cth day of the seffion, being appointed for the report from the committee on the bill for the increase and encouragement of sailors, Sir JOHN BARNARD presented a petition from the merchants of London, and spoke as follows :—

SIR, this petition I am directed to lay before this house by many of the principal merchants of that great city which I have the honour to represent ; men too wise to be terrified with imaginary dangers, and too honest to endeavour the obstruction of any measures that may probably advance the publick good, merely because they do not concur with their private interest ; men, whose knowledge and capacity enable them to judge rightly, and whose acknowledged integrity and spirit set them above the suspicion of concealing their sentiments.

I therefore present this petition in the name of the merchants of London, in full confidence that it will be found to deserve the regard of this assembly, though I am equally with the other members a stranger to what it contains ; for it is my opinion that a representative is to lay before the house the sentiments of his constituents, whether they agree with his own or not, and that therefore it would have been superfluous to examine the petition, which, though I might not wholly have approved it, I had no right to alter.

The petition was read, and is as follows :

" The humble petition of the merchants and traders of the city of London—sheweth, that your petitioners are informed a bill is depending in this honourable house, for the encouragement and increase of seamen, and for the better and speedier manning his majesty's fleet, in which are clauses, that, should the bill pass into a law, your petitioners apprehend will be highly detrimental to the trade and navigation of this kingdom, by discouraging persons from entering into or being bred to the sea service, and entirely prevent the better and speedier manning his majesty's fleet, by giving the seamen of Great Britain, and of all other his majesty's dominions, a distaste of serving on board the royal navy.

" That

" That your petitioners conceive nothing can be of so bad
consequence to the welfare and defence of this nation, as the
treating so useful and valuable a body of men, who are its natural strength and security, like criminals of the highest nature,
and so differently from all other his majesty's subjects; and at the
same time are persuaded, that the only effectual and speedy method of procuring, for the service of his majesty's fleet, a pro-
portionable number of the sailors in this kingdom, is to distinguish that body of men by bounties and encouragements, both
present and future, and by abolishing all methods of severity
and ill usage, particularly that practice whereby they are deprived, after long and hazardous voyages, of enjoying for a
short space of time the comforts of their families, and equal
liberty with other their fellow subjects in their native country.

" That your petitioners believe it will not be difficult to have
such methods pointed out as will tend to supply the present
necessities, and at the same time effectually promote the increase
of seamen, when this honourable house shall think fit to enquire
into a matter of such high importance to the naval power, trade,
and riches of this kingdom.

" That your petitioners are convinced this bill will not only
be ineffectual to answer the ends proposed by it, but will be destructive of the liberties of all his majesty's subjects, as it em-
powers any parish officer, accompanied with an unlimited number of persons, at any hour, by day or by night, to force open the
dwelling houses, warehouses, or other places, provided for the
security and defence of their lives and fortunes, contrary to the
undoubted liberties of the people of Great Britain, and the
laws of this land.

" In consideration therefore of the premises, and of the particular prejudices, hardships, and dangers, which must inevitably attend your petitioners, and all others the merchants and
traders of this kingdom, should this bill pass into a law, your
petitioners most humbly pray this honourable house, that they
may be heard by their council against the said clauses in the said
bill."

Mr. BATHURST then presented a petition, and spoke as follows : —
Sir, the alarm which the bill now depending has raised, is not con-

fined

fined to the city of London, or to any particular province of the king's dominions; the whole nation is thrown into commotions, and the effects of the law now proposed are dreaded far and wide as a general calamity.   Every town which owes its trade and its provisions to navigation, apprehends the approach of poverty and scarcity, and those which are less immediately affected, consider the infraction of our liberties as a prelude to their destruction.   Happy would it be, if we who are entrusted with their interest, could find any arguments to convince them that their terror was merely panic.

That these fears have already extended their influence to the county which I represent, the petition which I now beg leave to lay before the house, will sufficiently evince, and I hope their remonstrances will prevail with this assembly to remove the cause of their disquiet, by rejecting the bill.

This was entitled " a petition of several gentlemen, freeholders, and other inhabitants of the county of Gloucester, in behalf of themselves and all other the freeholders of the said county," setting forth in substance,

" That the petitioners being informed that a bill was depending in this house, for the encouragement and increase of seamen, and for the better and speedier manning his majesty's fleet, containing several clauses, which, should the bill pass into a law, would, as the petitioners apprehend, impose hardships upon the people too heavy to be borne, and create discontents in the minds of his majesty's subjects ; would subvert all the rights and privileges of a Briton, and overturn Magna Charta itself, the basis on which they are built ; and by these means destroy that very liberty, for the preservation of which the present royal family was established upon the throne of Britain ; for which reasons such a law could never be obeyed, or much blood would be shed in consequence of it."

Mr. HENRY PELHAM then spoke to this purport :—Sir, I have attended to this petition with the utmost impartiality, and have endeavoured to affix to every period the most innocent sense, but cannot forbear to declare it as my opinion, that it is far distant from the stile of submission and request : instead of persuading, they attempt to intimidate us, and menace us with no less than bloodshed and rebellion.

bellion. They make themſelves the judges of our proceedings, and appeal from our determinations to their own opinion, and declare that they will obey no longer than they approve.

If ſuch petitions as theſe, Sir, are admitted, if the legiſlature ſhall ſubmit to receive laws, and ſubjects reſume at pleaſure the power with which the government is veſted, what is this aſſembly but a convention of empty phantoms, whoſe determinations are nothing more than a mockery of ſtate ?

Every inſult upon this houſe is a violation of our conſtitution, and the conſtitution, like every other fabrick, by being often battered, muſt fall at laſt. It is indeed already deſtroyed, if there be in the nation any body of men who ſhall with impunity refuſe to comply with the laws, plead the great charter of liberty againſt thoſe powers that made it, and fix the limits of their own obedience.

I cannot, Sir, paſs over in ſilence the mention of the king, whoſe title to the throne, and the reaſons for which he was exalted to it, are ſet forth with uncommon art and ſpirit of diction, but ſpirit, which, in my opinion, appears not raiſed by zeal, but by ſedition, and which therefore it is our province to repreſs. ·

That his majeſty reigns for the preſervation of liberty, will be readily confeſſed ; but how ſhall we be able to preſerve it, if his laws are not obeyed ?

Let us therefore in regard to the dignity of the aſſembly, to the efficacy of our determinations, and the ſecurity of our conſtitution, diſcourage all thoſe who ſhall addreſs us for the future, on this or any other occaſion, from ſpeaking in the ſtile of governors and dictators, by refuſing that this petition ſhould be laid on the table.

The queſtion was put, and it was agreed by the whole houſe that it ſhould not lie on the table.

Mr. HENRY PELHAM roſe up again, and ſpoke thus :—Sir, I cannot but congratulate the houſe upon the unanimity with which this petition, a petition of which I ſpeak in the ſofteſt language when I call it irreverent and diſreſpectful, has been refuſed the regard commonly paid to the remonſtrances of our conſtituents, whoſe rights I am far from deſiring to infringe, when I endeavour to regulate their conduct, and recal them to their duty.

This is an occaſion, on which it is in my opinion neceſſary to exert our authority with confidence and vigour, as the ſpirit of oppoſition muſt always be proportioned to that of the attack. Let us therefore
not

not only refufe to this petition the ufual place on our table, but reject it as unworthy of this houfe.

The queftion was put, and the petition rejected, with fcarcely any
oppofition.

The houfe then entered upon the confideration of the bill, and
when the report was made from the committee, and the blanks
filled up, Sir WILLIAM YONGE fpoke in the following manner : —

Sir, The bill has been brought by fteady perfeverance and diligent
attention to fuch perfection, that much more important effects may
be expected from it than from any former law for the fame purpofe,
if it be executed with the fame calmnefs and refolution, the fame
contempt of popular clamour, and the fame invariable and intrepid
adherence to the publick good, that has been fhewn in forming and
defending it.

But what can we hope from this or any other law, if particular
men, who cannot be convinced of its expedience, fhall not only refufe
to obey it, but declare their defign of obftructing the execution of it?
fhall determine to retire from the fphere of their authority, rather than
exercife it in compliance with the decree of the fenate, and threaten
in plain terms to call the country into their affiftance, and to pour
the rabble by thoufands upon thofe who fhall dare to do their duty,
and obey their governors?

Such declarations as thefe, Sir, are little lefs than fallies of rebellion, and, if they pafs without cenfure, will perhaps produce fuch
commotions as may require to be fuppreffed by other means than
forms of law and fenatorial cenfures.

Nor do I think, that, by rejecting the petition, we have fufficiently
eftablifhed our authority ; for in my opinion we yielded too much in
receiving it. The bill before us, whatever may be its title, is in
reality a money-bill, a bill by which aids are granted to the crown,
and we have therefore no neceffity of rejecting petitions on this occafion, becaufe the ftanding orders of the houfe forbid us to admit
them.

They then proceeded to the amendments, and when the claufe for
limiting the wages of feamen was read, Sir JOHN BARNARD
rofe up, and fpoke to this effect : —

Sir, we are now to confider the claufe to which the petition relates
which I have now prefented, a petition on a fubject of fo general importance,

portance, and offered by men fo well acquainted with every argument
that can be offered, and every objection which can be raifed, that
their requeft of being heard by their council cannot be denied,
without expofing us to the cenfure of adhering obftinately to our own
opinions, of fhutting our ears againft information, of preferring expedition to fecurity, and difregarding the welfare of our country.

It will not be neceffary to defer our determinations on this claufe
for more than three days, though we fhould gratify this juft and common requeft. And will not this lofs be amply compenfated by the
fatisfaction of the people, for whofe fafety we are debating, and by
the confcioufnefs that we have neglected nothing which might contribute to the efficacy of our meafures?

The merchants, Sir, do not come before us with loud remonftrances and harraffing complaints, they do not apply to our paffions but
our underftandings, and offer fuch informations as will very much
facilitate the publick fervice. It has been frequent in the courfe of
this debate to hear loud demands for better expedients and more efficacious than thofe which have been propofed; and is it to be conceived that thofe who called thus eagerly for new propofals intended
not to inform themfelves but to filence their opponents?

From whom, Sir, are the beft methods for the profecution of naval affairs to be expected but from thofe whofe lives are fpent in the
ftudy of commerce, whofe fortunes depend upon the knowledge
of the fea, and who will moft probably exert their abilities in contriving expedients to promote the fuccefs of the war, than they whom
the mifcarriage of our fleets muft irreparably ruin?

The merchants, Sir, are enabled by their profeffion to inform us,
are deterred by their intereft from deceiving us; they have, like all
other fubjects, a right to be heard on any queftion, and a better right
than any other when their intereft is more immediately affected; and
therefore to refufe to hear them will be at once impolitick and cruel;
it will difcover at the fame time a contempt of the moft valuable part
of our fellow fubjects, and an inflexible adherence to our own opinions.

The expedient of afferting this to be a money-bill, by which the
juft remonftrances of the merchants are intended to be eluded, is too
trivial and grofs to be adopted by this affembly: if this bill can be
termed a money-bill, and no petitions are therefore to be admitted
againft it, I know not any bill relating to the general affairs of the
nation

nation which may not plead the fame title to an exemption from petitions.

I therefore defire that the confideration of this claufe may be deferred for two days, that the arguments of the merchants may be examined, and that this affair may not be determined without the cleareft knowledge and exacteft information.

Sir ROBERT WALPOLE fpoke next to this effect :—Sir, the petition, whether juftifiable or not, with regard to the occafion on which it is prefented, or the language in which it is expreffed, is certainly offered at an improper time, and therefore can lay no claim to the regard of this affembly.

The time prefcribed by the rules of this houfe for the reception of petitions is that at which the bill is firft introduced, not at which it is to be finally determined.

The petition before us is faid not to regard the bill in general, but a particular claufe ; and it is therefore afferted, that it may now properly be heard : but this plea will immediately vanifh, when it fhall be made appear that the claufe is not mentioned in it, and that there is no particular relation between that and the petition, which I fhall attempt——

Here Sir JOHN BARNARD, remarking that Sir Robert Walpole had the petition in his hand, rofe, and faid :—Sir, I rife thus abruptly to preferve the order of this affembly, and to prevent any gentleman from having in this debate any other advantage above the reft, than that of fuperior abilities, or more extenfive knowledge.

The petition was not ordered by the houfe to be placed in the right honourable gentleman's hand, but on the table ; nor has he a right to make ufe of any other means for his information, than are in the power of any other member : if he is in doubt upon any particulars contained in it, he may move that the clerk fhould read it to the houfe.

Sir Robert Walpole laid down the paper ; Mr. PELHAM rofe, and faid :—Sir, I am fo far from thinking the rules of the houfe afferted, that, in my opinion, the right of the members is infringed by this peremptory demand. Is it not in the higheft degree requifite, that he who is about to reafon upon the petition, fhould acquaint himfelf with the fubject on which he is to fpeak.

What inconveniencies can enfue from fuch liberties as this, I am not able to difcover; and as all the orders of the houfe are doubtlefs made

made for more eafy and expeditious difpatch, if an order be contrary
to this end, it ought to be abrogated for the reafons for which others
are obferved.

The confidence with which this petition was prefented, will not
fuffer us to imagine that the perfon who offered it fears that it can
fuffer by a clofe examination, and, I fuppofe, though he has fpoken
fo warmly in favour of it without perufing, he does not expect that
others fhould with equal confidence admit———

Sir JOHN BARNARD obferving that Sir Robert Walpole leaned forward towards the table, to read the petition as it lay, rofe, and faid :
—Sir, I rife once more to demand the obfervation of the orders of
the houfe, and to hinder the right honourable gentleman from doing
by ftratagem what he did more openly and honeftly before.

It was to little purpofe that he laid down the petition, if he placed it
within reach of his infpection ? For I was only defirous, Sir, to hinder him from reading, and was far from fufpecting that he would take
it away. I infift, that henceforward, he obey the rules of this
affembly, with his eyes as well as with his hands, and take no advantage of his feat, which may enable him to perplex the queftion in
debate.

Then the PRESIDENT fpoke thus :—Sir, it is undoubtedly required by the orders of the houfe, that the petitions fhould lie upon
the table, and that any member, who is defirous of any farther fatif-
faction, fhould move, that they be read by the clerk, that every
member may have the fame opportunity of underftanding and confidering them, and that no one may be excluded from information by
the curiofity or delays of another. But the importance of this affair
feems not to be fo very great as to require a rigorous obfervance of
the rules ; and it were to be wifhed, for the eafe and expedition of
our deliberations, that gentlemen would rather yield points of indifference to one another, than infift fo warmly on circumftances of
a trivial nature.

Sir ROBERT WALPOLE then defired that the clerk might read the
petition, which being immediately done, he proceeded in the
following manner : —

Sir, having fat above forty years in this affembly, and never been
called to order before, I was fomewhat difconcerted by a cenfure fo
new and unexpected, and, in my opinion, undeferved. So that I am
fomewhat at a lofs, with regard to the train of arguments which I
                                                                    had

had formed, and which I will now endeavour to recover. Yet I
cannot but remark, that those gentlemen who are so sollicitous for
order in others, ought themselves invariably to observe it ; and
that if I have once given an unhappy precedent of violating the rules
of this house, I have, in some measure, atoned for my inadvertence,
by a patient attention to reproof, and a ready submission to authority.

I hope, Sir, I may claim some indulgence from the motive of my
offence, which was only a desire of accuracy, and an apprehension
that I might, by mistaking or forgetting some passages in the petition, lose my own time, and interrupt the proceedings of the house to
no purpose.

But having now, according to order, heard the petition, and
found no reason to alter my opinion, I shall endeavour to convince
the house, that it ought not to be granted.

The petition, Sir, is so far from bearing any particular relation to
the clause now before us, that it does not in any part mention the
expedient proposed in it, but contains a general declaration of difcontent, suspicion, apprehensions of dangerous proceedings, and dislike of our proceedings ; insinuations, Sir, by no means consistent
with the reverence due to this assembly, and which the nature of
civil government requires always to be paid to the legislative power.

To suspect any man, Sir, in common life, is in some degree to detract from his reputation, which must suffer in proportion to the supposed wisdom and integrity of him who declares his suspicion. To
suspect the conduct of this senate, is to invalidate their decisions, and
subject them to contempt and opposition.

Such and such only appears to be the tendency of the petition which
has now been read ; a petition, Sir, very unskilfully drawn, if it was
intended against the clause under our consideration, for it has not a
single period or expression that does not equally regard all the other
clauses.

If any particular objection is made, or any single grievance more
distinctly pointed at, it is the practice of impresses, a hardship I own
peculiar to the sailors ; but it must be observed that it is a practice
established by immemorial custom, and a train of precedents not to
be numbered ; and it is well known that the whole common law of
this nation, is nothing more than custom, of which the beginning
cannot be traced.

Impreſſes, Sir, have in all ages been iſſued out by virtue of the imperial prerogative, and have in all ages been obeyed, and if this exertion of the authority had been conſidered as a method of ſeverity not compenſated by the benefits which it produces, we cannot imagine but former ſenates, amidſt all their ardour for liberty, all their tenderneſs for the people, and all their abhorrence of the power of the crown, would have obviated it by ſome law, at thoſe times when nothing could have been refuſed them.

The proper time for new ſchemes and long deliberations, for amending our conſtitution, and removing inveterate grievances, are the days of proſperity and ſafety, when no immediate danger preſſes upon us, nor any publick calamity appears to threaten us ; but when war is declared, when we are engaged in open hoſtilities againſt one nation, and expect to be ſpeedily attacked by another, we are not to try experiments, but apply to dangerous evils thoſe remedies, which, though diſagreeable, we know to be efficacious.

And though, Sir, the petitioners have been more particular, I cannot diſcover the reaſonableneſs of hearing them by their council ; for to what purpoſe are the lawyers to be introduced ? Not to inſtruct us by their learning, for their employment is to underſtand the laws that have been already made, and ſupport the practices which they find eſtabliſhed. But the queſtion before us relates not to the paſt but the future, nor are we now to examine what has been done in former ages, but what it will become us to eſtabliſh on the preſent occaſion ; a ſubject of enquiry on which this houſe can expect very little information from the profeſſors of the law ?

Perhaps the petitioners expect from their council, that they ſhould diſplay the fecundity of their imagination, and the elegance of their language ; that they ſhould amuſe us with the illuſions of oratory, dazzle us with bright ideas, affect us with ſtrong repreſentations, and lull us with harmonious periods ; but if it be only intended that juſt facts and valid arguments ſhould be laid before us, they will be received without the decorations of the bar. For this end, Sir, it would have been ſufficient had the merchants informed their repreſentatives of the methods which they have to propoſe ; for the abilities of the gentlemen whom the city has deputed to this aſſembly, are well known to be ſuch as ſtand in need of no aſſiſtance from occaſional orators. Nor can it be expected that any men will be found more

capable

capable of underftanding the arguments of the merchants, or better
qualified to lay them before the fenate.

That every petitioner has (except on money bills) a right to be
heard, is undoubtedly true ; but it is no lefs evident that this right is
limited to a certain time, and that on this occafiou the proper time
is elapfed. Juftice is due both to individuals and to the nation; if
petitions may at any time be offered, and are whenever offered to be
heard, a fmall body of men might, by unfeafonable and importunate petitions, retard any occafional law, till it fhould become
unneceffary.

Petitions, Sir, are to be offered when a new bill is brought into
the houfe, that all ufeful information may be obtained; but when it
has paffed through the examination of the committees, has been approved by the collective wifdom of the fenate, and requires only a
formal ratification to give it the force of a law, it is neither ufual nor
decent to offer petitions, or declare any diflike of what the fenate has
admitted.

We are not, when we have proceeded thus far, to fuffer pleaders
to examine our conduct, or vary our determinations, according to
the opinions of thofe whom we ought to believe lefs acquainted with
the queftion than ourfelves. Should we once be reduced to afk advice,
and fubmit to dictators, what would be the reputation of this affembly
in foreign courts, or in our own country? What could be expected
but that our enemies of every kind would endeavour to regulate our
determinations by bribing our inftructors.

Nor can I think it neceffary that lawyers fhould be employed in laying before us any fcheme which the merchants may propofe, for fupplying the defects and redreffing the inconveniencies of the laws, by
which failors are at prefent levied for the royal navy; for how
fhould lawyers be more qualified than other men, to explain the particular advantages of fuch expedients, or to anfwer any objections
which may happen to rife ?

It is well known that it is not eafy for the moft happy fpeaker to
imprefs his notions with the ftrength with which he conceives them,
and yet harder is the tafk of tranfmitting imparted knowledge, of conveying to others thofe fentiments which we have not ftruck out by our
own reflection, nor collected from our own experience, but received
merely from the dictates of another.

Yet

Yet fuch muft be the information that lawyers can give us, who can only relate what they have implicitly received, and weaken the arguments which they have heard, by an imperfect recital.

Nor do I only oppofe the admiffion of lawyers to our bar, but think the right of the merchants themfelves in the prefent cafe very queftionable; for though in general it muft be allowed, that every petitioner has a claim to our attention, yet it is to be enquired whether it is likely that the publick happinefs is his chief concern, and whether his private intereft is not too much affected to fuffer him to give impartial evidence, or honeft information. Scarcely any law can be made by which fome man is not either impoverifhed, or hindered from growing rich; and we are not to liften to complaints, of which the foundation is fo eafily difcovered, or imagine a law lefs ufeful, becaufe thofe who fuffer fome immediate inconvenience from it, do not approve it.

The queftion before us is required by the prefent exigence of our affairs to be fpeedily decided, and though the merchants have with great tendernefs, compaffion, and modefty, condefcended to offer us their advice, I think expedition preferable to any information that can reafonably be expected from them, and that as they will fuffer in the firft place by any mifconduct of our naval affairs, we fhall fhew more regard to their intereft by manning our fleet immediately, than by waiting three or four days for farther inftructions.

Mr. SANDYS anfwered to this effect :---Sir, the merchants of London, whether we confider their numbers, their property, their integrity, or their wifdom, are a body of too much importance to be thus contemptuoufly rejected, rejected when they afk nothing that can be juftly denied to the meaneft fubject of the empire, when they propofe to fpeak on nothing but what their profeffion enables them to underftand.

To no purpofe is it urged, that the bill is far advanced, for if we have not proceeded in the right way, we ought to be in more hafte to return, in proportion as we have gone farther; nor can I difcover why we fhould expedite with fo much affiduity meafures which are judged ineffectual, by thofe who know their confequences beft, and for whofe advantage they are particularly defigned.

That we have already fpent fo much time in confidering methods for manning the fleet, is furely one reafon why we fhould endeavour at laft to eftablifh fuch as may be effectual, nor can we hope to fuc-

ceed without a patient attention to their opinion, who muft neceffarily be well experienced in naval affairs.

It is furely therefore neither prudent nor juft to fhut out intelligence from our affemblies, and ridicule the good intention of thofe
that offer it, to confult upon the beft expedients for encouraging and
encreafing failors, and when the merchants offer their fcheme to treat
them as faucy, impertinent, idle medlers, that affume——

Here the ATTORNEY GENERAL called him to order, and fpoke after
this manner :—Sir, it is not very confiftent to prefs the difpatch of
bufinefs, and to retard it at the fame time by invidious infinuations,
or unjuft reprefentations of arguments or expreffions: whenever any
expreffion is cenfured, it ought to be repeated in the fame words ; for
otherwife, does not the animadverter raife the phantom that he encounters? Does he not make the ftain which he endeavours with fo
much officious zeal to wipe away.

That no epithets of contempt or ridicule have in this debate been
applied to the merchants, nor any violation of decency attempted, it
is unneceffary to prove, and therefore it is neither regular nor candid
to reprefent any man as aggravating the refufal of their petition with
reproaches and infults. But not to dwell longer on this incident, I will
take the liberty of reminding the gentleman, that perfonal invectives
are always at leaft fuperfluous, and that the bufinefs of the day requires
rather arguments than fatire.

Mr. SANDYS then fpoke as follows :—Sir, I am by no means convinced that the learned gentleman who charges me with irregularity,
is better acquainted than myfelf with the rules and cuftoms of this
houfe, which I have ftudied with great application, affifted by long
experience. I hope, therefore, it will be no inexcufable prefumption,
if, inftead of a tacit fubmiffion to his cenfure, I affert in my own vindication, that I have not deviated from the eftablifhed rules of
the fenate, that I have fpoken only in defence of merit infulted, and
that I have condemned only fuch injurious infinuations. I did not,
Sir, attempt to repeat expreffions, as ought not to be heard without
reply.

Then the PRESIDENT faid :—I believe the gentleman either heard
imperfectly, or mifunderftood thefe expreffions, which he fo warmly
condemns, for nothing has been uttered that could juftly excite his
indignation. My office obliges me on this occafion to remark, that
the regard due to the dignity of the houfe ought to reftrain every
member

member from digreffions into private fatire ; for in proportion as we proceed with lefs decency, our determinations will have lefs influence.

Mr. PELHAM fpoke next, In fubftance as follows :—Sir, the reputation which the honourable gentleman has acquired by his uncommon knowledge of the ufages of the fenate, is too well founded to be fhaken, nor was any attack upon his character intended, when he was interrupted in the profecution of his defign. To cenfure any indecent expreffion by whomfoever uttered, is doubtlefs confiftent with the ftricteft regularity ; nor is it lefs proper to obviate any mifreprefentation which inattention or miftake may produce.

I am far, Sir, from thinking that the gentleman's indignation was excited rather by malice than miftake ; but miftakes of this kind may produce confequences which cannot be too cautioufly avoided. How unwillingly would that gentleman propagate through the nation an opinion that the merchants were infulted in this houfe, their intereft neglected, and their intelligence defpifed, at a time when no afperfion was thrown upon them, nor any thing intended but tendernefs and regard ? And yet fuch had been the reprefentation of this day's debate, which this numerous audience would have conveyed to the populace, had not the miftake been immediately rectified, and the rumour crufhed in the birth.

Nothing, Sir, can be more injurious to the character of this affembly, by which the people are reprefented, than to accufe them of treating any clafs of men with infolence and contempt, and too much diligence cannot be ufed in obviating a report which cannot be fpread in the nation, without giving rife to difcontent, clamours, and fedition.

Thofe who fhall be inclined to reject the petition, may perhaps act with no lefs regard to the merchants, and may promote their intereft and their fecurity with no lefs ardour than thofe who moft follicitoufly labour for its reception : for, if they are not allowed to be heard, it is only becaufe the publick intereft requires expedition, and becaufe every delay of our preparations is an injury to trade.

That this is not a proper time for petitions againft the bill to be heard, is univerfally known, and I can difcover nothing in the petition that reftrains it to this particular claufe, which is fo far from being fpecified, that it appears to be the only part of the bill of which they have had no intelligence.

Y 2   Let

Let the warmeſt advocates for the petition point out any part of it that relates to this ſingle clauſe, and I will retract my aſſertion; but as it appears that there are only general declarations of the inexpediency of the meaſures propoſed, and the pernicious tendency of the methods now in uſe, what is the petition, but a complaint againſt the bill, and a requeſt that it ſhould be laid aſide.

The practice of impreſſes, Sir, is particularly cenſured, as ſevere and oppreſſive; a charge which, however true, has no relation to this clauſe, which is intended to promote the voluntary engagement of ſailors in the ſervice of the crown; yet it may not be improper to ob-ſerve, that as the practice of impreſſing is, in itſelf, very efficacious, and well adapted to ſudden emergencies, as it has been eſtabliſhed by a long ſucceſſion of ages, and is therefore become almoſt a part of our conſtitution; and as it is at this time neceſſary to ſupply the navy with the utmoſt expedition, it is neither decent nor prudent to com-plain too loudly againſt, or to heighten the diſcontent of the people at a neceſſary evil.

We have, Sir, examined every part of this bill with the attention which the defence of the nation requires, we have ſoftened the rigour of the methods firſt propoſed, and admitted no violence or hardſhip that is not abſolutely neceſſary to make the law effectual, which like every other law muſt be executed by force, if it be obſtructed or op-poſed. We have inſerted a great number of amendments, propoſed by thoſe who are repreſented as the moſt anxious guardians of the pri-vileges of the people, and it is not ſurely to no purpoſe that the great council of the nation has ſo long and ſo ſtudiouſly laboured.

Thoſe who are choſen by the people to repreſent them, have undoubt-edly, Sir, ſome claim as individuals to their confidence and reſpect; for to imagine that they have committed the great charge of ſenato-rial employments, that they have truſted their liberties and their hap-pineſs to thoſe whoſe integrity they ſuſpect, or whoſe underſtandings they deſpiſe, is to imagine them much more ſtupid than they have been repreſented by thoſe who are cenſured as their enemies.

But far different is the regard due to the determinations formed by the collective wiſdom of the ſenate; a regard which ought to border upon reverence, and which is ſcarcely conſiſtent with the leaſt mur-mur of diſſatisfaction.

If we are to hear the preſent petitioners, is it not probable that be-fore we have diſpatched them, we ſhall be ſolicited by others, who will then

then plead the fame right, fupported by a new precedent? And is it not poffible that by one interruption upon another, our meafures may be delayed, till they fhall be ineffectual?

It feems to me to be of much more importance to defend the merchants than to hear them, and I fhall therefore think no conceffions at this time expedient, which may obftruct the great end of our endeavours, the equipment of the fleet.

Mr. PULTENEY then fpoke as follows :—Sir, notwithftanding the art and eloquence with which the grant of the merchants petition has been oppofed, I am not yet able to difcover that any thing is afked unreafonable, unprecedented, or inconvenient, and I am confident, that no real objection can have been over-looked by the gentlemen who have fpoken againft it.

I have fpent, Sir, thirty five years of my life in the fenate, and know that information has always upon important queftions been willingly received, and it cannot furely be doubted that the petitioners are beft able to inform us of naval bufinefs, and to judge what will be the right method of reconcjling the failors to the publick fervice, and of fupplying our fleets without injuring our trade.

Their abilities and importance have been hitherto fo generally acknowledged, that no fenate has yet refufed to attend to their opinion, and furely we ought not to be ambitious of being the firft affembly of the reprefentatives of the people, that has refufed an audience to the merchants.

With regard to the expedience of delaying the bill at the prefent conjuncture; he muft think very contemptuoufly of the petitioners, who imagines that they have nothing to offer that will counter-balance a delay of two days, and muft entertain an elevated idea of the vigilance and activity of our enemies, enemies never before eminent for expedition, if he believes that they can gain great advantages in fo fhort a time.

The chief reafon of the oppofition appears, indeed, not to be either the irregularity or inexpediency of hearing them, but the offence which fome have received from an irreverent mention of the power of impreffing, a power which never can be mentioned without complaint or deteftation.

It is not, indeed, impoffible that they may intend to reprefent to the houfe, how much the failors are oppreffed, how much our commerce is impeded, and how much the power of the nation is exhaufted

by

by this cruel method. They may propose to shew that sailors, not having the choice of their voyages, are often hurried through a sudden change of climates from one extreme to another, and that nothing can be expected from such viciffitudes, but sickness, lameness, and death. They may propose, that to have just arrived from the south may be pleaded as an exemption from an immediate voyage to the north, and that the seaman may have some time to prepare himself for so great an alteration, by a refidence of a few months in a temperate climate.

If this should be their intention, it cannot, in my opinion, Sir, be called either unreasonable or difrespectful, nor will their allegations be easily disproved.

But it is infinuated, that their grievances are probably such as affect them only as diftinct from the reft of the community, and that they have nothing to complain of but a temporary interruption of their private advantage.

I have, indeed, no idea of the *private advantage* of a legal trader : for unlefs, Sir, we neglect our duty of providing that no commerce shail be carried on to the detriment of the publick, the merchants profit muft be the profit of the nation, and their interefts inseparably combined.

It may, however, be poffible, that the merchants may, like other men, prefer their immediate to their greater advantage, and may be impatient of a painful remedy, though neceffary to prevent a more grievous evil. But let us not cenfure them by fufpicion, and punish them for a crime which it is only pofible they may commit ; let us, Sir, at leaft have all the certainty that can be obtained, and allow them an audience ; let us neither be fo positive as not to receive information, nor fo rigorous as not to liften to entreaties.

If the merchants have nothing to offer, nothing but complaints, and can propofe no better meafures than thofe which they lament, if their arguments should be found to regard only their prefent intereft, and to be formed upon narrow views and private purpofes, it will be eafy to detect the impofture, and reject it with the indignation it shall deferve : nor will our proceedings be then cenfured by the nation, which requires not that the merchants should be implicitly believed, though it expects that they should be heard. Let us at leaft have a *conention*, though we should not be able to conclude a treaty.

I know not, Sir, why we have not taken care to obviate all thefe
difficulties,

difficulties, and to remove the neceffity of petitions, debates, fearches, and impreffes, by the plain and eafy method of a voluntary regifter; by retaining fuch a number of feamen as may probably be requifite upon fudden emergencies.   Would not the nation with more chear-fulnefs contribute half-pay to thofe who are daily labouring for the publick good, than to the caterpillars of the land fervice, that grow old in lazinefs, and are difabled only by vice?

Let ten thoufand men receive daily a fmall falary, upon condition that they fhall be ready, whenever called upon, to engage in the fer-vice of the crown, and the difficulty of our naval preparations will be at an end.

That it is neceffary to exert ourfelves on this occafion, and to ftrike out fome meafures for fecuring the dominion of the ocean, cannot be denied by any one who confiders that we have now no other pretenfions to maintain; that all our influence on the continent, at whatever expence gained and fupported, is now in a manner loft, and only the reputation of our naval ftrength remains to preferve us from being trampled and infulted by every power, and from finding Spaniards in every climate.

Sir WILLIAM YONGE fpoke in fubftance, as follows:—Sir, the violence and feverity of impreffes, fo often and fo pathetically complained of, appears to be now nothing more than a punifhment inflicted upon thofe who neglect or refufe to receive the encourage-ment offered with the utmoft liberality by the government, and de-cline the fervice of their country from a fpirit of avarice, obftinacy, or refentment.

That fuch men deferve fome feverities, cannot be doubted, and therefore a law by which no penalty fhould be enacted, would be im-perfect and ineffectual.   The obfervation, Sir, of all laws is to be enforced by rewards on one fide, and punifhments on the other, that every paffion may be influenced, and even our weaknefs made inftru-mental to the performance of our duty.

In the bill before us no punifhment is indeed exprefsly decreed, be-caufe the failors who fhall difregard it, are only left to their former hardfhips, from which thofe who engage voluntarily in the fervice of the navy are exempted.

Why fo many rewards and fo much violence fhould be neceffary to allure or force the failors into the publick fervice, I am unable to comprehend: for, excepting the fudden change of climates, which

may

may doubtless sometimes bring on distempers, the service of the king has no disadvantages which are not common to that of the merchants.

The wages in the navy are indeed less, but then it is to be remembered, that they are certainly paid, and that the sailor is in less danger of losing by a tempest, or a wreck, the whole profits of his voyage, because, if he can preserve his life, he receives his pay. But in trading voyages, the seamen mortgage their wages, as a security for their care, which, if the ship is lost, they are condemned to forfeit.

Thus, Sir, the hardships of the navy appear not so great when compared with those of the merchants service, as they have been hitherto represented; and I doubt not, that if counsellors were to be heard on both sides, the measures taken for supplying the fleet would be found to be reasonable and just.

Sir John Barnard rose to speak, when Mr. Fox called to order, and proceeded.

Sir, it is well known to be one of the standing and unvariable orders of this house, that no member shall speak twice in a debate on the same question, except when for greater freedom we resolve ourselves into a committee. Upon this question the honourable gentleman has already spoken, and cannot therefore be heard again without such a transgression of our orders as must inevitably produce confusion.

Sir John Barnard spoke thus :—Sir, I know not for what reason the honourable gentleman apprehends any violation of the order of the house; for as I have not yet spoken upon the present question, I have an undoubted right to be heard, a right which that gentleman cannot take away.

Sir William Yonge next spoke to this effect:—Sir, I know not by what secret distinction the gentleman supports in his own mind this declaration, which, to the whole house, must appear very difficult to be defended; for we must, before we can admit it, allow our memories to have forsaken us, and our eyes and ears to have been deceived.

Did he not, as soon as the clause before us was read, rise and affect the characters of the petitioners, and their right to the attention of the house? Did he not dwell upon their importance, their abilities, and their integrity; and enforce, with his usual eloquence, every motive to the reception of the petition? How then can he

assert

affert that he has not fpoken in the prefent debate, and how can be
expect to be heard a fecond time, fince, however his eloquence may
pleafe, and his arguments convince, that pleafure and conviction
cannot now be obtained, without infringing the ftanding orders of
the houfe.

Then the PRESIDENT rofe, and fpoke to this purport:—It is
not without uneafinefs that I fee the time of the houfe and of the
publick wafted in fruitlefs cavils and unneceffary controverfies.
Every gentleman ought now to confider that we are confulting upon
no trivial queftion, and that expedition is not lefs neceffary than accuracy. It cannot be denied, Sir, [to Sir John Barnard,] that you
have already fpoken on this queftion, and that the rules of the houfe
do not allow you to fpeak a fecond time.

Sir ROBERT WALPOLE faid:—Sir, I am far from thinking the
order of the houfe fo facred, as that it may not be neglected on fome
important occafions, and if the gentleman has any thing to urge fo
momentous, that, in his own opinion, it outweighs the regard due
to our rules, I fhall willingly confent that he fhall be heard.

Sir JOHN BARNARD fpoke as follows:—Sir, I am far from being
inclined to receive as a favour, what, in my own opinion, I may
claim as a right, and defire not to owe the liberty of fpeaking to the
condefcenfion of the right honourable gentleman.

What I have to urge is no lefs againft the bill in general than the
particular claufe now immediately under our confideration, and though
the petition fhould relate likewife to the whole bill, I cannot difcover why we fhould refufe to hear it.

Petitions from men of much inferior rank, and whofe intereft is
much lefs clofely connected with that of the publick, have been
thought neceffary to be heard, nor is the meaneft individual to be
injured or reftrained without being admitted to offer his arguments
in his own favour. Even the journeymen fhoemakers, one of the
loweft claffes of the community, have been permitted to bring their
council to our bar, and remonftrate againft the inconveniencies to
which they were afraid of being fubjected.

Mr. WINNINGTON fpoke thus:—Sir, I am always willing to hear
petitions, when refpectfully drawn up, and regularly fubfcribed, but
can by no means difcover that this is a real petition, for I have
heard of no names affixed to it; it is therefore a requeft from nobody, and by rejecting it no man is refufed. It may, fo far as can be
                                                        difcovered,

difcovered, be drawn up by the gentleman who offered it, and perhaps no other perfon may be acquainted with it.

Mr. HAY fpoke to the following purport :—Sir, it is, in my opinion, neceffary that a petition in the name of the merchants of London fhould be fubfcribed by the whole number, for if only a few fhould put their names to it, how does it appear that it is any thing more than an apprehenfion of danger to their own particular intereft, which perhaps the other part, their rivals in trade, may confider as an advantage, or at leaft regard with indifference. This fufpicion is much more reafonable, when a petition is fubfcribed by a fmaller number, who may eafily be imagined to have partial views, and defigns not wholly confiftent with the intereft of the publick.

Admiral WAGER then fpoke thus : —Sir, if I am rightly informed, another petition is preparing by feveral eminent merchants, that this claufe may fland part of the bill ; and certainly they ought to be heard as well as the prefent petitioners, which will occafion great and unneceffary delays, and therefore I am againft the motion.

Advocate CAMPBELL anfwered to this effect :—Sir, I agree with that honourable gentleman, that if the merchants are divided in opinion upon this point, one fide ought to be heard as well as the other, and hope the houfe will come to a refolution for that purpofe : for I fhall invariably promote every propofal which tends to procure the fulleft information in all affairs that fhall come before us.

Then the queftion was put, that the further confideration of the report be adjourned for two days, in order to hear the merchants, and it paffed in the negative, ayes 142, noes 192.

On the report this day the eleven claufes of feverity were given up without any divifion, and a claufe was added, viz. " Provided that nothing in this bill fhall be conftrued to extend to any contracts or agreements for the hire of feamen [or perfons employed as fuch] in voyages from parts beyond the feas, to any other parts beyond the feas, or to Great Britain."

The engroffed bill " for the encreafe and encouragement of feamen," was read, according to order, when Mr. DIGBY rofe, and fpoke as follows :—

Sir, I have a claufe to be offered to the houfe as neceffary to be inferted

erted in the bill before us, which was put into my hands by a member, whom a sudden misfortune has made unable to attend his duty, and which in his opinion, and mine, is of great importance, and I shall therefore take the liberty of reading it.

' Be it enacted, that every seaman offering himself to serve his majesty, shall, upon being refused, receive from such captain, lieutenant, or justice of the peace, a certificate, setting forth the reasons for which he is refused, which certificate may be produced by him, as an exemption from being seized by a warrant of impress."

I hope the reasonableness and equity of this clause is so inconcestably apparent, that it will find no opposition ; for what can be more cruel, unjust, or oppressive, than to punish men for neglect of a law which they have endeavoured to obey. To what purpose are rewards offered, if they are denied to those who come to claim them ? What is it less than theft, and fraud, to force a man into the service who would willingly have entered, and subject him to hardships without the recompence which he may justly demand from the solemn promise of the legislature.

Admiral WAGER next spoke to this effect: —Sir, to this clause, which the gentleman has represented as so reasonable and just, objections may, in my opinion, be easily made, of which he will himself acknowledge the force. The great obstruction of publick measures is partiality, whether from friendship, bribery, or any other motive ; against partiality alone the clause which is now offered, is levelled, and indeed it is so dangerous an evil, that it cannot be obviated with too much caution.

But this clause, instead of preventing private correspondence, and illegal combinations, has an evident tendency to produce them, by inciting men to apply with pretended offers of service to those who are before suborned to refuse them, then make a merit of their readiness, and demand a certificate.

By such artifices multitudes may exempt themselves from the impress who may be known to be able sailors, even by those that conduct it, and may, under the protection of a certificate, fallaciously obtained, laugh at all endeavours to engage them in the publick service.

Mr. DIGBY spoke thus :—Sir, if this authority, lodged in the
hands

hands of thofe who are propofed in the claufe to be entrufted with it, be in danger of being executed, without due regard to the end for which it is granted, let it be placed where there is neither temptation nor opportunity to abufe it. Let the admiralty alone have the power of granting fuch certificates, the officers of which will be able to judge whether the failor is really unfit for the fervice, and deliver thofe whom age or accidents have difabled from the terror of impreffes; for furely, he that is fit to ferve, when taken by violence, is no lefs qualified when he enters voluntarily, and he who could not be admitted when he tendered himfelf, ought not to be dragged away, when perhaps he has contracted for another voyage.

Mr. WAGER replied:—Sir, it is, doubtlefs, more proper to place fuch authority in the officers of the admiralty, than in any other; but it does not appear that the benefit which the failors may receive from it, to whatever hands it is entrufted, will not be over-balanced by the injury which the publick will probably fuffer.

Sailors are frequently levied in remote parts of the kingdom; in ports where the admiralty cannot fpeedily be informed of the reafons for which thofe that may petition for certificates have been refufed, and therefore cannot grant them without danger of being deceived by fraudulent accounts.

The grievance for which the remedy is propofed cannot frequently occur; for it is not probable that in a time of naval preparations, any man qualified for the fervice fhould be rejected, fince the officers gain nothing by their refufal.

Mr. HAY fpoke as follows:—Sir, it is very poffible that thofe inftances which may be produced of men, who have been impreffed by one officer, after they have been rejected by another, may be only the confequences of the high value which every man is ready to fet upon his own abilities: for he that offers himfelf, no doubt, demands the higheft premium, though he be not an able failor; and, if rejected, and afterwards impreffed as a novice, thinks himfelf at liberty to complain, with the moft importunate vehemence, of fraud, partiality, and oppreffion.

The queftion being put was refolved in the negative, almoft unanimoufly.

Mr. SOUTHWELL offered a claufe, importing, "That all failors who fhould take advance-money of the merchants, fhould be obliged

obliged to perform their agreements, or be liable to be taken up
by any magistrate or justice of the peace, and deemed deserters,
except they were in his majesty's ships of war."

He was seconded by Lord GAGE :—Sir, as this clause has no other
tendency than to promote the interest of the merchants, without obstructing the publick preparations ; as it tends only to confirm legal
contracts, and facilitate that commerce from whence the wealth and
power of this nation arises, I hope it will readily be admitted, as we
may, by adding this sanction to the contracts made between the
merchants and sailors, in some degree balance the obstructions where-
with we have embarrassed trade by the other clauses.

Admiral WAGER replied :--This clause is unquestionably reasonable,
but not necessary ; for it is to be found already in an act made for the
encouragement of the merchants, which is still in force, and ought,
whenever any such frauds are committed, to be rigorously observed.

Sir ROBERT WALPOLE then desired that the clerk might read the
act, in which the clause was accordingly found, and Mr. Southwell withdrew his motion.

Then the question was put, whether the bill " for the encrease
and encouragement of sailors" do pass, which was resolved
in the affirmative, 153 against 79.

HOUSE OF COMMONS.

March 13, 1740-1.

*The house being resolved into a committee for the consideration of the bill
for the punishment of mutiny and desertion, and for the better payment
of the army and their quarters, &c. Sir WILLIAM YONGE desired
that the 20th and 26th clauses of the late act might be read, which
were read as follows :*

XX. *It is hereby enacted, that the officers and soldiers, so quartered
and billeted, shall be received by the owners of the inns, livery-stables,
ale-houses, victualling-houses, and other houses in which they are allowed to be quartered and billeted by this act ; and shall pay such rea-*
sonable

sonable prices as *shall be appointed, from time to time, by the justices of the peace, in their general and quarter-sessions of each county, city, or division, within their respective jurisdictions: and the justices of the peace aforesaid, are hereby impowered and required to set and appoint, in their general or quarter-sessions aforesaid, such reasonable rates, for all necessary provisions for such officers and soldiers, for one or more nights, in the several cities, towns, villages, and other places, which they shall come to in their march, or which shall be appointed for their residence and quarters.*

XXVI. *That the quarters, both of officers and soldiers in Great Britain, may be duly paid and satisfied, be it enacted, that every officer, to whom it belongs to receive the pay or subsistence-money, either for a whole regiment, or particular troops and companies, shall immediately, upon each receipt of every particular sum, on account of pay or subsistence, give publick notice thereof to all persons keeping inns, or other places where officers or soldiers are quartered by virtue of this act: also appoint them and others to repair to their quarters, within four days at the farthest, after the receipt of the same, to declare the accounts or debts (if any shall be) between them and the officers and soldiers quartered in their respective houses: which accounts the said officer or officers are hereby required immediately to discharge, before any part of the said pay or subsistence be distributed to the officers or soldiers: provided the said accounts exceed not for a commission officer of horse, under a captain, for one day's diet and small beer, two shillings; for one commission officer of dragoons, under a captain, one shilling; for one commission officer of foot, under a captain, one shilling; and for hay and straw, for one horse, six pence; for one dragoon or light horseman's diet and small beer, each day six pence, and hay and straw for his horse, six pence; and also not to exceed four pence a day, for one foot soldier's diet and small beer.*

He then spoke to the following effect: —Sir, whether there is any real difficulty in the clauses which you have now heard read, or whether there are such passages as may be easily understood by those who have no interest to mistake them, and which are only clouded by an artificial obscurity, whether they are in themselves capable of different meanings, or whether avarice or poverty have produced unreasonable interpretations, and found ambiguities only because they were determined not to be disappointed in their search; whether this law is

disobeyed,

difobeyed, becaufe it is mifunderftood, or only mifunderftood by thofe who had refolved to difobey it, the committee muft determine.

It has been for many years underftood that inn-holders and keepers of publick houfes were obliged by this law to fupply foldiers quartered upon them with diet and fmall beer, and hay and ftraw for their horfes, at fuch rates as are mentioned in the act; nor can I difcover that thefe claufes admit of any other interpretation, or that any other could be intended by the fenate by which it was enacted.

The pay of the foldiers, Sir, was well known to thofe who gave their confent to this law, it was intended by them that the foldiers fhould be fupplied with neceffaries, and it could not be meant that they fhould pay for them more than they received; they therefore eftablifhed the rate at which they were to be furnifhed, and fixed the higheft rate which the wages of a foldier allow him to pay.

This interpretation was, as I fuppofe, from its apparent confonance to reafon, univerfally allowed, till the inhabitants of Ledbury, whither foldiers had been fent to fupprefs a riot and enforce the laws, found their apprehenfions fo fharpened by their malice, that they difcovered in the act an ambiguity, which had, till that time, efcaped the penetration of the moft fagacious, and, upon comparifon of one circumftance with another, found themfelves under no obligation to give any affiftance to the foldiers.

They therefore, Sir, not only refufed to afford them victuals at the accuftomed rates, but proceeding from one latitude of interpretation to another, at length denied them not only the privilege of diet, but the ufe of kitchen utenfils, to drefs the provifions which they bought for themfelves, and at laft denied their claim to the fire itfelf.

The foldiers, exafperated not only at the breach of their eftablifhed and uncontefted privileges, but at the privation of the neceffaries of life, began to think of methods more fpeedy and efficacious than thofe of arguments and remonftrances, and to form refolutions of procuring by force, what, in their opinions, was only by force withheld from them.

What might have been the event of this controverfy, to what extremities a conteft about things fo neceffary might have been carried, how wide the conteft might have fpread, or how long it might have lafted, we may imagine, but cannot determine; had not a fpeedy deci-
                                                                        cifion

cifion been procured, its confequences might have been fatal to multitudes, and a great part of the nation been thrown into confufion.

Having received an account of the affair from the officers who commanded at that place, I confulted the attorney general what was the defign of the law, and the extent of the obligation enforced by it, and was anfwered by him, that the fums which were to be paid for the diet of the men, and the hay and ftraw for the horfes, being fpecified, it muft necceffarily be intended, by the legiflature, that no higher rates fhould be demanded ;—that the power granted to the juftices of peace was wholly in favour of the foldier, and that they might leffen the payment at difcretion in places of uncommon cheapnefs, or years of extraordinary plenty, but could not encreafe it on any occafion.

Another difpute, Sir, of the like nature was occafioned by the late fcarcity at Wakefield, where the juftices, upon the application of the inn-keepers, made ufe of the authority which they fuppofed to have been repofed in them by the act, and raifed the price of hay and ftraw to eight pence, which the foldiers were not able to pay, without fuffering for want of victuals.

On this occafion likewife I was applied to, and upon confulting the prefent attorney general, received the fame anfwer as before; and tranfmitting his opinion to the place from whence I received the complaint, it had fo much regard paid to it, that the additional demand was thenceforward remitted.

The letters which thofe two learned lawyers fent to me on this fubject I have now in my hand ; and hope their opinion will be thought fufficient authority for the interpretation of an act of the fenate.

Nor is their authority, Sir, however great, fo ftrong a proof of the juftnefs of this interpretation, as the reafonablenefs, or rather neceffity of admitting it. The only argument that can be produced againft it, is the hardfhip impofed by it on the inn-holder, who, as it is objected, muft be obliged by the law, fo underftood, to furnifh the foldiers with provifions for a price at which he cannot afford them.

But let it be confidered, how much more eafily the landlord can furnifh them at this price, than they can provide for themfelves, and the difficulty will immediately vanifh. If foldiers are neceffary, they muft neceffarily be fupported, and it appears, upon reflection, that their pay will not fupport them by any other method.

If they are obliged to buy their victuals, they muft likewife buy fire
and

and implements to drefs them; and what is ſtill a greater hardſhip; they muſt ſell them, and buy new, at every change of their quarters: if this is impoſſible, it will be allowed not to be the meaning of the ſenate, upon whoſe wiſdom it would be a cenſure too ſevere to ſuppoſe them capable of enacting impoſſibilities.

But to the inn-holder, Sir, whoſe utenſils are always in uſe, and whoſe fire is always burning, the diet of a ſoldier coſts only the original price paid to the butcher, and in years of common plenty may be afforded without loſs at the price mentioned in the act. It cannot, indeed, be denied that, at preſent, every ſoldier is a burthen to the family on which he is quartered, in many parts of the kingdom; but it may be reaſonably hoped, that the preſent ſcarcity will quickly ceaſe, and that proviſions will fall back to their former value; and even, amidſt all the complaints with which the ſeverity and irregularity of the late ſeaſons have filled the nation, there are many places where ſoldiers may be maintained at the ſtated rates, with very little hardſhip to their landlords.

However, Sir, as this interpretation of the act, though thus ſupported both by authority and reaſon, has been diſputed and denied, as ſome lawyers may be of a different opinion from thoſe whom I have conſulted, and as it is not likely that the practice thus interrupted will now be complied with as a preſcription; I think it neceſſary to propoſe, that the price of a ſoldier's diet be more explicitly aſcertained, that no room may remain for future controverſies.

Mr. SANDYS then roſe and ſpoke as follows:—Sir, I am very far from thinking the authority of theſe learned gentlemen, whoſe letters are produced, incontrovertible proof of the juſtneſs of an interpretation of an act of the ſenate, where that interpretation is not in itſelf warranted by reaſon, nor conſiſtent with the preſervation or enjoyment of property. Much leſs ſhall I agree to ſupport their interpretation by a new law, or eſtabliſh, by an act of the legiſlature, a kind of oppreſſion, for which, however tacitly ſubmitted to, nothing could be pleaded hitherto but cuſtom.

The burthen, Sir, of a ſtanding army, is already too heavy to be much longer ſupported, nor ought we to add weight to it by new impoſitions; it ſurely much better becomes the repreſentatives of the nation to attend to the complaints of their conſtituents, and where they

are found to arife from real grievances, to contrive fome expedient
for alleviating their calamities.

A heavy and dreadful calamity, Sir, lies now in a particular manner upon the people ; the calamity of famine, one of the fevereft
fcourges of Providence, has filled the whole land with mifery and la-
mentation, and furely nothing can be more inhuman than to chufe
out this feafon of horror, for new encroachments on their privileges,
and new invafions of the rights of nature, the dominion of their own
houfes, and the regulation of their own tables.

The honourable gentleman, Sir, has mentioned places where provifions, as he fays, are ftill to be bought at eafy rates. For my part,
I am fixed in no fuch happy corner of the kingdom, I fee nothing
but fcarcity, and hear nothing but complaints, and fhall therefore be
very far from admitting now fuch methods of fupporting the army,
as were thought too burthenfome in times of plenty, nor will combine in laying a new tax upon any clafs of my countrymen, when
they are finking under an enormous load of impofts, and in want of
the neceffaries of life.

Sir WILLIAM YONGE replied in the manner following :—Sir, nothing is more eafy than outcry and exaggeration, nor any thing lefs
ufeful for the difcovery of truth, or the eftablifhment of right. The
moft neceffary meafures may often admit of very florid exclamations
againft them, and may furnifh very fruitful topics of invective.

When our liberties, Sir, are endangered, or our country invaded,
it may be very eafy, when it is propofed that we fhould have recourfe
to our fwords for fecurity, to bewail in pathetic language the miferies
of war, to defcribe the defolation of cities, the wafte of kingdoms,
the infolence of victory, and the cruelty of power inflamed by hof-
tilities. Yet to what will thofe reprefentations contribute, but to
make that difficult which yet cannot be avoided, and embarrafs meafures which muft however be purfued.

Such, Sir, appear to me to be the objection made to the method
now propofed of providing neceffaries for the foldiers, methods not
eligible for their own fake, but which ought not to be too loudly
condemned, till fome better can be fubftituted : for why fhould the
publick be alarmed with groundlefs apprehenfions, or why fhould we
make thofe laws which our affairs oblige us to enact, lefs agreeable
to the people by partial reprefentations ?

Is

In the difcuffion of this queftion, Sir, is to be confidered whether foldiers are to be fupported, and whether it will be more proper to maintain them by the method of afcertaining the rates at which they are to be fupplied, or by encreafing their pay.

One of thefe two ways it is neceffary to take, the provifions are already fixed at as high a price as their pay will allow ; if, therefore, they are expeced to pay more, their wages muft be encreafed.

For my part I fhall comply with either method, though I cannot but think it my duty to declare that in my opinion it is fafer to fix the price of provifions, which muft fink in their value, than to raife the pay of the army, which may never afterwards be reduced.

Mr. GYBDON then fpoke to this effect:—Sir, I agree with the honourable gentleman, that if foldiers are neceffary, we muft make provifion for their fupport. This is indifputably certain, but it is no lefs certain, that where foldiers are neceffary, reftraints and regulations are neceffary likewife, to preferve thofe from being infulted and plundered by them, who maintain them for the fake of protection.

The ufefulnefs, Sir, of this caution feems not to be known, or not regarded, by the gentleman whofe propofal gave occafion to this debate; for by enacting laws in general terms, as he feems to advife, we fhould leave the unhappy inn-keeper wholly at the mercy of his guefts, who might plunder and infult him under the protection of the legiflature, might riot as in a conquered country, and fay—To this treatment you are fubjected by the determination of the fenate.

The unhappy man, Sir, could have no profpect either of quiet or fafety, but by gratifying all the expectations of his mafters, returning civilities for infolence, and receiving their commands with the fame fubmiffion that is paid in capitulating towns to the new garrifon.

If it be neceffary to afcertain the price, is it not neceffary at the fame time to afcertain the fpecies and quantity of provifions to be allowed for it? Is a foldier to fatten on delicacies, and to revel in fuperfluities, for four-pence a day? Ought not fome limits to be fet to his expectations, and fome reftraints prefcribed to his appetite? Is he to change his fare with all the capricioufnefs of luxury, and relieve by variety the fqueamifhnefs of excefs?

Such demands as thefe, Sir, may be thought ludicrous and trifling, by thofe who do not reflect on the infolence of flaves in authority, who do not confider that the licenfe of a military life is the chief inducement that brings voluntiers into the army ; an inducement which would, indeed, make all impresses superfluous, were this proposal to be adopted : for how readily would all the lazy and voluptuous engage in a state of life which would qualify them to live upon the labour of others, and to be profuse without expence ?

Our army may by this method be encreased, but the number of those by whom they are to be maintained, must quickly diminish : for by exaction and oppression the poorer inn-keepers must quickly become bankrupts, and the soldiers that lose their quarters must be added to the dividend allotted to the more wealthy, who by this additional burthen will soon be reduced to the same state, and then our army must subsist upon their pay, because they will no longer have it in their power to encrease it by plunder.

It will then be inevitably necessary to divide the army from the rest of the community, and to build barracks for their reception ; an expedient, which, though it may afford present ease to the nation, cannot be put in practice without danger to our liberties.

The reason, for which so many nations have been inslaved by standing armies, is nothing more than the difference of a soldier's condition from that of other men. Soldiers are governed by particular laws, and subject to particular authority ; authority, which, in the manner of its operation, has scarcely any resemblance of the civil power. Thus they soon learn to think themselves exempt from all other laws ; of which, they either do not discover the use, and therefore easily consent to abolish them ; or envy the happiness of those who are protected by them, and so prevail upon themselves to destroy those privileges which have no other effect, with regard to them, but to aggravate their own dependence.

These, Sir, are the natural consequences of a military subjection ; and if these consequences are not always speedily produced by it, they must be retarded by that tenderness which constant intercourse with the rest of the nation produces, by the exchange of reciprocal acts of kindness, and by the frequent inculcation of the wickedness of contributing to the propagation of slavery, and the subversion of the rights of nature ; inculcations which cannot be avoided by men who live in constant fellowship with their countrymen.

But soldiers shut up in a barrack, excluded from all conversation with such as are wiser and honester than themselves, and taught that nothing

nothing is a virtue but implicit obedience to the commands of their
officer, will soon become foreigners in their own country, and
march against the defenders of their constitution, with the same alacrity as against an army of invaders ravaging the coasts; they will
lose all sense of social duty and of social happiness, and think nothing illustrious but to inslave and destroy.

So fatal, Sir, will be the effects of an establishment of barracks,
or petty garrisons, in this kingdom; and therefore, as barracks must
be built when inn-keepers are ruined, and our concurrence with this
proposal must produce their ruin, I hope it will not be necessary to
prove by any other argument, that the motion ought to be rejected.

Mr. PELHAM spoke next in terms to this purpose:—Sir, though
I am not inclined by loud exaggerations and affected expressions of
tenderness to depress the courage, or inflame the suspicions of the people, to teach them to complain of miseries which they do not feel,
or ward against ill designs which were never formed, yet no man is
more really sollicitous for their happiness, or more desirous of removing every real cause of fear and occasion of hardships.

This affection to the people, an affection steady, regular, and unshaken, has always prompted me to prefer their real to their seeming
interest, and rather to consult the security of their privileges than the
gratification of their passions; it has hitherto determined me to vote
for such a body of troops as may defend us against sudden inroads
and wanton insults, and now incites me to propose that some efficacious method may be struck out for their support, without exaspera-
ting either the soldiers or their landlords by perpetual wrangles, or
adding to the burthen of a military establishment the necessity of contentions in courts of law.

I know not with what view those have spoken by whom the proposal first made has been opposed; they have indeed produced objections, some of which are such as may be easily removed, and others
such as arise from the nature of things, and ought not therefore to be
mentioned, because they have no other tendency than to inflame the
minds of those that hear them against an army, at a time when it is
allowed to be necessary, and prove only what was never denied, that
no human measures are absolutely perfect, and that it is often impossible to avoid a greater evil but by suffering a less.

The question before us, Sir, is in its own nature so simple, so little
connected with circumstances that may distract our attention, or in-

duce

duce different men to different confiderations, that when I reflect upon it, I cannot cafily conceive by what art it can be made the fubject of long harangues, or how the moft fruitful imagination can expatiate upon it.

It is already admitted that an army is neceffary; the pay of that army is already eftablifhed; the accidental fcarcity of forage and victuals is fuch, that the pay is not fufficient to maintain them; how then muft the deficiencies be fupplied? It has been propofed either to fix the price of provifions with refpect to them, or to advance their wages in fome proportion to the price of provifions. Both thefe methods feem to meet with difapprobation, and yet the army is to be fupported.

Thofe who reafon thus, do furely not expect to be anfwered, or at leaft expect from a reply no other fatisfaction than that of feeing the time of the feffion wafted, and the adminiftration harraffed with trivial delays; for what can be urged with any hope of fuccefs to him who will openly deny contradictory propofitions, who will neither move nor ftand ftill, who will neither difband an army nor fupport it?

Whether thefe gentlemen conceive that an army may fubfift without victuals till the time of fcarcity is over, or whether they have raifed thofe forces only to ftarve them, I am not fagacious enough to conjecture, but fhall venture to obferve, that if they have fuch a confidence in the moderation and regularity of the foldiers, as to imagine that they will ftarve with weapons in their hands, that they will live within the fight of full tables, and languifh with hunger, and perifh for want of neceffaries, rather than diminifh the fuperfluities of others, they ought for ever to ceafe their outcries about the licentioufnefs, infolence, and danger of a ftanding army.

But, not to fink into levity unworthy of this affembly, may I be permitted to hint that thefe arts of protracting our debates, are by no means confiftent with the reafons for which we are affembled, and that it is a much better proof, both of ability and integrity, to remove objections, than to raife them, and to facilitate, than to retard, the bufinefs of the publick.

The propofal made at firft was only to elucidate a law which had been regularly obferved for fifty years, and to remove fuch ambiguities as tended only to embarrafs the inn-holders, not to relieve them.

To this many objections have been made, and much declamation has been employed to difplay the hardſhips of maintaining ſoldiers, but no better method has been yet difcovered, nor do I expect that any will be ſtarted, not attended with greater difficulties.

In all political queſtions, queſtions too extenſive to be fully comprehended by ſpeculative reaſon, experience is the guide which a wiſe man will follow with the leaſt diſtruſt, and it is no trivial recommendation of the preſent method, that it has been ſo long purſued without any formidable inconvenience or loud complaints.

Hardſhips, even when real, are alleviated by long cuſtom ; we bear any preſent uneaſineſs with leſs regret, as we leſs remember the time in which we were more happy ; at leaſt by long acquaintance with any grievance we gain this advantage, that we know it in its whole extent, that it cannot be aggravated by our imagination, and that there is no room for ſuſpecting that any miſery is yet behind more heavy than that which we have already borne.

Such is the preſent ſtate of the practice now recommended to this aſſembly, a practice to which the inn-keepers have long ſubmitted, and found it at leaſt tolerable, to which they knew themſelves expoſed when they took out a licence for the exerciſe of that profeſſion, and which they conſider as a tax upon them, to be balanced againſt the advantages which they expect from their employment.

This tax cannot be denied at preſent to be burthenſome in a very uncommon degree, but this weight has not been of long continuance, and it may be reaſonably hoped that it will now be made every day lighter. It is indeed true, that no unneceſſary impoſitions ought to be laid upon the nation even for a day, and if any gentleman can propoſe a method by which this may be taken off or alleviated, I ſhall readily comply with his propoſal, and concur in the eſtabliſhment of new regulations.

With regard to barracks, I cannot deny that they are juſtly names of terror to a free nation, that they tend to make an army ſeem part of our conſtitution, and may contribute to infuſe into the ſoldiers a diſregard of their fellow ſubjects, and an indifference about the liberties of their country ; but I cannot diſcover any connection between a proviſion for the ſupport of ſoldiers in publick-houſes, in a ſtate of conſtant familiarity with their countrymen, and the erection of barracks, by which they will be, perhaps for ever, ſeparated from them, nor can diſcover any thing in the method of ſupporting them now re-

Z 4

commended

commended that d-es not tend rather to the promotion of mutual good offices, and the confirmation of friendship and benevolence.

The Advocate CAMPBELL next spoke, in substance as follows :— Sir, whence the impropriety of raising objections to any measures that are proposed is imagined to arise I am unable to discover, having hitherto admitted as an incontrovertible opinion, that it is the duty of every member of this assembly to deliver, without reserve, his sentiments upon any question which is brought before him, and to approve or censure according to his conviction.

If it be his duty, Sir, to condemn what he thinks dangerous or inconvenient, it seems by no means contrary to his duty, to show the reason of his censure, or to lay before the house those objections which he cannot surmount by his own reflection. It certainly is not necessary to admit implicitly all that is afferted; and to deny, or disapprove without reason, can be no proof of duty, or of wisdom; and how shall it be known, that he who produces no objections, acts from any other motives, than private malevolence, discontent, or caprice?

Nor is it, Sir, to be imputed as a just reason for censure to those who have opposed the motion, that no other measures have been offered by them to the consideration of the committee. It is necessary to demolish a useless or shattered edifice, before a firm and habitable building can be erected in its place: the first step to the amendment of a law is to show its defects; for why should any alteration be made where no inconvenience is discovered?

To the chief objection that was offered, no answer has yet been made, nor has the assembly been informed how the inn-keeper shall be able to discover when he has paid the tax which this law lays upon him. This is indeed a tax of a very particular kind, a tax without limits, and to be levied at the discretion of him for whose benefit it is paid. Soldiers quartered upon these terms, are more properly raising contributions in an enemy's country, than receiving wages in their own.

Is it intended by this motion, that the inn-keepers shall judge what ought to be allowed the soldier for his money? I do not see then that any alteration is proposed in the present condition of our army; for who has ever refused to sell them food for their money at the common price, or what necessity is there for a law to enforce a practice equally the advantage of all parties? If it be proposed that the soldier shall

shall judge for himself, that he shall set what value he shall think fit on his own money, and that he shall be at once the interpreter and executioner of this new law, the condition of the inn-keeper will then be such as no slave in the mines of America can envy, and such as he will gladly quit for better treatment under the most arbitrary and oppressive government.

Nor will the insolence of the soldier, thus invested with unlimited authority, thus intitled to implicit obedience, and exalted above the rest of mankind, by seeing his claim only bounded by his own moderation, be confined to his unhappy landlord. Every guest will become subject to his intrusion, and the passenger must be content to want his dinner, whenever the lord of the inn shall like it better than his own.

That these apprehensions, Sir, are not groundless, may be proved from the conduct of these men, even when the law was not so favourable to their designs; some of them have already claimed the sole dominion of the houses in which they have been quartered, and insulted persons of very high rank, and whom our antient laws had intended to set above the insults of a turbulent soldier. They have seen the provisions which they had ordered taken away by force, partly perhaps to please the appetite of the invader, and partly to gratify his insolence, and give him an opportunity of boasting among his comrades, how successfully he blustered.

If it be necessary, Sir, to insert a new clause in the act to prevent lawsuits, which, however advantageous they may sometimes be to me, I shall always be ready to obviate, it is surely proper to limit the claim of one party as well as that of the other, for how else is the ambiguity taken away ? The difficulty may be indeed transferred, but is by no means removed, and the inn-keeper must wholly repose himself upon the lenity and justice of the soldier, or apply to the courts of law for the interpretation of the act.

The question between us is said to be so free from perplexity, that it can scarcely give occasion for harangues or disputations ; and indeed it cannot but be allowed, that the controversy may soon be brought to a single point, and I think nothing more is necessary than to enquire, if inn-holders shall be obliged to provide victuals for soldiers at a stated price, what, and how much the soldier shall demand.

The power of raising money at pleasure, has been hitherto denied to our kings, and furely we ought not to place that confidence in the loweft, that has been refufed to the moft exalted of mankind, or inveft our foldiers with power, which neither the moft warlike of our monarchs could conftrain us, nor the moft popular allure us to grant.

The power now propofed to be granted, is nothing lefs than the power of levying money, or what is exactly equivalent, the power of raifing the money in their own hands, to any imaginary value. A foldier may, if this motion be complied with, demand for a penny, what another man muft purchafe at forty times that price. While this is the ftate of our property, it is furely not very neceffary to raife armies for the defence of it; for why fhould we preferve it from one enemy only to throw it into the hands of another, equally rapacious, equally mercilefs, and only diftinguifhed from foreign invaders by this circumftance, that he received from our own hands the authority by which he plunders us.

Having thus evinced the neceffity of determining the foldiers privileges, and the inn-keepers rights, I think it neceffary to recommend to this affembly an uncommon degree of attention to the regulation of our military eftablifhment, which is become not only more burthenfome to our fellow fubjects by the prefent famine, but by the encreafe of our forces; an encreafe which the nation will not behold without impatience, unlefs they be enabled to difcern for what end they have been raifed.

The people of this nation are for very juft reafons difpleafed, even with the appearance of a ftanding army, and furely it is not prudent to exafperate them, by augmenting the troops in a year of famine, and giving them at the fame time new powers of extortion and oppreffion.

Mr. WINNINGTON fpoke to this purpofe:—Sir, I have heard nothing in this debate, but doubts and objections, which afford no real information, nor tend to the alleviation of thofe grievances, which are fo loudly lamented.

It is not fufficient to point out inconveniences, or to give ftriking reprefentations of the hardfhips to which the people are expofed; for unlefs fome better expedient can be propofed, or fome method difcovered by which we may receive the benefits, without fuffering the difadvantages of the prefent practice, how does it appear that
thefe

thefe hardfhips, however fevere, are not infeparable from our prefent condition, and fuch as can only be removed, by expofing ourfelves to more formidable evils?

As no remedy, Sir, has been propofed by thofe who appear diffatiffied with the prefent cuftom, it is reafonable to imagine that none will be eafily difcovered; and therefore I cannot but think it reafonable that the motion fhould be complied with. Be it no new impofition is intended, nor any thing more than the eftablifhment of a practice which has continued for more than fifty years, and never, except on two occafions, been denied to be legal. It is only propofed that the fenate fhould confirm that interpretation of the act which has been almoft univerfally received, that they fhould do what can produce no difturbance, becaufe it will make no alterations, but may prevent them; becaufe it may prevent any attempts of innovation, or diverfity of opinions.

Sir JOHN BARNARD fpoke next to the following effect:—Sir, whether the interpretation of the act which is now contended for, has been univerfally admitted, it is impoffible to know, but it is at leaft certain, that the practice which is founded upon it, has in many places never been followed, nor indeed can it be made general without great impropriety.

Many of thofe, Sir, who are ftiled keepers of publick houfes, and on whom foldiers are quartered under that denomination, have no conveniency of furnifhing provifions, becaufe they never fell them; fuch are many of the keepers of livery-ftables, among whom it is the common method to pay foldiers a fmall weekly allowance, inftead of lodging them in their houfes, a lodging being all which they conceive themfelves obliged to provide, and all that the foldiers have hitherto required; nor can we make any alteration in this method without introducing the licence and infolence of foldiers into private houfes; into houfes hitherto unacquainted with any degree of riot, incivility, or uproar.

The reafon for which publick houfes are affigned for the quarters of foldiers, is partly the greater conveniency of accommodating them in families that fubfift by the entertainment of ftrangers, and partly the nature of their profeffion, which by expofing them to frequent encounters with the rude and the debauched, enables them either to bear or reprefs the infolence of a foldier.

But

But with regard, Sir, to the perfons whom I have mentioned, neither of thefe reafons have any place ; they have not, from their daily employment, any opportunities of furnifhing foldiers with beds or victuals, nor by their manner of life are adapted to fupport intrufion or ftruggle with perverfenefs. Nor can I difcover why any man fhould force foldiers into their houfes, who would not willingly admit them into his own.

Mr. Cocks fpoke to this effect :— Sir, the practice mentioned by the honourable gentleman, I know to be generally followed by all thofe that keep alehoufes in the fuburbs of this metropolis, who pay the foldiers billetted on them a compofition for their lodging, nor ever fee them but when they come to receive it ; fo far are they from imagining that they can claim their whole fubfiftence at any ftated price.

It is apparent, therefore, that by admitting this motion, we fhould not confirm a law already received, but eftablifh a new regulation unknown to the people; that we fhould lay a tax upon the nation, and fend our foldiers to collect it.

General WADE rofe, and fpoke to this purpofe :—Sir, I have been long converfant with military affairs, and therefore may perhaps be able to give a more exact account from my own knowledge of the antiquity and extent of this practice, than other gentlemen have had, from their way of life, an opportunity of obtaining.

It was, Sir, in the reign of king William, the conftant method by which the army was fupported, as may be eafily imagined by thofe who reflect, that it was common for the foldiers to remain for eight or ten months unpaid, and that they had therefore no poffibility of providing for themfelves the neceffaries of life. Their pay never was received in thofe times by themfelves, but iffued in exchequer bills for large fums, which the inn-keepers procured to be exchanged and divided among themfelves, in proportion to their debts.

Such was the practice, Sir, in that reign, which has been generally followed to this time, and the rates then fixed have not fince been changed ; and as no inconveniency has arifen from this method, I can difcover no reafon againft confirming and continuing it.

Mr. PULTENEY fpoke next, in the manner following :— Sir, thofe that have fpoken in defence of the motion, have accufed their
opponents

opponents, with great confidence, of declaiming without arguments, and of wafting the time of the feffions in a ufelefs repetition of objections.

I do not indeed wonder that the objections which have been raifed fhould have given fome difguft, for who can be pleafed with hearing his opponent produce arguments which he cannot anfwer? But furely the repetitions may be excufed; for an objection is to be urged in every debate till it is anfwered, or is difcovered to be unanfwerable.

But what, Sir, have thofe urged in defence of their own opinions, who fo freely animadvert upon the reafonings of others? What proofs, Sir, have they given of the fupcriority of their own abilities, of the depth of their refcarches, or the acutenefs of their penetration?

They have not produced one argument in favour of their motion, but that it is founded on cuftom; they have not difcovered, however wife and fagacious, that it is always neceffary to enquire whether a cuftom be good or bad; for furely without fuch enquiry no cuftom ought to be confirmed.

The motion which they would fupport, is indeed ufelefs in either cafe, for a good cuftom will continue of itfelf, and one that is bad ought not to be continued. It is the bufinefs of the legiflature to reform abufes, and eradicate corruptions, not to give them new ftrength by the fanction of a law.

It has been urged, Sir, that the law in reality exifts already; that the act has been interpreted in this fenfe by the attorney general; and that his interpretation is generally received. This is then the ftate of the queftion: if the practice, founded upon this fenfe of the act, generally prevails, there is no need of a new claufe to enforce what is already complied with; if it does not prevail, all that has been urged in defence of the motion falls to the ground.

I do not doubt, Sir, that this cuftom has been received without many exceptions, and therefore think it ought ftill to remain a cuftom, rather than be changed into a law, becaufe it will be complied with as a cuftom, where there are no obftacles to the obfervation of it; and it ought not to be enforced by law, where it is inconvenient and oppreffive.

While the foldier, Sir, is moderate in his demands, and peaceable and modeft in his behaviour, the inn-keeper will chearfully furnifh

him

him even more than he can afford at the stated price; and certainly rudenefs, infolence, and unreasonable expectations, may justly be punished by the forfeiture of some conveniencies. Thus, Sir, the inn-keeper will preserve some degree of authority in his own house, a place where the laws of nature give every man dominion, and the soldier will continue a regular and inoffensive member of civil society.

The absurdity of leaving the soldier at large in his demands, and limiting the price which the inn-keeper is to require, has been already exposed beyond the possibility of reply; nor indeed has the least attempt been made to invalidate this objection; for it has been passed in filence by those who have most zealously espoused the motion.

The account given by the honourable gentleman of the reason for which this regulation was first introduced in the reign of king William, is undoubtedly just; but it proves, Sir, that there is no neceffity of continuing it; for the soldiers are now conftantly paid, and therefore need not that affiftance from the inn-keeper, which was abfolutely requifite when they were fometimes fix months without money.

It has been urged, Sir, with great importunity and vehemence, that some expedient should be proposed in the place of this, which so many gentlemen who have spoken on this occasion feem inclined to reject, and which indeed cannot be mentioned without contempt or abhorrence. That the soldiers should know as well as their landlord their own rights, is undoubtedly just, as well as that they should have fome certain means of procuring the neceffaries of life; it may therefore be proper to enact, that the inn-keeper shall either furnish them with diet at the eftablished rates, or permit them to dress the victuals which they shall buy for themfelves, with his fire and utenfils, and allow them candles, falt, vinegar, and pepper. By this method the soldiers can never be much injured by the incivility of their landlord, nor can the inn-keeper be fubjected to arbitrary demands. The soldier will ftill gain, by decency and humanity, greater conveniencies than he can procure for himfelf by his pay alone, and all opportunities of oppreffion on either fide will in a great meafure be taken away.

I cannot but exprefs my hopes that this method will be generally approved. Those that have oppofed the eftablishment of an army will be pleafed to fee it made lefs grievous to the people; and those that have declared in its favour, ought furely to adopt without oppofition,

fition, any meafures, by the purfuit of which it may be borne with fewer complaints and lefs reluctance.

[The confideration of this queftion was deferred, and the chairman having moved for leave to fit again, it was refolved to proceed on this bufinefs upon the next day but one, in a committee of the whole houfe.

H O U S E   O F   C O M M O N S.

March 15, 1740-1.

The order of the day being read for the houfe to refolve itfelf into a committee of the whole houfe, to confider the bill for punifhing mutiny and defertion, and the better paying the army and their quarters,

Sir WILLIAM YONGE fpoke in fubftance as follows:—Sir, the laft day which was affigned to the confideration of this bill, was fpent in long altercations, in vague and unneceffary difquifitions, in retrofpective reflections upon events long paft, and in aggravating of grievances that may never happen; much fagacity was exerted, and much eloquence difplayed, but no determination was attained, nor even that expedient examined, by which thofe objections might be removed which appeared fo important, or thofe dangers obviated which were reprefented fo formidable and fo near.

I hope, Sir, part of the time which has intervened between that debate and the prefent day, has been employed by the gentlemen, whofe fcruples were fo numerous, and whofe caution is fo vigilant, in contriving fome methods of maintaining the army without oppreffing the victuallers, and of providing for our defence againft foreign enemies without fubjecting us to the evils of difcontent and difaffection, which they impute to the prefent ftate of the military eftablifhment.

To object for ever and to advance nothing, is an eafy method of difputation upon any queftion, but contributes very little to the increafe of knowledge: an artful and acute objector may confound, and darken, and difturb, but never affifts enquiry, or illuftrates truth.

In political queſtions, Sir, it is ſtill more eaſy and leſs ingenuous ; for all political meaſures are in ſome degree right and wrong at the ſame time : to benefit ſome they very frequently bear hard upon others, and are therefore only to be approved or rejected as advantages appear to over-balance the inconveniencies, or the inconveniencies to out-weigh the advantages.

It is, Sir, the proper province of a ſenator to promote, not to obſtruct the publick counſels, and when he declares his diſapprobation of any expedient, to endeavour to ſubſtitute a better : for how can he be ſaid to ſuſtain his part of the general burthen of publick affairs, who lays others under the neceſſity of forming every plan, and inventing every expedient, and contents himſelf with only cenſuring what he never endeavours to amend ?

That every man, who is called forth by his country to ſit here as the guardian of the publick happineſs, is obliged, by the nature of his office, to propoſe in this aſſembly whatever his penetration or experience may ſuggeſt to him as advantageous to the nation, I doubt not but all that hear me are ſufficiently convinced ; and therefore cannot but ſuppoſe that they have ſo far attended to their duty, as to be able to inform us how the preſent inconveniencies of this bill may be remedied, and its defects ſupplied.

To ſhew, Sir, at leaſt my inclination to expedite an affair ſo important, I ſhall lay before the houſe an amendment that I have made to the clauſe, purſuant to a hint offered the laſt day by an honourable member, *That all inn-holders, victuallers, &c. ſhall be obliged to furniſh ſoldiers with ſalt, vinegar, ſmall beer, candles, fire, and utenſils to dreſs their victuals, and ſo doing ſhall not be obliged to ſupply the troops with proviſion, except on a march.*

I am far, Sir, from thinking the clauſe, as it will ſtand after this amendment, compleat and unexceptionable, being conſcious that ſome articles in it may require explanation. The quantity of ſmall beer to be allowed to each ſoldier muſt neceſſarily be aſcertained in order to prevent endleſs and indeterminable diſputes ; for one man, Sir, may demand a greater quantity than another, and a man may be prompted by malice or wantonneſs to demand more than health requires ; it will therefore be proper to limit the quantity which muſt be furniſhed, that neither the ſoldier may ſuffer by the avarice of his landlord, nor the landlord be oppreſſed by the gluttony of the ſoldier.

                                                            WEB

With regard to this question, Sir, I expect to find different opinions in this assembly, which every man is at liberty to offer and to
vindicate: and I shall take this opportunity of propofing on my part,
that every man may have a daily allowance of three quarts. One
quart to each meal may be allowed in my opinion to be sufficient, and
fure no gentleman can imagine that by this limitation much fuper-
fluity is indulged.

There are some parts, Sir, of this kingdom, in which cyder is
more plentiful, and cheaper than small beer, confequently it may be
for the eafe of the victualler to have the choice allowed him of furnifhing one or the other; it will therefore be a very proper addition
to this claufe, that the inn-keepers shall allow the foldier every day
three quarts of either small beer or cyder.

That penal fanctions, Sir, are effential to laws, and that no man will
fubmit to any regulations inconvenient to himfelf, but that he may avoid
fome heavier evil, requires not to be proved; and therefore to compleat this claufe, I propofe that the victualler who shall neglect or refufe to obferve it shall be subject to fome fine for his non-com-
pliance.

Mr. PELHAM fpoke to this effect: —Sir, I cannot omit this opportunity of obferving how much the burthen of the army is diminifhed
by the judicious regulations invariably obferved in the late reigns,
and how little the affignment of troops is to be dreaded by the
victualler.

In the reign of king William, Sir, before funds were eftablifhed,
while the credit of the government was low, the meafures of the
court were often obviated or defeated by the fuperiority of the dif-
contented party, and the fupplies denied which were neceffary to
fupport them, and in expectation of which they had been undertaken,
it was not uncommon for the towns in which the troops were ftationed, to murmur at their guefts; nor could they be charged with
complaining without juft reafons; for to quarter foldiers upon a
houfe, was in thofe days little lefs than to fend troops to live at
difcretion.

As all fupplies, Sir, were then occafional and temporary, and nothing was granted but for the prefent exigence, the prevalence of
the oppofition for a fingle feffion embarraffed all the meafures of the
court in the higheft degree, their defigns were at a ftand, the forces

were unpaid, and they were obliged to wait till another feffion for an opportunity of profecuting their fchemes.

Thus, Sir, the foldiers were fometimes five months without their pay, and were neceffarily fupported by the inn-keeper at his own expence, with how much reluctance and difcontent I need not mention. It cannot but be immediately confidered, upon hearing this account of the foldier's condition, with how many reproaches he would receive his victuals, how roughly he would be treated, how often he would be infulted as an idler, and frowned upon as an intruder. Nor can it be imagined that fuch affronts, however they might be provoked, would be borne without return, by thofe who knew themfelves not the authors of the provocation, and who thought themfelves equal fufferers with thofe who complained. When the inn-keeper growled at the foldier, the foldier, it may be fuppofed, feldom failed to threaten or to plunder the inn-keeper, and to rife in his demands as his allowance was retrenched.

Thus, Sir, the landlord and his gueft were the conftant enemies of each other, and fpent their lives in mutual complaints, injuries, and infults.

But by the prefent regularity of our military eftablifhment, this great evil is taken away; as the foldier requires no credit of the victu-aller, he is confidered as no great incumbrance on his trade, and being treated without indignities, like any other member of the community, he inhabits his quarters without violence, infolence, or rapacity, and endeavours to recommend himfelf by officioufnefs and civility.

In the prefent method of payment, Sir, the troops have always one month's pay advanced, and receive their regular allowance on the ftated day; fo that every man has it in his power to pay his land-lord every night for what he has had in the day; or if he ima-gines himfelf able to procure his own provifions at more advantage, he can now go to market with his own money.

It appears therefore to me, Sir, that the amendment now propofed is the proper mean between the different interefts of the inn-keeper and foldier, by which neither is made the flave of the other, and by which we fhall leave to both opportunities of kindnefs, but take from them the power of oppreffion.

Mr. CAREW next fpoke as follows:—Sir, the amendment now offered is not, in my opinion, fo unreafonable or unequitable as to

demand

demand a warm and ſtrenuous oppoſition, nor ſo compleat as not to be
ſubjeċt to ſome objeċtions; objeċtions which, however, may be eaſily
removed, and which would perhaps have been obviated, had they
been foreſeen by the gentleman who propoſed it.

The allowance, Sir, of ſmall liquors propoſed, I cannot but
think more than ſufficient; three quarts a day are ſurely more than
the demands of nature make neceſſary, and I know not why the
legiſlature ſhould promote, or confirm in the ſoldiery, a vice to which
they are already too much inclined, the habit of tipling.

The inn-keeper, Sir, will be heavily burthened by the obligation
to ſupply the ſoldier with ſo many of the neceſſaries of life without payment, and therefore it may be juſtly expeċted by him, that
no ſuperfluities ſhould be enjoyed at his expence.

But there remains another objeċtion, Sir, of far more importance,
and which muſt be removed before this clauſe can be reaſonably paſſed into a law. It is not declared, or not with ſufficient perſpicuity,
that it is to be left to the choice of the inn-keeper, whether he will
furniſh the ſoldier with proviſions at four pence a day, or with the
neceſſaries enumerated in the clauſe for nothing. If it is to be left
to the choice of the ſoldier, the victualler receives no relief from
the amendment, to whoſe option, ſince he muſt ſuffer in either caſe,
it ought to be referred, becauſe he only can tell by which method
he ſhall ſuffer leaſt.

Mr. CORNWALL ſpoke in the manner following:—Sir, it is not
without the greateſt diffidence that I riſe to oppoſe the gentleman
who offered the amendment, for his abilities are ſo far ſuperior to
mine, that I objeċt without hope of being able to ſupport my objeċtion, and contend with an abſolute certainty of being overcome.
I know not whether it may be allowed me to obſerve, that the difference between our faculties is with regard to ſtrength and quick-
neſs, the ſame as between the cyder of his country and that of mine,
except that in one part of the parallel the advantage is on our ſide,
and in the other on his.

The cyder, Sir, of our county is one of our moſt valuable commodities, ſo much eſteemed in diſtant places, that our merchants
often ſell it by the bottle, for more than the ſoldier has to give for
the proviſion of a day, and of ſuch ſtrength, that I, who am accuſtomed to the uſe of it, never was able to drink three quarts in any
ſingle day.

If therefore, Sir, the foldier is to have three quarts of this cyder, when fmall beer is not eafily to be procured, not only the inn-keeper, but the army will be injured ; for what greater harm can be done to any man, than to initiate him in a habit of intemperance ? and what outrages and infolencies may not be expected from men trufted with fwords, and kept from day to day, and from month to month, in habitual drunkennefs by a decree of the fenate ?

Sir WILLIAM YONGE replied to this purpofe:—Sir, I know not why the gentleman has thought this a proper opportunity for difplaying his eloquence in the praife of his own cyder. That he loves his own county cannot be wondered, for no paffion is more univerfal, and few lefs to be cenfured ; but he is not to imagine that the produce of his native foil will be generally allowed to excel that of other counties, becaufe early habits have endeared it to him, and familiarifed it to his particular palate.

The natives of every place prefer their own fruits and their own liquor, and therefore no inference can be drawn from approbation fo apparently partial. From this prejudice I am far from fufpecting myfelf free, nor am defirous or induftrious to overcome it : neither am I afraid of expofing myfelf to all the cenfure that fo innocent a prepoffeffion may bring upon me, by declaring, that, in my opinion, the cyder of my native county is of equal excellence with that which this gentleman has fo liberally extolled.

Mr. CORNWALL anfwered to the following effect:—Sir, how little I expect victory in this controverfy I have already declared, and I need not obferve of how fmall importance it is what foil produces cyder of the greateft excellence and value, fince if there be other places where the cyder is equally efteemed, and purchafed at the fame rate, it is yet more neceffary to provide by fome exception, that the foldier fhall not be intitled to demand, of the victualler, liquor to more than thrice the value of his pay, nor be allowed to revel in continual drunkennefs, and to corrupt his morals, and enervate his limbs by inceffant debauchery.

But fince, Sir, the preference due to the cyder of my county has been denied, in my opinion, with great partiality and injuftice, I think myfelf obliged, by all the laws of honour and gratitude, to ftand up once more to vindicate its fuperiority, and affert its value.

The laws of honour, Sir, require this from me, as they oblige every man to ftand forth a vindicator of merit flighted and oppreffed;

and

and gratitude calls loudly upon me to exert myself in the protection
of that to which I have been often indebted for a pleafing fufpenfe
of care, and a welcome flow of fpirit and gaiety.

The cyder, Sir, which I am now refcuing from contemptuous
comparifons, has often exhilarated my focial hours, enlivened the
freedom of converfation, and improved the tendernefs of friendfhip,
and fhall not therefore now want a panegyrift. It is one of thofe
few fubjects on which an encomiaft may expatiate without deviating
from the truth.

Would the honourable gentleman, Sir, who has thus vilified this
wonder-working nectar, but honour my table with his company, he
would quickly be forced to retract his cenfures, and, as many of
his countrymen have done, confefs that nothing equal to it is produced in any other part of the globe, nor will this confeffion be the
effect of his regard to politenefs, but of his adherence to truth.

Of liquor like this, Sir, two quarts is undoubtedly fufficient for
a daily allowance, in the lieu of fmall beer, nor ought even that to
be determined by the choice of the foldier, but of the inn-keeper,
for whofe benefit this claufe is faid to be inferted, and from whofe
grievances I hope we fhall not fuffer our attention to be diverted
by any incidental queftions, or ludicrous difputes.

Mr. GORE then fpoke to the following effect :—Sir, that the allowance of two quarts a day is fufficient, and that to demand more
is a wanton indulgence of appetite, is experimentally known, and
therefore no more ought to be impofed upon the inn-keeper.

Nor is this, Sir, the only part of the claufe that requires our
confideration, for fome of the other particulars to be provided by
the victualler, may eafily furnifh perverfe tempers with an opportunity of wrangling : vinegar is not to be had in every part of the
kingdom, and where it cannot be procured, ought not to be required ; for neither reafon nor experience will inform us that vinegar ought to be ranked among the neceffaries of life.

Sir WILLIAM YONGE made the following reply :—Sir, by the
alteration now made in the claufe, the inn-keepers are effectually
relieved from a great part of the burthen which, in my opinion,
his act has hitherto laid upon them ; the neceffity of furnifhing the
foldiers quartered upon them with provifions at the ftated price,
whatever might be the fcarcity of the feafon or of the country. That
his was the intention of the act, is afferted by thofe whofe reputa-

tion and promotion are sufficient evidences of their ability in the
interpretation of our laws.

The inn-keeper may now either accept or refuse the limited price,
as it shall appear to him most consistent with his interest; nor will
there be for the future any room for murmuring at unreasonable demands, since he may oblige that soldier whom he cannot satisfy, to
please himself better at his own expence.

The choice of the liquor is likewise wholly referred to the inn-
keeper; for the words in the clause requiring that he shall furnish
three quarts of small beer or cyder, he complies indisputably with
the law by supplying either ; and therefore the value of cyder in any
particular county is not of much importance in the question before
us ; if cyder be more valuable than small beer, it may be with-held;
if it be cheaper, it may be substituted in its place ; so that the inn-
keeper has nothing to confult but his own interest.

That this is the meaning of the clause, is, I suppose, obvious to
every man that hears it read, and therefore I see no reason for any
alterations, because I know not any effect which they can possibly
have, except that of obscuring the sense which is now too clear to
be mistaken.

Sir John Barnard spoke next to the effect following : —Sir,
though it should be granted, that the clause before us is intelligible
to every member of this assembly, it will not certainly follow, that
there is no necessity of further elucidations ; for a law very easily
understood by those who make it, may be obscure to others who
are less acquainted with our general intention, less skilled in the nice-
ties of language, or less accustomed to the stile of laws.

It is to be considered, that this law will chiefly affect a class of
men very little instructed in literature, and very unable to draw in-
ferences ; men to whom we often find it necessary in common cases
to use long explanations, and familiar illustrations, and of whom it
may be not unreasonably suspected, that the same want of education,
which makes them ignorant, may make them petulant, and at once
incline them to wrangle, and deprive them of the means of decid-
ing their controversies.

That both inn-holders and soldiers are for the greatest part of
this rank and temper, I suppose, Sir, every gentleman knows from
early observation ; and therefore it will, I hope, be thought necef-
sary to descend to their understandings, and to give them laws in
                                                        terms

terms of which they will know the meaning ; we shall otherwise more
consult the interest of the lawyers than the inn-holders, and only by
one alteration produce a necessity of another.

I am therefore desirous, Sir, that all the difficulties, which have
been mentioned by every gentleman on this occasion, should be removed by clear, familiar, and determinate expressions ; for what
they have found difficult, may easily be to an inn-holder or soldier
absolutely inexplicable.

I cannot but declare, while I am speaking on this subject, that
in my opinion, two quarts of liquor will be a sufficient allowance.
If we consider the demands of nature, more cannot be required ;
if we examine the expence of the inn-holder, he ought not to supply
soldiers with a greater quantity for nothing. It is to be remembered,
that small beer, like other liquors, is charged with an excise in publick houses, and that two quarts will probably cost the landlord a
penny, and as we cannot suppose, that fire, candles, vinegar, salt,
pepper, and the use of utensils, and lodging, can be furnished for
less than three pence a day, every soldier that is quartered upon a
publick house, may be considered as a tax of six pounds a year ;
a heavy burthen, which surely ought not to be aggravated by unnecessary impositions.

The committee having gone through the bill, and settled the
amendments, the chairman was ordered to make his report the
next day.

HOUSE OF COMMONS.

March 16, 1740-1.

*The report was read, and the amendments to the clauses in debate, which
then ran thus :*

*That the officers and soldiers to be quartered and billeted as aforesaid,
shall be received, and furnished with diet and small beer by the owners
of the inns, livery stables, ale houses, victualling houses, &c. paying and allowing for the same the several rates mentioned.*

*Provided, that in case the inn-holder on whom any non-commission
officers or soldiers shall be quartered by virtue of this act (except on a*

march)

march) shall be desirous to furnish such officers or soldiers with candles, vinegar, and salt, and with either small beer or cydar, not exceeding three quarts for each man a day gratis, and to allow them the use of fire, and the necessary utensils for dressing and eating their meat, and shall give notice of such his desire to the commanding officers, and shall furnish and allow them the same accordingly ; then, and in such case the non commission officers and soldiers so quartered shall provide their own victuals, and the officer to whom it belongs to receive, or that does already receive the pay and subsistence of such non-commission officers as aforesaid, shall pay the several sums, payable out of the subsistence-money for diet and small beer, to the non-commission officers and soldiers aforesaid, and not to the inn-holder or other person on whom such non-commission officers or soldiers are quartered.

The question being put whether this clause should stand thus,

Mr. CAREW spoke to this effect :—Sir, though it may perhaps be allowed, that the circumstances of our present situation oblige us to support a more numerous army in former years, surely no argument can be drawn from them that can show the necessity of a profuse allowance to our soldiers, or of gratifying their desires by the oppression of the inn-holders.

If, Sir, the designs of our enemies are so malicious, and their power so formidable, as to demand augmentations of our troops and additions to our natural securities, they ought surely to impress upon us the necessity of frugal measures, that no useless burthens may be imposed upon the people.

To furnish two quarts of beer, Sir, every day for nothing, is undoubtedly an imposition sufficiently grievous, and I can therefore discover no reason for which an allowance of three should be established ; a proposal injurious to the victualler, because it exacts more than he can afford to allow, and of no benefit to the soldier, because it offers him more than he can want.

Sir WILLIAM YONGE spoke next to this purpose :—Sir, if it is an instance of misconduct to spend upon any affair more time than the importance of it deserves, I am afraid that the clause to which our attention is now recalled may expose us to censure, and that we may be charged with neglecting weighty controversies, and national questions, to debate upon trifles ; of wasting our spirits upon subjects unworthy

worthy of contention ; of defeating the expectations of the publick, and diverting our enemies rather than opposing them.

But, Sir, as nothing has a more immediate tendency to the security of the nation than a proper establishment of our forces, and the regulation of their quarters is one of the most necessary and difficult parts of the establishment ; it is requisite that we think no question of this kind too trivial for our consideration, since very dangerous disturbances have often been produced by petty disputes.

The quantity, Sir, of small beer to be allowed by the victualler to those soldiers who shall provide their own victuals, was disputed yesterday, and as I thought agreed upon ; but since this question is revived, I must take the opportunity to declare that we ought not to assign less than three quarts a day to each man ; for it is to be remembered by those who estimate the demands by their own, how much their way of life is different from that of a common soldier, and how little he can be charged with wantonness and superfluity, for drinking more small liquor than themselves.

There are few members of this house, who do not, more than once a day, drink tea, coffee, chocolate, or some other cooling and diluting infusion ; delicacies which the soldier cannot purchase, to which he is entirely a stranger, and of which the place must be supplied by some other cheap and wholesome liquors.

If, Sir, those gentlemen whose close attention to the interest of the inn-holder has perhaps abstracted them, in some degree, from any regard to the necessities of a soldier, will consent to allow him five pints a day, I shall contend no longer ; for though I cannot agree that it is a sufficient provision, yet, as other gentlemen, equally able to judge in this subject with myself, are of a different opinion, I shall show my regard for their sentiments by desisting from opposition.

Lord BALTIMORE spoke in substance as follows :—Sir, I am not able to discover any necessity of compromising this debate, by taking the mean between the two different opinions, or for denying to the soldiers what every labourer or serving-man would murmur to be refused for a single day.

I believe, Sir, every gentleman, who examines the expence of his family, will find that each of his servants consumes daily at least
three

three quarts of small-beer, and surely it is not to be required that a soldier should live in a perpetual state of war with his constitution, and a constant inability to comply with the calls of nature.

General HANDASYD spoke to the following purpose:—Sir, the inclination shown by several gentlemen for a penurious and scanty provision for the soldiers, must, in my opinion, proceed from an inattentive consideration of their pay, and will therefore be removed by laying before them an account of his condition, and comparing his daily pay with his daily expences.

The whole pay of a foot soldier, Sir, is six pence a day, of which he is to pay four pence to his landlord for his diet, or, what is very nearly the same, to carry four pence daily to the market, for which how small a supply of provisions he can bring to his quarters, especially in time of scarcity, I need not mention.

There remain then only two pence, Sir, to be disbursed for things not immediately necessary for the preservation of life, but which no man can want without being despicable to others and burthensome to himself. Two pence a day is all that a soldier has to lay out upon cleanliness and decency, and with which he is likewise to keep his arms in order, and to supply himself with some part of his cloathing. If, Sir, after these deductions, he can from two pence a day procure himself the means of enjoying a few happy moments in the year with his companions over a cup of ale, is not his œconomy much more to be envied than his luxury ? Or can it be charged upon him that he enjoys more than his share of the felicities of life ? Is he to be burthened with new expences lest he should hoard up the publick money, stop the circulation of coin, and turn broker or usurer with two pence a day ?

I have been so long acquainted, Sir, with the soldier's character, that I will adventure to secure him from the charge of avarice, and to promise that whatever he shall possess not necessary to life, he will enjoy to the advantage of his landlord.

Then the Advocate CAMPBELL spoke in substance as follows:— Sir, I am far from intending to oppose this proposal of five pints, though, upon a rigorous examination, it might appear more than the mere wants of nature require ; for I cannot but declare that this question has too long engaged the attention of the house, and that the representatives of a mighty nation beset with enemies, and encumbered

with

with difficulties, feem to forget their importance and their dignity, by wrangling from day to day upon a pint of fmall-beer.

I conceive the bill, which we are now confidering, Sir, not as a perpetual and ftanding law, to be interwoven with our conftitution, or added to the principles of our government, but as a temporary eftablifhment for the prefent year; an expedient to be laid afide when our affairs ceafe to require it; an experimental effay of a new practice which may be changed or continued according to its fuccefs.

To allow, Sir, five pints of fmall beer a day to our foldiers for a fingle year, can produce no formidable inconveniency, and may, though it fhould not be entirely approved, be of lefs difadvantage to the publick, than the wafte of another day.

An alteration was made to five pints inftead of three quarts; and the bill, thus amended, was ordered to be engroffed, and a few days afterwards, being read a third time, was paffed, and ordered to the Lords, where it occafioned no debate.

HOUSE OF COMMONS.

April 12, 1741.

A copy of his majefty's fpeech being read, Mr. CLUTTERBUCK rofe, and fpoke as follows:—

SIR, the prefent confufion in Europe, the known defigns of the French, the numerous claims to the Auftrian dominions, the armies which are levied to fupport them, and the prefent inability of the queen of Hungary to maintain thofe rights which defcend to her from her anceftors, and have been confirmed by all the folemnities of treaties, evidently require an uncommon degree of attention in our confultations, and of vigour in our proceedings.

Whatever may be the profeffions of the French, their real defigns are eafily difcovered, defigns which they have carried on, either openly, or in private, for near a century, and which it cannot be expected that they will lay afide, when they are fo near to fuccefs. Their view, Sir, in all their wars and treaties, alliances and intrigues, has been the attainment of univerfal dominion, the deftruction of the rights

of

of nature, and the subjection of all the rest of mankind; nor have we any reason to imagine that they are not equally zealous for the promotion of this pernicious scheme, while they pour troops into Germany, for the assistance of their ally, as when they wasted kingdoms, laid cities in ashes, and plunged millions into misery and want, without any other motive than the glory of their king.

But the French are not the only nation at this time labouring for the subversion of our common liberties. Our liberties, Sir, are endangered by those equally interested with ourselves in their preservation; for in what degree soever any of the princes who are now endeavouring to divide among themselves the dominions of Austria may be pleased with the acquisition of new territories, and an imaginary increase of influence and power, it must be evident to all who are not dazzled by immediate interest, that they are only fighting for France, and that by the destruction of the Austrian family, they must in a short time fall themselves.

It is well known, Sir, though it is not always remembered, that political as well as natural greatness is merely comparative, and that he only is a powerful prince, who is more powerful than those with whom he can have any cause of contention. That prince, therefore, who imagines his power enlarged by a partition of territories, which gives him some additional provinces, may be at last disappointed in his expectations: for, if this partition gives to another prince already greater than himself an opportunity of encreasing his strength in a degree proportionate to his present superiority, the former will soon find, that he has been labouring for nothing, and that his danger is still the same.

Such, Sir, is the case of the king of Prussia, who, when he has over run that part of Germany, to which he now lays claim, will only have weakened the house of Austria, without strengthening himself.

He is at present secure in the possession of his dominions, because neither the Austrians would suffer the French, nor the French permit the Austrians to encrease their power by subduing him. Thus while the present equipoise of power is maintained, jealousy and caution would always procure him an ally whenever he should be attacked; but when by his assistance the Austrian family shall be ruined, who shall defend him against the ambition of France?

While the liberties of mankind are thus equally endangered by

folly

folly and ambition, attacked on one fide, and neglected on the other, it is neceffary for thofe who forefee the calamity that threatens them, to exert themfelves in endeavours to avert it, and to retard the fatal blow, till thofe who are now lulled by the contemplation of private advantage, can be awakened into a juft concern for the general happinefs of Europe, and be convinced that they themfelves can only be fecure by uniting in the caufe of liberty and juftice.

For this reafon, Sir, our fovereign has afferted the pragmatic fanction, and promifed to affift the queen of Hungary with the forces which former treaties have entitled her to demand from him; for this reafon he has endeavoured to rouze the Dutch from their fupinenefs, and excite them to arm once more for the common fafety, to intimidate by new augmentations thofe powers whofe ardour, perhaps, only fubfifts upon the confidence that they fhall not be refifted, and to animate by open declarations in favour of the houfe of Auftria, thofe who probably are only hindered from offering their affiftance, by the fear of ftanding alone againft the armies of France.

That by this conduct he may expofe his dominions on the continent to invafions, ravages, and the other miferies of war, every one who knows their fituation muft readily allow; nor can it be doubted by any man who has heard of the power of the Pruffians and French, that they may commit great devaftations with very little oppofition, the forces of the electorate not being fufficient to give them battle: for though the fortified towns might hold out againft them, that confideration will very little alleviate the concern of thofe who confider the miferies of a nation, whofe enemies are in poffeffion of all the open country, and who from their ramparts fee their harveft laid wafte, and their villages in flames. The fortifications contain the ftrength, but the field and the trading towns comprife the riches of a people, and the country may be ruined which is not fubdued.

As therefore, Sir, the electoral dominions of his majefty are now endangered, not by any private difpute with the neighbouring princes, but by his firmnefs in afferting the general rights of Europe; as the confequences of his conduct, on this occafion, will be chiefly beneficial to Britain, we ought furely to fupport him in the profecution of this defign; a defign, which we cannot but approve, fince our anceftors have always carried it on without regard either to the danger or the expence.

In conformity to this maxim of politics, fo clearly founded in equity, and

and fo often juftified by the votes of the fenate, has his majefty been pleafed to declare to us his refolution to adhere to his engagements, and oppofe all attempts that may be forming in favour of any unjuft pretenfions to the prejudice of the houfe of Auftria. 'Tis for this end he defires the concurrence of his fenate. I hope every gentleman in this houfe will agree with me that we ought to declare our approbation of thefe meafures, in fuch terms as may fhow the world, that thofe who fhall dare to obftruct them, muft refolve to incur the refentment of this nation, and expofe themfelves to all the oppofition which the fenate of Britain can fend forth againft them. We ought to pronounce that the territories of Hanover will be confidered on this occafion as the dominions of Britain, and that any attack on one or the other will be equally refented. I therefore move, that an humble addrefs be prefented by this houfe to his majefty,

> To return our thanks for his fpeech; to exprefs our dutiful fenfe of his majefty's juft regard for the rights of the queen of Hungary, and for maintaining the pragmatic fanction; to declare our concurrence in the prudent meafures which his majefty is purfuing for the prefervation of the liberties and balance of power in Europe; to acknowledge his majefty's wifdom and refolution, in not fuffering himfelf to be diverted from fteadily perfevering in his juft purpofes of fulfilling his engagements with the houfe of Auftria; alfo, further to affure his majefty, that, in juftice to and vindication of the honour and dignity of the Britifh crown, we will effectually ftand by and fupport his majefty againft all infults and attacks, which any prince or power, in refentment of the juft meafures which he has fo wifely taken, fhall make upon any of his majefty's dominions, though not belonging to the crown of Great Britain. And that in any future event, which might make it neceffary for him to enter into ftill larger expences, this houfe will enable him to contribute in the moft effectual manner, to the fupport of the queen of Hungary, to the preventing, by all reafonable means, the fubverfion of the houfe of Auftria, and to the maintaining the pragmatic fanction and the liberties and balance of Europe.

Mr. Fox feconded the motion in this manner:—Sir, the expediency if not the neceffity of the addrefs now moved for, will, I believe,

lieve, be readily allowed by thofe who confider the juft meafures which are purfued by his majefty, the end which is intended by them, and the powers by which they are oppofed.

How much it is our duty to fupport the houfe of Auftria it is not neceffary to explain to any man who has heard the debates of this affembly, or read the hiftory of the laft war. How much it is our duty to fupport it, is evident as foon as it is known by whom it is attacked; by the antient enemy of thefe nations, by the general difturber of the univerfe, by the formidable oppreffors of liberty, exulting in new acquifitions, inflamed with the madnefs of univerfal monarchy, and elated with an opportunity of fubjecting Germany, by exalting to the fupreme power a prince who fhall hold his authority only by their permiffion.

The houfe of Auftria, which has fo often ftood forth in defence of our common rights, which has poured armies into the field in confederacy with Britain to fupprefs the infolence of that family which nothing could fatisfy but boundlefs power, now demands the affiftance which it has fo often afforded; that affiftance is demanded from us by every claim which the laws of fociety can enact, or the dictates of nature can fuggeft, by treaties maturely confidered, and folemnly confirmed, by the ties of antient friendfhip, and the obligations of common intereft.

To violate the publick faith, and to neglect the obfervation of treaties, is to fink ourfelves below barbarity, to deftroy that confidence which unites mankind in fociety. To deny or evade our ftipulations, Sir, is to commit a crime which every honeft mind muft confider with abhorrence, and to eftablifh a precedent which may be ufed hereafter to our own deftruction.

To forfake an antient ally only becaufe we can receive no immediate advantage from his friendfhip, or becaufe it may be in fome degree dangerous to adhere to him ; to forfake him when he moft wants our good offices, when he is diftreffed by his enemies, and deferted by others from whom he had reafon to hope for kinder treatment, is the moft defpicable, the moft hateful degree of cowardice and treachery.

The obligations of intereft, Sir, it is not often needful to enforce, but it may be obferved on this occafion, that a fingle year of neglect may never be retrieved. We may, Sir, now be able to fupport thofe whom, when once difpoffeffed, it will not be in our power to reftore ;

and

and that if we fuffer the houfe of Auftria to be over-borne, our pofterity through every generation may have reafon to curfe our injudicious parfimony, our fatal inactivity, and our perfidious cowardice.

With what views the king of Pruffia concurs in the French meafures, or upon what principles of policy he promifes to himfelf any
fecurity in the enjoyment of his new dominions, it is not eafy to
conjecture; but as it is eafy to difcover, that whatever he may propofe to himfelf, his conduct evidently tends to the ruin of Europe, fo
he may, in my opinion, juftly be oppofed, if he cannot be diverted or
made eafy.

Nor can we, Sir, if this oppofition fhould incite him, or any other
power, to an invafion of his majefty's foreign dominions, refufe
them our protection and affiftance: for as they fuffer for the caufe
which we are engaged to fupport, and fuffer only by our meafures,
we are, at leaft as allies, obliged by the laws of equity and the general
compacts of mankind, to arm in their defence; and what may be
claimed by the common right of allies, we fhall furely not deny
them, only becaufe they are more clofely united to us, becaufe they
own the fame monarch with ourfelves.

Mr. PULTENEY fpoke to the following purpofe:—Sir, with what
eagernefs the French fnatch every opportunity of encreafing their influence, extending their dominions, and oppreffing their neighbours,
the experience of many years has convinced all Europe; and it is
evident that unlefs fome power be preferved in a degree of ftrength
nearly equal to theirs, their fchemes, pernicious as they are, cannot
be defeated.

That the only power from which this oppofition can be hoped, is
the houfe of Auftria, a very fuperficial view of this part of the globe,
will fufficiently demonftrate; of this we were long fince fo ftrongly
convinced, that we employed all our forces and all our politicks to
aggrandize this houfe. We endeavoured not only to fupport it in all
its hereditary rights, but to inveft it with new fovereignties, and extend its authority over new dominions.

Why we afterwards varied in our councils and our meafures, I
have long enquired without any fatisfaction, having never, Sir, with
the utmoft application, been able to difcover the motives to the memorable treaty of Hanover, by which we ftipulated to deftroy the fabrick that we had been fo long and fo laborioufly endeavouring to
erect; by which we abandoned that alliance which we had fo diligently

gently cultivated, which we had preferred to peace, plenty, and riches, and for which we had chearfully fupported a tedious, a bloody, and an expenfive war.

This conduct, Sir, raifes a greater degree of admiration, as the authors of it had exhaufted all their eloquence in cenfuring the treaty of Utrecht, and had endeavoured to expofe thofe who tranfacted it to the general hatred of the nation; as they always expreffed in the ftrongeft terms their dread and deteftation of the French; as they animated all their harangues, and ftunned their opponents with declarations of their zeal for the liberties of Europe.

By what impulfe, or what infatuation, thefe affertors of liberty, thefe enemies of France, thefe guardians of the balance of power, were on the fudden prevailed on to declare in favour of the power whom they had fo long thought it their chief intereft and higheft honour to oppofe, muft be difcovered by fagacity fuperior to mine. But after fuch perplexity of councils and fuch fluctuation of conduct, it is neceffary to enquire more particularly what are the prefent intentions of the miniftry, what alliances have been formed, and what conditions are required to be fulfilled.

If we are obliged only to fupply the queen of Hungary with twelve thoufand men, we have already performed our engagements; if we have promifed any pecuniary affiftance, the fum which we have ftipulated to furnifh ought to be declared; for I fuppofe at leaft our engagements have fome limits, and that we are not to exert all the force of the nation, to fight as if fire and fword were at our gates, or an invader were landing armies upon our coafts.

I have, Sir, from my earlieft years been zealous for the defence and exaltation of the Houfe of Auftria, and fhall be very far from propofing that any danger or diftrefs fhould influence us to defert it; but I do not eafily difcover by what means we fhall be able to afford any efficacious affiftance; for the power of Britain confifts chiefly in naval armaments, which can be of very little ufe to the queen of Hungary, and I know not any ftate that will eafily confent to unite with us on this occafion.

If there be, Sir, any ftates remaining in Europe which the French can neither intimidate nor bribe, we ought ftudioufly to follicit and diligently to cultivate their friendfhip; but whether any, except the Mofcovites, are now independent, or fufficiently confident of their

Vol. I.   B b   own

own ftrength, to engage in fuch a hazardous alliance, may be juftly doubted.

The late grand alliance, Sir, was fupported at the expence of this nation alone, nor was it required from the other confederates to exhauft the treafure of their country in the common caufe ; I hope the debt which that war has entailed upon us will inftruct us to be more frugal in our future engagements, and to ftipulate only what we may perform without involving the nation in mifery, which victories and triumphs cannot compenfate.

The neceffity, Sir, of public œconomy obliges me to infift, that before any money fhall be granted, an account be laid before the fenate in particular terms of the ufes to which it is to be applied. To afk for fupplies in general terms, is to demand the power of fquandering the publick money at pleafure, and to claim in fofter language nothing lefs than defpotick authority.

It has not been uncommon for money granted by the fenate to be fpent without producing any of thofe effects which were expected from it, without affifting our allies, or humbling our enemies ; and therefore there is reafon for fufpecting that money has fometimes been afked for one ufe and applied to another.

If our concurrence, Sir, is neceffary to increafe his majefty's influence on the continent, to animate the friends of the houfe of Auftria, or to reprefs the difturbers of the publick tranquillity, I fhall willingly unite with the moft zealous advocates for the adminiftration in any vote of approbation or affiftance, not contrary to the act of fettlement, that important and well-concerted act, by which the prefent family was advanced to the throne, and by which it is provided, that Britain fhall never be involved in war for the enlargement or protection of the dominions of Hanover, dominions from which we never expected nor received any benefit, and for which therefore nothing ought to be either fuffered or hazarded.

If it fhould be again neceffary to form a confederacy, and to unite the powers of Europe againft the Houfe of Bourbon, that ambitious, that reftlefs family, by which the repofe of the world is almoft every day interrupted, which is inceffantly labouring againft the happinefs of human nature, and feeking every hour an opportunity of new encroachments, I declare, Sir, that I fhall not only, with the greateft chearfulnefs, bear my fhare of the publick expence, but endeavour to
reconcile

reconcile others to their part of the calamities of war.   This, Sir, I
have advanced, in confidence that sufficient care shall be taken, that
in any new alliance we shall be parties, not principals, that the
expence of war, as the advantage of victory, shall be common ; and
that those who shall unite with us will be our allies, not our mercenaries.

Mr. WALPOLE then spoke to the following purpose: —Sir, it is not
without reason that the honourable gentleman defires to be informed
of the stipulations contained in the treaty by which we have engaged
to support the pragmatick sanction, for I find that he either never
knew them or has forgotten them ; and therefore those reasonings
which he has formed upon them fall to the ground.

We are obliged, Sir, by this treaty, to supply the house of Austria
with twelve thousand men, and the Dutch, who were engaged in it by
our example, have promised a supply of five thousand.   This force,
joined to those armies which the large dominions of that family enable them to raise, were conceived sufficient to repel any enemy by
whom their rights should be invaded.

But because in affairs of such importance nothing is to be left to
hazard, because the prefervation of the equipoife of power, on which
the liberties of almost all mankind, who can call themselves free,
must be acknowledged to depend, ought to be rather certain, than
barely probable ; it is stipulated farther, both by the French and ourfelves, that if the supplies specified in the first article shall appear in-
sufficient, we shall unite our whole force in the defence of our ally,
and struggle once more for independence, with ardour proportioned
to the importance of our caufe.

By thefe stipulations, Sir, no engagements have been formed that can
be imagined to have been prohibited by the act of settlement, by which
it is provided, that the house of Hanover shall not plunge this nation
into a war, for the fake of their foreign dominions, without the confent of the senate ; for this war is by no means entered upon for the
particular security of Hanover, but for the general advantage of
Europe, to reprefs the ambition of the French, and to preferve
ourfelves and our posterity from the most abject dependence upon
a nation exafperated against us by long oppofition, and hereditary
hatred.

Nor is the act of settlement only preferved unviolated by the rea-

fons.

fons of the prefent alliance, but by the regular concurrence of the fenate which his majefty has defired, notwithftanding his indubitable right of making peace and war by his own authority. I cannot therefore imagine upon what pretence it can be urged, that the law, which requires that no war fhall be made on account of the Hanoverian dominions without the confent of the fenate, is violated, when it is evident that the war is made upon other motives, and the concurrence of the fenate is folemnly defired.

But fuch is the malevolence with which the conduct of the adminiftration is examined, that no degree of integrity or vigilance can fecure it from cenfure. When in the prefent queftion truth and reafon are evidently on their fide, paft tranfactions are recalled to memory, and thofe meafures are treated with the utmoft degree of contempt and ridicule, of which the greateft part of the audience have probably forgotten the reafons, and of which the authors of them do not always ftand up in the defence, becaufe they are weary of repeating arguments to thofe who liften with a refolution never to be convinced.

How well, Sir, thofe by whom the miniftry is oppofed, have fucceeded in hardening their minds againft the force of reafon, is evident from their conftant cuftom of appealing from the fenate to the people, and publifhing in pamphlets thofe arguments which they have found themfelves in this affembly unable to fupport ; a practice which difcovers rather an obftinate refolution to obftruct the government, than zeal for the profperity of their country, and which, to fpeak of it in the fofteft terms, feems to be fuggefted more by the defire of popularity than the love of truth.

Mr. SANDYS fpoke to the effect following :—Sir, notwithftanding the confidence with which this motion has been offered and defended, notwithftanding the fpecious appearance of refpect to his majefty, by which it is recommended, I am not afhamed to declare, that it appears to me inconfiftent with the truft repofed in us by our conftituents, who owe their allegiance to the king of Britain, and not to the elector of Hanover.

It will be urged, Sir, by the people, whom we fit here to reprefent, that they are already embarraffed with debts contracted in a late war, from which, after the expence of many millions, and the deftruction of prodigious multitudes, they receive no advantage ; and that
they

they are now loaded with taxes for the fupport of another, of which they perceive no profpect of a very happy or honourable conclufion, of either fecurity or profit, either conquefts or reprifals, and that they are therefore by no means willing to fee themfelves involved in any new confederacy, by which they may entail on their pofterity the fame calamities, and oblige themfelves to hazard their fortunes and their happinefs in defence of diftant countries, of which many of them have fcarcely heard, and from which no return of affiftance is expected.

Mr. WALPOLE fpoke again to this purpofe:—Sir, though it is not neceffary to refute every calumny that malice may invent, or credulity admit, or to anfwer thofe of whom it may reafonably be conceived that they do not credit their own accufations, I will yet rife once more in vindication of the treaty of Hanover, to fhew with how little reafon it is cenfured, to reprefs the levity of infult, and the pride of unreafonable triumph.

The treaty of Hanover, Sir, how long foever it has been ridiculed, and with whatever contempt thofe by whom it was negotiated have been treated, was wife and juft. It was juft, becaufe no injury was intended to any power, no invafion was planned, no partition of dominions ftipulated, nothing but our own fecurity defired. It was wife, becaufe it produced the end propofed by it, and eftablifhed that fecurity which the Auftrians and Spaniards were endeavouring to deftroy.

The emperor of Germany, Sir, had then entered into a fecret treaty of alliance with Spain, by which nothing lefs was defigned than the total deftruction of our liberties, the diminution of our commerce, the alienation of our dominions, and the fubverfion of our conftitution. We were to have been expelled from Gibraltar and totally excluded from the Mediterranean, the pretender was to have been exalted to the throne, and a new religion, with the flavery that always accompanies it, to have been introduced amongft us, and Oftend was to have been made a port, and to have fhared the poor remains of our commerce to foreign nations.

This unjuft, this malicious confederacy, was then oppofed with the utmoft vehemence by the Imperial general, whofe courage and military capacity are celebrated throughout the world, and whofe political abilities and knowledge of the affairs of Europe, were equal to his knowledge of war. He urged with great force, that such a confederacy would disunite the empire for ever from the maritime powers, by which it had been supported, and which were engaged by one common interest in the promotion of its prosperity : but his remonstrances availed nothing, and the alliance was concluded.

When our antient allies, who had been so often succoured with our treasure, and defended by our arms, had entered into such engagements ; when it was stipulated not only to impoverish but enslave us; not only to weaken us abroad, but to deprive us of every domestic comfort : when a scheme was formed that would have spread misery over the whole nation, and have extended its consequences to the lowest orders of the community, it was surely necessary to frustrate it by some alliance, and with whom could we then unite, but with France ?

This is not the only fact on which gentlemen have ventured to speak with great freedom without sufficient information ; the conduct of our allies in the late war has been no less misrepresented than that of our ministers in their negotiations. They have been charged with imposing upon us the whole expence of the confederacy, when it may be proved beyond controversy, that the annual charge of the Dutch was five millions.

Nor did they, Sir, only contribute annually thus largely to the common cause, but when we forsook the alliance, and shamefully abandoned the advantages we had gained, they received our mercenaries into their own pay, and expended nine millions in a single year.

Of the truth of these assertions it is easy to produce incontestable evidence, which, however, cannot be necessary to any man who reflects, that from one of the most wealthy nations in the world, the Dutch, with all their commerce, and all their parsimony, are reduced to penury and distress ; for who can tell by what means they have sunk into their present low condition, if they suffered nothing by the late war ?

How this gentleman, Sir, has been deceived, and to whose insinuations his errors are to be imputed, I am at no loss to discover. I hope he will by this confutation be warned against implicit credulity, and remember with what caution that man is to be trusted, whose perfidious counsels have endangered his country.

Mr.

Mr. VINER fpoke thus :—Sir, it is, in my opinion, an inconteft-able maxim, that no meafures are eligible, which are unjuft, and that therefore before any refolutions are formed, we ought to examine not what motives may be fuggefted by expedience, but what argu-ments may be advanced by equity on one part or the other.

If I do not miftake the true intent of the addrefs now propofed, we are invited to declare that we will oppofe the king of Pruffia in his attempts upon Silefia, a declaration in which I know not how any man can concur, who knows not the nature of his claim, and the laws of the empire. It ought therefore, Sir, to have been the firft endeavour of thofe by whom this addrefs has been fo zealoufly promoted, to fhow that his claim, fo publickly explained, fo firmly urged, and fo ftrongly fupported, is without foundation in juftice or in reafon, and is only one of thofe imaginary titles, which ambition may always find to the dominions of another.

But no attempt has been yet made towards the difcuffion of this important queftion, and therefore I know not how any man can call upon us to oppofe the king of Pruffia, when his claim may pro-bably be juft, and, by confequence, fuch as, if it were neceffary for us to engage in the affairs of thofe diftant countries, we ought to join with him in afferting.

Lord GAGE fpoke next in fubftance as follows :—Sir, as no mem-ber of this affembly can feel a greater degree of zeal for his majefty's honour than myfelf, none fhall more readily concur in any expreffion of duty or adherence to him.

But I have been always taught that allegiance to my prince is con-fiftent with fidelity to my country, that the intereft of the king and the people of Great Britain is the fame, and that he only is a true fubject of the crown, who is a fteady promoter of the happinefs of the nation.

For this reafon I think it neceffary to declare, that Hanover is al-ways to be confidered as a fovereignty feparate from that of Britain, and as a country with laws and interefts diftinct from ours ; and that it is the duty of the reprefentatives of this nation, to take care that interefts fo different may never be confounded, and that Britain may incur no expence of which Hanover alone can enjoy the advan-tage.

If the elector of Hanover fhould be engaged in war with any of the neighbouring fovereigns, who fhould be enabled by a victory to

B b 4

enter

enter into the country, and carry the terrors of war through all his
territories, it would by no means be neceffary for this nation to in-
terpofe; for the elector of Hanover might lofe his dominions with-
cut any difadvantage or difhonour to the emperor or people of
Britain.

H O U S E   O F   C O M M O N S.

April 16, 1741.

DEBATE ON A MOTION FOR SUPPORTING THE QUEEN OF HUNGARY.

His majefty went this day to the houfe of Lords, and after his af-
fent to feveral bills, he, in a fpeech from the throne to both
houfes of the fenate, acquainted them, that the war raifed
againft the queen of Hungary, and the various claims on the
late German emperor's fucceffion, might expofe the dominions
of fuch princes as fhould incline to fupport the pragmatick fanction to imminent danger. That the queen of Hungary required
the 12,000 men ftipulated by treaty, and thereupon he had demanded of the king of Denmark, and of the king of Sweden as
Sovereign of Heffe Caffell, their refpective bodies of troops, of
6000 men each, to be in readinefs to march to her affiftance.
That he was concerting fuch further meafures as may difappoint
all dangerous defigns forming to the prejudice of the houfe of
Auftria, which might make it neceffary for him to enter into
ftill larger expences for maintaining the pragmatick fanction.
He therefore, in a conjuncture fo critical, defired the concurrence of his fenate, in enabling him to contribute, in the moft
effectual manner, to the fupport of the queen of Hungary, the
preventing, by all reafonable means, the fubverfion of the houfe
of Auftria, and to the maintaining the liberties and balance of
power in Europe.

The houfe of Commons, in their addrefs upon this occafion, expreffed a dutiful fenfe of his majefty's juft regard for the rights
of the queen of Hungary, and for the maintaining the pragma-

The

tick fanction; they declared their concurrence in the prudent
measures which his majesty was pursuing for the preservation of
the liberties and balance of power in Europe; they assured his
majesty, that, in justice to, and vindication of the honour and
dignity of the British crown, they would effectually stand by
and support his majesty against all insults and attacks, which
any power, in resentment of the just measures which he had so
wisely taken, should make upon any of his majesty's dominions,
though not belonging to the crown of Great Britain. They further assured his majesty, that in any future events which might
make it necessary for him to enter into still larger expences, they
would enable him to contribute in the most effectual manner to
the support of the designs he proposed.

His majesty, in his answer to this address, observed their readiness in enabling him to make good his engagements with the
queen of Hungary, and the assurances given him not to suffer
his foreign dominions to be insulted on account of the measures
he was pursuing for the support of the pragmatick sanction, &c.

In consequence of this procedure, the house, pursuant to order,
resolved itself into a committee, to consider of the supplies granted to his majesty.

Upon this occasion, a motion was made by Sir Robert Walpole
for a grant of three hundred thousand pounds for the support of
the queen of Hungary, on which arose the following debate.

Sir ROBERT WALPOLE supported his motion by a speech in substance as follows:—Sir, the necessity of this grant appears so plainly
from the bare mention of the purposes for which it is asked, that I
can scarcely conceive that its reasonableness will be disputed. I can
discover no principles upon which an objection to this motion can be
founded, nor the least arguments by which such objection can be
supported.

The indispensable obligations of publick faith, the great ties by
which nations are united, and confederacies formed, I cannot suppose any man inclined to invalidate. An exact performance of national promises, an inviolable adherence to treaties, is enforced at
once by policy and justice, and all laws both of heaven and earth.

Publick

Publick perfidy, Sir, like private dishonesty, whatever temporary advantages it may promise or produce, is always upon the whole the parent of misery. Every man, however prosperous, must sometimes wish for a friend, and every nation, however potent, stand in need of an ally; but all alliances subsist upon mutual confidence, and confidence can be produced only by unlimited integrity, by known firmness, and approved veracity.

The use of alliances, Sir, has in the last age been too much experienced to be contested; it is by leagues well concerted, and strictly observed, that the weak are defended against the strong, that bounds are set to the turbulence of ambition, that the torrent of power is restrained, and empires preserved from those inundations of war, that, in former times, laid the world in ruins. By alliances, Sir, the equipoise of power is maintained, and those alarms and apprehensions avoided, which must arise from daily vicissitudes of empire, and the fluctuations of perpetual contest.

That it is the interest of this nation to cultivate the friendship of the house of Austria, to protect its rights, and secure its succession, to inform it when mistaken, and to assist it when attacked, is allowed by every party. Every man, Sir, knows that the only power that can sensibly injure us, by obstructing our commerce, or invading our dominions, is France, against which no confederacy can be formed, except with the house of Austria, that can afford us any efficacious support.

The firmest bond of alliances is mutual interest. Men easily unite against him whom they have all equal reason to fear and to hate, by whom they have been equally injured, and by whom they suspect that no opportunity will be lost of renewing his encroachments. Such is the state of this nation, and of the Austrians. We are equally endangered by the French greatness, and equally animated against it by hereditary animosities, and contests continued from one age to another; we are convinced that, however either may be flattered or caressed, while the other is invaded, every blow is aimed at both, and that we are divided only that we may be more easily destroyed.

For this reason we engaged in the support of the pragmatick sanction, and stipulated to secure the Imperial crown to the daughters of Austria, which was nothing more than to promise, that we would
endeavour

endeavour to prevent our own deftruction, by oppofing the exaltation of a prince who fhould owe his dignity to the French, and in confequence of fo clofe an alliance, fecond all their fchemes, admit all their claims, and facrifice to their ambition the happinefs of a great part of mankind.

Such would probably be the confequence, if the French fhould gain the power of conferring the Imperial crown. They would hold the emperor in perpetual dependence, would, perhaps, take poffeffion of his hereditary dominions as a mortgage for their expences, would awe him with the troops which they fent under a pretence of affifting him, and leave him only the titles of dominion, and the fhadows of empire.

In this ftate would he remain, whilft his formidable allies were extending their dominions on every fide. He would fee one power fubdued after another, and himfelf weakened by degrees, and not only deprived of his throne, becaufe it would be unneceffary to dethrone him ; or he would be obliged to follicit our affiftance to break from his flavery, and we fhould be obliged, at the utmoft hazard, and at an expence not to be calculated, to remedy what it is, perhaps, now in our power to prevent with very little difficulty.

That this danger is too near to be merely chimerical, that the queen of Hungary is invaded, and her right to the Imperial dignity contefted, is well known ; it is therefore the time for fulfilling our engagements : engagements of the utmoft importance to ourfelves and our pofterity ; and I hope the government will not be accufed of profufion, if for three hundred thoufand pounds the liberties of Europe fhall be preferved.

We cannot deny this grant without acting in oppofition to our late profeffions of fupporting his majefty in his endeavours to maintain the pragmatick fanction, and of affifting him to defend his foreign dominions from any injuries to which thofe endeavours fhould expofe them, for how can he without forces defend his dominions, or affift his ally, or how can he maintain forces without fupplies?

Mr. SHIPPEN next rofe and fpoke thus :—Sir, as I have always endeavoured to act upon conviction of my duty, to examine opinions before I admit them, and to fpeak what I have thought the truth, I do not eafily change my conduct, or retract my affertions; nor am I deterred from repeating my arguments when I have a right to fpeak, by the remembrance that they have formerly been unfuccefsful.

Every

Every man, when he is confident himself, conceives himself able to perfuade others, and imagines that their obftinacy proceeds from other motives than reafon; and that, if he fails at one time to gain over his audience, he may yet fucceed in fome happier moment, when their prejudices fhall be diffipated, or their intereft varied.

For this reafon, though it cannot be fufpected that I have forgotten the refentment which I have formerly drawn upon myfelf, by an open declaration of my fentiments with regard to Hanover, I fland up again, with equal confidence, to make my proteftations againft any interpofition in the affairs of that country, and to avow my diflike of the promife lately made to defend it: a promife, inconfiftent, in my opinion, with that important and inviolable law, the *Act of Settlement!* — a promife, which, if it could have been foreknown, would perhaps have for ever precluded from the fucceffion that illuftrious family, to which we owe fuch numberlefs bleffings, fuch continued felicity!

Far be it from me to infinuate that we can be too grateful to his majefty, or too zealous in our adherence to him; only let us remember that true gratitude confifts in real benefits, in promoting the true intereft of him to whom we are indebted; and furely, by hazarding the welfare of Britain in defence of Hanover, we fhall very little confult the advantage, or promote the greatnefs of our fovereign.

It is well known how inconfiderable, in the fight of thofe by whom the fucceffion was eftablifhed, Hanover appeared, in comparifon with Britain. Thofe men, to whom even their enemies have feldom denied praife for knowledge and capacity, and who have been fo loudly celebrated by many, who have joined in the laft addrefs, for their honeft zeal, and the love of their country, enacted, that the king of Britain fhould never vifit thofe important territories, which we have fo folemnly promifed to defend, at the hazard of our happinefs. It was evidently their defign that our fovereign, engroffed by the care of his new fubjects, a care, which, as they reafonably imagined, would arife from gratitude for dignity and power fo liberally conferred, fhould in time forget that corner of the earth on which his anceftors had refided, and act, not as elector of Hanover, but as king of Britain, as the governor of a mighty nation, and the lord of large dominions.

It was exprefsly determined, that this nation fhould never be involved in war for the defence of the dominions on the continent,

and

and doubtlefs the fame policy that has reftrained us from extending our conquefts in countries, from which fome advantages might be received, ought to forbid all expenfive and hazardous meafures, for the fake of territories from whence no benefit can be reaped.

Nor are the purpofes, Sir, for which this fupply is demanded, the only objections that may be urged againft it, for the manner in which it is afked, makes it neceffary at leaft to delay it. The minifters have been fo little accuftomed to refufals that they have forgot when to afk with decency, and expect the treafure of the nation to be poured upon them, whenever they fhall think it proper to hint that they have difcovered fome new opportunity of expence.

It is neceffary, that when a fupply is defired, the houfe fhould be informed, fome time before, of the fum that is required, and of the ends to which it is to be applied, that every member may confider, at leifure, the expediency of the meafures propofed, and the propor- tion of the fum to the occafion on which it is demanded; that he may examine what are the moft proper methods of raifing it, and perhaps enquire with what willingnefs his conftituents will advance it.

Whether any man is enabled by his acutenefs and experience, to determine all thefe queftions upon momentaneous reflection, I cannot decide. For my part, I confefs myfelf one of thofe on whom nature has beftowed no fuch faculties, and therefore move that the confide- ration of this fupply may be deferred for a few days: for if it be now preffed upon us, I fhall vote againft it, becaufe I do not yet fully difcover all the reafons for it, nor all the confequences which it may produce, and I think myfelf obliged to know for what purpofe I give away the money which is not my own.

Mr. VINER fpoke as follows :— Sir, whatever may be the necef- fity of maintaining the pragmatick fanction, or whatever the obliga- tions of national pacts, of which I hope no man is defirous of counte- nancing the neglect, yet they cannot oblige us to arm without an enemy, to embarrafs ourfelves with watching every poffibility of danger, to garrifon dominions which are not threatened, or affert rights which are not invaded.

The expediency of maintaining the houfe of Auftria on the Impe- rial throne, it is not at prefent neceffary to affert, becaufe it does not appear that any other family is afpiring to it. There may indeed be whifpers of fecret defigns and artful machinations, whifpers, perhaps, fpread only to affright the court into treaties, or the fenate into grants;

grants; or defigns, which, like a thoufand others that every day produces, innumerable accidents may defeat, which may be difcovered, not only before they are executed, but before they are fully formed, and which therefore are not worthy to engrofs much of our attention, or to exhauft the wealth of the people.

The pragmatick fanction is nothing more than a fettlement of the Imperial dignity upon the eldeft daughter of the late German emperor and her fon, and if fhe has no fon, upon the fon of the fecond daughter; nor has the crown of Britain, by engaging to fupport that fanction, promifed any thing more than to preferve this order of fucceffion, which no power at prefent is endeavouring to interrupt, and which therefore at prefent requires no defence.

The difpute, Sir, between the king of Pruffia and the queen of Hungary is of a different kind, nor is it our duty to engage in it, either as parties or judges. He lays claim to certain territories ufurped, as he alleges, from his anceftors by the Auftrian family, and afferts, by force, this claim, which is equally valid, whether the queen be emprefs or not. We have no right to limit his dominions, or obligation to examine the juftice of his demands. If he is only endeavouring to gain what has been forcibly with held from him, what right have we to obftruct his undertaking? And if the queen can fhow a better title, fhe is, like all other fovereigns, at liberty to maintain it; nor are we neceffarily to erect ourfelves into judges between fovereigns, or diftributors of dominion.

The conteft feems to have very little relation to the pragmatick fanction: if the king of Pruffia fucceeds, he will contribute to fupport it; and if the queen is able to fruftrate his defigns, fhe will be too powerful to need our affiftance.

But though, Sir, the pragmatick fanction were in danger of violation, are we to ftand up alone in defence of it, while other nations, equally engaged with ourfelves by intereft and by treaties, fit ftill to look upon the conteft, and gather thofe advantages of peace which we indifcreetly throw away? Are we able to maintain it without affiftance, or are we to exhauft our country, and ruin our pofterity in profecution of a hopelefs project, to fpend what can never be repaid, and to fight with certainty of a defeat?

The Dutch, whofe engagements and whofe interefts are the fame as our own, have not yet made any addition to their expences, nor augmentation of their troops; nor does a fingle potentate of Europe,

however

however united by long alliances to the houfe of Auftria, or however endangered by revolutions in the empire, appear to roufe at the approach of alarm, or think himfelf obliged to provoke enemies by whom he is not yet injured.

I cannot therefore perfuade myfelf that we are to ftand up fingle in the defence of the pragmatick fanction, to fight the quarrel of others, or live in perpetual war, that our neighbours may be at peace.

I fhall always think it my duty to difburfe the publick money with the utmoft parfimony, nor ever intend, but on the moft preffing neceffity, to load with new exactions a nation already overwhelmed with debts, harraffed with taxes, and plundered by a ftanding army.

For what purpofe thefe numerous forces are maintained, who are now preying on the publick ; why we increafe our armies by land when we only fight by fea ; why we aggravate the burthen of the war, and add domeftick oppreffions to foreign injuries, I am at a lofs to determine. Surely fome regard fhould be had to the fatisfaction of the people, who ought not, during the prefent fcarcity of provifions, to be ftarved by the encreafe of an army, which feems fupported only to confume them.

As therefore part of our prefent expence is in my opinion unneceffary, I fhall not contribute to aggravate it by a new grant, for purpofes of which I cannot difcover that they will promote the advantage of the publick.

Sir ROBERT WALPOLE replied to the following effect :—Sir, the pragmatick fanction, which we are engaged to fupport, is not confined to the prefervation of the order of fucceffion, but extends to all the rights of the houfe of Auftria which is now attacked, and by a very formidable enemy, at a time of weaknefs and diftraction, and therefore requires our affiftance.

That others equally obliged by treaty and by intereft to lend their help on this occafion fit reluctive, either through cowardice or negligence, or fome profpect of temporary advantage, may, perhaps, be true ; but is it any excufe of a crime, that he who commits it is not the only criminal ? Will the breach of faith in others excufe it in us ? Ought we not rather to animate them by our activity, inftruct them by our example, and awaken them by our reprefentations ?

Perhaps the other powers fay to themfelves, and to one another, Why fhould we keep that treaty which Britain is violating ! Why
fhould

should we expose ourselves to danger, of which that mighty nation, so celebrated for courage, is afraid? Why should we rush into war, in which our most powerful ally seems unwilling to support us?

Thus the same argument, an argument evidently false, and made specious only by interest, may be used by all, till some one, more bold and honest than the rest, shall dare to rise in vindication of those rights which all have promised to maintain; and why should not the greatest nation be the first that shall avow her solemn engagements? Why should not they be most diligent in the prosecution of an affair who have most to lose by its miscarriage?

I am always willing to believe, that no member of this assembly makes use in any solemn debate of arguments which do not appear rational to himself, and yet it is difficult to conceive that any man can imagine himself released from a promise, because the same promise is broken by another, or that he is at liberty to desert his friend in distress, because others desert him, whose good offices he has equal reason to expect, and that the more his assistance is needed, the more right he has to deny it.

Surely such arguments as these deserve not, need not a confutation. Before we regulate our conduct by that of others, we must either prove that they have done right, which proof will be a sufficient defence without the precedent, or own that they are more capable of judging than we, and that therefore we pay an implicit submission to their dictates and example; a sacrifice which we shall not willingly make to the vanity of our neighbours.

In the present case it is evident that if other nations neglect the performance of their contracts, they are guilty of the breach of publick faith; of a crime, that, if it should generally be imitated, would dissolve society, and throw human nature into confusion, that would change the most happy region into deserts, in which one savage would be preying on another.

Nor are they only propagating an example, which in some distant times may be pleaded against themselves, but they are exposing themselves to more immediate dangers; they are forwarding designs that have no tendency but to their ruin, they are adding strength to their inveterate enemies, and beckoning invasion to their own frontiers.

Let

Let us, therefore, inftead of hardening ourfelves in perfidy, or lulling ourfelves in fecurity by their example, exert all our influence to unite them, and all our power to affift them. Let us fhow them what they ought to determine by our refolutions, and teach them to act by our vigour; that, if the houfe of Auftria be preferved, our alliance may be ftrengthened by new motives of gratitude; and that, if it muft be that the liberties of this part of the world be loft, we may not reproach ourfelves with having neglected to defend them.

Mr. PELHAM fpoke next to this purpofe :—Sir, it is not to be fuppofed that fuch members of this affembly as are not engaged in publick affairs fhould receive very exact intelligence of the difpofitions of foreign powers, and therefore I do not wonder that the conduct of the Dutch has been mifreprefented, and that they are fufpected of neglecting their engagements at a time when they are endeavouring to perform them.

The Dutch have now under confideration the moft proper methods of affifting the queen of Hungary, and maihtaining the pragmatick fanction: it may be indeed juftly fufpected from the nature of their conftitution, that their motions will be flow, but it cannot be afferted, that they break their engagements, or defert their confederates.

Nor is there any reafon for imagining that the other princes who have incurred the fame obligations, will not endeavour to perform their promifes; it may be eafily conceived that fome of them are not able at a fudden fummons to afford great affiftance, and that others may wait the refult of our deliberations, and regulate their conduct by our example.

Not that we ought to neglect our engagements, or endanger our country, becaufe other powers are either perfidious, or infenfible; for I am not afraid to declare, that if that fhould happen, which there is no reafon to fufpect, if all the other powers fhould defert the defence of the Auftrian line, fhould confent to annul the pragmatick fanction, and leave the queen of Hungary to the mercy of her enemies, I would advife that Britain alone fhould pour her armies into the continent, that fhe fhould defend her ally againft the moft formidable confederacy, and fhow mankind an example of conftancy not to be fhaken, and of faith not to be violated.

If it be therefore our duty to fupport the pragmatick fanction, it is now the time for declaring our refolutions, when the Imperial crown is claimed by a multitude of competitors, among whom the elector of Bavaria, a very powerful prince, has by his minister notified his pretensions to the court of Britain.

The antient alliance between this prince and the French is well known, nor can we doubt that he will not now implore their affiance for the attainment of the throne to which he aspires ; and I need not say what may be expected from an emperor whose elevation was procured by the forces of France.

Nor is this the only prince that claims the Imperial crown upon plausible pretences, or whose claims other powers may combine to support ; it is well known that even the Spanish monarch believes himself intitled to it, nor can we, who have no communication with him, know whether he has not declared to all the other princes of Europe, his resolution to assert his claim.

It is far from being impossible that the pretensions of the house of Bourbon may be revived, and that though no single prince of that family should attempt to mount the Imperial throne, they may all conspire to dismember the empire into petty kingdoms, and free themselves from the dread of a formidable neighbour, by erecting a number of diminutive sovereigns, who may be always courting the assistance of their protectors, for the sake of harrassing each other.

Thus will the house by which Europe has been hitherto protected, sink into an empty name, and we shall be left to stand alone against all the powers that profess a different religion, and whose interest is opposite to that of Britain.

We ought indeed to act with the utmost vigour, when we see one of the most powerful of the reformed princes so far forgetful of the interest of our religion as to co-operate with the designs of France, and so intent upon improving the opportunity of distressing the house of Austria, as to neglect the common cause, and expose himself or his posterity to the danger of becoming a dependent on the house of Bourbon.

For this reason, I cannot agree that our army, though numerous and burthensome, is greater than the necessity of affairs requires : if we cast our eyes on the continent, nothing is to be seen but general confusion, powerful armies in motion, the dominions of one prince invaded, of another threatened, the tumults of ambition in one place, and a panic stillness in another.

What will be the event of these commotions who can discover? And how can we know what may determine the course of that flood of power, which is now in a state of uncertain fluctuation, or seems driven to different points by different impulses? How soon may the Dutch see their barrier attacked, and call upon us for the ten thousand men which we are obliged to send them? How soon may the house of Austria be so distressed as to require all our power for its preservation?

That we are to leave nothing unattempted for the security of our own religion and liberty, will easily be granted, and, therefore, unless it can be proved that we may be equally secure, though the house of Austria be ruined, it will necessarily follow that we are with all our power to enforce the observation of the pragmatick sanction.

This is not an act of romantic generosity, but such as the closest attention to our own interest shows to be necessary: in defending the queen of Hungary we defend ourselves, and only extinguish that flame, by which, if it be suffered to spread, we shall ourselves be consumed. The empire may be considered as the bulwark of Britain, which, if it be thrown down, leaves us naked and defenceless.

Let us therefore consider our own danger, and remember, that while we are considering this supply, we are deliberating upon nothing less than the fate of our country.

Mr. PULTENEY spoke next to the effect following:—Sir, I am on this occasion of an opinion different from that of the honourable member who spoke the second in this debate, though on most questions our judgment has been the same. I am so far from seconding his proposal for delaying the consideration of this supply, that I think it may justly be enquired, why it was not sooner proposed.

For the support of the house of Austria, and the assertion of the pragmatick sanction, no man can be more zealous than myself; I am convinced how closely the interest of this nation and that of the Austrian family are united, and how much either must be endangered by the ruin of the other, and therefore, I shall not delay, for a single moment, my consent to any measures that may re-establish our interest on the continent, and rescue Germany once more from the jaws of France.

I am afraid that we have lost part of our influence in the neighbouring countries, and that the name of Britain is less formidable than heretofore; but if reputation is lost, it is time to recover it, and I

doubt

doubt not but it may be recovered by the same means that it was at first obtained. Our armies may be yet equally destructive, and our money equally persuasive.

We have not yet suffered, amidst all our misconduct, our naval force to be diminished ; our sailors yet retain their antient courage, and our fleets are sufficient to keep the dominion of the ocean, and prescribe limits to the commerce of every nation. While this power remains unimpaired, while Britain retains her natural superiority, and asserts the honour of her flag in every climate, we cannot become despicable, nor can any nation ridicule our menaces or scorn our alliance. We may still extend our influence to the inland countries, and awe those nations which we cannot invade.

To preserve this power let us watch over the disposal of our money ; money is the source of dominion ; those nations may be formidable for their affluence which are not considerable for their numbers; and by a negligent profusion of their wealth, the most powerful people may languish into imbecillity, and sink into contempt.

If the grant which is now demanded will be sufficient to produce the ends to which it is proposed to be applied, if we are assured of the proper application of it, I shall agree to it without hesitation. But though it cannot be affirmed that the sum now demanded is too high a price for the liberties of Europe, it is at least more than ought to be squandered without effect, and we ought at least to know before we grant it what advantages may be expected from it.

May not the sum demanded for the support of the queen of Hungary be employed to promote very different interests? May it not be lavished to support that power to which our grants have too long contributed, that power by which ourselves have been awed, and the administration has tyrannized without controul?

If this sum is really intended to support the queen of Hungary, may we not enquire how it is to be employed for her service? Is it to be sent her for the payment of her armies and the support of her court? Should we not more effectually secure her dominions by purchasing with it the friendship and assistance of the king of Prussia, a prince, whose extent of dominions and numerous forces make him not more formidable than his personal qualities.

What may be hoped, Sir, from a prince of wisdom and courage, at the head of a hundred and ten thousand regular troops, with eight
millions

millions in his treafury? How much he muft neceffarily add to the
ftrength of any party in which he fhall engage, is unneceffary to mention; it is evident, without proof, that nothing could fo much
contribute to the re-eftablifhment of the houfe of Auftria, as a
reconciliation with this mighty prince, and that to bring it to pafs
would be the moft effectual method of ferving the unfortunate queen
that requires our affiftance.

Why we fhould defpair, Sir, of fuch a reconciliation I cannot perceive; a reconciliation equally conducive to the real intereft of
both parties. It may be proved, with very little difficulty, to the
king of Pruffia, that he is now affifting thofe with whom interefts
incompatible and religions irreconcilable have fet him at variance,
whom he can never fee profperous but by the diminution of his own
greatnefs, and who will always project his ruin while they are enjoying the advantages of his victories. We may eafily convince him that
their power will foon become by his affiftance fuch as he cannot hope
to withftand, and fhow, from the examples of other princes, how
dangerous it is to add to the ftrength of an ambitious neighbour. We
may fhow him how much the fate of the empire is now in his hands,
and how much more glorious and more advantageous it will be to preferve it from ruin, than to contribute to its deftruction.

If by fuch arguments, Sir, this potent monarch can be induced to
act fteadily in defence of the common caufe, we may once more ftand
at the head of a proteftant confederacy; of a confederacy that may
contract the views and reprefs the ambition of the houfe of Bourbon,
and alter their fchemes of univerfal monarchy into expedients for the
defence of their dominions.

But in tranfacting thefe affairs, let us not engage in any intricate
treaties, nor amufe ourfelves with difplaying our abilities for negotiation; negotiation, that fatal art which we have learned as yet very imperfectly, and which we have never attempted to practife but to our
own lofs. While we have been entangled in tedious difquifitions,
and retarded by artful delays, while our commiffaries have been debating about what was only denied to produce controverfies, and enquiring after that which has been hid from them only to divert their
attention from other queftions, how many opportunities have been
loft, and how often might we have fecured by war, what was, at a
much greater expence, loft by treaties.

Treaties, Sir, are the artillery of our enemies, to which we have nothing to oppofe; they are weapons of which we know not the ufe, and which we can only efcape by not coming within their reach. I know not by what fatality it is, that to treat and to be cheated, are, with regard to Britons, words of the fame fignification; nor do I intend, by this obfervation, to afperfe the characters of particular perfons, for treaties, by whomfoever carried on, have ended always with the fame fuccefs.

It is time, therefore, to know, at length, our weaknefs and our ftrength, and to refolve no longer to put ourfelves voluntarily into the power of our enemies: our troops have been always our ableft negotiators, and to them it has been, for the moft part, neceffary at laft to refer our caufe.

Let us then always preferve our martial character, and neglect the praife of political cunning; a quality which, I believe, we fhall never attain, and which, if we could obtain, would add nothing to our honour. Let it be the practice of the Britons to declare their refolutions without referve, and adhere to them in oppofition to danger; let them be ambitious of no other elogies than thofe which may be gained by honefty and courage, nor will they then ever find their allies diffident, or their enemies contemptuous.

By recovering and afferting this character we may become once more the arbiters of Europe, and be courted by all the proteftant powers as their protectors; we may once more fubdue the ambition of the afpiring French, and once more deliver the houfe of Auftria from the inceffant purfuit of thofe reftlefs enemies.

The defence of that illuftrious family, Sir, has always appeared to me, fince I ftudied the ftate of Europe, the unvariable intereft of the Britifh nation, and our obligations to fupport it on this particular occafion have already been fufficiently explained.

Whence it proceeded, Sir, that thofe who now fo zealoufly efpoufe the Auftrian intereft, have been fo plainly forgetful of it on other occafions, I cannot determine. That treaties have been made very little to the advantage of that family, and that its enemies have been fuffered to infult it without oppofition, is well known; nor was it long ago that it was debated in this houfe, whether any money fhould be lent to the late emperor.

No publick or private character can be fupported, no enemy, Sir, can be intimidated, nor any friend confirmed in his adherence, but by a fteady and confiftent conduct, by propofing in all our actions fuch ends as may be openly avowed, and by purfuing them without regard to temporary inconveniencies, or petty obftacles.

Such conduct, Sir, I would gladly recommend on the prefent occafion, on which I fhould be far from advifing a faint, an irrefolute, or momentary affiftance, fuch fupplies as declare diffidence in our own ftrength, or a mean inclination to pleafe contrary parties at the fame time, to perform our engagements with the queen, and continue our friendfhip with France. It is, in my opinion, proper to efpoufe our ally with the fpirit of a nation that expects her decifions to be ratified, that holds the balance of the world in her hand, and can beftow conqueft and empire at her pleafure.

Yet, Sir, it cannot be denied that many powerful reafons may be brought againft any new occafions of expence, nor is it without horror and aftonifhment that any man, converfant in political calculations, can confider the enormous profufion of the national treafure. In the late dreadful confufion of the world, when the ambition of France had fet half the nations of the earth on flame, when we fent our armies to the continent, and fought the general quarrel of mankind, we paid, during the reigns of king William and his great fucceffor, reigns of which every fummer was diftinguifhed by fome important action, but four millions yearly.

But our preparations for the prefent war, in which fcarcely a fingle fhip of war has been taken, or a fingle fortrefs laid in ruins, have brought upon the nation an expence of five millions. So much more are we now obliged to pay to amufe the weakeft, than formerly to fubdue the moft powerful of our enemies.

Frugality, which is always prudent, is, at this time, Sir, indifpenfable, when war, dreadful as it is, may be termed the lighteft of our calamities; when the feafons have difappointed us of bread, and an univerfal fcarcity afflicts the nation. Every day brings us accounts from different parts of the country, and every account is a new evidence of the general calamity, of the want of employment for the poor, and its neceffary confequence, the want of food.

He that is fcarce able to preferve himfelf, cannot be expected to affift others; nor is that money to be granted to foreign powers, which is wanted for the fupport of our fellow-fubjects, who are now languifhing with difeafes, which unaccuftomed hardfhips and unwholefome provifions have brought upon them, while we are providing

viding againſt diſtant dangers, and bewailing the diſtreſſes of the houſe
of Auſtria.

Let us not add to the miſeries of famine the mortifications of inſult
and neglect; let our countrymen at leaſt divide our care with our
allies, and while we form ſchemes for ſuccouring the queen of Hungary, let us endeavour to alleviate nearer diſtreſſes, and prevent or
pacify domeſtick diſcontents.

If there be any man whom the ſight of miſery cannot move to com-
paſſion, who can hear the complaints of want without ſympathy, and
ſee the general calamity of his country without employing one hour
on ſchemes for its relief; let not that man dare to boaſt of integrity,
fidelity, or honour; let him not preſume to recommend the preſervation of our faith, or adherence to our confederates: that wretch can
have no real regard to any moral obligation, who has forgotten thoſe
firſt duties which nature impreſſes; nor can he that neglects the happineſs of his country, recommend any good action for a good reaſon.

It ſhould be conſidered, Sir, that we can only be uſeful to our allies, and formidable to our enemies, by being unanimous and mutu-
ally confident of the good intentions of each other, and that nothing
but a ſteady attention to the publick welfare, a conſtant readineſs to
remove grievances, and an apparent unwillingneſs to impoſe new
burthens, can produce that unanimity.

As the cauſe is therefore neceſſarily to precede the effect, as foreign
influence is the conſequence of happineſs at home, let us firſt endeavour to eſtabliſh that alacrity and ſecurity that may animate the people to aſſert their antient ſuperiority to other nations, and reſtore that
plenty which may raiſe them above any temptation to repine at aſſiſtance given to our allies.

No man, Sir, can very ſollicitouſly watch over the welfare of
his neighbour, whoſe mind is depreſſed by poverty, or diſtracted by
terror; and when the nation ſhall ſee us anxious for the preſervation
of the queen of Hungary, and unconcerned about the wants of our
fellow-ſubjects, what can be imagined, but that we have ſome method of exempting ourſelves from the common diſtreſs, and that we
regard not the publick miſery when we do not feel it?

Sir ROBERT WALPOLE replied, to the following effect:—Sir, it
is always proper for every man to lay down ſome principles upon
which he propoſes to act, whether in publick or private; that he may
not be always wavering, uncertain, and irreſolute; that his adherents

may know what they are to expect, and his adverfaries be able to tell why they are oppofed.

It is neceffary, Sir, even for his own fake, that he may not be always ftruggling with himfelf; that he may know his own determinations, and enforce them by the reafons which have prevailed upon him to form them; that he may not argue in the fame fpeech to contrary purpofes, and weary the attention of his hearers with contrafts and antithefes.

When a man admits the neceffity of granting a fupply, expatiates upon the danger that may be produced by retarding it, declares againft the leaft delay, however fpecioufly propofed, and inforces the arguments which have been already offered to fhow how much it is our duty and intereft to allow it; may it not reafonably be imagined, that he intends to promote it, and is endeavouring to convince them of that neceffity of which he feems himfelf convinced?

But when the fame man proceeds to difplay, with equal eloquence, the prefent calamities of the nation, and tells to how much better purpofes the fum thus demanded may be applied; when he dwells upon the poffibility that an impolitick ufe may be made of the national treafure, and hints that it may be afked for one purpofe and employed to another, what can be collected from his harangue, however elegant, entertaining, and pathetick? How can his true opinion be difcovered? Or how fhall we fix fuch fugitive reafonings, fuch variable rhetoric?

I am not able, Sir, to difcern, why truth fhould be obfcured; or why any man fhould take pleafure in heaping together all the arguments that his knowledge may fupply, or his imagination fuggeft, againft a propofition which he cannot deny. Nor can I affign any good purpofe that can be promoted by perpetual renewals of debate, and by a repetition of objections, which have in former conferences, on the fame occafion, been found of little force.

When the fyftem of affairs is not fully laid open, and the fchemes of the adminiftration are in part unknown, it is eafy to raife objections formidable in appearance, which perhaps cannot be anfwered till the neceffity of fecrecy is taken away. When any general calamity has fallen upon a nation, it is a very fruitful topic of rhetoric, and may be very pathetically exaggerated, upon a thoufand occafions to which it has no neceffary relation.

Su

Such, in my opinion, Sir, is the ufe now made of the prefent fcarcity, a misfortune inflicted upon us by the hand of Providence alone; not upon us only, but upon all the nations on this fide of the globe, many of which fuffer more, but none lefs than ourfelves.

If at fuch a time it is more burthenfome to the nation to raife fupplies, it muft be remembered, that it is in proportion difficult to other nations to oppofe thofe meafures for which the fupplies are granted; and that the fame fum is of greater efficacy in times of fcarcity than of plenty.

Our prefent diftrefs will, I hope, foon be at an end; and perhaps a few days may produce at leaft fome alteration. It is not without reafon, that I expect the news of fome fuccefsful attempts in America, which will convince the nation, that the preparations for war have not been idle fhows, contrived to produce unneceffary expences.

In the mean time, it is neceffary that we fupport that power which may be able to affift us againft France, the only nation from which any danger can threaten us, even though our fleets in America fhould be unfuccefsful.

If we defeat the Spaniards, we may affift the houfe of Auftria without difficulty, and if we fail in our attempts, their alliance will be more neceffary. The fum demanded for this important purpofe cannot be cenfured as exorbitant, yet will, I hope, be fufficient: if more fhould hereafter appear neceffary, I doubt not but it will be granted.

The queftion paffed without oppofition.